Warning: Climbing is dangerous and can result in serious injury or death

Climbing is a sport that can be inherently dangerous and cause severe injury or death. This book is not meant for instructional purposes. Instruction should be sought out by a seasoned professional. It is the reader's responsibility to attain qualified instruction before climbing. This book is not a substitution for instruction or experience. Attempt routes and boulder problems at you own risk. This book, the author, and or the publisher are not responsible for any injury or fatality while climbing at any of the areas within this book or anywhere else. The author and publisher are also not responsible for routes being harder than graded or protection being in any way different than the grade in this book. The reader needs to know that protection and grades may vary greatly from what is written in this book. Cliffs and boulders are in a state that regularly changes. Cliffs can become more hazardous after the printing of this book and can become visibly different. This book also holds no responsibility for its directions. It is easy to become lost in the woods coming to or going from a cliff or bouldering area. The author and publisher are not responsible for incorrect or wrong directions. The author and publisher are also not responsible for incorrect route information or incorrect route data. Rout-finding is your own responsibility. Getting off route can be dangerous and deadly. The author and publisher hold no responsibility to landowners. This book is made for reference only. The author and publisher are not liable for anyone trespassing on private or public property or any injuries that are sustained on private or public lands. Permissions may change on lands both public and private and may differ after the printing of this book. Fixed protection on routes should always be looked at with skepticism. Bolts, pitons, and fixed hardware are left in elements all year and can become corroded or dangerous. Use good judgment and test all equipment. Landings below boulder problems can also be hazardous and ridden with obstacles. Use crash pads and be aware of your surroundings. Grades on climbs may vary from climber to climber and can seem more difficult to individual climbers. Be aware that climbs can be unsafe if the grade seems or is harder than graded in this book. This book makes no guarantees

Rock Climbing and Bouldering Pennsylvania "Secrets of the Keystone State"

ISBN 978-1-4507-1272-9

Blue Biner Guidebooks

Blue Biner guides are innovative, new guidebooks that focus on quality print and E-book formats. We are looking to expand our rock climbing and bouldering guidebook series. For more information visit our website at www.bluebiner.com or e-mail us at bluebiner@gmail.com.

Cover Photo: Randy Ross soloing at the Delaware Water Gap. Photo taken by the author.

To order additional copies of this book or to purchase E-books visit us online at www. bluebiner.com.

Rock Climbing and Bouldering

Pennsylvania

Secrets of the Keystone State

Rob Holzman

For Jess, Mia, and Khloe

Eastern Pennsylvania Region

Central Pennsylvania Region

Western Pennsylvania Region

Thank you, thank you, thank you

With so many people who made this book possible, I don't know who to thank first, well, actually I do. First I want to thank my wife Jess, who traipsed throughout the Pennsylvania woodlands, putting up with climbing mediocre areas I needed for the book instead of going on good climbing trips or more importantly, attending classes at med school. I would also like to thank her for all her support.

Next I would like to thank three lifelong climbing partners Tom Kneiss, Nick Morell, and Ryan Lucas for spending a great deal of time finding new areas and climbing new routes. You were always willing to take long trips and share ropes and give me lifelong memories. You guys are the best.

I want to especially thank Tim Bonner for editing the guidebook and giving insightful ideas and forethought. Without his help it might have looked like a caveman wrote this book.

I would also like to thank Dave Pfurr for making several trips across the state and always being eager to explore new areas. Dave has been a true friend for many years.

Bob D'Antonio for all your help in the Mocanaqua area and the use of his historic photos of the state. Bob is a true pioneer of Pennsylvania and worldwide climbing. Thanks for all the help and great photos.

Al Pisaneschi for all the help in Mocanaqua and northeast Pennsylvania where he has been a prolific climber since the 70s.

George Peterson for his insights in the Northeast Pennsylvania region and great stories about Pennsylvania climbing.

Randy Ross for spending lots of time showing me some of his secret crags that he was eager to share with fellow climbers.

Tim Fitzinger for his willingness to explore areas in the Pocono's.

Joe Forte for all his help and photos of eastern Pennsylvania and for always being willing to share a rope and explore the mysteries of the state. You're the best Joe.

Darryl Roth for his historic information and help with the areas around Allentown and the Lehigh Gorge.

Curt Harler for his historic information about Pennsylvania in general and for providing valuable contact information for the whole state of Pennsylvania.

Sandra Healy for information about her mothers climbing exploits in the State College region.

Steve Klaver for the use of his excellent photos of the Delaware Water Gap.www. steveklaverphotos.com

Bob Value for insights into the regions of western Pennsylvania and for historic information about crags all over western Pennsylvania. I highly recommend purchasing his guidebook for The Mills if you plan to visit western PA.

Tim Anderson for information about western Pennsylvania.

Eric Horst for his insights and information about central Pennsylvania. Eric has been a true pioneer of rock climbing in Pennsylvania and the Mid Atlantic. If you are a novice climber or seasoned expert, I recommend any of his books on training.

Michael Kennedy for information regarding Mugs Stump and Hunter Rocks.

The Stump family for information about Mugs Stump climbing in Pennsylvania and State College.

John Gill for information about East Coast bouldering.

Rob Ginieczki for all his help about western Pennsylvania and eastern Pennsylvania. Rob is a guidebook author of several mountain biking guidebooks for Pennsylvania and the Pennsylvania ice climbing guidebook (ordering information in the back of this book).

Hal Beimel and Paul Danday for all their help and willingness to share their local areas with other climbers. You guys are some of the friendliest climbers I've ever met. Thanks for all the help and guided tours.

Tim Garland for his help on all the South Mountain areas and turning me on to some very interesting and unusual central Pennsylvania crags.

Cheyenne Wills for information on South Mountain crags.

Glen Stoner for help regarding South Mountain history and providing undocumented information about Chimney Rocks.

Joel Toretti for all his help and willingness to share Elk State Forest and other central Pennsylvania areas with other climbers. Also for his excellent photos.

Mike Stewart and Josh Karns for their help and tour of the Cliffside area at Elk State Forest.

Dana Harrington for all his help and information about areas in Allegheny State Forest.

Mike Rich for taking several trips across the state to very lousy climbing areas.

Hugh Herr for information on central Pennsylvania areas.

Keith Uhl for all his help and historic tours of Emmaus and the Delaware Water Gap and for fun memories and great climbing days.

John Croom for his software help; we named a route after you in this book.

I would also like to specially thank other climbers who contributed historic information for various areas throughout the state: Jeff Holt, Hans Herr, Jim Goldsmith, Scott Schellenberger, Jim Nonnemaker, Tom Bebe, Ed VanSteenwick, Jeff Martin, Gene Genay, Rich Pleis, Bill Barrios, Mike Pantelich.

For use of photos I want to thank: Bob D' Antonio, Tom Kneiss, Ryan Lucas, Joe Forte, Jessica Shoemaker, Gabe Franklin, Gus Gruner, Manasseh Franklin, Nancy Joseph, Eric Olsheskne, Keith Uhl, Mike Steele.

Introduction

I'm writing this introduction and thinking: *who actually reads the introduction to a climbing guidebook anyway?* Well, obviously you. Yes, *you*. So, since *you* have taken the time to actually read this, I'm going to make it rather long, hopefully somewhat useful, and possibly entertaining.

Finally finishing this guide feels like a calm breeze wafting up a mountain pass. I feel as though a giant weight has been lifted off my shoulders—for a while attempting to finish this book felt like Sisyphus pushing that boulder uphill for eternity. Having a recurring nightmare that gremlins brake into my house and delete the guidebook from my PC has not been particular helpful either.

The main problem with writing this guidebook for Pennsylvania has been the lack of documented information. I had visited so many areas in Pennsylvania that climbers started to say: "you should do a guide". What I thought would be less than a years work turned out to be several years of bushwhacking through the backwoods, calling hundreds of older climbers for first-ascent information, and delving through old topos of mine trying to remember what I named what climb and what the grades were.

I have been fortunate enough to have developed over 500 routes and 2,000 boulder problems in Pennsylvania. Because of this, I am lucky enough to have firsthand knowledge about a great deal of the climbing in the state. I am also fortunate enough to know many of the older climbers who paved the ways to modern climbing in the state. The main crux of this book was going to all the areas, grading the climbs, and trying to fill the gaps where a lot of information has been long forgotten. The common myth has been that climbers never named routes in Pennsylvania in the early years. This couldn't be farther from the truth. In fact, most of the climbing and bouldering was named and graded. Unfortunately, for most Pennsylvania climbers, the information was only passed around by word of mouth. Since many first-ascentionists moved out-of-state, much of this knowledge was lost.

The main focus of this book is to seek out this forgotten knowledge and provide climbers with accurate names and grades of routes statewide. I don't know how many times I've been to climbing areas where the names of routes or boulder problems have changed time and time again. At one climbing area in particular, a problem I developed some years back has been renamed 6 times since it was originally named. In most cases climbers are just unsure of route names due to lack of knowledge being passed around via word of mouth. In a few cases however, climbers simply have not been concerned with what routes were actually named, and just want to name the routes themselves. I've even offered correct route names to climbers doing mini guidebooks for small areas in PA, only to find that they just made up their own names for the routes anyway. This is unfortunate because it adds even more inaccurate information to the already heightened problem of inaccurate information to begin with. Because of these reasons, it was clearly time for a comprehensive guidebook to be written. Because of a lack of consistency with route names, many of the names in this guide will differ with current names being passed around presently. I realize of course, that this may upset a few climbers. To the best of my knowledge, what I have contributed to this guide is the most accurate information available. I hope the information I have to offer will interest and excite climbers—if not the book makes a pretty good Frisbee. With any guide, some of the information may be inaccurate or left out. If you feel anything is in error please feel free to contact me so I can remedy this for future additions.

For grading purposes I have climbed, or attempted, nearly every route and boulder problem mentioned in this guide. Whenever possible, I had other climbers input in assessing grades. I did change some grades that were previously documented both easier and harder. These grades were changed for reasons such as rockfall, broken holds, a consensus about that grade, or inaccurate grading. I did not change grades for sandbagging or other purposes. I simply tried to give the most honest figure, so that climbers can get the most enjoyment and performance out of those particular climbs.

This book is meant to give accurate descriptions, directions, ratings, and history for a state where information is known to be ambiguous. I realize the subtitle "Secrets of the Keystone State" can alarm certain climbers in a state where climbers are known to be tight-lipped about sharing beta on local crags. In the past few years this trend has finally started to break like the carabiner in the opening scene of the movie *Cliffhanger*. The real secret is that there are so many obscure crags lying scattered throughout the Pennsylvania mountainsides, keeping areas a secret should be the last thing on climbers' minds—next to clipping toe nails and taking that overdue trip to the Dushore outhouse race you're always talking about. The fact is, you could easily give directions to 100 unknown spots, and not even begin to touch a fraction of the rock within the state. The time has finally come to enjoy Pennsylvania's hidden jewels. Personal agendas for hiding the best climbing areas have finally gone the way of Goldline, EB's, and Pitons. I know there are still a few die-hards who have sequestered themselves to caves, committing themselves to only wear neon Spandex, watch *Masters of Stone Volume I*, and give directions to only those who solemnly swear to exclusively climb on rigid-stem Friends. Luckily, these climbers are few and far between.

It is not the intention of this book to expose private areas on private lands. In most cases the secrets of the keystone state are secrets of my own, that I have chosen to include in this book. I intentionally sought out areas that were known only to me and a few other climbers. I have also spent a great deal of time looking for obscure areas with quality rock, to develop into areas so that Pennsylvania climbers can enjoy some of these lesser known gems.

Of course, not all of the areas in this book fall into this level of obscurity. I have also included many popular areas and documented many of the routes whose names were unknown, incorrectly named, or not graded. Pennsylvania is noted for some of the best kept secrets in the East. Although the Keystone State doesn't boast the great cliffs found in California or Colorado it does have bragging rights to some of the most interesting rock formations…anywhere. Sandstone pillars the shape of needles, boulder gardens the size of cities, roof systems the length of city blocks, and rock the quality of any four-star area; what Pennsylvania lacks in hype, it makes up for in quantity and quality—it can be coined the Keystone State for more than one reason.

Many climbing areas in the state have character that is unsurpassed. Imagine climbing the 200'-high Minsi Cliff: views of the cool Delaware fill the space between your quivering feet. Envision yourself at the Atlantis Bouldering Area: sun paints the rock brilliant orange as you send four-star problems that rest at waters edge, along a tranquil mountain lake. Picture yourself climbing Boxcar Rocks: an infinite sea of pebbles speckle train-car-shaped boulders that carry on for three miles, streaming along the mountaintop like a stone freight train. These are but some of the amazing climbing destinations found throughout the state.

My greatest hope is that climbers will enjoy visiting the areas in this book as much as I have. I hope climbers will read about these amazing areas and visit as many as they can.

For some of the best alpinesque trad climbing the Delaware Water Gap holds great potential. A Mecca of 200' trad lines beckons the adventurous at heart. If you brave the massive roof-caps, you will experience some of the most exhilarating trad climbing in the East. Chickies Rock, Dauphin Narrows, and White Rocks are excellent areas to cut your teeth on classic Pennsylvania trad as well. Smaller areas like The Hermitage, Main Wall Mocanaqua, and McConnels Mills, are also road-worthy excursions for the seasoned trad aficionado.

Pennsylvania is a great state for sport climbing. Areas like Paradise Rock, Mocanaqua, The Lost Crag, Boxcar Rocks, The Library, and many others offer great sport climbing. Birdsboro and Stony Ridge also offer a theatre for the modern rock jock; however, I have excluded these areas from print due to sensitive access. In the near future—as gears have started turning in the right directions—I would expect to find Birdsboro in print.

Many areas like The Sex Wall, Euro Wall, Star Wall, Infinity Wall, Pillar of Insandity, Safe Harbor, Cauldron, Susquehanna Islands, Tilbury, Bellfonte, State College region quarries, and numerous other sport areas would have been wonderful to include in this guide. Sine I have been an advocate for access, I am unwilling to publicize these popular but closed areas. Hopefully future generations—or wishfully, this generation—will be able to enjoy these great climbing areas.

Some of the most intriguing areas lie hidden amongst the forested Pennsylvania woodlands. Unfortunately this book is not large enough—in lieu of resembling *War and Peace*—to feature some of the amazing rock hidden around the state. I certainly would have liked to include areas I have recently been recently developing like The Castle, The Whale Wall, or many other spots. Unfortunately, to fit many of these areas in print would take volumes.

Perhaps some of the states best secret gems are yet to be discovered. In recent years I've spent a lot of time exploring and discovering new and undeveloped areas. Many climbers find it hard to believe that new route potential—and even more surprisingly new areas—still exist in this state. With a state that is so foliated and so large, it's hard not to believe. Several 100' - 200'-high quarries, as well as a few dozen bouldering areas, have been recently developed in Pennsylvania. Many secretes like these still await the adventurous at heart. I guarantee if you hike any ridgeline in the state you will find quality rock. If you spend some time in this state exploring you won't be disappointed. An incredible amount of first ascent potential still exists. So quit your job, sell all your personal belongings, and devote your time to seeking out the hidden jewels of Pennsylvania rockdom—well, at least take a weekend or two and do some exploring.

Without argument, any Pennsylvania climber can tell you that the bouldering in the Keystone state is comparable to, if not better than, anyplace you have ever bouldered! This may sound like a big statement for a seemingly unpopular climbing state. Make no mistake however; the bouldering in Pennsylvania is first-rate. There are several hundred areas to boulder in Pennsylvania. Nearly all have high-quality areas with excellent problems.

This book is about rock. If you purchased this under the false pretences that it may include small engine repair, Soduko, or sexy love passages—which is the name of a climb in this book and not a subject—you are mistaken. This book is about rock. Rock does not think, smell, feel, calculate, cogitate, or collaborate. Is this sad? Not really. Because if you think about it, rock does, however, at times: cooperate, confiscate, cohabitate, and corrugate (think about it). It can also drink, radiate, permeate, sweat, vibrate, and sometimes, when least expecting, even violate. Does this make it a living thing? Probably not, but it creates something in us that makes it feel alive; makes *us* feel alive. And during this coexistence between mammal and mountain, climber and crag, we experience a feeling of being one with something bigger than us. Something we strive to dominate, but no that even if we can achieve this, by climbing the blankest section, the hardest move. We've only achieved this for now. And for now we are just guests. And even if we can be stronger than the rock at this time, it will outstay our visit. It will outlive us. It will be stronger. But now, in this moment, it will give us strength that can help us overcome our greatest obstacles on stone and in life. Help embrace our fears, instill focus, and bring harmony.

Rock can do many things for us. It has the potential to bring out the best and worst in us. It has the power to influence us for good and bad. Sadly, it can cause us to exploit it, damage it, and use it for our own personal agendas. And, although the rocks feelings won't be hurt, ours will. In this way it has a strange power over us. It does not care if you hit it, kick it, caress it, chalk it, or even drill it. But you care if you do these things. The rock does not feel these things, but you and I do. We as climbers do. And as a community, we care if these things are done to it. Bolt wars are not about the rock, they are about us and our feelings toward each other. Ratings and numbers are not about the stone and difficulty, they are about feelings and attitudes. The rock will be here long after us, the memories sometime in between, but the feelings are here now. If we strive to be the best we can be, and do the best things we can do, and respect something that is, perhaps, bigger than us, then and only then can we feel proud of our achievements.

I hope you enjoy this book as much as I have enjoyed writing it. I hope it takes you to some of the places it has taken me. I hope it is both useful in helping you find the wonderful areas in the state, and informative in helping you enjoy the routes within these areas. If not, as I mentioned before, the book makes a pretty good Frisbee. I hope all your travels throughout the Keystone State are always safe and always fun. To misquote an American radio icon: keep both feet off the ground and keep cranking for the stars.

Safety and Dangers while Climbing

Make no mistake, climbing is dangerous. Although most moments shroud us in a blanket of laughter, friendship, and exciting movement; the playing field can quickly shift to shroud us in a tunnel of fear, danger, and fatal decision. Reality can hit you quickly in this sport. Climbing is, without doubt, a sport of risk. Even if your best defense in this sport is a good offense, there are still many climbing dangers you can be unprepared for. The sport centers on a theatre of high exposure. Injuries can, at any time, be incurred from falling, falling objects, weather, gear malfunction, exposure, exhaustion, malnutrition, dehydration, and many other problems.

The danger of climbing may not be obvious at times. Many climbers have been lost attempting to locate a climbing/bouldering areas and sustained injuries. Rockfall can be unexpected and fatal. Although we can prepare ourselves with years of experience, danger is always a factor. We strive to educate ourselves, hone our skills, develop new techniques, and mould ourselves into model, responsible athletes. As diverse climbers we reach a level of comfort and competence. At times this confidence can lead us to a unique level of focus that can block our receptors of fear, and sometimes proper judgment. Similarly, motorcyclists find that their safest years have been their earliest years; judgment and focus can often be at their highest levels when tasks are new. For this reason judgment and focus should always center on the climbing experience and never, at any time in ones climbing career, be overlooked.

Rock Climbing and Bouldering Pennsylvania

This generation has experienced a boom in climbing like no other before it. More and more novice climbers scamper off to cliffs statewide. Indoor climbing has further advanced this growth. More information is available through increased trade publications, online resources, and regional events. In modern times, there are more climbers, but more information is available to these climbers. Because of this, it should come as no surprise that many climbers are getting amazingly strong in an amazingly short time. The level of sport is proportionately advancing with this. Proportionately increasing with this is a level of risk. Essentially, more climbers are placing themselves in more challenging situations quicker than ever before. These increasing levels have become a focal-point for climbers, land managers, and anyone involved with the sport.

Pennsylvania has certainly seen its fair share of accidents in the past few decades. Their have been several injuries, rescues, and fatalities across the state. Anyone who has climbed for any significant amount of time most likely knows someone who has been injured, had a close call, or worse. Climbers in Pennsylvania have been lost, stranded on cliffs, and overcome by exposure or hypothermia. Climbers have succumbed to insect bites, lyme disease, poison ivy and agitating plantlife. Climbers have had serious or fatal reactions to bee and wasp stings, snake bites, animal bites, infections and other maladies. Climbers have also been seriously or fatally injured by rockfall, falling while climbing, or from equipment failure. Most may not consider bouldering a rescue oriented outing; however, several climbers have had to be rescued while lost in boulder fields while succumbing to frostbite, hypothermia, and exhaustion.

Although you may not consider Pennsylvania on par with concerns you may face on a trip to the West; Pennsylvania climbing should, by no means, be underestimated. I have personally been attacked by more than a dozen bees (at one time), stepped on venomous snakes, come face-to-face with a fox while mantling a ledge, been bitten by a Black Widow sister spider, and endured poison ivy rashes that resembled radiation burns. Having dealt with these things and others, I offer a few suggestions while climbing in Pennsylvania. Be aware of time while out in the woods. Avoid leaving crags and bouldering areas after dark. Pack a headlamp, first aid supplies, and plenty of water and high energy foods. Plan for the worst; hope for the best. Use caution and judgment on every climb. Asses risks, be aware of fall potential, always, and wear a helmet! Bring warm clothing and or water repellent clothing. In warmer months bring appropriate clothing. Climb with responsible partners who are experienced or at least have an experienced climber involved. Always examine fixed protection. Many areas in Pennsylvania have less-than-ideal fixed hardware.

It is a good idea to start a mental checklist before climbing (this includes mental preparation before you leave the house). Plan what you will bring: water, food, head lamps, gear, phone (tell someone where you are going), clothing, etc. Go through a checklist while at the crag: double-backed, knot tied properly, on belay, etc. Sticking to good mental routines is a good safety measure while climbing that helps minimize risks.

Statistically, rappelling is one of the most hazardous times while climbing. Always double check rap stations, your knots, rappel devices, etc. Always try to rappel before dusk.

Bouldering risks can often be overlooked. Try to boulder with a partner if possible, if none are available; tell someone where you will be and what time you are expected back. Use a crashpad, spot landings, and know your abilities. Scouting out topouts can also be helpful and a good safety practice.

The above ideas are, by no means, a complete agenda to follow. Many other safety practices should be inherited. Educate yourself as much as possible and climb with responsible parties and your experiences will be greatly rewarded. I hope all your adventures in Pennsylvania will be safe and enjoyable.

Access Issues

There is no question; many of Pennsylvania's more popular areas are closed to climbing. With a state having over 400 climbing/ bouldering areas it's no wonder why a large portion of them are closed. For this reason alone I have chosen to fashion a guidebook that only includes areas with good access. I have worked long and hard with many landowners to assure that most of the areas in this guidebook will remain open to climbing for many years to come. That being said, at any time this could change. Perhaps, the best solution to keep statewide areas with good access open in the future is to keep a successive chain of communication open between climbers and landowners. No one person can effectively tackle the job of communicating with all the landowners statewide. Hopefully local climbers will continually communicate with appropriate land managers and keep abreast of any changes to policies, restrictions, or problems that may occur in the future.

Many areas in Pennsylvania have no written policies toward climbing. Many of these areas are in remote parts of the state far from concern from many land managers. Some of these areas are in many ways a non-issue in respect to addressing issues with appropriate parties. The reasoning behind this is that some bouldering areas or crags are so far from visibility that only a few climbers regularly visit the lands. Additionally, the areas are so displaced from formal scrutiny that problems will—most likely—never arise (fingers crossed).

The Access Fund has been very involved with many issues that have plagued the state in the past few years. Many policies have been implemented to limit restrictions and many climbing areas have adopted climbing into their allowed list of activities. Some examples of these areas are Emmaus bouldering area, Bauer's Rock, Rothrock State Forest, Micheaux State Forest, Select parcels of the Pennsylvania State Game Commission, Mount Gretna region, Francis E. Walther National Recreation Area, Mocanaqua areas, and many others. Trail projects, cleanups, rebolting projects, and other issues have been regularly addressed with land managers at the areas listed above.

Without question, Pennsylvania has many access problems that are works-in-progress. Safe Harbor, Bellefonte Quarry, Stony Ridge, and many other quarries and crags have long been the focus of The Access Fund and various climbers' coalitions. To keep updated on events and access issues statewide check www.paclimbing.com in the access section of the webpage. Access Fund Regional coordinators in Pennsylvania, as well as regularly updated access information, can be found on The Access Fund's webpage at www.accessfund.org.

Ethics

Warning: What you are about to read may be controversial to some climbers, offend most household pets, and frighten certain plantlife. Yes, you guessed it, we're about to talk about climbers ethics. And—much like the Twilight Zone— it lies between the pit of man's fears and the summit of his knowledge. As you might have guessed, ethics are one of the most controversial issues in the sport of climbing. Not surprisingly, Pennsylvania is no exception to ethical scrutiny. Some of the major ethical dilemmas in Pennsylvania are: Bolting existing trad routes, bolting boulder problems, respecting landowners and the environment, and altering rock.

One of the most prevalent of these problems has been bolting. In past years, areas all over the state have seen an increase in retro-bolting (adding bolts to existing climbs). It is a nationally accepted standard that it is poor ethics to bolt a route that has already been established in a traditional (non-bolted) style. It is also poor ethics to add bolts to existing sport lines that have been climbed previously. If a climb can be done in a traditional manner by placing gear, bolts should not be added.

There are many areas in Pennsylvania that benefit from bolts and are long established bolted climbing areas. Bolting climbing areas should only be done if it is a legal practice at any given area. Local climbers should be consulted first. This is not to attain permission but to directly inquire whether a climb has been done previously in a more traditional manner or may present a specific reason as to why it had not been previously developed.

When bolting a route each placement should be considered carefully. Only climbers with experience in bolting should bolt climbs. If not setting up a route ground up several climbers should toprope the route and determine where the best placements are. Considerations like different climber height, clipping stance, and crux should be considered. Consider the quality of the proposed route and take a consensus on whether it will be worth bolting—many routes in Pennsylvania have never bolted for a reason. Always consult local climbers and follow local traditions and prevent from straying from accepted ethics. Refrain from bolting climbs too close together or next to existing trad or sport lines and never bolt boulder problems.

Bolting wars can be a consequential conundrum. Differences in opinions can lead to destruction of rock, land management issues, and even closures. If climbers can agree on one thing, it should be to actively communicate between each other and keep an open channel of dialogues to prevent destructive behaviors. Remember in order to make friends in the climbing community you have to be one. Climbing on statewide lands is a privilege that's a shame to jeopardize.

Do not alter the rock. Gluing, chipping, or altering rock in any manner is extremely unethical and can have extreme consequences. Several people were recently fined in excess of 1,000, each, for altering rock and the environment in central Pennsylvania.

It seems as though no matter how far into the backwoods of Pennsylvania you travel off roads, pathways, or even faint deer paths, you will always come across a long since depleted beer can. I challenge any climber to romp through the most remote areas of the state and not come across the remains of a one of these long-discarded tin sarcophagi. Every time you see one of these—and you certainly will—let it be a reminder to respect the environment by packing out trash and leaving little impact on the local flora and fauna. Camp only in designated camping areas and keep on marked trails where applicable. If it is necessary to stray from trails or none exist, tred lightly. To quote an ancient Chinese scholar—or maybe it was scripture inside a hardened dough shell from Min's Express—the forest is full of vast knowledge; with vast knowledge comes experience; If you substitute experience before knowledge, the forest will look vast.

Pennsylvania's Unique and Amazing Geology

The Keystone State is noted for many unusual things: a town that boasts an annual outhouse race, a town inhabited exclusively by midgets (don't believe me; Google it), and a city that was abandoned because an underground mine fire has been burning under it for over 30 years. It should come as no surprise that Pennsylvania hosts the most unusual geology in the known universe. If you climb in this state for any length of time, you can expect to encounter boulder gardens the size of trailer parks, trailer parks the size of boulder gardens, 100'-high stone leviathans that resemble colossal whales, Tolkienian outcrops that resemble Middle Earth, boulders that form a cacophony of shapes and sizes, and frighteningly deep quarries that appear to slice into the very crust of the planet. Climb here long enough and you will see an uncountable amount of stone anomalies like spiny fins, sandstone knobs, deep-chiseled overhangs, and a plethora of many other jaw-dropping stone mutations. If my synopsis of our statewide geology doesn't excite you, there are plenty of bowling alleys in Pennsylvania too.

I, at no moment, pretend to be an expert on Pennsylvania geology. I'm that guy who picks the rock up and stares googly-eyed at the pretty sparkles. Any recreational geologist could easily bully my layman's knowledge of rock, and proceed to kick sand in my face—probably stating what kind of sand it is to further scoff at my geologic ignorance. People inaccurately presume that, because I have climbed at so many areas statewide, I am some sort of geological *Wunderkindt* who mysteriously inherited a geologic wealth of knowledge via osmosis while I was belaying fellow climbers. I can't begin to tell you how many times I hear, "Rob, what type of rock is *this*?" Regrettably, I ignorantly reply: "Hard? White? Steep?" Or, on occasion will make up a name like Paleoconglomeraticizedmezazooamorphiced cross-bedded sandstonediabasicized ironized shist to fake climbers into thinking I might actually know something about rock. Surprisingly, the latter answer has given me much-unwanted geologic crag-cred.

Anyway, if you want to read what little I know about Pennsylvania's intriguing geology—and believe me you don't—here it is.

Eastern Pennsylvania
Arguable, the best quality stone can be found in the eastern part of the state. Conglomerate cliffs near Scranton, Wilkes-Barre, and Mocanaqua have some of the cleanest rock you could hope to sink a nut in. The bouldering in these areas is, in my opinion, better than the Gunk's. The stone is almost identical to the nearby Gunk's as well. In fact, the lower end of the Shawangunk formation actually creeps into Pennsylvania at the Delaware Water Gap. The stone here is much different from the Scranton/Wilkes-Barre rock (not as clean or white colored) but is good quality. This gap is arguably, the most striking gap along the Appalachian ridges.

Near the Water Gap, Promised Land State Park hosts some amazing glacial cross-bedded sandstone. Bruce Lake has beautiful boulders that showcase this rock. The glaciated Pocono Plateau holds many sandstone and conglomerate bouldering areas and cliffs.

One of the most intriguing of these is part of stony Ridge near Palmerton. This rock looks like boulders were dropped out of the sky from Colorado or California. What adds even further to this pseudo-Western setting is the zinc tragedy that wiped of the vegetation off the trees for several miles. This setting looks more like Mars than Mars. There hasn't been one occasion while bouldering there when I haven't half-expected to find a green alien sit-starting a boulder problem and saying, "Greetings earthling."

Several miles to the south, near Allentown, Emmaus has several areas with rock composed of Diabase and granite, yes granite, boulders. These boulders resemble Joshua Tree boulders. Like Palmerton, the rock quality is fantastic.

19

Triassic Diabase boulders are abundant near Lake Nockamixon, Harleysville, and several places in-between. This Diabase extends into the central region of the state, and eventually Maryland.

One of the lowest quality formations in the eastern part of the state is Ralph Stover (High Rocks) in the Tohickon Creek Gorge. Geologists call the rock here Brunswick Shale; I call it choss. Although the quality is no where near as nice as the rock found in the rest of eastern Pennsylvania, many climbers enjoy this slick, slabby shale.

Central Pennsylvania

The most unusual geologic feature in the known Universe, perhaps aside from that ridiculous face on Mars, is located in Schukill County. It is called the Whaleback and it resembles a 100'-high, half-a-mile wide stone whale. Geologists from all over the country line up, rock hammer in hand, pens in pocket protectors, to study this giant stone leviathan. This unusual rock beast is known to be the second largest anticline in the country. People come for all over the U.S. to gawk, photograph, and study this incredibly weird rock formation. This monster sits on the Western Middle Anthracite Field, the largest anthracite coal field in the world. Part of this field caught fire in 1962 and is still burning underground. This caused the town of Centralia to be evacuated when a noxious sinkhole partially swallowed a small child. The whaleback is of the Pennsylvania Llewellyn formation. You can climb on gloss black coal on one side or smooth gold-colored rock on the other. Nearby Centralia contains conglomerate of the Pottsville group. Climb here and you can climb on Gunks-like conglomerate and breathe in life threatening fumes all in one session.

Typical quarries in central Pennsylvania can range from sandstone to limestone. Popular quarries near Bellfonte and Lock Haven are made of Ordovician Bellfonte limestone.

Sandstone quarries found south of State College are Devonian sandstone. Many quarries of this type offer sport climbing on cliffs in excess of 200'.

Cross-bedded sandstone boulders of the Pottsville group can be found at the many bouldering areas along Chestnut Ridge. This type of sandstone contains excellent bouldering.

Chickies quartzite is found at areas like Chickies Rock, Atomic Rocks, The Precipice, other outcrops along the Susquehanna River.

One of the most popular rock types for bouldering is Triassic Diabase. Pennsylvania is very fortunate to have the largest concentration of bouldering areas with this rock type in the world. The "Diabase belt" runs from New Jersey to Maryland. The only other place in the world that has this type of rock is South Africa. This rock has become increasingly popular with the bouldering crowd because of the rocks delicate edges, smooth features, and reliability for difficult problems. Several dozen bouldering areas with this rock type are located in south-central Pennsylvania. Mount Gretna and Govoners Stables are the most popular areas.

Western Pennsylvania

The western side of the state is known for many amazing rock types. McConnells Mills is one of the finest examples of geologic wonderment. Courtesy of the Wisconsin Ice Sheet, cross-bedded sandstone "rock cities"—a geologic term for boulder gardens that resemble small cities—were formed in this area. Devonian, Silurian, and Cambrian sandstones are common in this part of the state. These fine sandstones rival any West Virginia rock.

Northwestern Pennsylvania, specifically areas throughout Allegheny National Forest—and there are tons of areas—contain Pottsville sandstone and conglomerate (Pennsylvanian and Mississippian ages) mixed rock. Areas like The Ice Cubes, Jake's Rocks, Rim Rock, Minister Creek, Kelly Pines, and at least a dozen other areas have rock cities. These cube-shaped and rectangular blocks create passageways, open streets and stone boulder-buildings created from heavy conglomerate layers over shale, causing soil creep and ideal conditions for the creation of these amazing features.

Weather

The weather in Pennsylvania is not as reliable as "Local on the 8's", but it isn't as unreliable as, say…Patagonia. Weather in this state is often quite pleasant. You can certainly climb year round, but there are uncomfortable times: Winter is often as bitter as a Moscow call-girl and summer can be as sweltering as a Bronx Mafioso snitch. Fall and spring are certainly the most comfortable months; weather is nearly perfect.

Although winter and summer can be unpleasant on extreme days, you can always find shade or sun. Many "winter crags" exist due to afternoon sun baking the stone. Pleasant "summer crags" can be found letting shade drape over secluded rock faces.

Thunderstorms can be alarming. Bad storms frequently roll in during summer months. These storms can be quite violent. A cliff is not a good place to be at these times. I have come several inches from being London Broiled on more than one occasion. Use caution and bail off cliffs if signs of extreme weather roll in.

What is not Covered in this Guide

I left a great deal out of this guide. I had to. Pennsylvania simply has too many areas to feature in one guide—without the book resembling The Encyclopedia. First and foremost, I left out a great deal simply because Pennsylvania has so areas that are closed to climbing. My primary focus when I first started this guide was to seek out many unknown or undeveloped areas on public lands. It took a long time, but during the development of some of these crags, I contacted numerous landowners and public land managers, to draft policies that allowed climbing. In the end, I am quite pleased with the results and content in furnishing a guidebook with areas that exclusively allow climbing.   Because of the focus of this guidebook, many areas that could not be included will hopefully be included in future additions. Many areas that aspire to be in future publications you will find below.

Safe Harbor: An impressive sport crag on the banks of the lower Susquehanna River Valley. Unfortunately this area is currently closed to climbing. An incredible amount of effort has gone into opening this area. The effort has been spearheaded by Eric Horst, The Access Fund, and Lancaster Climbers Club; however, the area may take several years to be open. If and when the land is finally turned from the Norfolk Southern to the pre-determined owners, climbing will be allowed. It will just take time.

Sex Wall: A great sport climbing area, with the same situation as above. The railroad owns the property. When the land is transferred, the property will allow climbing.

Euro Wall: Great sport climbs. Essentially the same situation as above.

Bellefonte Quarry: A State College Gem that is in jeopardy. Much of the quarries have been filled in. The quarry is now being policed of the first time in years. A local climbers coalition is working on its situation.

Other Central PA Quarries: A great deal of 200' and 300' quarries with bolted sport lines exist throughout central PA. Unfortunately access is a major concern.

Stony Ridge/ Area 51: Most of the area is privately owned and for this reason not included in this guide.

Schuylkill County Crags: An immeasurable amount of areas. Most are privately owned.

Birdsboro: Although access is no longer an issue, I wanted to test the waters while others compile guidebooks before adding it to this book. Birdsboro Quarry will most likely be in a future addition of this book or on our website www.paclimbing.com. A new quarry is also going to be developed in nearby state park thanks to the efforts of a devoted local climber. Perhaps in the future a guidebook will be available for this area.

Using this Guide

Rock Climbing and Bouldering Pennsylvania is the first comprehensive guidebook for the state…ever. More than 1000 routes and boulder problems are mentioned in this guide. Photo maps, illustrations, and route descriptions are included for most areas. The only areas that do not include this information area smaller areas that are not highly traveled or are not of high enough quality to warrant this information.

Most climbing and bouldering areas include: **Location**, which includes a general location the area is near; **General Overview**, which includes useful information about the area—like how many routes, what grades are, and other useful tips; **Recommended Rack**, which includes what gear may be useful; **Access Issues and Restrictions,** which includes land ownership information and restrictions for individual areas; **Area Hazards**, which includes known dangers for a particular area; **In Case of Emergency**, which includes contact information for emergency services; **Nearby Areas**, which includes major nearby climbing areas.

Included for every area is a major description and overview of that particular area. This includes more detailed information than what is included in the **General Overview**. Most areas include a detailed **History** of the area which includes first ascent information, historical facts, interesting stories, dates of ascents, and other historical information. I spent many nights making long-distance phone calls to climbers who spanned a history of several decades of developing Pennsylvania climbing. I have tried to compile the first detailed and accurate history for a state that had virtually no documented information of this type. Because of this, some information may be inaccurate—it happens in every guidebook. You will also find a **Directions** section to every area. I have made every attempt to log distances as correctly as possible and be as detailed as possible.

Maps are abundant throughout this guide. The maps are not always to scale but are very close and attempt to identify as many natural landmarks as possible. Topo maps and illustrations of boulder fields and crags are as detailed as I could make them. I purposely used many new techniques to create boulder topos that clearly identify boulders. I hope I have been successful in accurately drawing the maps.

Routes are listed in numerical order. Numbers coincide with topo maps. Not all routes are listed on the maps due to crowding issues. Larger areas are broken into subdivided maps. After the route number the name appears. Next is the route grade and protection rating. First ascent information comes next. The term FA refers to first ascent: the person who first climbed the route. This can mean that that person either lead the route or toproped it. The term FFA refers to first free ascent meaning the first person to redpoint the route on lead. Almost all the routes in this guide are listed by the FA annotation. I did this because it makes things more clear and concise. Although these terms have different meanings virtually every route in this book with first ascent (FA annotation) means that that person did the first free ascent; however, a few do refer to TR ascents. I have tried to note if the first ascent was something other than a free ascent on lead. In compiling this book it was cumbersome and many times impossible to determine who first climbed routes but it was easier to determine who did the first free ascents. The first ascentionist's name appears first in order if a party of more than one was involved. Many instances it was not possible for climbers to remember who did the FFA so in some instances more than one name appears, noting all climbers involved in first ascent endeavors.

The Rating Game
Ratings are one of the most controversial aspects of climbing—next to bolting of course. Ratings are very subjective—there I said it, now when you're at the crux of a 5.12 I feel is 5.10 you can't banish me to a lifetime of climbing only at "Stover". What appears to be hard to one climber can be easy to another. Height, strength, style and many other facets dictate what is difficult to one climber and easy to another. Please remember this is just a guideline. Do not assume that a rating system—excuse the needless pun—is set in stone. I personally have climbed nearly every route and boulder problem mentioned in this guide to assure proper protection ratings and accurate grades. I also relied on a great deal of input from people who climbed routes in Pennsylvania extensively, were very competent at grading routes, or did first ascents of the routes themselves. Keeping this in mind, there are bound to be mistakes in this guide due to typographical errors, personal thoughts, or changes in rock. I have made every attempt to keep sandbagging and ego from grades in this guide. If you feel a route grade is in error, I would be happy to change it. If you strongly feel a grade is off, it may very well be. Don't take grades to hart, climb for fun.

Route Grades

I use the Yosemite Decimal System—like people buy books with the Easter Island or El Salvador System anyway. This system is the adopted system of the U.S. Routes begin at 5.0 (technical rock) and end at 5.15+ (at present). A (+) or (−) sign after a route annotates a route being slightly harder or easier respectively. Letters following a YDS grade like a,b,c, or d stand for additional difficult of the grade. A protection rating is also listed to determine how safe or unsafe a lead may be. The ratings are as follows:

G Excellent protection. Gear and rest stances are abundant.

PG Pretty good gear placements, pretty good stances.

PG/R Not quite PG yet not quite R. Gear is not great.

R Poorly protected and or strenuous placements. Injury may result from a fall.

X Extremely poor gear, unreliable gear or no gear. A fall will most likely result in serious injury or death.

Boulder Ratings

John Sherman once told me he wished he'd never invented the V scale. It was a necessary evil. The V scale or "Verm" scale is the most commonly accepted scale for bouldering. It is much more involved than its predecessor the B scale invented by John Gill. The V Scale is as follows. Keep in mind the V grades and YDS grades do not always crossover. A V6 may not convert to a hard twelve just as a 5.9 may not always convert directly to a V0 or V0-.

V1	**5.11a**
V2	**5.11b,c**
V3	**5.11d**
V4	**5.12a**
V5	**5.12a,b**
V6	**5.12d**

V7   **5.13a**

V8   **5.13b,c**

V9   **5.13d**

V10   **5.14a**

V11   **5.14b,c**

V12   **5.14d**

V13   **5.15**

V14   **Off the scale**

V15   **if you climb this grade, you don't need this chart.**

Bouldering Protection Scale

G Good landing. Not exactly a bed of feathers, but not a pungie pit either.

PG Pretty good.

R Dangerous with the possibility of dangerous objects to land on and or a high fall. The stuff E.R. visits are made of.

X Extremely dangerous. Death may result from a fall of this type.

Notes

Notes

Eastern Pennsylvania

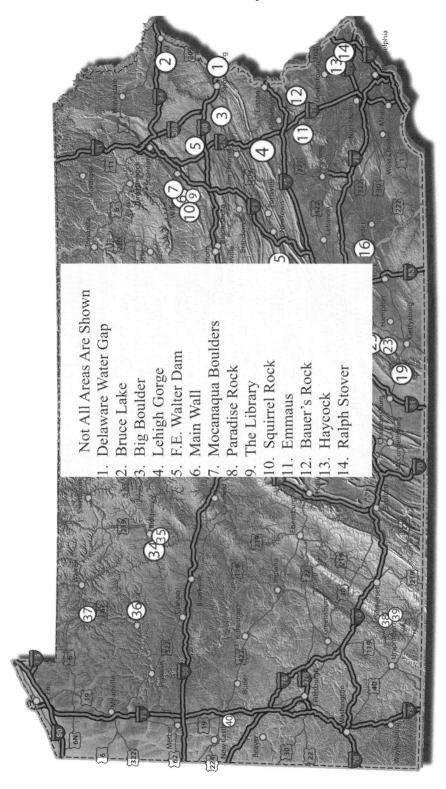

Not All Areas Are Shown
1. Delaware Water Gap
2. Bruce Lake
3. Big Boulder
4. Lehigh Gorge
5. F.E. Walter Dam
6. Main Wall
7. Mocanaqua Boulders
8. Paradise Rock
9. The Library
10. Squirrel Rock
11. Emmaus
12. Bauer's Rock
13. Haycock
14. Ralph Stover

1. Delaware Water Gap

Area Beta

Location
Pennsylvania and New Jersey border.

Type of Rock
Some of the highest rock in the state. Best trad climbing in Pennsylvania and New Jersey.

Other Beta
Don't listen to the rumors, visit this area!

Falcon Closures
Depending on the year, there are sometimes falcon closures. View the park website to see if and when it is in effect.

Introduction

Exposed climbing and breathtaking views characterize The Delaware Water Gap. Long regarded as a playground of overhangs, this spot has lured climbers for decades. Anyone who drives the winding I-80 corridor, through the deeply carved Delaware River Valley, peers with astonished eyes at the looming cliff-face above. A regular site at the roadside overlook finds tourist's hearts racing as they spy climbers high above on disheartening faces.

Many climbers have cut their teeth on the intimidating, steep, walls and overhangs for which this area boasts. One of the most distinct features at this intriguing place is the thrilling overhangs. I would, without question, rank the roofs here amongst some of the best in the East.

Located on both sides of the Delaware River, just outside the town of Stroudsburg, The Water Gap, or "The Gap" as locals call it, offers climbing in both Pennsylvania and New Jersey. Mt. Minsi in Pennsylvania, and Mt. Tammany in New Jersey, both offer numerous grades and difficulties on high, multi-pitch rock. Mt. Minsi, home to the highest natural cliff in Pennsylvania, is 200' in height; Mt. Tammany possesses the higher of the two cliffs and the highest cliff in New Jersey at 280'.

Although loose rock can be found on many climbs at The Gap, most of the established routes have solid rock that is somewhat reminiscent of the nearby Gunk's. In fact, this rock is a gray conglomerate and sandstone of the Silurian Shawangunk formation. Instead of climbing the usually overcrowded Gunk's, a trip to The Water Gap can be a very pleasurable and worthwhile excursion.

This guidebook lists 154 routes ranging from 4th Class to 5.12d. Some routes in this book are not known to climbers, and are not listed in any other guidebooks. I tried to include most of the climbs on the Pennsylvania side of the river. To compensate for excluding part of the New Jersey side, I have included many lesser known Minsi gems. Due to size limits of this guide shy of resembling *War and Peace*, I opted to leave a large portion of the New Jersey side out—heck, it's in another state anyway. One major asset found in this book is the bouldering section and section of the *Minsi Ridge Cliff*. This bouldering area and small crag have never before been documented and are previously unknown to the majority of the climbing community.

There are a few things to be mindful of when climbing at The Gap. One of the first things you will notice about The Gap that differs from most Pennsylvania crags, is the large amount of rock over a large area. Because of this, it is important to plan your day around weather, climate, and time constraints. Although the steep approach isn't long—at least not on the grand scheme of things—it's quite long for Pennsylvania standards, and many climbers find it exhausting. It is important to pack extra water, especially if you plan to hike to the extreme high end of the ridge. Also, be aware that route finding at such a large climbing area can be tricky; it is important to keep track of what section of cliff you are at as you progress along the ridge. Allow plenty of time to return to your car if you are at the high end of the ridge late in the day. A headlamp is a great asset and sensible accompaniment at The Gap; a helmet is a must!

Sadly, there have been three climbing fatalities to date at The Gap. In 1978 a climber was killed from injuries sustained from a fall due to gear failure at the nearby Yards Creek Reservoir section of The Gap. Two climbers have been killed on the Pennsylvania side of The Gap. One incident involved rockfall that had severed the climber's rope, another involved a faulty rap-anchor. All have been extremely unfortunate accidents.

The Gap is certainly an adventurous place to climb. A climbing partner of mine brought an interesting fact to my attention recently. He said that when the majority of climbers speak about The Gap, they regard the cliff as choss. When asked when he'd last climbed there, his response was "Never". My point is, don't knock the area if you haven't climbed here. This area offers exhilarating, diverse, alpinesqe climbing--in Pennsylvania and New Jersey of all places. You'd be crazy not to climb such an amazing place so close to home.

History

The Water Gap has a long history of climbing but, unfortunately, a short recorded history of ascents. It is known that climbing took place here on the jagged rock faces as long ago as three centuries, when Native American Indian's roamed the river valley. It is believed the Delaware Indians climbed some of the rock faces as tests of courage and bravery.

One tale involves great heartbreak. A Lenape Indian princess, in love with an Englishman was shunned by her tribe. The princess leapt from the Tammany cliff to profess her love. It is told that on misty nights a flame can be seen descending the point where she leapt to her death. This spot is known as Lover's Leap.

One of the earliest rumors of technical rock climbing at The Gap involves the legendary John Turner. It is believed that he had climbed some routes here at an undetermined time prior to the 1960s. Although it has never been proven, it is also rumored that Fritz Wiessner and Hans Kraus may have climbed at the cliffs around a similar timeframe—how could someone avoid such tempting faces after all? Another common belief is that Bob Cambers and perhaps Ritner Walling, a colorful climber from Philadelphia who pioneered routes at The Gunk's and The Tetons, may have been a developer in the early years. Considering the alluring nature of the cliffs and close proximity to these climbers, it is likely any or all of these climbers would have visited here. But it never has been authenticated that they had.

It is known that prior to 1975 classics like *Surprise* 5.4, *Triumvirate* 5.4, and *Colorado* 5.6 were climbed during this timeframe. Remnants of old pitons and resident fixed gear support these facts; however, it is not known who placed the gear. For this reason many theories exist about who may have pioneered the routes, but it is anyone's guess who climbed them.

Keith Uhl on the first ascent of "Morning Sickness." Photo by Mike Steele.

In 1978, Hugh Dougher wrote the first guidebook for The Gap. It included 40 rock routes as well as a few ice routes. The guide was called *Rock and Ice in The Gap*. Hugh was one of the early pioneers of extensive development at the cliffs. Hugh Dougher along with Henry McMahon, developed many classics on Mt. Minsi including *Boca Roca Grande* 5.7+, *High Falls* 5.8+, and *Osprey* 5.6 to name a few.

Shortly after the Dougher guide went out of print, Michael Steel, a park ranger at The Water Gap in the 1980s, printed the first comprehensive guide to the area in 1987, and a revised second edition in 1989. Michael Steele did an excellent job of compiling all the routes in his book. He had even climbed all the routes with the exception of a few. Some of Steele's achievements include *Voyage of the Damned* 5.11a, *Chieftain* 5.8+, *Billy Goat Gruff* 5.7, and many other climbs. Steele was perhaps the most influential climber to explore and develop this quartzite Mecca. Steele developed countless classics between 1984 and 1989. Second only to his climbing achievements was his devout land stewardship. Mike was an excellent caretaker of this stone fortress. After Mike moved to the West, a noticeable decline in route cleanliness was obvious.

Along with Steele, many other climbers such as Bill Ravitch, Nick Miskowski, and Todd Swain, who has written a popular Gunk's guidebook and several other books on popular climbing destinations, established some of the true difficult classics on the Minsi cliff.

Keith Uhl added some of the finest routes at The Gap in 1989. His first ascents on *The Morning Wall* challenge climbers to this day. Keith made many notable ascents in Yosemite, The Gunks and many other places (many he was never credited for due to his modest nature), but he once told me some of his most memorable ascents were on these high walls above the Delaware. Keith's first ascents of *Morning Wall* truly brought a new standard of climbing to these daunting walls.

Another "heavy user" and prolific local was Mark Ronca. Mark was a true pioneer of the 1990s at the area. Mark introduced serious aid climbing and pushed the grades of hard-man trad climbing at the cliffs. *Screaming Eagle* 5.12d R is a prime example of Mark's high ethical standards and raw climbing skills. This climb remains the most difficult grade at The Gap and remains one of the hardest trad lines in the mid-Atlantic.

Matt Hill, Carlie Ronca, Paul Newman, Jeff Gagliano, Ryan Lukas, Tom Kneiss, Nick Morell, Randy Ross, Rob Muti, and myself were also active route developers from the early '90s to 1999. I added several spicy leads like *Edge of Night* 5.12a, *Jesus Built my Hotrod* 5.10c, and *Hanging Gardens* 5.9+. Many of these and other routes were developed with Nick Morell, Ryan Lukas, Rob Muti, Tom Kneiss and Randy Ross. Because we did them after work, many of these outings took place as late night excursions on difficult runout terrain.

A multitude of new route potential still exists here. If you're looking for a good bit of untapped rock, this is the place.

Trip Planning

General Location: 10 miles east of Stroudsburg, Pennsylvania, and 10 miles west of Buttsville, New Jersey.

Cliff Description: 200' faces. Lots of overhangs, face climbs, crack climbs and a small amount of bouldering. 125 routes on the Pennsylvania side and 140 on the New Jersey side, not including areas farther north along the *Kittatinny Ridge*. Routes range from 4th class to 5.12d. Mostly trad routes with some semi-bolted routes. The area also boasts some of the best ice climbs in the mid-Atlantic.

Gear Recommendations: A standard rack of variable sized nuts and cams are recommended. Large cams will be helpful on many climbs. Horizontals are abundant so bring extra cams and TCUs. Webbing is a cautious supplement to some fixed tree anchors. Many rappel trees and rappel stations are reliable, but expect to find un-maintained or unreliable stations on less traveled routes. Wear a helmet!

Weather and Climbing Season: The spring and fall are the most enjoyable times to climb here. Summer is popular, but heat, humidity, poison ivy, and insects dissuade many climbers from slogging up the steep talus slope. Winter is cold and the exposed, rock faces yield an uninviting location for winter craging, but it's a good time to avoid the insects and ivy.

Access, Ownership, and Restrictions: The Delaware Water Gap is a National Recreation Area. This area has recognized and permitted climbing since the 1970s. The Park and climbers have a long-standing relationship that has continued to grow for several years. Follow rules and regulations of the park in order to keep this existing relationship.

The Access Fund has worked with the park regarding fixed anchors and raptor closures. The outcome of these talks about anchors is to allow safe replacement of poor existing anchors by designated individuals. The outcome regarding Falcons is a restriction due to Peregrine Falcon nesting at a section of the *Minsi Cliff*. There is a mandatory closure that lasts from spring until August. The closure has varied in the past years—some years the birds appear to nest and other years, they don't. It is important to check if the cliff is closed, or if part of the cliff is closed due to nesting raptors. The park can be contacted at 570-588-2452 or by checking on the web at www.nps.gov/dewa/index.htm.

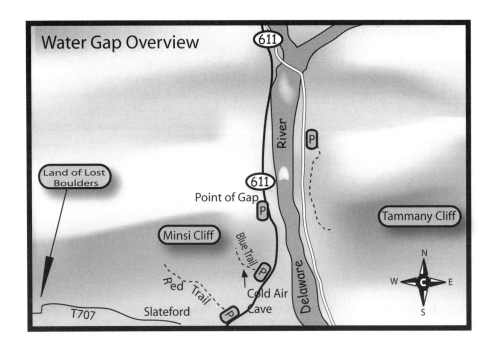

Ethical Considerations: The main ethical concern to date revolves around bolting. In recent years, several instances have encountered bolts being placed on existing trad climbs, bolts being placed next to textbook gear placements, and excessive over-bolting of climbs. These unfortunate occurrences ended in bolt chopping. Unfortunately, this is a poor solution to the bolting problem.

Perhaps the best conclusions to future problems lie in good communication between climbers. Before adding fixed hardware to a climb: talk to locals, find out what has and has not been established, and come to an amicable agreement. Hopefully, friendly communication will bring positive solutions and existing routes will remain unchanged.

The Water Gap has a long history of priding itself on stiff, trad climbs. In recent times many mixed (some bolt some trad) routes have been developed. As more and more of the untapped, trad-lines disappear, the bleak, unprotected faces seem to yield the majority of presently undeveloped routes. As this begins to happen, bolt placement will become more and more prevalent.

At present, the park frowns on the use of motorized drills; however, permission has been granted to select individuals for anchor replacement of existing anchors only!

In a nutshell, if you are going to establish a new climb, seek out local climbers who know the area well, and find out if a proposed new route has been done in a traditional form already. Do not place bolts in areas that the park deems inappropriate. Lastly, don't place bolts where gear can be placed.

Camping Information: The nearest spot for public camping is in Worthington State Forest. The campground offers a moderate amount of sites. The campground can be reached at 908-496-4458. It is located a few miles north of The Water Gap, along the Delaware River.

Safety Concerns: Some common hazards at The Gap are snakes, Poison Ivy (quite a bit at the base of climbs), ticks, chiggers, and loose rock. Although the climbs are solid—for the most part—loose rock can be found on many climbs. One fatality has occurred at the gap due to loose rock. Be very careful near anything that looks loose and please wear a helmet!

In Case of an Emergency: Dial 911 or call the park headquarters at 570-588-2435. 24-hour emergency services are also found at 1-800-543-HAWK(4295).

Other Nearby Areas: Rick's Rocks (NJ), Allamuchy (NJ), Yards Creek (Now Closed), Bangor Crag, Wind Gap Ridge, Bangor Quarry, Wolf Rocks, and 115 Boulders.

Mt. Minsi

When you climb on Mount Minsi, you climb some of the nicest trad in the Mid Atlantic. This cliff that brags being the highest in Pennsylvania holds true to its alpinesque feel, multi-pitch leads, and thrilling exposure. Climb on Minsi and you are bound for a day of adventure that is unrivaled with any other keystone crag.

Descent Options: The most popular descent routes on Minsi are the rappels on a few highly traveled routes. The **Intimidation Wall** has a **60-meter rappel** on **Teardrop Buttress**. **Two Double Rope rappels** can be achieved on **Pussytoes** where there is a two-bolt rappel. **Crackpot** has a **two-bolt rappel** on top the first pitch. **Surprise** is the most popular route for rappel of the Land of Giants wall. A two-rope rappel is advised. **Morning Wall** has a **two-bolt anchor** on top and on pitch one. **Hell and High Water** has a **two-bolt anchor** near the top pitch and on top of the first pitch of Sleeping Beauty there is one also. **Osprey** has a **two-bolt anchor** near the top pitch. Do not climb or rappel here if Falcons are present.

When rappelling from routes farther down the ridge from *Osprey* I strongly recommend bringing slings and rappelling supplements. Many of the rappels farther down the ridge are dubious.

Directions: From the town of Delaware Water Gap follow Route 611 south for several miles. You will drive through the Gap and come to the Point of Gap parking area. Park at the second of two small, dirt parking areas on the right just after the Point of Gap parking lot. The cliff is visible above. Walk to the Cold Air cave and follow the trail that goes off and right from here. About 10 minutes hike up the steep talus will bring you to the base of *The Practice Face.*

Note: Another trail departs the paved parking lot just after the Cold Air Cave pull-off (regular parking area for the cliff). The trail that can be found here is not often used and is more difficult than the main approach trail. The only reason for using this second trail is to access climbs near *Boca Roca Grande.* Most climbers follow the regular approach trail to *Boca Roca* from the Cold Air Cave, but it is shorter to use this alternate trail; however, most find it more difficult to access the cliff this way.

Falcon Closure Information:

Part of the Minsi cliff is sometimes closed due to nesting falcons. This closure varies from year to year. As of 2010, there is a seasonal closure that may effect all or part of the PA cliff. Contact the park website or climbing message boards to determine how long the closure is in effect as it varies greatly.

Intimidation Wall

This is the intimidating wall to the right of the approach trail. It begins at the right end of *Practice Face*, and continues to *Teardrop Buttress*. Many of the routes on this face are steep and wander a bit. The cliff can be descended by rappelling down *Teardrop Buttress* via a rappel tree (60m rappel) or by rappelling via a single rope from trees 10' below and right of the *Teardrop Buttress* rappel.

1. Teardrop Buttress 5.3 G
FA: Unknown pre 1970
This is the buttress just right of a large dirty gully. Ascend the buttress or crack near it, then swing around the right side of the buttress and squeeze through the overhang near a tree. Rap from slings at the rappel tree (60m rappel). This climb is often wet and has some loose rock.

2. Shredded Meat 5.5 G
FA: Hugh Dougher, Henry McMahon
Climb the left side of the big gully via the big, dirty chimney. Head right at the top to the big rappel tree.

3. Bird Dog 5.10b G/PG
FA: Hugh Dougher, Henry McMahon
Start left of the previous climb and bark right to a big corner tilted rightward. After climbing its awesome moves, belay left at its top. Paw your way left to the top of the climb.

4. Gap View Heights 5.10d G/PG
FA: Hugh Dougher, Henry McMahon
This long, strenuous climb ascends the large, foreboding corner left of *Bird Dog*. Gain the large corner by stepping off right of the low initial corner. Swing left when you reach the ceiling at the top of the corner and then traverse 25' left to a belay. Rappel or follow *Tower of Flowers* to the top.

5. Tower of Flowers 5.10b G
FA: Hugh Dougher, Henry McMahon
Most people do the first pitch then rappel. **Pitch 1:** Start the same as *Gap View* at the large corner. Move left into a corner and follow it past a small ceiling midway up, then move up into an overhanging corner. Continue up this to its top and move left. **Pitch 2:** Continue up and along the left side of a right-arching corner, traverse right to the end of a ceiling, and then move straight up to the top.

6. Touch and Blow 5.10a R
FA: Mark Ronca
If you need an excuse to relieve your bowels, climb this route. Often toproped. Start in the same spot as the previous two climbs and climb a few feet up and traverse far left past the *Tower of Flowers* corner. From here move up and into a right-facing corner at 50'. Continue up this past a ceiling and the communal rappel on *Gap View Heights*/Tower of *Flowers*.

7. Lemonade 5.6 R

FA: Hugh Dougher, Lyle Schultze

Not recommended due to bad rock, unappealing climbing, and limited pro. If that doesn't dissuade you, the bad rappel tree should. Climb a dirty ramp up and past two right-facing corners to the large, right-facing corner (*Pink Lemonade*). Continue up this corner to the top.

8. Pink Lemonade 5.7 PG

Best done in two pitches. Climb the long corner to pull out left of the ceiling high above.

9. Razors Edge 5.11a PG

FA: Michael Steele

Ascend the previous route to the small ledge where *Lemonade* and *Pink Lemonade* meet. From this ledge, traverse up and left heading for a big horizontal up high. At this horizontal move left and merge with the belay on *Drifting Arrow*.

The Practice Face

This is the 60' wide, 25' high face where the blue approach trail joins the base of the cliff. It is a popular spot for toproping and for beginners before they depart to seek out higher ground. To set up a toprope here, traverse the obvious ledge that can be gained at the left edge of the face. Rappelling from the second pitch of the routes in this section is questionable. It is best to walk to *Pussytoes* and rappel with two double-rope rappels. Also, a rappel can be achieved off the first belay on *Cat O'Nine Tails*.

Intimidation Wall

10. Lactic Acid Ladybugs 5.11b PG
FA: Mark Ronca

Pumpy and technical. **Pitch 1:** Start on the right side of *The Practice Face* and climb the three-tiered overhang above to a belay that is 35' above the overhang. **Pitch 2:** Continue up to a large roof with a deep notch and then climb up and right through the notch.

11. Drifting Arrow 5.6+ PG
Pitch 1: Start at the right side of *The Practice Face*, slightly left of *Lactic Acid*, and cruise up a corner to a belay. **Pitch 2:** Continue up to a large roof with a deep notch, then climb up and right, through this notch.

12. Expresso 5.9 PG
FA: Michael Steele

An optional belay can be set 40' off the ground. Climb a crack in the middle of *The Practice Face* past a ledge to a blocky corner. Continue up through a small overhang and climb up the face to a large right-facing corner (*High Falls* final corner). Follow the big corner to the top and move left at the final overhang.

13. High Falls 5.8+ PG
FA: Hugh Dougher

It's best to set up a belay to begin this climb, because it starts above *The Practice Face*. Many people do this climb in three pitches to reduce rope drag. **Pitch 1:** Climb the left side of *The Practice Face* to a ledge (optional belay), then climb a long left-facing corner to a ceiling (optional belay) escaped at its right side. From here move up a right-facing corner 15', and belay under a roof. **Pitch 2:** Move right around the big roof (crux), and into a large right-facing corner   climb up this and escape left out the final roof.

14. Scardy Cat A1
Aid problem number 16 (*Cat O' Nine Tails*). The original aid line was done without bolts.

15. Hillbent Hooks 5.11a PG A2
FA: Matt Hill (rope solo)

This climb was named for the special hooks Matt Hill crafted for the first ascent. Climb up the rock to the first large roof on *High Falls*. Climb the roof and aid with hooks or free climb the face at 5.11a. Belay under the next roof above. From a hanging belay, aid out the center of the roof and climb straight up.

16. Cat O' Nine Tails 5.12a (a.ka. Scardy Cat)
FA: Paul Nick

The route was previously done as an aid route; attempted by climbers but never freed until Paul Nick successfully freed it after adding bolts. He renamed it *Cat O' Nine Tails*. **Pitch 1:** 20' left of the previous climb find your way up a dihedral to the left side of a big roof. **Pitch 2:** Move right and pull past the roof and two bolts (Crux), and diagonal up and right passing blocky features near the summit.

Cat Wall
This wall contains climbs 17 - 20. It is the short wall that forms the large left-facing corner.

The main rappel is achieved by two double-rope rappels down *Pussytoes*. There is a bolted anchor above *Pussytoes* and *Alley Cat*.

17. Tom Cat 5.7 PG/ R
FA: Michael Steele, Kim Alicandri
One to leave you purring. Climb up the prow/corner left of the previous route to an overhang. Belay or climb the crack left of the roof and diagonal right to the prow again, and climb past the right side of two ceilings to reach the summit.

18. Pussytoes 5.5+ PG
FA: Michael Steele, Ellen Waible
Don't forget your catnip. Climb ledges in the center of a short face around the left corner from *The Practice Face* to a ledge 30' up. Next, ascend a small corner, then a short crack (crux), and pass an overhang and a belay tree at their right sides. Hiss up and right and then scratch your way straight to the top. Lots of trees to sling.

19. Alley Cat 5.6 PG
Pitch 1: Start on *Pussytoes* and go left before the tree-ledge and belay below the ceiling at 55'. **Pitch 2:** Head left to a ceiling escaped at its left side. Wander straight up to finish.

20. Sex Kitten 5.7+ PG
FA: Michael Steele
If you like choss, and most Gap climbers do, this is the route for you. **Pitch 1:** Climb the unappealing corner paralleling *Alley Cat* and pass an overhang on the right side. Move out left to a belay. **Pitch 2:** Traverse out left and up from the belay on poor-quality rock to join *Shoes for the Millipedes*.

The Grunge Wall
This is the unappealing-looking wall left of the *Cat Wall*. If you have climbed every other climb at The Gap and decide to do any of the climbs on this wall, don't waste your time; go climb someplace else. Should you decide to wade this vast sea of dilapidated rock and decomposing flora, a questionable rappel can be done from a tree above *Stronger than Dirt* (the tree may not be as optimal as the name implies). Similar trees can be rappelled on routes 29 and 30.

21. Shoes for the Millipedes 5.4 PG
Pitch 1: Climb the dirt, moss, muck, and funk 40' left of *Sex Kitten*, straight up to a big ledge half-way up the cliff. **Pitch 2:** Head a bit right, and up to a small ceiling passed on the right; then dig your way to the summit.

22. The Great Escape 5.4 PG
Pitch 1: Squirm up the obvious chimney 15' left of *Shoes*, and go through the ceiling above. Move left to a nice belay ledge. **Pitch 2:** Climb straight up from the ledge 30' up, and move right to a ceiling passed on its right.

23. Stronger than Dirt 5.6 + PG
This climb goes up the wall left of *The Great Escape*. Climb corners and small ceilings to the large ledge above. You can rap with two ropes or continue up the wall that is left of the

belay ledge (not recommended).

24. Baby Face 5.7 PG
FA: Michael Steele, Nick Maskowski
Climb the face 25' left of the previous route to a good belay ledge. Next, climb up to and around the left side of a small overhang, to another ledge. You can walk right to rappel off a pine tree on the previous route or scum up to the summit.

25. Sphagnum Force 5.7 PG
25' left of *Baby Face* is a low roof with a crack. Climb up to and over the roof via the crack, and rappel.

26. Captain Crunch 5.7- PG
Start left of *Sphagnum* at the left side of a low overhang. Climb up to and over the overhang and traverse right for 15'. Climb up corners (Crux) to the top and belay or continue to join with *Baby Face* above.

27. Fall Into the Gap 5.5 PG
90' left of the previous route, climb an obvious corner to a ceiling midway up. Pull the ceiling and continue to a rappel above.

28. For Whom the Bridge Tolls 5.5 PG
Climb the corner and face 20' left of the previous climb. Rappel from the same tree as the previous route.

29. Scouter 5.2 G
70' left of the previous climb, just left of a big corner in the cliff, climb a small inside-corner to a weakness above, and follow this weakness to a rappel tree.

30. Twilight Time 5.5 PG
Slightly left of *Scouter*, climb up to a big, slanting right-facing corner. Move up this (Crux) and move left at the top to a rappel.

31. Frigid Dare 5.5 PG
Diagonal upward and right on the face between *Twilight Time* and the *Crackpot* corner.

Land of the Giants
This is the massive roof-system, left of the *Grunge Wall*. The best rappel point is from the route *Surprise*. A single double-rope rappel or two single-rope rappels will bring you to the ground. Be mindful that the rappel tree in the gulley at the top of the first pitch is hollow in spots.

32. Crackpot 5.4+ PG/R
This route was recently, unnecessarily retro-bolted. Cruise up and right to follow a prow over a ledge, and pass an overhang at its right side. Move out right to a big tree. A single-rope rappel barely brings you to the ground. Two bolt anchor below large roof system.

Var. 1: The Jerseylvania Shuffle 5.6 PG/R

FA: R. Holzman, N. Morell

Climb the same line as *Crackpot*, but move left at the final roof pulling the roof at its arete. Continue straight up, and downclimb slightly to the rappel.

Var. 2: Not My Forte 5.8 PG/R

FA: D. Kotch, J. Forte, R. Holzman

Climb up to the right of the previous two routes. When you find steep rock, follow a big crack up and left. Use the anchors for *Crackpot*. A hard 5.10 variation can be done to the right on the steep, slick rock. It is not protectable.

33. Crickety Crack 5.5 G

Start around the corner from the previous route and run up past ledges and trees to a small cave. Jam out an overhanging crack (crux) that splits the cave, and rap from the tree above.

34. Crackly Corner 5.5 G

FA: Ed Walters, Ed Brock

Start as for *Crickety*, but move left before the cave, and climb the left crack near the corner of the wall. Belay the same as *Crickety*. The second pitch rises up and left traveling far across the wall, above giant overhangs, and following the easiest-looking path. Most people rap off the first pitch.

35. Big Time Football 5.7 A3

FA: Matt Hill (rope solo)

Bring Knifeblades, Lost Arrows and your mojo. Begin left of the *Crackley Corner* corner, and head straight up to the right side of the giant roof (90'). Aid out the roof, and hook up left over steep terrain, then continue up to the top.

36. Money Baby 5.7 A2+

FA: Matt Hill (rope solo)

Hooks, Knifeblades, Lost arrows, and Copperheads may be useful. Start on the previous route, and break left of the big roof. Climb a seam farther left in the roof and rejoin the previous climb.

37. Point of No Return 5.9- PG

FA: Hugh Dougher, Henry McMahon

Pitch 1: Begin left of the previous climb, near a left-facing corner system. Climb up the corner and move onto the face. Next, head above the corner, moving out left to another corner at the right end of the *Voyage of the Damned* roof. This roof is the very large roof with a large corner leading up to its center (there is a higher roof directly above this called *Land of the Chiefs* roof). From the right side of the *Voyage* roof, head up a corner to a belay at the end of the corner under a ceiling. **Pitch 2:** Traverse left out the roof/corner and continue for 20' to another right-facing corner. Climb up this corner and move out left at the final roof. Continue left to a good rappel tree.

38. Land of the Chiefs 5.9+ PG

FA: Michael Steele, Kim Alicandri

Climb off a ledge with trees, 60' left of *Point of No Return*, and right of the *Voyage* corner.

27. Fall Into the Gap 5.5 PG
28. For Whom 5.5 PG
29. Scouter 5.2 G
30. Twilight Time 5.5 PG
32. Crackpot 5.4+ PG/R

22. The Great Escape 5.4 PG
23. Stronger than Dirt 5.6+ PG
24. Baby Face 5.7 PG
26. Captain Crunch 5.7- PG

The Grunge Wall

Climb straight up a face past roofs and pull through two final roofs (crux) to join *Point of No Return* at the belay ledge.

39. Who's Andy Lemon? 5.10a A2+

FA: Matt Hill, Mark Ronca

Well, who is he? Start on *Land of the Chiefs* and climb to the first belay. From here, move out right and up the obvious notch to a roof. Move out the big roof and continue up a right-facing corner above, to another roof. Move out left to a good rappel tree.

40. Voyage of the Dammed 5.11a PG

 FA: Michael Steele

One of the most exhilarating climbs anywhere! Climb an obvious crack, then a corner, just right of *Chieftain*, to a ledge below a giant overhang system and belay. Pull the roof (crux) at a crack with good holds; then move right using a good horizontal; then up to a bigger horizontal passing a corner to another corner and a belay. Climb the corner and join *P.O.N.R.* to finish. Bring double ropes or your voyage may be dammed.

41. Damned Voyager Direct 5.7 A3

FA: Mark Ronca

Lots of nailing, hooks, and other fun aid stuff make this route a distinctive aid-route. Climb *Voyage of the Damned* to its big roof and move left to aid out a seam in the roof.   From here move out right and aid two more roofs to gain the summit.

42. Oops 5.11a PG

FA: Bob Almond, Keith Thompson, Bill Markland

Move up to and out the left side of the beefy part of the *Voyage of the Damned* roof, just left of the previous route. From the top of the roof, climb a right-facing corner and move left to a good rappel-tree.

43. Chieftain 5.8+ PG/R

FA: Michael Steele, Nick Miskowski

Start on a ledge 15' above the trail, in a large gully. Climb a face past two overhangs, passing the first hang at its right, and the second at its left. Pass a third hang going out a crack at its right side, and belay at a large ledge below a big overhang. Pull directly over the center of the overhang, and then finish up the final corner and small hangs.

44. Bloodsport 5.9 PR/R

FA: Mike Cichon, Rob Holzman

A spicy and exciting lead. Climb the face slightly left of *Chieftain*, to the final overhang on *Chieftain*. Pull the overhang slightly left of the original line.

45. Surprise 5.4 PG

FA: Unknown pre.1975

Begin a few feet right of the large gully, near a big tree. Climb a faint open-book to a small, blocky ceiling. Pull through the ceiling at its center, 50' up. Climb a few feet more and belay or continue to the top, following a weakness. A two-rope rappel brings you to the ground.

46. Surprise Surprise 5.7+ PG/R

FA: Rob Holzman, Nick Morell

A nice variation of the original route, and an independent line that gives airy exposure with great views of The Gap. Begin two feet right of *Surprise*, on the arete, and climb the nice arete all the way to the small ledge at the end of the first pitch on *Surprise*. From here climb the not-so-well-protected slabby face to the summit.

47. Wine Couloir 5.3 PG

FA: Unknown

Often very dirty and wet. On the right side of the very large gully that is visible from the road is a well-featured slab. Climb this to a tree with rap-slings and belay (optional). From here move left into a flaring corner system at an overhang. Follow this and then skirt off right to finish. The Rappel tree at the first belay is very hollow and dangerous; the normal rap off Surprise is recommended.

48. Hidden Passage 5.0 PG

Usually dirty and gross. Watch for loose rock! Scum your way up the obvious chimney system in the left corner of the large gully. Near the top, traverse right across a ledge for a short distance and then climb to finish.

49. High Dungeon 5.9+ PG

FA: Michael Steele, Henry McMahon

Climb *Hidden* for 35' to a ledge, then move right until it is possible to gain a bombay chimney. Climb the chimney (crux) to a rappel tree. Finish on *Hidden* or rap. Short but fun.

50. Guru Party 5.9 PG

Climb the corner just left of *Dungeon* to a big hemlock, then move right and up a clean face, then left and up to join *Hidden*.

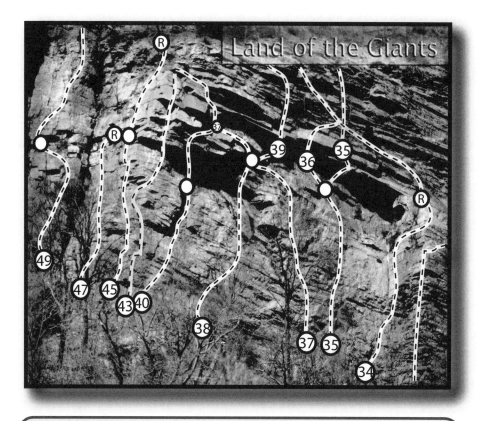

34. Crackly Corner 5.5 G
35. Big Time Football 5.7 A3
36. Money Baby 5.7 A2+
37. P.O.N.R 5.9- PG
38. Land of the Chiefs 5.9+ PG
39. Who's Andy Lemon? 5.10a A2
40. Voyage of Dammed 5.11a PG
43. Chieftain 5.8+ PG/R
45. Surprise 5.4 PG
47. Wine Couloir 5.3 PG
49. High Dungeon 5.9+ PG

The Morning Wall

Keith Uhl was the first to break new terrain and establish routes on this steep, looming wall. This large tower-like feature hosts some of the nicest climbs at The Gap. A double-rope rappel will bring you down or a single-rope will take you to a set of anchors on a ledge in *The Wine Couloir*. A second rappel will bring you to the ground. You can also rappel from the top-anchors to a large tree at the left edge of the ledge near *Melissa*.

51. Morning Wall 5.9+ PG

FA: Keith Uhl, Jetro Oldrich

On a ledge halfway up *Hidden* there is a two-bolt anchor. Move left around a corner and climb flakes past a piton to an overhang and bolt. Move right and around the overhang, then follow a crack left to a two-bolt anchor. Bring some big gear. New bolts were installed on this route in the spring of '99.

Robbie Pepper seconding "Voyage of the Damned". Photo courtesy of Nancy Joseph.

Var. 1: 5.9 Ultraworld Humanoid Lobes
FA: K. Uhl
This route has been incorrectly named in previous guides as *Subterranean Humanoid Lobes*. Keith actually used the name as an acronym for his last name Uhl. Climb the bolts next to *Morning Sickness*. A great variation!

52. Morning Sickness 5.11b PG
FA: Keith Uhl, Jetro Oldrich
The first bolt at The Gap was added to make this route possible. Start on Morning Wall and then climb to a bolt below the overhang at a crack. Pull the hang (crux) and jam the crack, then move up left to the anchor.

53. The Hanging Gardens of Babylon 5.9+ R
FA: Rob Holzman, Tom Kneiss
Named for the hanging vegetation that looms over the final roof. Begin this climb off the base trail and 70'left of the giant gulley. Climb the face through dirty ledges to the belay ledge for the first pitch of *Melissa*. Move out right past *Melissa's* corner-pitch to a face with a shallow crack and climb this to a small roof/bulge. Move left around the ceiling (5.8-) or pull straight over the small hang (5.9+) and continue to the left side of *The Morning Wall*.

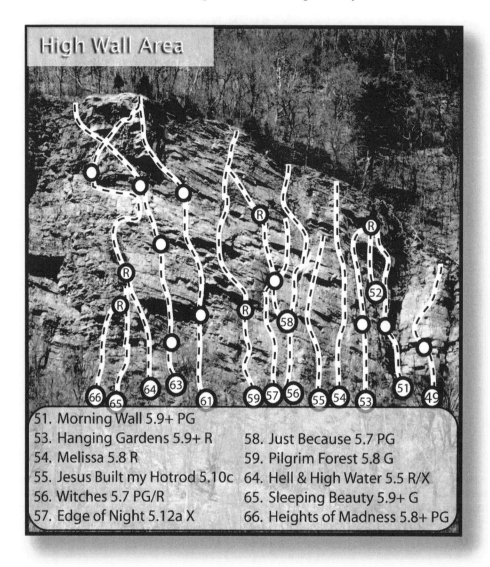

High Wall Area

51. Morning Wall 5.9+ PG
53. Hanging Gardens 5.9+ R
54. Melissa 5.8 R
55. Jesus Built my Hotrod 5.10c
56. Witches 5.7 PG/R
57. Edge of Night 5.12a X
58. Just Because 5.7 PG
59. Pilgrim Forest 5.8 G
64. Hell & High Water 5.5 R/X
65. Sleeping Beauty 5.9+ G
66. Heights of Madness 5.8+ PG

Climb the left side of the roof near a big, loose crack, and move right to fixed anchors.

54. Melissa 5.8 R
FA: Hugh Dougher, Henry McMahon
Start at a crack 25' left of the giant gulley and climb the long face past grassey/chossey rock to a ledge 40' up. Belay here of continue up the delicate left-facing corner, passing a small roof on the right, and belay out right. **Pitch 2:** From here continue left on marginal gear to a roof up high. Move left and climb through the roof to the summit.

55. Jesus Built my Hotrod 5.10c X
FA: Rob Holzman, Randy Ross
Pitch 1: Start the same as *Melissa* but slightly left, on the long face, and climb to *Melissa's* alternate belay 40' at the grassy ledge, on the left edge of the ledge near a tree. **Pitch 2:** Rev up the vertical face above and on to a small ceiling passed on the left and then move straight up to the center of a steep overhang. Pull the center of the hang and motor to the top. Note: The rock to the right at the beginning of the second pitch is loose and should be avoided.

The High Wall
This wall encompasses routes 56 through 74. Several rappel trees and fixed-rap stations lie within this area.

56. Witches 5.7 PG/R
FA: Hugh Dougher, Henry McMahon
Although there are many features for gear on this route, placements in many spots are suspect. Either way, this climb will put a spell on you. **Pitch 1:** At the long face where *Melissa* starts, walk a bit left to a large, dirty groove and climb it to the ledge 40'up. **Pitch 2:** Craft the large, enchanting crack/corner that faces left. After the ceiling the crack/corner passes, move out right past spellbinding exposure, to pass another roof at a breach.

57. The Edge of Night 512a X
FA: Rob Holzman, Tom Kneiss
The top pitch is amongst the most exciting at The Gap. 15' left of *Just Because*, climb to a grassy ledge and find a steep, mossy face that leads past horizontals to a lichen-covered ceiling. Pull the ceiling (5.10- R) and belay just above at a tree between *Witches* and *Just Because*. You will now be below a roof. Climb up to the roof and over (Crux) to a bolted face above.

58. Just Because 5.7 PG
FA: Hugh Dougher, Henry McMahon
Pitch 1: Begin at the left side of a long face (10'left of the start of *Witches*), and climb up to a belay tree where *Witches* breaks off right and up the crack/corner. **Pitch 2:** Climb up a crack that slants slightly left, and around a roof at a notch. Cruise up and left to the top.

59. Pilgrim Forest 5.8 G
Pitch 1: 18' left of *Just Because*, climb through a notch and past ledges to a belay above a flake. **Pitch 2:** Climb a crack through a roof at an old tree (Crux), and continue left to a corner, then a ceiling above that is passed at its left.

60. And Justice for All 5.10a PG
FA: Paul Newman, Kenny Fox
Climb left of *Pilgrim* using the same belay to the second pitch; then follow a crack left of the flake near the crux on *Pilgrim*; then move out left over the overhang.

61. Raptor of the Steep 5.10a PG
An exhilarating, bold lead, that takes you to extreme heights along the apex of the Minsi cliff. **Pitch 1:** Start at an obvious left-facing corner to the left of *Justice* and climb it past

Barry Rusnock leading the mega-classic "Surprise Surprise." Photo by the author.

several ledges to a belay at a steep right-facing corner capped by a roof. **Pitch 2:** Follow the corner and escape left out the roof to some loose, thrilling face-climbing. Diagonal left to the center of a roof at a flake and pull the lip. Climb straight up from there to a belay in an alcove under a roof. **Pitch 3:** Move left along the roof to the massive overhanging arete on the horizon. Climb some of the most thrilling, exposed moves at The Gap to gain the summit.

62. Flying to Houston 5.9 PG
FA: Paul Newman, Chris Buck
Short but sweet. Climb the 20'-high buttress just right of the start of *Cataleptic Communicator*.

63. Cataleptic Communicator 5.11a R
FA: Mark Ronca, Matt Hill
Pitch 1: Begin just right of *Hell and High Water* and climb a dirty slab to an optional belay at 45'. Climb left to a notch and climb an overhang (bolt) to a belay above. **Pitch 2:** Traverse up and left (R-rated) or move to *Hell and High Water* for a semi-well-protected variation (Belay). **Pitch 3:** Power up a difficult poorly-protected crack (crux), and then climb to an arete above.

64. Hell and High Water 5.5R/X
Breaching one of the highest sections of the cliff, this route used to be one of the most thrilling at The Gap; however, since a tragic death occurred on this route from rockfall, this route is no longer recommended. Should you decide to climb it, begin at the obvious crack/slab 15' right of the bolts on *Sleeping Beauty*. Move left, slightly, passing corners, until you reach a belay ledge at an obvious pine tree and rappel station. If you rap here the route is not a dangerous climb. The following pitches are the hazardous ones. **Pitch 2:** Move up and right around slightly-more-difficult rock. Traverse far left under a small overhang and pass the overhang at its left side. Move up slightly to a belay. **Pitch 3:** Climb up very loose, frightening rock and begin to diagonal right, passing under steep sections, to a corner above an overhang and below the overhang escaped at its right. Gain the loose corner and climb it to the top.

65. Sleeping Beauty 5.9+ G
FA: Ed Esmond, Doug Allcock
If grandma is in town and looking of an easy lead, show her this route. Just left of the previous climb, follow an over-bolted face to a crux at the third bolt and below a small ceiling. Continue straight up to gear placements in horizontals and another small roof. Clip the bolt at the roof or place good gear in the crack an arm's reach away and continue to an anchor above. You can rap the first pitch with a single rope from a two-bolt anchor.

66. Heights of Madness 5.8+ PG
FA: Michael Steele, John Steele
Pitch 1: This climb was retro-bolted and renamed *Snow White*. Surprisingly, no one has ever noticed this and chopped the bolts. Climb up left of S*leeping Beauty* to a small ceiling (Crux) and follow it to a belay at the *Hell and High* belay tree. **Pitch 2:** Climb a crack and share *Busses* to an overhang passed on its left. Continue up past loose orange-colored rock

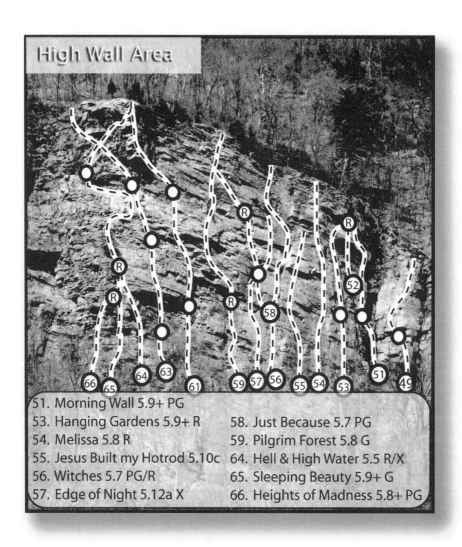

High Wall Area

51. Morning Wall 5.9+ PG
53. Hanging Gardens 5.9+ R
54. Melissa 5.8 R
55. Jesus Built my Hotrod 5.10c
56. Witches 5.7 PG/R
57. Edge of Night 5.12a X

58. Just Because 5.7 PG
59. Pilgrim Forest 5.8 G
64. Hell & High Water 5.5 R/X
65. Sleeping Beauty 5.9+ G
66. Heights of Madness 5.8+ PG

and pass another overhang on the right.

67. Busses 5.7 R
FA: Hugh Dougher, Henry McMahon
The top two pitches should be avoided due to dangerously loose rock. **Pitch 1:** Follow *Heights* to the ceiling, and move left 15' before the ceiling to pull up and right, moving diagonally above the ceiling, to access the *Hell and High* belay tree. **Pitch 2:** climb straight up and left of *Hell and High* to cross over the route to a belay below and left of a high-hanging ceiling and buttress. **Pitch 3:** Pass the hanging buttress on the left; then continue to pass another overhang on the left; then move right and follow *Hell and High* up the final arete to the top.

68. Tombstone 5.8 R
FA: Michael Steele, Randy Seese
Pitch 1: Left of the previous route, climb a face to a small, long ceiling that is climbed on its right side. Move up and left to belay high in a left-facing corner capped by a blocky roof. **Pitch 2:** Move left then right to the right edge of a giant roof. Blast straight to the top, passing very loose rock and following the path of least resistance.

69. Blue Sparks from Hell 5.10a PG
FA: Michael Steele, Bill Ravich
Pitch 1: 18' left of the previous climb, follow a face to the belay on the first pitch of *Tombstone*. **Pitch 2:** Move straight up off the belay and then diagonal far left, until you are under the center of a large roof. Pull through the roof (crux) and belay above. **Pitch 3:** Continue left, passing an overhang on its right side, and then climb straight up to and through the next small overhang. Pass more small overhangs on their left sides and gain a loose blocky corner. Follow this 25'; then traverse 20' left and 15' below a large overhang; then pull through the overhang at a cleft in its left side.

70. Heroine Hypnosis 5.5 G
Pitch 1: A bit left of *Blue Sparks*, climb up a face to a right-facing corner 45' up and follow it through a small roof at the top that is passed on its left. Continue to a left-facing corner and belay. **Pitch 2:** Move left under the overhang and pass it; then pass another overhang on the right; then pass two more overhangs on the right. Climb straight to another overhang that can be breached via a weakness and diagonal left up loose rock. Next traverse 20' left and 15', below a large overhang, and pull through the overhang at a cleft in its left side.

71. Osprey 5.6 G
FA: Hugh Dougher, Henry McMahon
Some of the best rock at The Gap! Falcons sometimes nest near this route. If you spot a Falcon, do not climb near this route. A two-bolt anchor was recently added to the upper pitch to keep rappels away from the nest. **Pitch 1:** 15' left of *Heroine*, climb 35' to a dropped-in section of rock. Move out left from this and continue to a ledge-belay below an overhang. **Pitch 2:** Move out the left side of the overhang and follow *Heroine* to the finish.

72. Pain Builds Character 5.10a PG
FA: Hugh Dougher, Henry McMahon

Tim Bonner on "Surprise." Photo by the author.

Pitch 1: Run up easy rock to a belay at 35' (same as *Osprey*). Climb up to a ceiling and climb the center of it. Next climb a face above and follow a crack off to the right to a belay or move left to climb ceilings to finish.

73. Dragon's Lair 5.9 G
FA: Michael Steele, Randy Seese
Climb this often overlooked route near *Guttersnipe*.

74. Guttersnuipe 5.9 PG
Climb 25' left of *Dragon's Lair* to a corner, gain a weakness in the rock, and then continue to the top.

The Playground
This section contains several lesser-traveled routes. Rappels are dubious here. For this reason, I recommend bringing extra slings to supplement the existing slings and rappel trees.

75. Black Hole 5.6 PG
FA: Michael Steele, Kim Alicandri
This climb is named for an interesting dark-colored hole at the crux. Climb ramps to the ceiling and black hole. Pull the ceiling (optional belay) and move off right through a notch to the top. A two-rope rappel brings you down.

76. Meteorite 5.6 G
FA: Michael Steele, Randy Seese

Climb to a prow and pass a small overhang. Belay off right of the prow or continue straight up, and then move off right to the rappel for *Black Hole* (two ropes).

77. Ladykiller 5.8- G
Just left of *Meteorite*, climb the corner 80' to an overhang passed on its left. Move left to the top. A two-rope rappel brings you down.

78. Fiddlesticks 5.4 G
Start on a ledge above the trail, at a pine tree, and climb 45' to another pine, and then continue to the top.

79. Hopscotch 5.6 PG
A nice route near *Fiddlesticks*.

80. Cry Baby Crack 5.5 G
Climb to a ledge below a large off-width crack and move out left to the corner of the face at a roof. Pass the right tip of the roof and diagonal up and left to trees.

81. Little Goof 5.5 G
FA: Michael Steele, Todd Swain
Left and around the corner from *Cry Baby*, climb up to an overhang and climb its right side. Continue straight up and rappel (one rope).

Screaming Eagle Area
This area is easily located by finding a large roof that caps the face below. Descend by rappelling from the trees on *Screaming Eagle* or *Daring Do*.

82. Elders of the Tribe 5.9- G
FA: Michael Steele, Bill Ravich
Start 12' left of *Goof* and climb up to the right/center of a roof. Pull through the roof and escape around the left side of a second roof. Continue to pass a blocky feature on the left, and pass a roof on the right. Continue to the top to a rappel that can be done with one rope.

83. Dancing Fool 5.7 PG/R
FA: Michael Steele, Kim Alacandri
Start left of the previous route and climb up and left to a large corner capped by a huge, long roof. Move up the corner to breach the roof at its right side and climb to another roof above, passed on its left. Run off left to a rappel tree.

84. Anything for a Laugh 5.8 PG
FA: Michael Steele, 1990
Begin left of the previous route at the right-center of the massive roof, along a left-facing corner. Climb up to and pull the roof and continue straight up to the communal rap-tree.

85. Monmouth Madman 5.11d PG
FA: Mark Ronca
Climb a slab a few feet left of *Anything for a Laugh*. Move up to the center of the roof,

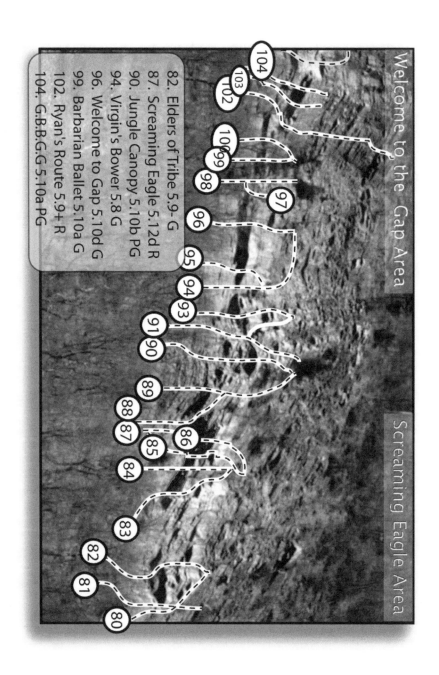

Welcome to the Gap Area

Screaming Eagle Area

82. Elders of Tribe 5.9- G
87. Screaming Eagle 5.12d R
90. Jungle Canopy 5.10b PG
94. Virgin's Bower 5.8 G
96. Welcome to Gap 5.10d G
99. Barbarian Ballet 5.10a G
102. Ryan's Route 5.9+ R
104. G.B.B.G.G 5.10a PG

pull it, and climb straight to the top. The crux makes difficult moves out a seam. The gear is good but strenuous to place.

86. Rude Dude 5.10c R
FA: Brint Prise, Mark Ronca
The brunt of this route and the crux are well protected; there is a small section after the crux that is very easy, but not well protected. Start left of *Monmouth* and climb up to a horizontal with triangular-shaped block-like flakes that go out a roof. Move out the roof on large pro and pull the lip (Crux/bolt). Continue left and then straight up to reach the *Screaming Eagle* communal rappel (5.4 with bad pro).

87. Screaming Eagle 5.12d R
FA: Mark Ronca
One of Mark Ronca's finest routes and one of the best 5.12 roof climbs in the Mid-Atlantic. This route is a staple of difficult Pennsylvania trad-climbing. The crux is well protected but the top is run out. If you climb 5.12d the unprotected 5.4 section shouldn't matter. Start left of *Rude Dude* and climb a weakness up to the left side of a huge roof. Head for the center of the roof and follow a piton and two bolts out a flake and horizontal to the lip (Large cam). Pull the difficult lip and climb past easy but unprotected climbing to a communal rap.

88. Full Tilt 5.5 G
FA: Michael Steele, Henry McMahon
Start near *Screaming Eagle* and climb up and far left via a ramp to breach through a section of rock between the big roof and a lesser roof to its left. Finish at a tree above *Daring Do*.

89. Daring Do 5.9 PG
FA: Michael Steele, Todd Swain
Wander up easy rock (loose pro placements), and climb through a crack in the center of the roof, left of the *Screaming Eagle* roof. Climb to the rappel tree above.

Welcome to the Gap Area
This area is the area surrounding the long roof that is a short way above the base trail. A good rappel can be done with a single rope from *Welcome to the Gap*.

90. Jungle Canopy 5.10b PG
FA: Paul Nick, Jeff Gagliano
Begin around the corner 45' left of *Daring Do* and climb up to the nice roof above. Pull the roof and move right to the *Daring Do* rappel tree.

91. Wing and a Prayer 5.8 PG
Start 20' left of *Jungle* and climb straight up, passing some small ceilings on the right, to gain a large hanging buttress that comes to a point at the bottom. Go right at the bottom of the clean buttress and climb to a ceiling 18'above. Move around the right side of this ceiling and continue to a rappel tree above the *Daring Do* rappel tree. A two-rope rappel brings you back down.

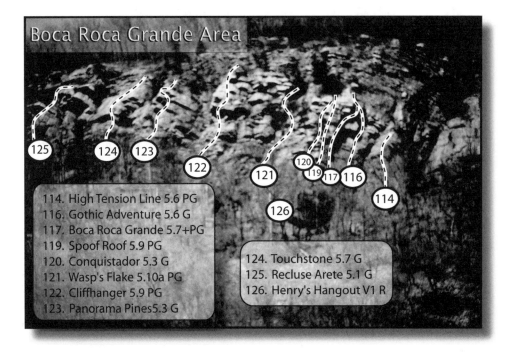

Boca Roca Grande Area

114. High Tension Line 5.6 PG
116. Gothic Adventure 5.6 G
117. Boca Roca Grande 5.7+PG
119. Spoof Roof 5.9 PG
120. Conquistador 5.3 G
121. Wasp's Flake 5.10a PG
122. Cliffhanger 5.9 PG
123. Panorama Pines5.3 G

124. Touchstone 5.7 G
125. Recluse Arete 5.1 G
126. Henry's Hangout V1 R

92. Flying Circus 5.8 G

FA: Michael Steele, Bill Ravich

Start the same as for *Wing* and climb to the hanging buttress. From here break off left and climb up a wide corner for 14' and escape out right via a notch. Continue straight up to rappel.

93. Slot Machine 5.8 G

Begin by climbing the corner just left of *Flying Circus*, and then climb up to the big slot this route is named and famed for. Climb the slot through the center of the roof and then climb to the rappel tree for the previous route.

94. Virgin's Bower 5.8 G

Left of the previous climb there is a breach where the *Slot Machine* and *Welcome to the Gap* roofs meet. Climb up the breach between the two roofs, then continue straight up and slightly left along a corner for 30'. Follow the grassy ledge far left to the *Welcome to the Gap* rappel.

95. Nick's Ceiling 5.10c G

FA: Paul Nick, Mark Ronca

Climb up to and pull the right side of the *Welcome to the Gap* ceiling and follow *Virgin's Bower* to finish.

96. Welcome to the Gap 5.10d G

FA: Michael Steele, Todd Swain

Easier if tall. Run up easy rock to the left end of the big roof (crux). Pull the roof and head straight up through easier ground to a rappel tree.

97. Damned if You Do 5.7 G
Moving left after the *Welcome to the Gap* overhang, walk down to where the next overhang is visible. Climb up to the overhang and move out right and up.

98. Damned if You Don't 5.7 G
Same as the previous route but move left out the overhang, then straight up.

99. Barbarian Ballet 5.10a G
FA: Michael Steele, Bill Ravich
Around a small corner left of the previous route. Move left into ceilings and head up to the clean ceiling above. Pull the ceiling (crux) and head up to the tree above. There is a fixed pin at the crux.

100. Pseudo Slab 5.4 G
Climb to an indent in the rock and pass a notch in the small overhang above. Move right to rappel from *Barbarian*.

101. Make or Break Flake 5.7 G
Pull the overhang left of *Pseudo* S*lab* via a flake, and move right to the *Barbarian* rappel.

Billy goat Gruff Area
This is the large, obvious roof, left of the previous routes. Descend by walking to the left edge of the ledge above, and rappel with one rope from *Hero Smasher*.

102. Ryan's Route 5.9+ R
FA: Ryan Lukas, Rob Holzman, Rob Mutti 1995
Climb the center of the face under the *Billy Goat* roof, and then move across *Billy Goat Gruff* to pull the roof at the right side. Continue up along a right-leaning seam/crack and go straight to the top.

103. Billy goat Gruff 5.7 PG
FA: Michael Steele, Randy Seese
Right of the start of the previous climb and at the right end of the roof and climb up to a notch. Pull through the notch (crux) and move left to a belay.   Note: This belay tree is in bad shape; this is a bad descent spot.

104. Great Big Billy Goat Gruff 5.10a PG
Climb past the left side of small ceiling 20'up, and continue to the big roof (Crux) that is pulled out its center. Continue to a communal rap on a marginal tree.

105. Man with a Crowbar 5.12b PG
FA: Mark Ronca 1999
Lever up easy rock left of the previous route, and pass an alcove below the big roof on its left. Pry over the big roof (Crux) at its left end, near some flakes, and continue to the top.

106. Don't be a Hero 5.9 PG

FA: Mark Ronca 1999

Watch for loose rock! Same as *Crowbar* but cut out left below the crux roof and climb the roof left of the original route. Rejoin *Crowbar* to finish.

107. Hero Smasher 5.11 R/X

Mostly done as a toprope. Big moves and hideously loose rock. Walk around the corner from The Gruff's and spy a nice roof. Climb the center of the roof straight, then meander left to a tree.

Boca Roca Grande Area

This area includes the final routes of the ridge. *Boca Roca* is one of the finest routes at this area and is well worth the hike. Descend the routes in this area by walking left at the top and finding the overgrown power line. Walk down this to return. **Note:** The ridge continues for a great distance from here. It is tremendously overgrown but does contain some quality, difficult roof-climbs. Some excellent bouldering is also hidden amongst the ridge and talus several-hundred feet below at an area called *The Land that Time Forgot*. Problems from V0- to V10 exist here. I would, by no means, recommend the anguish involved in

Tim Bonner on steep terrain. Photo by the author.

wading the neck-high razor-like plant-life that torments your every move when trying to find these problems.

108. Troll's Opera 5.0 G

Sprint up the unappealing gully 100' left of *Hero Smasher*.

109. White Elephant 5.7 PG

Climb the right side of the interesting two-tiered overhang 75' left of the previous route.

110. Dean's Ceiling 5.10d PG

FA: Dean Hernandez 1997

Climb the left end of the ceiling, staying 20' left of *White Elephant*.

111. Delaware Dreamer 5.2G
Sail an openbook 40' left of *White Elephant*.

112. From Beyond 5.8- PG
Work through a notch (Crux) left of an overhang and move right to the top of the previous climb.

113. Short Circuit 5.7+ PG
Make fun moves up the crack and corner immediately left of the previous climb.

114. High Tension Line 5.6 PG
Fun, clean climbing takes the nice prow 15' left of *Short Circuit*.

115. Vision Quest 5.3 PG
Follow the easy corner left of the previous climb.

116. Gothic Adventure 5.6 G
Gothic best describes the rock at this area of the cliff. Climb the right side of the big overhang just right of *Boca Roca Grand*, then climb the exciting corner and traverse left to reach the last 10' of *Boca*.

117. Boca Roca Grande 5.7+ PG
FA: Hugh Dougher, Henry McMahon
One of the best climbs at The Gap. Climb the thrilling, long corner left of the previous route, then break right around the highest ceiling above. Continue up a large off-width to the top. This route can be done in two pitches.

118. Raving Lunatic 5.12a PG
FA: Jeff Gagliano
This climb works best with a belay set before the crux roof. Climb *Boca* to the first big roof and step out right to climb the left side of the big roof (crux). Climb straight to the top rejoining *Boca* at the final roof.

119. Spoof Roof 5.9 PG
FA: Mark Ronca, Carlie Ronca 1996
Watch for loose rock! Start on the dirty face left of the *Boca* gully and climb to a roof. Step up to another roof and continue straight to the top. This climb is often done in two pitches.

120. Conquistador 5.3 G
Climb up the dirty, loose face 12' left of S*poof Roof.*

121. Wasp's Flake 5.10a PG
FA: Mark Ronca 1998
Work up the dirty corner 110' left of *Conquistador* and climb to a roof near the summit. Pull the roof (Crux).

122. Cliffhanger 5.9 PG

Walk left past the previous climb. The next large overhang above is *Cliffhanger*. Climb up to and over the left side of the big overhang.

123. Panorama Pines 5.3 G

80' left of *Cliffhanger*, climb the nice, easy corner to a small ceiling pulled through at its easiest point.

124. Touchstone 5.7 G

Past some overhangs on the next corner, left of the previous route, climb the corner, passing it on the left edge at the first ceiling onto the arete. Dance along the nice slab at the arete and move up and right to the summit.

125. Recluse Arete 5.1 G

A secluded, short, and pleasant scramble at the end of the Water Gap cliff. Located a short way from a power line, climb the cliff's final arete.

126. Henry's Hangout V1 R

Locate the obvious boulder with a crack. Climb the center of the crack.

Mount Tammany

Mount Tammany is named for the Lenni Lenape Indian chief Tamenund.   This daunting, natural cliff dominates the New Jersey hillside until breaking through the pavement of I-80, breaching the roads shoulder like the wall of a dam. The rock literally plunges from the highway, rising over 200' above the gridlock, creating an excellent escape from the fast pace of everyday life.

The immense walls of Mount Tammany loom over the garden state with their playground of enchanting rock: giant overhangs, frighteningly steep walls, multi-tiered roofs, and rock that causes any climber and non-climber to gawk. This jaw-dropping cliff is the highest natural rock formation in the state of New Jersey, the highest area featured in this guide, and the higher of the two Delaware Water Gap cliffs.

There are at least 130 documented routes on the New Jersey side of the river. I am only including a handfull due to the size restraints of this guide. Should you have more interest in other routes on Mount Tammany, Mike Steele's *Climbing Guide to the Delaware Water Gap* is an excellent resource. You can also check out www.paclimbing.com for more detailed descriptions and topos for Mount Tammany and an upcoming guidebook for The Gap.

The routes here range from 5.0 to 5.12 on multi-pitch trad. Some of the best climbs at The Gap exist on the Jersey side. I recommend a broad mix of gear; cams are very useful considering the many horizontals; large gear is helpful also. Additionally, I recommend adding extra webbing to old rap stations scattered around the cliff.

A few drawbacks exist at this cliff: loose rock, unclean climbs, and traffic noise from the road below. Bring plenty of water and long draws because the routes tend to wander around obstacles. Routefinding can be tricky here also. From the ground, the climbs look straightforward, but after about 50' they seem more and more like a Rorschach Test. Study all routes well before departing into the friendly skies. Due to high traffic noise, a two-way radio is a recommended device to use while climbing here--the din of traffic is unavoidable on many climbs.

Absolutely wear a helmet here. Due to the alpine nature of the rock, many routes spew loose rock on inattentive climbers. Also be mindful of traffic below. Trundling stone on traffic below can be an awful lot like the '80s videogame Frogger to unsuspecting motorists.

A dancing stone bouncing across three lanes of I-80 traffic would not be a welcome sign during the evening commute.

Even though there is a fair share of loose and unclean rock, this area offers many clean and exciting climbs. Some of the finest climbs in the East exist here. It truly is adventure climbing at its best. Try this area at least once. If you don't like it, you can always Frisbee my book into the Delaware once you get to the top.

History

Climbers have visited this cliff for many decades—it would have been hard to pass up a massive rock face like this so close to a major highway. The 1960s hosted the first recorded climbs at the crag. Classics like *The Rib* 5.3, *Triumvirate* 5.4 and other obvious lines were ticked off during this time. Several harder lines were done as aid routes during this time and into the '70s (*Corkscrew* 5.8+ is a prime example). Up to the mid-80s Hugh Dougher and Henry McMahon were very active in establishing lines like *Death Don't Have No Mercy* 5.9, *Real Rangers* 5.9, and many other classic climbs. Perhaps one of the most impressive ascents during this time period was the first free ascent of *Corkscrew* 5.8+ made by Hugh Dougher and Ron Matthews in the early 80s. This climb challenges climbers to this day.

In 1984 a park ranger named Mike Steele, who later authored a guidebook for The Gap, began a wave of development on the mountain. Mike was one of the most active climbers on Mount Tammany and Mount Minsi. During a period from the mid-80s until 1990, Mike developed an incredible amount of routes on the New Jersey side of The Water Gap. Some of his landmark achievements include *Warpath* 5.11a, *Welcome to the Gap* 5.10b, *Premature Exasperation* 5.11a, *Ride of the Valkyries* 5.10b, *Rad Dudes from Hell* 5.11d, and *Last of the Vikings* 5.10c.

Mike Steele was active with many climbers on the first ascents of these and other routes. Some of these other climbers were: Kim Alicandri, Jeff Chiniewiz, Nick Miskowski, Henry McMahon, Amy Pierson, Bill Ravich, Todd Swain, and Randy Seese.

Another prolific climber with boundless energy was Mark Ronca. Between 1991 and 1999, Mark was active with his wife Carlie, Matt Hill and Dave Pfurr. Some of the best achievements during this time were *Ribbed Pleasures* 5.10d*, Forces of Pfurry* 5.9, *Disappointment Beaver* 5.11c, and many other classics. A unique boulder problem called *Cheatstone Traverse*--postulated by Dave Pfurr then sent by Mark Ronca and Dave Pfurr --was developed around this time also.

Descent Options: The **Class Four Ramp** provides one of the **easiest descents**. It is an easy gully to descend or rappel. There is also a **two-bolt rappel** above **Triumvirate**. Corkscrew can also be used for rappel. Use double ropes anywhere on Mount Tammany.

Directions: From the Mount Tammany rest area off of I-80, walk east towards the cliff. You will very shortly have to climb into a trench/faint path behind the highway retaining wall. NO MATTER WHAT, DO NOT WALK ON THE HIGHWAY! Continue walking in the trench being mindful of glass, refuse and possibly the body of Jimmie Hoffa. After a short walk, you will have to walk dangerously close to the wall and the highway. Enjoy the whispering gusts of passing trucks and wafting scent of exhaust while you approach a steep trail that climbs up to the base of the cliff. The approach on the New Jersey side of The Gap is easily a 5.12 in terms of nerviness.

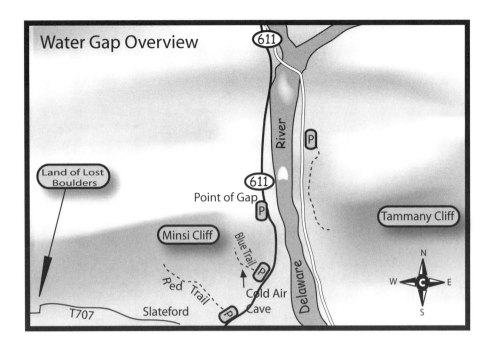

Roadside Area

This is the short section of the cliff just above the road. Rappel by climbing down to the *Little Shop of Horrors* rappel.

1. Dead Mans Curve 5.9- PG

A short way above the highway, this is a short but sweet intro to the Tammany cliff. Climb a right-arching crack/slab to a makeshift anchor above. Belay at a block or traverse far left to the summit. Walk right and downclimb to the *Little Shop of Horrors* rappel.

2. Lie Detector 5.4 PG

40' right of the previous route climb easy rock to an overhang up high. Move through the overhang at a groove. Rappel the same as for the previous climb.

3. The Chiseler 5.4+ R

The crux is a short way off the ground. This climb is easily located as one of the first climbs you see on the wall, after walking uphill from the road, on the approach. The route got its name because J.G. is chiseled at the bottom. Locate the chisel mark and a box-chimney. Climb the chimney and step right to a weakness and an overhang above. Move right around the overhang to finish above.

4. Premature Exasperation 5.11a PG/R

FA: M. Steele, H. McMahon

Exasperating to protect if jumped on prematurely. Climb up to and over the overhang right

Black Wall

Water Gap Triumvirate Area

Black Wall

9. Class-four Ramp 5.1 G
10. Class Warefare 5.2 PG
17. 5th-grade Crusader 5.2 PG
18. Dunce's Corner 5.2 G
19. Easy Day 5.7+ PG
20. Black Wall 5.7+ PG
24. Tamenund 5.4 PG/R
25. Triumvirate 5.4 PG
27. Cryptic Corner 5.5 PG

Randy Ross soloing at the Gap. Photo by the author.

of the previous climb. Either lower after the crux or follow *Chiseler* to the top. Can be set as a toprope from easier climbs to the left.

5. Climbantic Orgasm 5.11a PG/R
Make sure to bring *protection* for this climb. Climb to a corner and move up this to the high overhang looming above. Penetrate the high overhang via either of two cracks (crux). Climax at the summit.

6. Four Play 5.4 PG
Climb the obvious, left-facing corner, moving left around the overhangs and through the notch to the top.

7. Chinese Handcuffs 5.11a TR
Easy to toprope from either of the climbs to the right or left. Around the corner from the previous route climb up to and over the obvious overhang (crux).

8. Little Shop of Horrors 5.8- G
Climb the crack through a roof, to a tree. Belay at the tree (a toprope for nearby climbs can be set here). Climb up a groove, move left at the top, and continue to a rappel.

9. Class-four Ramp 5.1 G
Several-hundred feet past the previous climb, climb low-angle rock up a ramp through a

large cleft above. This climb is the obvious low-angle section, left of the large left-facing corner. Several trees on the ledges allow for this to be a popular descent. A rappel is also located at the top.

10. Class Warefare 5.2 PG
Right of the left-facing corner, climb the easiest path to the top.

11. The Cheatstone Block
Several must-do boulder problems can be found on the large block that is detached from the cliff, 30' right of the previous climb. An easy descent can be found off to the side.

12. Cheatstone V0
Climb off the left side of the block and top out above.

13. The Cheatstone Traverse V4
SDS on a crack and traverse a sloping rail to a top out at the right side.

14. Beneath the Cheatstone Traverse V5
SDS and climb the thin face beneath the sloping rail past small crimps to finish at the right side. The hardest part is keeping your feet from touching ground.

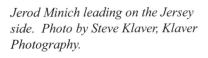

Jerod Minich leading on the Jersey side. Photo by Steve Klaver, Klaver Photography.

15. Cheatstone High Traverse V2 R
Traverse the block above the regular variation and top out.

16. Cheatstone Right V0
SDS and climb the right side of the block to the ledge above.

Class-four Ramp 5.1
This is the large chimney left of the *Cheatstone Block*. Climb the obvious corner to a tree, step left, then continue up the face to pass an overhang. Many people descend the cliff from this point after climbing other nearby routes. Rappel this point using two ropes.

17. Fifth-grade Crusader 5.2 PG
Follow easy terrain just right of *Class-four Ramp*.

18. Dunce's Corner 5.2 G
Follow the obvious left-facing corner to the top.

The Black Wall
This section of cliff contains some of the most foreboding rock features in the Mid-Atlantic! It is hard to miss this looming wall just right of the *Cheatstone Block*. The easiest descent or rappel is from the *Class Four Ramp* or *Triumvirate*.

Barry Rusnock and Tim Bonner finish up a great day of climbing at the Gap.

19. Easy Day for an Old Lady 5.7+ PG
FA: Bob Daneker, Tony Passariello
Stay left of the large corner and climb to a ledge. Pass an overhang at the right side before entering the steep *Black Wall* area. Follow up left of the steep wall along the path of least resistance to the top.

20. The Black Wall 5.7+ PG
FA: H. Dougher
Pitch 1: Climb the curving corner to a ledge 25' up. Angle 20' right to a corner and a ledge above that. There is an optional 1st belay here or you can belay at the large tree under the roof. Climb the left corner in the steep black-colored wall. Belay under the huge overhang in a cramped area near the tree. **Pitch 2:** climb up to and around the right side of the overhang (difficult and strenuous to protect). I recommend a belay near the big tree for pitch 2 to minimize serious rope drag around the tree.

21. Heart of Darkness 5.10a PG/R
Pitch 1: Climb *Black Wall* to the regular 1st belay. **Pitch 2:** Climb the left corner and find a wide crack on the left wall a bit left of the big tree at the right side of the big top overhang. Climb this to a traverse around the left end of the overhang. Continue up the steep wall.

22. Ride of the Valkyries 5.10b PG/R
FA: H. McMahon
Pitch 1: Climb to a big belay ledge, than up to a groove and overhang passed at its left side. Belay at a big slanting block. **Pitch 2:** From the right side of the block go straight up the steep face.

23. Valhala 5.10c PG/R
Pitch 1: Climb *Black Wall* to the first belay (5.7+). **Pitch 2:** Climb left to the steep slabs and climb the overhang above. Go left at the small overhang and climb to the left side of the giant roof above. Climb up to join *Heart of Darkness*.

Triumvirate Area

Tom Kneiss Leading "Triumvirate." Photo by the author.

Right of *The Black Wall* and around the corner from its hanging buttress is the *Triumvirate Area*. From the top, there are three options for rappel: The bolt anchor on *Triumvirate* (double-rope rappel), from walking to *Fourth Class Ramp* (double or single-rope rappel), or from *The Rib* (double or single-rope rappel).

24. Tamenund 5.6 PG/R

The climb gets its name from the Indian chief Tamenund. Start this climb around the corner from *The Black Wall* and massive overhang above this wall. Begin around the corner near big ledges and a slab. Move up this staying left of *Triumvirate* and pull past an overhang at its right side. Climb a smooth ramp and belay at the belay ledge after the ramp or continue up passing the right side of an overhang. Continue up another section of low-angle rock, move left around the overhang, and climb a crack to the top.

25. Triumvirate 5.4 PG

FA: Unknown pre '75

One of the best climbs at its grade in the Mid-Atlantic! Climb the ramp to a large off-width-weakness. Follow this to a ledge slightly right. **Pitch 2:** Move left into a traverse that brings thrilling exposure below your feet. Follow the traverse while climbing above one tier of overhang and with another tier above that. Move far left to escape the overhang at the left side. Bolt anchor at the top.

26. Triumvirate Direct 5.6- PG

The same route as the previous, but pull directly over the triangular overhang and continue up. You can belay on either *Triumvirate* or *Tamenund* and you can follow either route to the overhang.

27. Cryptic Corner 5.5 PG

Right of *Triumvirate*, climb a groove to a corner above. Move left from the overhangs and climb the obvious corner to a chimney. It is best to split this route into two pitches by using any of the abundant ledges.

28. The Rib 5.3 G

FA: Unknown pre '75

One of the best climbs in the Poconos. Follow the rib feature that starts 30' off the ground and above a ramp. Follow a crack to a good belay ledge. **Pitch 2:** climb up left of the obvious corner. A two-rope rappel brings you down.

29. Rib Cage 5.6- PG

A spectacular climb with thrilling exposure. Start the same as the previous route but follow the large inside corner just right of the original route to the good belay ledge used for *The Rib*. **Pitch 2:** Continue up from the belay and traverse far right on exposed horizontals under the roof. Climb thrilling moves to gain the right side of the wall.

Rad Dudes Block

This is the large block that stands out off the cliff a short way past *The Triumvirate Area*. It is about 30' high with a clean arete. Several climbs are also located on the high cliff above. A toprope is easy to set up by scrambling to the top via a ledge uphill from the block. Be careful while traversing the ledge!

Water Gap   The Great Arch Area

32. Friends 5.7 PG
33. Colorado 5.6 PG
34. Triple Hangover 5.8 R
35. Double Overhang 5.8 PG/R
36. Corkscrew 5.8+ PG/R
37. Tree Toad Fracture 5.9 G
38. Cornerstone 5.11b R

30. Rad Dudes From Hell 5.11d TR
FA (toprope): M. Steele, B. Ravich
Locate a short wall just off the ground and detached from the main cliff a few minutes past the previous climbs. Climb the blank face at its right corner. Mostly done as a toprope due to the absence of protection.

31. Quivering Hips 5.8+ PG
Crank your hips through the obvious overhang and crack right of *Rad Dudes*.

32. Friends in High Places 5.7 PG
FA: B. Daneker, T. Passariello, Sharon Ringel
15' right of the rib, bring yourself up a slab to the right side of an overhang. Continue to another overhang and pull through the center. Belay under roofs. **Pitch 2:** Quiver up to the first roof at the right side above a corner and pull over the next roof. Continue straight to the top.

33. Colorado 5.6 PG
An exhilarating route in an interesting setting. Follow the large inside-left-facing corner to a large overhang. Escape out left at the overhang and continue straight to the top. A belay can be set at the small ledge at the right side of the overhang.

Tom Kneiss, "Triumvirate." RH photo.

71

Double Overhang Area

This area is located just right of *The Rad Dudes Block*. Rappel from a double-rope rappel off *Corkscrew* or walk left for an easier rappel down *Class Four Ramp* or *The Rib*.

34. Triple Hangover 5.8 R

You may need some Alieve after this one. Climb to a roof passed at its right, then to a second roof that is breached at a crack. Upchuck onto the belay ledge above. **Pitch 2:** Stay right of the big corner and climb the overhanging face above.

35. Double Overhang 5.8 PG/R

Climb a groove off a ledge that is a few hundred feet past the previous climb. Belay below an inside corner. **Pitch 2**: Climb the corner to an overhang (crux). Move right out an undercling (optional belay) and climb to another overhang and the top.

36. Corkscrew 5.8+ PG/R

FA: H. Dougher, R. Matthews

80' right of the previous climb. Climb up to the big series of overhangs and veer left to a corner used to gain the first overhang. Move left around the overhang and climb smaller overhangs to a belay below a corner. **Pitch 2:** Climb an obvious corner to a big overhang passed at its right. An optional belay can be achieved at big horizontals. Follow a crack through and overhang and move right through the last overhang. An easier variation moves out right and outside the crack on the face and rejoins the final overhangs.

37. Tree Toad Fracture 5.9 G

FA: Dean Giftos, Bill Lafontaine

Climb the obvious corner to a belay tree. Belay here or continue to the top overhang where it is possible to pull out to the right over the overhang.

38. Cornerstone 5.11b R

FA: H. Dougher, M. Panz

There is a lot of fixed gear that is now missing, making this route poorly protected. Note: The climb to the left *Godzilla* is 5.11c and PG rated. Climb the start of *Tree Toad* and move out right. Climb to the center of the giant overhang and breach it at its left side then move right out the cleft in the overhang.

Donna Morell at Land of Lost

Delaware Water Gap Bouldering Areas

Previously, it had been rumored that bouldering did not exist at The Gap. This statement could not be further from the truth. There is, in fact, an extensive amount of bouldering along the Water Gap ridgeline. The unfortunate part is that much of this rock is secluded and involves several hours hiking to access.

Basically, the ridge south of the main cliffs on the Pennsylvania side and north of the cliffs on the New Jersey side, all contain boulders where the cliff height decreases. Massive amounts of vegetation and seriously undeveloped rock make most of these spots not worth the trouble of finding them. There are a few spots that have excellent quality large boulders and are extremely accessible within literally a few minutes walk. Perhaps the most impressive of these spots is *The Land of the Lost*. This area was discovered by myself and developed a short time after by myself, Randy Ross, Tim Fitzinger, Nick Morell, and Tom Kneiss. The area encompasses a mile long hillside with a small handful of large, rectangular quartzite boulders, a few-hundred feet beyond the park service road.

The Land of the Lost and a few other accessible spots with worthwhile problems are mentioned in this guide: *Table Rock*, *Roadside Boulder*, *The Ice Cube* and surrounding area, *The Junkyard*. As for the rest, great, mysterious problems lie on the flanks of the Water Gap ridgeline. Happy hunting.

The Land of the Lost
This area is located a few miles west of Slateford Farms, off the north side of the park service road that travels across the base of the ridge. Several high quality blocks of quartzite are located a few hundred feet behind the field just off the road. This spot is one of the easy bouldering areas to access due to the 4 minute walk involved in reaching the boulders. Surprisingly, the boulders are not visible from the road.

Tom Kneiss reaching the crux on "Driftwood."
Photo by the author.

The main group of boulders consists of three large boulders near each other. One boulder is only a few feet high, but very steep. The other two are 18' and 25' high, respectively. Many other boulders lie on the east side of the field along the hillside. Just walk east and uphill a bit until you see rock. The only drawback here is lack of rock and dense vegetation. If you want to do some problems after a day of craging, this is a good place to stop for an hour or so.

Some problems include: *The Supercrack* V1 R, *Waverunner* V7 R, *Delite* V4, *Driftwood* V3, *Shady Thicket* V2.

Directions: Drive the forest service road west toward Bangor from Slateford Farms, keeping right on the dirt road. At the third field on the right several miles from Slateford,

Nick Morell on "The Supercrack"
Photo by the author.

park on the side of the road. Do not block the field entrance and do not park in the field. Find a spot off the shoulder of the road and park. Walk to the back-left tip of the field. A faint trail will lead to a small overhanging boulder a few hundred feet northwest of the field. The rock is hard to find through the thick brush of summer. You have to be right on top the rock to see it. The next boulder left of the first is the *House Boulder*. *The Supercrack* is located on this boulder. Another good boulder is north and on top the hill a bit right of this boulder. Other boulders can be found east on the hillside. Do not walk west of the *House Boulder*. There are no good boulders to the west.

The Junkyard

This area is a collection of a few boulders located inches from I-80 westbound. They can be found a few yards east of the cliff, past the talus field, behind the highway fence, near the old parking spot off I-80 (you are not allowed to park here anymore). If you are traveling westbound in New Jersey on I-80, coming from Buttsville and Heading toward the cliff. You will see a pull-off on the right just before reaching the talus field and Tammany Cliff. The boulders are right behind the pull-off, but you have to access them from the main approach to the Tammany Cliff. Some problems include *Sound of Silence* V4, *Grid Lock* V1, and *Motor Man* V1.

Table Rocks

There are some boulders and a small overhang/cave located along the Appalachian Trail just east of the town of Delaware Water Gap. Find the AT and hike it from town and you will find the rock. There isn't much at this spot but it is an interesting, small outcrop.

Roadside Boulder

Located between Route 6 and the Delaware River, just below the highway retaining wall between the Minsi Cliff and the town of Delaware Water Gap, and below the lookout where ice climbing can be found. This large boulder has a piton in a nice crack and overhanging face. Many excellent boulder problems can be found here.

The Ice Cube

Located below the nice cliff seen from Minsi Lake. A small boulder garden with excellent problems was developed by Randy Ross and myself. Henry McMahon developed routes on the cliff. Many problems are located on the *Ice Cube*. This is the large cube. An excellent V5 named *Gun Metal Blue* can be found on the adjacent boulder.

Other Kittatinny Ridge Bouldering

Many other boulders lie far north along the Tammany ridge. Basically, where the main cliff ends a good distance from *Corkscrew*, boulders start and continue for miles along the ridge.

Some of the best boulders are located near The Yards Creek Reservoirs. Climbing is prohibited on the cliffs here, but bouldering can be had near the reservoir boundary on public land. The only problem with all the boulders here is the incredibly long walk to the rock and the massive amounts of vegetation. I developed a select amount of problems along the whole ridge from Mt Tammany to Rick's Rocks, but I do not recommend hunting the miles of rock for the select good problems that exist here. If you have a guide, some good problems can be found, but they are few and far between.

Rick's Rocks has some decent but small boulders in the talus below and south of the main cliff. On the north side of the main road that takes you to Rick's Rocks, there are also boulders.

Randy Ross on "the Ice Cube." Photo by RH

Notes

Notes

2. Bruce Lake Bouldering Area

Area Beta

Location
Promised Land State Park.

Type of Climbing
Bouldering.

Other Info
A long walk but a great area.

Bruce Lake Bouldering

The Bruce Lake Bouldering Area is a small sandstone cliff located in the Bruce Lake Nature Area, a desolate wildlife reserve just outside the Promised Land State Park boundary. The bouldering here is fair and limited to a short section of cliff. There is only enough rock here to keep you busy for part of an afternoon, but the rock is good quality.

Some consider the two-mile approach long for bouldering standards; however, the hike is quite pleasant and very scenic. The main redeeming quality of this area is that the crag is picturesque and rests just above the water at the edge of Bruce Lake, a pristine pool of water accessible only by footpath.

This isolated bouldering spot really takes you away from the ordinary. You won't find crowds, manicured problems, or perhaps even chalk on holds, but you will find wildlife, intriguing overhangs, and quite certainly a pleasant day of bouldering.

Should you visit this spot, there are about 30 established problems on a 10 to 25'-high outcrop with problems ranging from V0- to V6. There are also a few problems on a few smaller boulders in Egypt Meadows, a small area before you reach Bruce Lake. If you want to get away from the ordinary bouldering scene, this is the place to go.

History

There has never been documented information about Bruce Lake. Several climbers from the Philadelphia area and parts of New Jersey initiated bouldering at this area sometime during the late '80s or early '90s. Nearby resident Tom Kneiss and Nick Morell and myself were the first *recorded* developers of this area. During the early '90s, these three climbers developed the majority of problems at the lake and nearby Lake Wallenpaupack. Mark Ronca was active at the area in the mid to late '90s. Ryan Anglemeyer was also active during this time.

Posing it up on "Jewel Roof." Photo by Tom Kneiss.

Access and Ownership: The rock is located in The Bruce Lake Nature Area and Promised Land State Park. Please keep impact to a minimum.

Directions

Take exit 26 (Promised Land/ Tafton exit) off Interstate 84, and follow State Route 390 south (look for signs off U.S. 84 for Promised Land SP). Follow 390 south for .02 miles. Park on the left-hand side of the road at the parking area for Bruce Lake Natural Area/ Egypt Meadow trailhead.

Follow the Egypt Meadow/Bruce Lake trail east for 2 miles, passing through Egypt Meadow Lake, until you come to Bruce Lake. The rock outcrop is located at the north tip of the lake on the shore hidden from view off the main trail. Once you see the water from the trail, walk down to the northwest tip of the lake, and walk east a few-hundred feet and you will run into the rock.

Established Problems: *Egyptian Dyno* V6, *Lake Traverse* V2, *Jewel Roof* V2, *Ronca's Reach* V1, *Pristine Dream* V0+, *Short Top* V4, *Block Arete* V5, *Goldenface* V1.
Camping: There are four camping areas: Deerfield, Lower Lake, Pickerel Point, and The Pines. To reserve a site call toll-free 888-PA-Parks. The state park's website is www.dcnr. state.pa.us/stateparks.

Tom Kneiss on the first ascent of "Goldenface."

3. Big Boulder Bouldering Area

Are Beta

Location

On Lake Mountain near Big Boulder ski area.

Overview

Nearly 100 established problems in a peaceful setting.

Other Beta

A long walk but good-quality rock. Some unclean from lack of visits.

Big Boulder

Some of the best quality stone in the Poconos is located on Lake Mountain near the Big Boulder Ski Area. Climbers who know about Lake Mountain—and there are only 6 of them prior to the publication of this book—admire the mountains beautiful rock, large boulders, and tranquil setting.

The only downside to the areas charm is the lengthy approach. The approach to the boulders is quite long, for this reason I suspect this area's peaceful setting will remain that way for a long time to come. Only the really adventurous climber will make the long trek to this remote area. Should you decide to avoid this area due to the approach, you will seriously let yourself down. The bouldering on Lake Mountain is superb. Sure, some of the rock is unclean, but that is the allure of Pocono bouldering.

Should you decide to endure the 35-45 minute hike to the boulders, you will be seriously surprised at the large boulders and quality of the rock. Expect to find caves, overhangs, and steep faces to investigate. Another highpoint about this area is the view. On a clear day, you can see Bake Oven Knob, a small bouldering area to the south, and the Lehigh Gap, another nearby bouldering area. The boulders range from a few feet to 25' in height. Difficulty ratings range between V0- and V7. This area is one of the best-kept secrets in the Poconos.

Geology: Conglomerate and sandstone mix. Pink in color, very solid, and high quality.

Access and Ownership: The bouldering is primarily State Game Lands. There are no regulations against climbing on this property. Please respect the land and pack out trash.

Hazards and Concerns: Like any remote destination, you'll want to bring a few things: plenty of water, high energy snacks, and a flashlight. Also, plan enough time to get back to your car with adequate sunlight. Remember, you're a long way from help. There already has been one injury on the mountain that involved a lengthy, epic descent to safety. Also, be aware that the approach trail passes directly behind a firing range. The range is located along the first 15 minutes into the hike, just before reaching the power line. If you hear gun shots, make yourself known by yelling or plan an alternate route. It is also highly recommended that you wear orange during hunting season. Most of this area is in State Game Lands. You *will* meet people with guns if you boulder here enough.

General Overview: About 40 boulders (more lie farther down the ridge but are not mentioned in this book) with over 60 problems ranging from V0- to V7. The boulders range from 5 to 25' high.

History

Area native Randal Ross discovered the main area at Lake Mountain in the mid-'90s. During this time, he developed problems like *Jawbreaker* V4, *Randy's Roof* V0, and numerous other problems. Randy is a true pioneer of remote, adventure bouldering in Pennsylvania. Because of this passion for remote bouldering, Randy developed a great deal of rock in the Pocono Northeast.

Randy and Tim Fitzinger were the original climbers to develop Big Boulder. Randy introduced me to the area shortly after he first visited here. I personally discovered the Skilandia boulders and developed the majority of the problems at Skilandia. At the main area I developed problems like *Talkie Walkie* V7, *Space Invader* V5 and several others. Tom Kneiss and Dave Pfurr were also active at the boulders during the '90s. Dave and Tom established some true classic lines along the mountaintop.

Directions

From the corner of State Route 940 and 115 in Blakeslee, drive south on State Route 115 approximately 3 miles, then turn right onto State Route 903, heading towards Jim Thorpe and Big Boulder Ski Resort.

Drive south on Route 903, pass the entrance for the ski resort on the right, and crest the small hill just past the turn for the ski resort and Big Boulder Lake. At the crest of the hill, drive south for slightly less than one-quarter mile, and park at a Game Lands parking lot on the left (SGL No.129).

Park at the dirt lot and walk onto the opposite side of the road from where you parked. Here you will see a trailhead with a blue-dot trail and a trail sign for the Hickory Run Boulder Field. Do not be alarmed by the distance to the boulder field, you are not going to have to walk that far but you *will* have to walk 35-45 minutes.

Walk the blue-blazed trail taking the split that goes left (taking the blue-blazed trail to the right will lead you off to *Spook Hollow*, a small low quality bouldering spot just off the

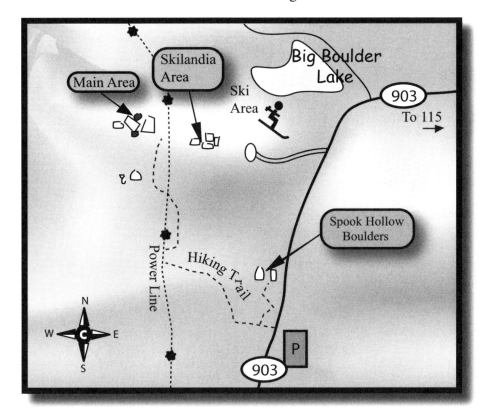

road). Follow the trail left, and it will turn into an orange-blazed trail that will lead you to a power-line cut within 15 minutes of walking. Be aware that just before reaching the power line, you will pass a shooting range that is located dangerously close to the trail. If you hear shots yell and make your presence known!

Follow the power line north until you come within a few-hundred feet of the crest. Off right the 15'-high outcrop is called the *Warm-up Boulder*. If you walk to the crest and look off right, you will see two high boulders. These are the trademark symbols of the Big Boulder Ski Resort, and the two main boulders to climb on.

Warm-up Boulder
When hiking to the boulders, this is the first large boulder you will come to near the crest of the mountain. It is located a few feet off the power-cut road on the right-hand side a few-hundred feet before a sharp, right turn that leads to the summit of the power line. The boulder is about 20' high.

1. Warm-up Crack V0- R
The obvious crack/weakness at the boulder's right side.

2. Ditchin V0+
The face between problems numbers one and three.

3. Unnamed V0
7'left of *Warm-up Crack*, climb a face to a notch or climb straight up to the slimy top.

4. The Cruise V0-
Cruise the corner near the tree.

5. Cruise Control V1/V2
This problem is V1 from a standing start, V2 from a sitting start. Make fun, technical moves on the slightly-overhanging face, left of the corner.

6. Mystery Blocks V0
Begin low in front of some detached boulders and climb the weakness in the center of an overhanging face.

7. Green Slime Pit V1
Start as low as possible in the pit at the left side of this boulder and climb to the ledge.

8. Hidden Ledge VB/V0-
Several easy problems can be done on the small ledge above and left of the previous problem.

Big Boulder Area
This area is located at the crest of the mountain. From the exact crest of the ridge on the power-line road, look left and you'll see rock. Walk about 100' and you'll see two large boulders. These two boulders are the trademark symbol on the Big Boulder Ski Resort's logo. This is the beginning of this side of the outcrop.

A. Big Boulder 1
Facing south, towards the direction you hiked in, this is the leftmost of two large boulders.

1. Casablanca V1 R
Climb the center of the steep, vertical face. The top out is high, scary, and loose.

2. Low Balls V1
From a low start, shoot up the right side of the steep face and pull onto the slab.

3. Cosmic Corner V0 R
Climb the left side of the steep face using the corner.

B. Big Boulder 2
This boulder is the large boulder behind the previous routes. There is a beautiful roof (*Randy's Roof*) on the center of the east face. An easy walk-off descends the back side of the boulder near the trench and problem r 13.

4. Randy's Roof V0-
Climb the right side of the roof.

5. Alcoholic's Garden Show V0+

Climb the center of the big roof.

6. Tom's Route V1 R

From a sitting start, make long moves to ascend the left center of the roof.

Var. 1: V1 Climb the left side of the roof.

7. Rhoddy Jungle V0+

Tunnel into Rhododendron bushes around the corner from the roof and climb the bulge and face.

8. Jawbreaker V4 R

This problem got its name when a climber broke his jaw working on the first ascent. Climb up to and over the left-center of the high roof 30' left of *Rhoddy Jungle*.

Warm-up Boulder

To Big Boulder Area

Power-cut Road

1. Warm-up Crack V0- R   5. Cruise Control V1/V2
2. Ditchin V0+   6. Mystery Blocks V0
3. Unnamed V0   8. Hidden Ledge VB/V0-
4. The Cruise V0-

9. Tom's Roof V0 R

Climb the left corner of the roof.

10. Unnamed V0- R

Climb the beautiful face left of the previous route.

11. Talkie Walkie V7

From a sitting start at the corner of the cave, delicately make your way up the overhanging face and corner.

12. The Great Escape V0+

Tunnel up the backside of the cave, climb over a bulge, and squirm out the escape-hatch hole near the top.

13. Grifter V2

SDS and climb the short, steep arete right of *Randy's Roof*.

14. The Gift V4

SDS and climb the steep face to the right of the previous route.

15. Dave's Hang V0

Looking at the *Jawbreaker* roof, you'll see a small overhang 12' off the ground and to the left. Climb the right side of this overhang.

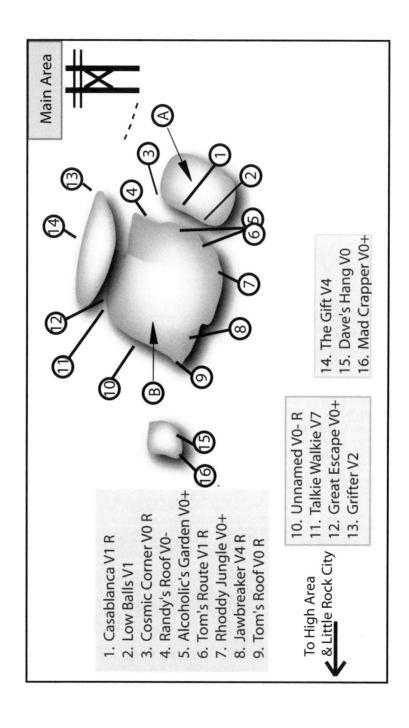

Main Area

1. Casablanca V1 R
2. Low Balls V1
3. Cosmic Corner V0 R
4. Randy's Roof V0-
5. Alcoholic's Garden V0+
6. Tom's Route V1 R
7. Rhoddy Jungle V0+
8. Jawbreaker V4 R
9. Tom's Roof V0 R

10. Unnamed V0- R
11. Talkie Walkie V7
12. Great Escape V0+
13. Grifter V2

14. The Gift V4
15. Dave's Hang V0
16. Mad Crapper V0+

To High Area
& Little Rock City

16. Mad Crapper V0+
A few inches left of *Dave's Hang*, climb up to and over the overhang.

C. High Area
Between the *Big Boulder 1* and *2* and the *Little Rock City* area there is a section of rock with a few highball problems. Most are moderate but fun. I don't mention any here because the area is small and only has a few problems.

D. Little Rock City Area
Just past the high section of rock there is a section of boulders that form a maze of rock (the geologic term for this is a rock city). Several easy problems have been done here and are mentioned below.

17. Laurel Roof V2
A Dave Pfurr classic! Begin in the back of this roof at a shallow crack/seam that splits the roof. Weave past the seam to gain the roof at a blunt corner and top out. This problem is easier from a standing start at the lip of the roof.

18. Demitri from Paris V3
Locate this problem by walking behind the *Laurel Roof* problem: you will see a boulder resting on another boulder. From a low start climb up to a bulge/ceiling in the center of the face where a large boulder rests atop another boulder. Climb over these boulders to top out near a corner.

19. Wookie Rape V2
Walk left, and around the backside of this boulder to climb the face using sidepulls a few feet left of the previous route.

20. The Shoe Box V0-
Diagonal to the previous two routes is a rectangular-shaped boulder with a few easy problems on it. This boulder is called *The Shoe Box*. The problems on it are no harder than V0-.

21. Unnamed V1
Looking at *The Shoe Box* boulder, there is a passage behind it created by two separate boulders. With your back to *The Shoe Box*, the boulder on your right contains this problem. Start on the downhill corner and climb over the bulge and corner.

22. Pocket Pal V1
Slightly to the right of the previous route, climb off two pockets in a horizontal.

23. Protrusion V0+
Directly behind the previous route climb the obvious overhang that protrudes over the passage.

24. Unnamed V0-
Climb the small ceiling around the corner.

25. Unnamed Boulder V0-
The boulder below the previous problem has two easy climbs that are obvious.

Skilandia Area
This spot can be a bit cumbersome to find. The easiest way to locate this area is by walking directly across the power line road from *Big Boulder 1*(the two large boulders on the west side of the power line). When across the power line, veer at an angle walking east-south-east, following an extremely faint trail through blueberry bushes. You should reach broken sections of rock within a few minutes of walking. Continue past insignificant rock for a few minutes until you reach this area. This spot contains several large rectangular-shaped boulders in a deeply wooded setting.

Powder Hound Boulder
This will be the first worthwhile boulder to climb on along this ridge. The problems are located on the downhill side of the boulder. There is a trench behind it with a nice cave and a round boulder left of the trench/cave.

1. Powder Hound V2
On the left side of this boulder utilize a sit start to climb a small ceiling near ground level. The V2 variation starts on a pinch and a crimp with your feet hooking the corner. An easier variation can be done climbing only the overhang.

2. Easy Traverse V0-
Traverse this boulder from left to right or right to left.

3. Intergalactic V3
This problem is in a cave on the backside of the boulder. Start sitting as far down in the pit as possible and climb the corner over a small overhang at the top.

4. Space Invader V5
SDS this problem a few feet left of the previous route and deep in a cave. Crank up on holds and pull over the center of a ceiling. The rocks behind are off route.

5. Paper Flake V0-
Climb over the center of a paper-thin flake behind *Intergalactic*.

Pitt Bull
This is the small, round boulder behind and left of the *Powder Hound* boulder.

6. Pitt Bull V1
Climb over a bulge on the very small boulder a few feet left of *Paper Flake*.

7. Pit Bully V3
SDS on edges in the center of the alcove just left of *Pitt Bull*.

8. Little Face V0-
You can find this problem by walking to your right from *Easy* Traverse. The problem starts around the right side of the boulder in a passage created by two boulders. This problem

Dave Pfurr on "Cosmic Corner."
RH photo.

climbs the short face in the passage.

9. Dirt Pilot V0
Climb the face around the corner from the previous problem.

10. Unnamed V0+
The problem near the previous route.

11. Easy Hang V0
Climb the center of the overhang.

12. Creepy Crawler V1
Move out of the cave from a lay-down start at a corner near the center of an overhang, at ground level.

13. Dirt Face V0-
Creep up the lichen-coated face around the right-hand corner from problem number 12.

14. Unnamed V0- R
Several climbs can be done on the boulder behind *Dirt Face*.

15. Two-second Problem V3
This problem is located directly across from *Dirt Face*. It is very short but worth doing. The corner is off route. Make a powerful move off crimps in a horizontal near the ground. Power up to another horizontal with a finger pocket or fire to the top.

16. Tranquility V2
This is the short, overhanging face inches right of the previous route.

17. Monster Move V4/V5
SDS near the previous route.

18. Taming the Wookie V4
Climb the steep face a few inches right of problem number 17.

19. Unclaimed Grace V2
The face inches left of the corner.

20. Downhill Racer V1
The arete/corner.

21. Unnamed V0+
The face to the right of the arete.

22. Unnamed V0-
Traverse the boulder to the right of the boulder the previous problems are located on.

23. Unnamed V0-
The unappealing face around the corner from the traverse.

Gondola Boulder
This is the last boulder of the main outcrop. It is square and has a roof on its downhill face.

24. Unnamed V0-
Climb the very high left side of the boulder.

25. Randy's Rage V0+
Climb the high face to the right of number 24.

26. Unnamed V0/V1
Several fun eliminate problems have been done at the small cave on the northeast side of this boulder.

27. Surprise Roof V3
Climb the center of the roof.

Other Lake Mountain Boulders
Numerous other boulders, and bouldering areas, lie scattered throughout the Big Boulder region. Unfortunately, the boulders are too spread out to logically give directions to, and

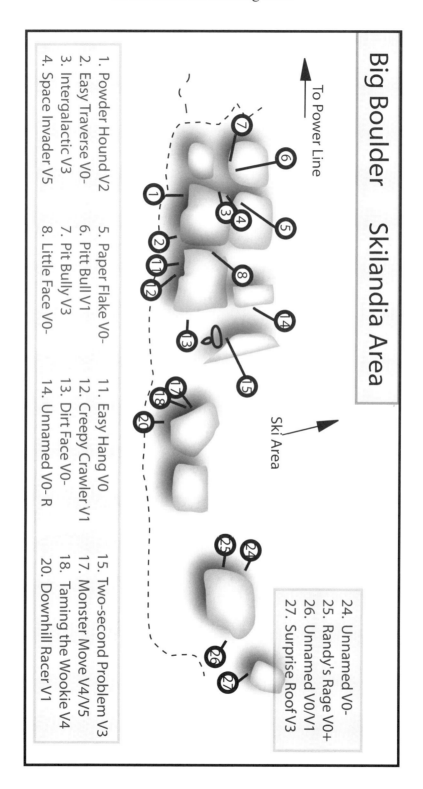

Big Boulder   Skilandia Area

To Power Line

Ski Area

1. Powder Hound V2
2. Easy Traverse V0-
3. Intergalactic V3
4. Space Invader V5
5. Paper Flake V0-
6. Pitt Bull V1
7. Pit Bully V3
8. Little Face V0-
11. Easy Hang V0
12. Creepy Crawler V1
13. Dirt Face V0-
14. Unnamed V0- R
15. Two-second Problem V3
17. Monster Move V4/V5
18. Taming the Wookie V4
20. Downhill Racer V1
24. Unnamed V0-
25. Randy's Rage V0+
26. Unnamed V0/V1
27. Surprise Roof V3

some lie on private land. A few worth fettering out, however, can be found in the places that follow: *The Pebble Boulder* is located in the talus far below the *Little Rock City* area. Other smaller boulders can be found there also. More boulders lie east of *Skilandia*, along the hillside and near to the ski resort. Happy Hunting.

"The Mayor" Randy Ross styling a classic problem.
RH photo.

4. Lehigh Gorge Areas

Area Beta

Location
Just outside of Jim Thorpe.

Type
Sport routes, trad routes, some bouldering, 2 areas.

Other Info
Although only 2 areas are listed, a fair amount of boulders and small cliffs lie scattered throughout the region.

The Lehigh Gorge State Park

A great deal of quality rock in a pristine mountain setting can be found in and near The Lehigh Gorge. This deep gorge has cascading waterfalls, scenic hiking, and high-quality climbing on clean conglomerate.

The two main climbing areas here are Eagle cliff and Gorgeous Rocks. Eagle Cliff is located a mountain top high above the Lehigh River. This area offers high-quality trad routes with panoramic views of the Poconos. Gorgeous Rocks offer a very short approach and a handful of good boulder problems and sport and trad routes.

Eagle Cliff

The approach to *Eagle Cliff* is long and difficult, but the views and setting make up for it. This area offers single-pitch trad climbing high above the Lehigh River. The Jim Thorpe and Lehigh Gorge area is nicknamed the Switzerland of Pennsylvania due to its mountainous nature and pristine surroundings.

The cliff offers 80'-high climbs that seem much higher above the steep mountain slope. About 30 climbs exist here ranging from 5.4 to 5.12a. All the routes are trad-climbs and most take gear well. Bring a standard rack of multiple sized stoppers and cams. Large gear is also recommended. The rock quality is quite good. The smooth conglomerate yields stone you'll need to fondle. Many of the climbs have overhangs and ledges. The main drawback here is lack of lengthy steep walls. If you're within an hours drive, the place is worth a visit if you don't mind a long hike up steep terrain.

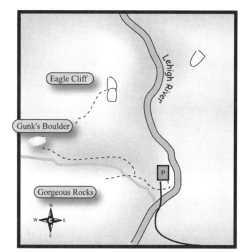

Bring plenty of food and water and headlamp and plan your day at this area. The area is a long walk from the parking area, so plan your day around the approach and getting back safely.

From the cliff, you will notice very large boulders and high-quality rock on the opposing side of the gorge. This area has been explored and developed. The rock is superb, but the approach is difficult and on private property.

Directions: From the parking lot follow the Glen Onoko Falls Trail up to the falls. Walk the steep trail passing all the falls on the right side. At the last fall, you will crest the gorge. Next you will walk past the *Gunk's Boulder*, a beautiful cube of rock with a few nice boulder problems. From here, follow blazes to the right and continue to walk north following the ridgeline. You will pass small cliffs along the way until you reach a massive cliff vista.

You can also follow the stream past the trail to a road that parallels the ridgeline. Follow the road about 40 minutes to another road that goes to the right and cliff top. Perhaps the best option is to walk the rail-bed/road north from the parking lot 1.5 miles to the large bend in the road/river. You will see the cliff above. A small trail on the left side of the hill leads up to the cliff. Note that this trail is a mere footpath that is steep and cumbersome. Either way, the hike will take you well over an hour.

1. Physics 105 5.9 PG
FA: D. Roth, J. Nick Oden Nov 83
Follow a ramp to a bulge 10' up and pull through following a short left-facing corner to another bulge. Continue straight up, passing ledges to a left-facing corner/notch in the big roof. Pull through this (crux).

2. Scare City 5.9 PG/R
FA: D. Roth L. Leymeister 10-16-83
Climb up to the large left-facing corner with a roof at its bottom. Half way up the corner, just above the roof, make your way right to the arete. Continue through crux ceilings to the top.

3. Barrage of Perpetual Protection 5.6 PG
FA: L. Leymeister, D. Roth 10-16-83
25' right of *Scare City* gain a rounded corner and move out left escaping the huge roof at its left. Follow the left-facing corner above passing steep rock until it is possible to move

Joe Forte on the first ascent of "Blap." Photo by the author.

right under the roof that caps the corner. Gain the face above.

4. Gretchen's Flowering Finger Fancy 5.7 R
FA: K. Steiner, Bob Shollenberger, B. Keener 10-14-84
Exciting climbing up clean rock with an exposed finish. 15' right of the previous route climb the white-colored ramp moving left across the face and passing under a slanting ceiling. Merge with the previous route to finish.

5. Porkus Non Grata 5.6
FA: J. Nickoden, D. Roth Nov '83
Climb past horizontals to a clean face with a short, vertical crack 25' up. Continue up the face to a ceiling above. Pull over another ceiling and continue to the top.

6. Andromeda Strain 5.6 PG
FA: Scott Wagstaff, Scott Shellenberger Oct. '83
Climb up to and past a long ceiling 15' up. Move left on the face and under another ceiling that is passed at its left. From here continue straight up over steep rock and some small overhangs above.

7. Roofed Out 5.7
FA: D. Roth, Todd Fosbenner 3-17-84
Climb dihedrals right of the previous climb and right of low ceilings. Climb to the large high roof and traverse left then pull through the big roof 10' right of its left edge.

8. Sloppy Slings 5.8
FA: Luke Leymeister 3-17-84

Ascend weakness to a notch. Move out right and climb into large ledge/alcove. Continue right and break through roof at its right side.

9. Upward Mobility 5.7
FA: D. Roth, S. Wagstaff 11-20-83
Run up broken, blocky rock to a roof 45' up. Pull through a notch in roof system and continue straight up.

10. The Bizzarre-O-World 5.12a PG
FA: D. Roth, L. Leymeister 10-15-83
A bold lead by Darryl Roth on a very cold afternoon. One of the hardest trad-roofs in the East! Climb up past horizontals to the large roof with a finger crack splitting it in the center of the cliff. Pull strenuous moves through the center of the roof.

11. White Punks on Rope 5.8+ PG
FA: D. Roth, L. Leymeister 10-15-83
At the right end of the cliff, climb up to a nice-sized roof with a right-facing corner at its left end. Climb 25' up to the roof and pull through the left end (crux) and out to a small, short right-facing corner attached to the roof's lip. Continue up the corner to the top.

12. Ethereal Route 5.9
D. Roth, L. Leimeister 10-15-83
Difficult to locate. At the very right side of the cliff, find a series of blocky roofs 20' up. Begin left of a roof near the ground and climb a corner under a roof and move right to a notch above a short arete. Climb the V-corner above to pull a roof at the left side. Pull more roofs above then angle out far left escaping the final roof.

Other Lehigh Gap Areas
If you hike the rail-trail north, along the Lehigh River, you will find good bouldering off to the left in the woods along the mountainside. Another notable area can be found on a side trail that departs the parking lot and moves off right before the falls trails. A small but interesting bouldering area is located off the trail (if you continue on this trail it leads to Eagle Cliff). The best quality boulder in the area is by far the *Gunk's Boulder*. This high-quality boulder has conglomerate identical to the Gunks. A handful of problems are located on it. Hike the falls trail past all the falls and this boulder is located above the falls on the trail that leads out to Eagle Cliff. I put up an excellent V5/V6 traverse on the low horizontal that splits the boulder. The traverse is called *Paradise Traverse*. Randy Ross put up an excellent V1 on the boulder also. A few good problems in the V0 range exist here also.

Joe Forte and I established some great climbing/bouldering across the valley from Eagle Cliff. The rock can be seen from Eagle Cliff, directly across the river, high on the ridge.

Gorgeous Rocks

If you don't find the pun in the name, you're probably spending too much time at Stony Ridge trying to impress your friends by redpointing *Space Monkey* for the 100th time. Either way, you need to visit this crag. The name says it all; the place is gorgeous. If the wall were in the back of a landfill, it would still be an alluring crag: large roofs, fist-sized cracks, New River Gorgy sandstone. But since it is in one of the most peaceful settings in the state you get that benefit also.

The crag is perched high above the Glen Onoko Gorge. The crag is not visible from any point because it is nestled on ledges just above the falls. The crag is shrouded in rhododendron, and several types on pine making it one of the most secluded settings in the Poconos. The gentle roar of the falls is the only sound to be heard from this cliff—unless you take a huge whipper off one of the overhangs.

Thanks to the efforts of Joe Forte, the approach to the crag no longer seems like an expedition through the jungles of Machu Pichu. The crag was once so crowded that you couldn't see your cams in front of your face. Now a soft-beaten trail weaves past the base of the cliff.

Hazards: Be aware that when you're at this crag, you are above steep cliffs that plummet to the base of the gorge as soon as you approach the rock. This is not a pet-friendly crag— unless you own a Bengal Tiger or a hawk. Also, do not throw rocks, debris, or climbing partners off the ledges or cliff. Often day-hikers flock to a section of the stream directly under the crag. The crag is not visible under the deep canopy of rhodys; the stream drowns out any sound from above as well. Objects darting out of the trees at hikers are not only irksome, they are very dangerous. Pay close attention to your belongings while climbing.

Joe Forte on "Seperate Reality.

Directions: From downtown Jim Thorpe, take 903 north. After crossing the Lehigh River, continue on Rt. 903. At the sharp bend, go straight and follow signs for Glen Onoko Falls and Lehigh Gorge State Park. Drive into the park and park at the main parking area for the falls. Park in the lot and follow the trail to the falls. Before reaching the main falls trail and at the shore of the river, walk left and follow a faint trail through a tunnel of trees/shrubs. Next, walk left across the bottom of the stream near where it feeds into Lehigh. Immediately after crossing the stream, walk up a steep, faint trail to the cliff. The cliff is hidden in the woods just above the falls.

History: This area was left alone by climbers who developed the nearby crags. Randy Ross and Mike Miscavage and his brother climbed here in the 90s. At the same time I developed a lot of bouldering on the cliff, nearby boulders, and large overhang above the cliff. Jess Holzman, and Ryan Lukas were active here at the same time also. The bouldering on the falls trail was also developed around this time.

Joe Forte along with the author and many of Joe Forte's friends developed a great deal

of routes on the main cliff. Erica Meyers, Jeff Carroll, and Dave Kotch were also active in recent years.

Bulbous Boulder

This boulder is located just off the shore near the approach trail. It is a round boulder perched a few feet off the trail, a few yards after passing under the steel bridge. It has two difficult problems on it.

1. Velocity Child V9

SDS and fire to the top from very thin holds.

2. Bulbous V7

Climb up just right of the previous problem.

Little Secret Boulder

This boulder is somewhat hidden below the main area. Before hiking up the hill, after you pass over the stream where you go to climb up to the main area, walk left. You will find a grey-colored boulder with excellent problems.

3. Little Secret V1

Climb the right side of the boulder.

4. Project

SDS and climb the steep arete.

The Schoolyard

Left of and slightly above *Separated at Birth* there is a small room with a few boulder problems. You can either walk around the left side of the cliff or go through a small passage to get to these problems.

5. Hemlock V1

SDS and climb the left wall.

6. Swept Away V4

SDS in the right side of the cave and climb up to and over the overhang.

7. Undertow V3

SDS and climb over the bulge at the left side of the main cliff.

8. Welcome Crack 5.6 G

FA: Erica Meyers, Joe Forte
Climb the first crack you come to on the cliff.

9. Separated At Birth 5.10a PG/R

FA: Joe Forte
Delicate moves between two thin cracks. RPs and TCUs.

10. Blap 5.9 G

Erica Meyers leading "Blap." Photo by the author.

FA: Joe Forte
A fun crux at the first bolt that is well protected! Climb the first bolted line at this area.

11. Variety Crack 5.6 G
FA: J. Forte
Climb the beautiful, mellow sandstone crack.

12. Separate Reality 5.10a G
FA: R. Holzman, J. Forte
Follow small crimps past two bolts to an anchor above.

13. The Space Between 5.10 PG or TR
Usually toproped, but can be easily lead using nearby bolts.

14. Mixed Bidness 5.8 G
FA: J. Forte
Climb the crack/arete to a bolt then up a slopey face to the anchors. 1 bolt, mixed.

15. Rabid Easter Bunny 5.6 PG
FA: J. Forte
Traverse left on jugs, then up slabby terrain to the big pine. Small to Med. cams.

16. Reach Around 5.5 PG
FA: J. Forte
Haul out fun overhanging rock on hidden buckets. .

17. Glen-O-Switchcrack 5.9 PG
FA: Gabe Franklin
Climbs a large prominent arete with an airy traverse.

18. Monkey's Fist 5.9 (5.9 G)
FA: J. Forte
Traverse over the first overhang and surmount the second and third. First roof has not gone free yet!

19. Too Many Tacos Not Enough Toilet Paper 5.7 G
FA: Dave Kotch, R. Holzman
Follow varied rock to 2-bolt anchor.

20. The Gorgeous Face 5.11a PG-13
FA: J. Forte
Height dependant. A bouldery start leads up and right on a bulletproof quartzite face.

21. The Gorgeous Crack 5.10a G
FA: J. Forte
A thin hands crack out steep rock leads to a mellow finish

22. The Gorgeous Arete. 5.7 PG

An easy overhanging arete that finishes on the previous route. A hard direct finish 5.10 G was done by Joe Forte..

23. The Bat Cave 5.5
FA: Len Forte
Chimney to 2-bolt anchor.

24. Party at Tim's 5.13a
FA: R. Holzman, J. Forte
Climb the steep difficult corner.

Jess Holzman on "Gorgeous Crack."

25. Painfully Obvious 5.12d
J. Forte, R. Holzman
Climb right of the previous route.

Other Routes
Several 5.11's and 5.12's have been soloed farther down the cliff by the author and Randy Ross. Some are unclean and need a little TLC.

Joe Forte on "Party at Tim's."

5. Francis E. Walter Recreation Area

Area Beta

Location
Between Bear Creek and White Haven.

Type of Climbing
High-quality bouldering and a few trad and sport routes.

Important Info.
Check to see what the water level is before visiting; sometimes it's too high to climb on the cliff and boulders.

Introduction

One of my favorite places to boulder in Pennsylvania is the Francis E. Walter Reservoir. Although this area is one of the finest in the East, few climbers have ever heard of it. If you've ever rafted on The Lehigh River, this is the dam that is opened to fill The Lehigh. Dozens of boulders dominate the shore of this quaint, little reservoir that greatly resembles the Horstooth Reservoir in Colorado. In fact, the Francis E. Walter Reservoir is such a doppelganger to its Colorado twin, it has been dubbed "Pennsylvania's Horsetooth".

Created by the Army Corps of Engineers in 1961, the dam is a 3000' long, 234'-high earthen dam that provides flood control for the Lehigh River Valley. The reservoir held back by the dam, originally named Bear Creek Reservoir, offers hundreds of boulders that clutter the vast shoreline. These boulders and small cliffs create a playground of climbing that offers rock in all shapes and sizes.

Weekend after weekend, the few climbers that know about this spot frequent the rock-tattered landscape to enjoy problems ranging from V0- to V9. Despite the broad range in grades, it is the aesthetic nature of the boulders that makes this area irresistible to visit. Sun bakes the golden conglomerate rock and paints it a brilliant orange color, making this one of the prettiest places to boulder in the Mid-Atlantic. With problems named *Atlantis*, *Waterworld*, and *Poseidon*, you can begin to envision the curious aquatic setting that surrounds this reservoir. Imagine climbing *The Poseidon Adventure*; your shoes skim the water as you traverse into a V4 highball that tops out above a pristine water landing. Visualize yourself on *The Gloaming*; you bask in the sun as you dance up a behemoth boulder that rests near the waters edge amid blueberry bushes

This book covers 10 areas at The F.E. Walter Dam. Over 20 areas exist, but many are complicated to locate and would go beyond the scope of this book. The areas you will find in this book are the *Atlantis Bouldering Area*, *The Klitergarden*, *Cube Boulder*, *City of Boulders*, *Atlantis Wall*, *Tangerine Dream Area*, *Ancient Wall*, *Brown Sugar Wall*, *The Devil's Elbow*, and *The Land of Overhangs*.

Until the printing of this book, many of these areas were completely unknown, even to local climbers. I hope climbers will investigate some of these secret crags and aspire to find some of the other treasures not mentioned in the book. Some of these lesser-known gems offer extraordinary bouldering.

Tom Kneiss on a mega-classic at the dam.

Most of the spots at this reservoir are bouldering areas. Two of the areas mentioned offer roped climbing, one of them being a semi-bolted crag with a few sport lines. Be aware that some times of the year—not often, but occasionally—the water level becomes higher than the boulders and cliff. During this time it is possible to climb only at the areas located in the woods. During the Agnes Flood in the 1970s, the water actually overflowed the top of the dam!

Bouldering found along the shore offers the best quality rock. Without a doubt, the *Atlantis Bouldering Area* offers the best concentration of quality boulder problems. The *Tangerine Dream* area comes in a close second for quality rock soon followed by *The Hideout*. For unique water landings, check out the *Atlantis Wall*; you are not likely to find a more surrealistic setting to boulder anywhere else in the state. *The Klittergarden, Land of Overhangs, Mystery Area*, and *Cube Boulder* offer a different blend of conglomerate that tends to be a bit dirty and more vegetated. During the rare high-water times, these are the only places to climb at the dam. *The Land of Overhangs* offers the highest concentration of difficult problems at the dam.

For route potential, *The Ancient Wall* checks in at 80' at its highest point. The nearby *Brown Sugar Wall* is not quite as high but offers a few sport routes and some semi-bolted, mixed trad/bolt climbs. The climbs on *The Brown Sugar Wall* range from 5.8 to 5.12a.

Important, Please Read:

Due to fish spawning activity, drought, and or water storage conflicts, the reservoir level is sometimes increased. Should this happen, expect surrealistic climbing with water landings at your feet amongst floating islands of boulders or completely submerged rock that is impossible to climb sans diving gear. The dam management frequently posts a loosely predicted annual forecast of approximate release times and water levels. This data can be obtained by checking www.nap.usace.army.mil/Projects/FEWalter/index.htm. If the water level is below 1309', the access road and parking lot is above water and you can climb at all the areas. Should the water exceed this number, it's hit or miss for climbing at the cliffs or bouldering areas along the shores. At these high water times, climbing is only possible at the *Klittergarden*, *Land of Overhangs*, *Mystery Area*, or *Cube Boulder*. If the water rises to cover these areas, build an ark!

General Location: 23 miles north of Allentown and 20 miles south of Wilkes-Barre. Half way between the towns of Blakslee and White Heaven, and a few miles from exit 35 off the northeast extension of the PA Turnpike.

Geology: Sandstone Silicate and Conglomerate mix. Rock type varies depending on what area you are at.

Land Ownership: National Recreation Area/Army Core of Engineers.

Access issues and Restrictions: The land is a National recreation Area (the same ownership is the same as the Delaware Water Gap). Climbing is allowed here. Please remain courteous to fisherman, hunters from the nearby hunting club, and other outdoor enthusiasts.

The only restriction toward climbing at this area is that you are not permitted to climb or walk on the giant tower that protrudes from the dam. This is owned by the Army Corps of Engineers, and it is a federal offense to climb on or walk on this property. I know it would be tempting to climb up the giant cement tower—we've all thought of it--but stay off!

It is also a restriction to climb on the *Atlantis Cliff* (do not get this confused with *Atlantis Bouldering Area* located on the other side of the dam; it is legal it climb there). A drowning accident occurred a few years where two young climbers were killed from diving off a nearby cliff. Please do not jeopardize access by climbing at this area.

Season: For the most part, the season starts in March/April and lasts until mid- November. You can climb at the *Atlantis Bouldering Area* in the winter on sunny days (the area is nicknamed the sunny boulders). Some winter days can be unpleasant with the cold air wafting off the nearby ice. The other areas are cold and unpleasant from November until March.

Nearby Areas: Lake Mountain, The Pink boulders, Effort Crag, The Devils Elbow, The City of Boulders, Spook Hollow, Hickory Run, River bottom Crag, Wilkes Barre Areas, The Rim, Split Rock Areas, Rt.-115 Crags, Bear Creek boulders, Lehigh/Toby Creek Crags.

History

Climbers have known about this area for a very long time. Evidence of early climbing dates back to the 1970s. Remnants of old pitons can be found on the *Atlantis Wall* and at the *Ancient Crag* on the *Original Route*. I was unable to locate the person who placed the original pitons at this area, and none of the older climbers in the region were able to attest to placing them either (if you know who put them in, please let me know).

Francis E. Walter Recreation Area

The first recorded climbers to develop climbing at the dam were Randall Ross, Nick Morell, the myself and Obe Carrion in the early '90s. Randall Ross was an area native who discovered many Pocono crags like Lake Mountain, Effort Crag, and a few other crags along the Pocono Plateau. Randy developed several climbs on the *Ancient Wall* during the early '90s. Randy also named the *Brown Sugar Wall*, a bolted cliff at the dam that resembles a brown sugar color with its orange hues. Some of Randy's other developments around the dam include *Florabunda* V0+/V1, *Rude Boy Rub* V0+ R, *Rude Boy Scrub* V0 R, and at least a dozen other problems at the dam.

At the same time, Obe Carrion, Nick Morell, George Morell and myself developed a lot of the bouldering here. Nick Morell and I developed the majority of bouldering at the dam and discovered many areas that were previously unknown and undeveloped.

Nick Morell was a very strong climber who developed an incredible amount of very difficult bouldering and climbing in the Scranton, Wilkes-Barre, and Mocanaqua regions and was the primary developer of *Hunter Rocks* in Central PA. At the dam, Nick developed some of the original area classics like *Aggravated*

Tom Kneiss putting up a new problem on the "Atlantis Wall." Photo by the author

Behavior V4, *Glider* V4, *Broken Corner* V0, *Monster Mash* V2, and *The One Inch Pinch* V5 (later named by another climber). Nick was also part of developing the original problems at the *Tangerine Dream* area as well as placing the first bolts at the dam with myself and Ryan Lukas.

I was fortunate enough to have developed over 150 problems and many climbing routes at the dam. Some of these routes and problems include *Heart of Atlantis* V2, *The Gloaming* V0, *Pitfall* V2, *Little Face* V5, *Gleaming the Cube* V6, *Melanie* V7, *Brown Sugar* V5, *Tangerine Dream* 5.13a or *Unnamed* V7, *Tomb of King Klutz* V5 and many others. I also discovered many hidden areas at the dam like the *Klittergarden* and several other outcrops in the region like *The Cube*, *Mystery Area*, *Tangerine Dream* area and a jackpot discovery of *The City of Boulders* (a giant area 5-times the size of the *Atlantis Boulders*). To this day I am thankful to have been lucky enough to stumble upon this Pennsylvania bouldering gem.

Tom Kneiss and Ryan Lukas also made significant contributions to developing the area. Tom and Ryan, two very talented climbers, developed several worthwhile problems at all areas around the dam and on the surrounding cliffs. These two climbers heavily developed routes and boulders over a vast area for the better part of a decade.

Jeremy Bisher and Ryan Anglemier established some of the hardest boulder problems at the dam in the late '90s. Their lines challenge and intimidate climbers to this day. Some of his classics include *The Stab* V6, and *My Screaming Double* V7. Jeremy also established a few hard lines at the *Land of Overhangs* area.

Ryan Anglemier was another active climber at *Atlantis* and *Land of Overhangs* in the late '90s, also developing a few hard problems at both these areas. Ryan is most noted for being the first person to establish problems at the *Land of Overhangs.* He developed many lines there like *Swamp Ass* V4, *Ryan's Problem* V5, and several problems in the V8 range.

Directions: The dam is located between White Haven and Blakeslee. There are only two points of access either from the north or south ends of the reservoir.

From the North: From the town of Bear Creek Village (located on State Route 115 - 12 miles south of Wilkes-Bare), turn west on White Haven Boulevard. This road can be located across from the wood dam in the village. There is a sign for the F.E. Walter Dam just before the turn. Follow White Haven Boulevard approximately 8 miles and turn left when you see the sign for the F.E Walter Dam. Follow the access road.

Parking for the *Land of Overhangs, Brown Sugar Wall, Ancient Wall*, and *Tangerine Dream* area are on the right side of the access road just before the road descends downhill to the reservoir. This is the big dirt lot just past the maintenance buildings. It has a concrete wall at the back of the lot that forms the right edge of the dam.

Parking for *Atlantis, Mystery Area, Cube Boulder*, and the *Klittergarden* is located at the base of the dam. It is the obvious square lot where the road is at its lowest point. **Note:** If the water level is too high, you must follow the road that drives over the dam. Parking at this time is only at the main lots near the dam.

From the South: From Exit 35 off the northeast extension of the PA Turnpike Rt. 476, take State Route 940 east, approximately 3 miles, until you see a sign (easy to miss) for the F.E Walter Dam. Make a left, and follow the access road until you reach the dam.

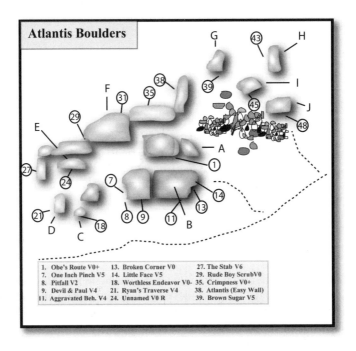

Atlantis Boulders

1. Obe's Route V0+	13. Broken Corner V0	27. The Stab V6
7. One Inch Pinch V5	14. Little Face V5	29. Rude Boy Scrub V0
8. Pitfall V2	18. Worthless Endeavor V0-	35. Crimpness V0+
9. Devil & Paul V4	21. Ryan's Traverse V4	38. Atlantis (Easy Wall)
11. Aggravated Beh. V4	24. Unnamed V0 R	39. Brown Sugar V5

See the directions above for specific parking areas for the climbs. Be aware that at times when the water level is elevated, the lower parking lot is submerged, and although it is not recommended or permitted by the reservoir, people have been known to drive to the water's high point to park. You should know that the water level is subject to sudden rise and turbulence. I once saw a late-model Porshe 911 speeding carefree around the final corner of the access road before reaching the water. The driver, unaware of the water level and submerged road ahead, locked his breaks in sheer terror as he slid out of control toward the vast, murky pool ahead. The nose of the car splashed into the water the instant the smoking tires came to a screeching halt. Luckily, his did not penetrate deep enough to pull a *Risky Business*. Please abide by the reservoirs rules and obey all posted signs.

Atlantis Bouldering Area

Bouldering at the Atlantis Bouldering Area is superb. A field of excellent problems, great quality rock, and one of the most picturesque settings in Pennsylvania is what you can expect here. The typical boulder height varies from a few feet to 20' high. The rock here is very similar to the rock at *The Gunk's*, but with a unique orange hue.

People have been coming here to boulder since 1990, but the area has recently seen a lot of activity and increased popularity. At times, the area is completely submerged under water, thus, getting its name *Atlantis*. When the water recedes, the boulders rest just above the water somewhat resembling the Horsetooth Reservoir in Colorado. The orange-colored rock is illuminated by the sun most of the day making the boulders climbable year round. If you climb at only one area at the dam, make it this one.

Directions: Park at the lower lot at the base of the access road below the dam. If the water level is above 1309 feet, climbing will not be possible at most of this area, and you will have to park at the last lot before the gate that marks the road as closed. Otherwise, cross the stream that feeds into the reservoir at the east end of the lot and follow the shoreline east along the water for 5 minutes. You will see boulders up to your right. Walk to the second set of boulders via a narrow trail through thick blueberry bushes. The trail will bring you to the *Titanic Boulder*. The *Monster Boulder* is located just behind it.

A. The Monster Boulder
This is the nicely-sized boulder directly behind the *Titanic Boulder*. When the sun hits the top of this boulder, it resembles a monster's head. Several great warm-up problems exist on this boulder.

1. Obe's Route V0+
This was one of the first problems done at the F.E. Walter Dam. Begin at the right end of the *Monster Boulder* and traverse left on a large rail to a horizontal under a small overhang. Continue left and top out at the center of the overhang. A classic at its grade.

2. My Screaming Double V7/V8
This route got its name on the first ascent, when Jeremy Bisher screamed in excitement for finally sticking the crux. During this shriek of success his echo screamed back at him from across the reservoir. Traverse the horizontal at head level using small crimps. Traverse

from right to left. The crux is about mid way into the traverse but the whole problem is rather sustained.

3. Monster Mash V2
Start on small edges at a horizontal and grab a small sloping bulge (crux). Gain the overhang to top out.

4. Sigmund the sea Monster VB
Climb the face and small overhang left of the previous route.

Nick Morell on "the One-inch Pinch."

B. The Titanic Boulder
This large ship-like boulder is the largest, most centrally located boulder at this area. Looking at this boulder from the water, the descent is off the left side.

5. Unnamed V0-
Climb easy rock to the point above.

6. Water Slug V0+
SDS deep in the cave located at the boulders left side near the descent. Start at a horizontal and climb the steep wall at its left side. The boulders to the left and behind are off. Mind your head on the boulder behind!

7. The One Inch Pinch V5
An area classic. Start on a horizontal far back in the cave and stretch to a small one-inch pinch (crux). Crank up and over the top.

8. Pitfall V2
A bit of a squirm. Begin just right of the previous route on a horizontal and a hidden undercling. Reach to a crimp and a rail, then up to a jug above. Try not to touch the boulder at your back.

9. The Devil and Paul Anka V4
This problem is located on the short face just around the corner and right of the previous

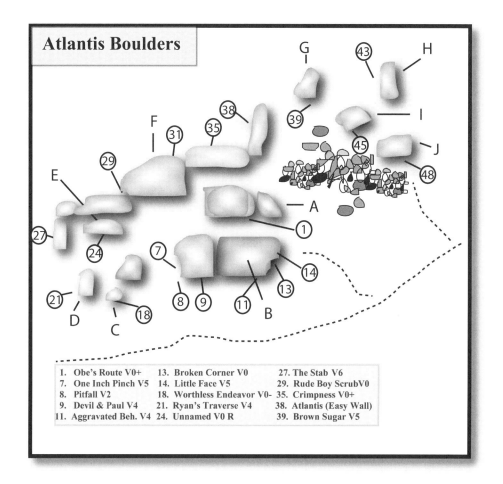

Atlantis Boulders

1. Obe's Route V0+	13. Broken Corner V0	27. The Stab V6
7. One Inch Pinch V5	14. Little Face V5	29. Rude Boy ScrubV0
8. Pitfall V2	18. Worthless Endeavor V0-	35. Crimpness V0+
9. Devil & Paul V4	21. Ryan's Traverse V4	38. Atlantis (Easy Wall)
11. Aggravated Beh. V4	24. Unnamed V0 R	39. Brown Sugar V5

route. SDS at a good horizontal and ascend the slightly overhung, crimpy face just right of a block on the ground. The block is off.

10. Aggravated Behavior V4
Climb the face right of the previous route without using the corner or crack to the right. This problem is tendon-popping fun.

11. Glider V4
SDS in the center of a slightly overhanging face with hands in a horizontal. Move to crimps then fire to the top. Variations of this problem have been done at the same grade.

12. Scaly Face V0-
From a SDS, climb the face just around the corner from the previous route.

13. Broken Corner V0
Just to the right of *Scaly Face* is an obvious corner. Climb up this to the top. Not as easy as it looks.

113

14. Little Face V5
Using small crimps, crank up the center of a small face just right of *Broken Corner*. A SDS can be done adding length, but not difficulty.

15. Obe's Arete V0+
Climb the arete just right of the previous route.
Var. 1: V1
Same problem using the crimpy face and arete to climb from a SDS.

16. Beginners Face VB
Several very easy problems can be done on the low-angle face on the back side of the *Titanic Boulder*.

17. Rob's Traverse V4
Traverse the entire boulder starting at any point.

18. Worthless Endeavor V0-
Slightly below the *Titanic Boulder* is a small cave that is easily overlooked. There are three problems in the cave: *Worthless Endeavor*, *The Crawl*, and an unnamed V1. Start deep in this small cave and pull over the roof.

19. The Crawl V0-
Start on a very loose flake near the previous route and pull over the top.

20. Unnamed V1
SDS and climb next to the previous problem.

C. Small-Unnamed Boulder
This boulder is just left of the last two problems near the left end of *The Atlantis Wall*.

21. Ryan's Traverse V4
Traverse a horizontal at mid-height from right to left avoiding the top or any large blocks for feet.

D. The Leaning Tower:
Above the previous boulder is a tower-like formation composed of two enormous boulders stacked on top of each other.

22. Tom's Finger V1
Climb over a finger of rock on the left side of the tower. The back wall is off.

23. The Leaning Tower V0 R
Start in the middle of a nice face and climb to the top. The crux is flopping over the left-center of the tower at a faint crack.

24. Unnamed VO R
Climb up a few inches right of *Leaning Tower*. Endure the creepy top out.

25. Candlelight Arete V0-
From a low start climb the arete to the right of *Leaning Tower*.

26. Theory of Atlantis V1
Traverse the entire tower on horizontals at head and chest level.

E. The Atlantis Wall
This is a section of cliff that runs behind the main boulders. The first problem starts at the far left end of the wall, left of the *Leaning Tower* boulder.

27. The Stab V6
A tricky, frustrating, but mega-classic problem. This route is located under a dead tree on top of a small roof at the very left end of the *Atlantis Wall*. Sit start on a big horizontal and stab a small finger pocket. Continue to the top.

28. Small Wall V0-
Cruise up the small wall just right of the previous route.

Dave Pfurr on "Little Face" Photo by the author.

29. Rude Boy Scrub V0
Randy Ross endured a lot of cleaning to unearth this fun problem. Scrub up an awkward crack/dihedral to the right of the *Leaning Tower* boulder.

30. Unnamed VB
Climb to a ledge and gain a small crack just right of *Rude Boy Scrub*.

31. The Gloaming V0 R
The sun hits this wall at the end of the day creating a fabulous orange glow on the rock. Do an awkward mantle to gain a crimpy wall below a notch made by a large block at the summit. Finish through the notch.

32. Rude Boy Rub V0+ R
Climb just right of *The Gloaming* and top out on the center of the block resting above this fantastic route.

33. Tangerine V0- R
Easy holds follow the arete and face at the right end of this section of the wall.
Var 1: V0 Don't use the arete but climb the same problem.

Ryan Lukas on "The Gloaming." Photo by the author.

34. Crimp Left V0-
Climb the crimpy face without using the corner.

35. Crimpness V0+
Climb the face just right of the previous route.

36. Jeff's Lunge V2
A great route first done by Jeff Sughenic. Easier if tall. Begin on holds at head-height between *Crimp left* and *Crimp Right*. Dyno to the top. A must-do problem.

37. Heart of Atlantis V2
At mid-height traverse the wall behind the *Monster Boulder* from right to left without using the top. The crux is at the deep pocket.

38. Atlantis Wall (Easy Wall)
Behind the *Monster Boulder*, the *Atlantis Wall* continues up and right to another small boulder field. A few easy problems can be done on this wall. They range from V0- to V1.

F. Brown Sugar Cube Boulder
This boulder is the cube-like boulder above the *Easy Wall*.

39. Brown Sugar V5
Start on low crimps on the arete. Levitate to the top and hump over it to finish.

40. The Fly V2
Interesting flakes create a nice climb up the face just right of the obvious arete.

41. White Water V0+
Splash up the center of this short wall.

42. Unnamed V0-
Climb the right side of this boulder.
Var. 1: V0 The same problem as above but without using the right corner.

43. Melanie V7
Directly across some talus from the *Brown Sugar Boulder* is a modest sized boulder with a blank vertical face. Climb the center of the face over a block at the top.

44. French Canadian Dame V0-
From a SDS cruise up right corner of this boulder.
Var. 1: VB Climb the same problem but swing right into a shallow blocky dihedral.

Ryan Lukas on "Candlelight Arete" RH photo.

G. The Nose
This boulder is the largest boulder of this group.
It has a point on its downhill side that forms a big nose. The boulder is perched on top of another boulder.

45. The Nose V1
SDS under the nose of a large boulder. Move off a flake to crimps and a scary mantle at the nose. Remain on the arete the whole way to the top.
Var. 1: V0+ Move out right at the nose.

46. Unnamed VB
Climb an obvious crack/weakness around the right side of a clean wall just right of the previous boulder.

47. Unnamed V0+
Climb the corner and face just left of the previous route.

Lukas Boulder
A few feet below *The Nose* you will see a very small boulder with some short problems on the downhill side.

117

48. Short and Simple V3

Start on the downhill side of this small boulder at a shallow horizontal with small incuts. Keep your feet off the good ledge and fire to the top.

49. Lukas Boulder Problem V1

Start a few inches right of the previous problem at a crack and low face. Begin with your left hand in a horizontal and a right in the good crack. Keeping your feet off the good ledge, shoot for the top or traverse to the left side of the boulder to top out.

Other Nearby Boulders

Farther north along the shore there is a small cube-shaped boulder that is a few feet tall. There is a V6 traverse called *Gleaming the Cube*, and a nice V6 Sit start up the center. Walk uphill from this boulder, into the woods, you will find a nice patch of boulders with excellent quality rock also.

Ancient Crag

Certainly one of the more scenic areas to climb in Pennsylvania. Located beside the reservoir, this 80-foot high cliff rises from the water with excellent trad and toprope routes. This small cliff offers about 10 decent routes. I only mention a few routes because not every route here has been climbed. Some portions of this rock are brittle making protection a concern. Bring very long webbing to set up topropes here. Because of the soft rock, a helmet is a good idea. The quality of this cliff is far less superior to the quality at the bouldering areas, but the setting is spectacular. Be aware at times of high water, you may have to rappel in and set an anchor above the water; otherwise, you can hike the shore to the rock.

From this cliff you can see *The Atlantis Boulders* directly across the water. I highly recommend visiting these boulders. Some excellent boulders can also be found near the *Ancient Crag*.

Directions: This area can be tricky to find because there are few landmarks and access is from above the cliff. Park at the main lot on the north side of the dam. Follow the gated dirt road on the opposite side of the main parking lot to the picnic area about five minutes down the dirt road. Walk straight down a faint trail that brings you to the *Land of Overhangs Area*. From here, walk straight down heading for the reservoir. This will bring you to the top of the cliff. Your best choice is to rap in from here. Be sure to check the water level before rapping

Tom Kneiss at City of Boulders.

in or you may end up rappelling into the reservoir. You can also access this cliff by walking farther along the shore past the *Tangerine Dream Area*. This area is accessed by a rock drainage that is south of the main lot (see directions for

118

Tangerine Dream Area).

1. Tiddlywinks 5.7 TR
FA: R. Holzman, N. Morell
Climb the face left of the crack.

2. Origional Route 5.8+ PG/R
FA: Unknown
Climb the obvious crack at the cliffs highest point past an old piton. Be aware that the brittle rock is not always reliable for protection.

3. Unnamed 5.12a TR
FA: R. Holzman
Climb the steep bulges right of *Original Route*.

4. The Dam Route 5.10a R
FA: R. Holzman, N. Morell
Climb the steep face left of *Original Route*.

The Klittergarden

This area is a bit tricky to find but is worth hunting for. The rock is not nearly as clean as many of the other spots in the area, but some of the routes here are well worth climbing. Several climbers in recent years thought they had recently discovered this spot. I can certainly understand why they thought this seeing as though the rock is so unclean. Actually, this spot was developed in the mid-'90s. Like so many other spots in Pennsylvania the original climbers just didn't feel the need to clean much at this area when such quality rock existed nearby.

There are about 50 established problems at this area. The height varies from 10' to about 25' at its highest point. Problems range from V0- to V7 with the majority being in the very easy range.

The rock is a conglomerate rock somewhat like what you would find at The Gunk's only much more vegetated. This area tends to be moist, so stay away from this spot after storms. Please note that part of the property here is owned by a hunting club. Only a very small section is owned by the club at the farthest border of their property. For this reason it is very unlikely to run into a hunter and only a few problems extend into their property. Please be cautious during hunting season, wear orange, and avoid drifting onto the hunting property during these times of year. Wearing a costume with antlers is also discouraged.

Directions: The easiest way to access this spot is to park at the main lot at the base of the dam and walk towards State Route 940. About 1000' from the lot, just before a road sign on the left, bushwhack up the hill. When you enter the forest, walk about 100' and immediately start walking right on a faint path. You will see rock within five minutes of walking. If the reservoir is flooded, you must park near the gate on the Rt. 940 side of the dam and walk down the road towards the lower parking lot. A few-hundred feet past the waterfall and picnic area, you can access the cliff via the same spot mentioned above.

A. Cube Boulder

This is the square-shaped boulder detached from the cliff. You will see it when you first approach this area. The problems on it range from V0- to V1 with some interesting eliminates.

1. Rhoddy Arete V1

At the left side of the cliff a few feet right of where this cliff-band starts climb the arete from a SDS.

2. Rhoddy Crack V0-

The crack just right of the nice arete.

3. Rhoddey Face Left V0

Climb the face a few inches right of the crack.

4. Rhoddey Face Right V1

Climb the crimpy-right side of the face without using the corner.

5. Unnamed V0-

Cruise the corner just right of the previous route.

6. Rhododendron Hell V0-/V1

This area is just past the past few problems. Simply walk past the first section and until you come to a smooth wall that is about 12' high and engulfed in rhododendron. Several problems have been done on this smooth face ranging from V0- to V1.

7. Spoof Roof V0-

After the *Rhododendron Hell* area you will come to a small area with a large detached boulder. This is the *Grunge Block* boulder. Look left from this boulder and you will see a small roof on the cliff. Climb it.

8. Grunge Block Boulder Problem V0+

Climb the center face of the nice but grungy boulder detached from the cliff. A harder variation can be done from a sitting start at the right side of the steep face and firing up to a small ledge.

9. Grungy V0

Climb the left side of the steep wall left of the previous route.

10. Slime Time V1

Often wet and loose. Climb the face on the backside of the boulder. Easier and harder variations have been done.

11. Unnamed V3

Sit start way back in the left corner of the cave behind the *Grunge Block* boulder and climb out to the lip of the overhang via the corner under the roof. Pull the lip of the roof without using the tree.

12. Unnamed V2

From a standing start pull over the right side of this roof.

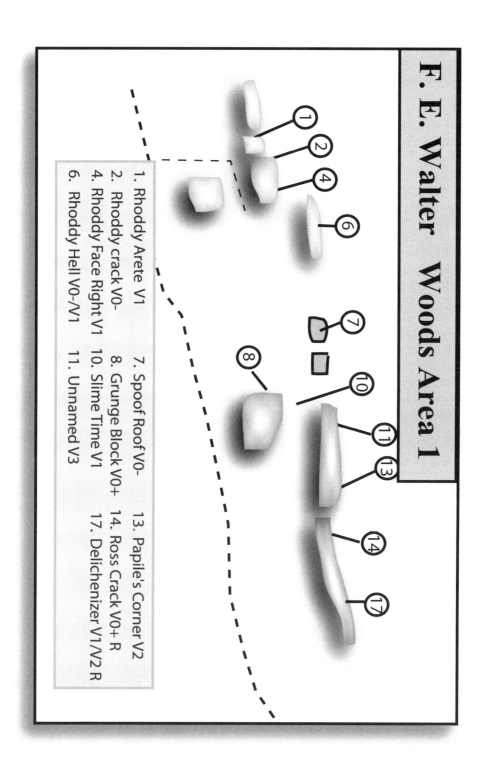

F. E. Walter Woods Area 1

1. Rhoddy Arete V1
2. Rhoddy crack V0-
4. Rhoddy Face Right V1
6. Rhoddy Hell V0-/V1

7. Spoof Roof V0-
8. Grunge Block V0+
10. Slime Time V1
11. Unnamed V3

13. Papile's Corner V2
14. Ross Crack V0+ R
17. Delichenizer V1/V2 R

13. Papile's Corner V2
A fun problem that was put up and cleaned by Mike Papile. SDS in the corner at the right edge of this roof and climb the corner to an overgrown top out.

14. Ross Crack V0+ R
Randy Ross put a lot of effort into delichenizing this area classic. Climb the high finger crack a few feet right of the previous route.

15. Unnamed V0- R
Grunt up the easy but high arete a few feet right of the beautiful crack.

16. Moss Corner V1 R
Stem up the corner just right of the previous climb.

Randy Ross/Klitter-garden. RH photo.

17. The Delichenizer V1/V2 R
The name reflects the effort it took to establish this route. The grade varies slightly depending on how this problem is done. A few feet right of *Moss Corner*, climb the polished face in front of a tree to an undercling-feature 12' up (crux). Continue to the top. The tree is off route.

B. Fern Grove Area:
Walk a little farther on the cliffband and you will come to a small grove of ferns. Several problems have been done on the cliff here.

18. Fern Grove V0-
On the first small outcrop near three small trees. Climb the nice face over horizontals.

19. Fern Traverse V0
Traverse the series of cliff-blocks, starting at the left end of the outcrop and continuing to the end of the cliff.

20. Wild Fern V0
SDS from low horizontals on the small outcrop 12' right of *Fern Grove*. Climb the center of the face.

21. Ferny Cracks V0-
Run up the cracks to the right of *Wild Fern*.

22. Florabunda V0+/V1
One of the best problems at this area. Easier variations can be done to the right or left of this problem. About 20' past *Ferny Crack*, climb the corner of a roof that is perched atop a boulder.

23. Unnamed V1
Climb up right of *Florabunda* near a small rock seat on the ground.

24. Gyrosphere V5

A classic at its grade. Deep under the small roof to the right of the previous routes, start sitting at the right end of the roof. Climbing into the right-hand corner is off route. Climb into flakes under the back end of the roof and reach out to the sloping lip trying not to use the edges up and right. Fly up and left to the big shelf on top the center of the roof. Control your swing and mantle.

25. Unnamed V4

Climb out the left-center of the roof just left of *Gyrosphere*.

26. Unnamed V2

Climb up and right into the corner that is off route for *Gyosphere*.

27. Gunkie Boulder

This is the large square-shaped boulder just beyond the last few problems. It resembles the rock found at The Gunk's. With lesser quality of course.

28. Gunkie V0-

Climb the face that faces the *Fern Grove Area*. Make your way up the center of the face.

29. Gunkie Arete V0-

Begin under the small ceiling at ground level and climb the arete to the top.

30. The Loose Goose V1

Quite loose. From a SDS climb the overhanging face on the backside of the *Gunkie Boulder*. Use the left side of the loose face.

31. Four-star Choss V1

Climb the center or right side of the overhanging face from a sitting start. Climb past horizontals and loose blocks just right of the previous problem.

32. The Tomb of King Klutz V5

Walk past the *Gunkie Boulder* to another outcrop of boulders. Just before the next outcrop you'll see a deep pit to your left. Sit/lay-start in the pit (the rock at your back is off route). Use an undercling in a horizontal low on the rock and fire up to a small pebble with an edge to top out. Be careful not to crack your back or neck on the rock behind.

33. Deer Lick V0-

Locate the boulder just above the previous route. Climb the

Randy Ross on "Inka Dinka Do" RH photo.

crack to a small ceiling and top out.

34. Musty Arete V0
From a SDS climb the nice arete to the right of *Deer Lick*.

35. Unnamed V0-
Just around the right-hand corner from the previous routes is a very small 6' tall boulder. SDS and climb up over the bulge.

36. Inka Dinka Do V2
Located on the last boulder of this outcrop climb the left-center of the slab perched above a cave. Step over the cave to begin.

37. Corkscrew V7
The same problem as above but with a SDS under the back of the cave.

38. Unnamed V1
Climb the right side of the slab from a standing start while stepping over the cave.

Land of Overhangs Area

The rock here is mostly composed of overhanging roofs. Top-outs on many problems are quite cumbersome due to hanging vegetation that extends over the lip of the rock. The rock is a solid conglomerate in some spots but can be quite loose in others. The problems here range from V0- to V8 with a few existing projects. The majority of the problems here were established by Ryan Anglemier, Jeremy Bisher, Tom Kneiss, and myself.
Directions: From the north lot (Bear Creek side of the dam), walk north beyond the gate at the dirt road, and walk the road to the picnic area that overlooks the reservoir. From the picnic area, walk down heading towards the water and slightly left, and within 200', you will run into the rock. Walk from here along the outcrop to see all the rock.
Classic Routes: *Swamp Ass* V4, *Rocket* V7, *Unnamed* V9, *Bat Hang* V8.

Atlantis Cliff

This is the enticing looking cliff that goes down to the water's edge just right of the Army Corps of Engineers tower near the dam access road. Climbing here is off limits due to access concerns, but I have taken the liberty to mention a few classics here that were established by me, Tom Kneiss, and Randy Ross. The rock is about 45' high and has great quality cracks, overhangs, and steep face climbs. Some area classics are *The Poseidon Adventure* V4 R, *Waterworld* V2 R, *The Creature from the Black Lagoon* V1 R, *What Lies Beneath* V5 R, and *Randy's Route* V1 R.

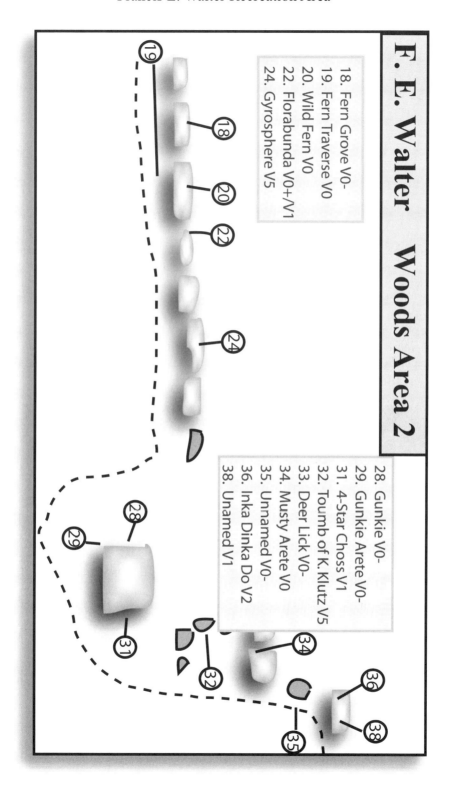

F. E. Walter Woods Area 2

18. Fern Grove V0-
19. Fern Traverse V0
20. Wild Fern V0
22. Florabunda V0+/V1
24. Gyrosphere V5

28. Gunkie V0-
29. Gunkie Arete V0-
31. 4-Star Choss V1
32. Toumb of K. Klutz V5
33. Deer Lick V0-
34. Musty Arete V0
35. Unnamed V0-
36. Inka Dinka Do V2
38. Unnamed V1

Brown Sugar Wall

This is one of Pennsylvania's small, hidden gems. The area is a small sport/toprope crag with a few bolted routes and a few trad/bolt lines; some of the routes with bolts take gear as a supplement to areas void of fixed hardware. The area offers a small 50' high, 200' wide vertical to slightly overhanging wall with 11 routes. The rock is a bit brittle at the bottom but is of great quality above. The routes here range from 5.7 to 5.12a. The routes are short but they are also steep and pumpy. In a nutshell, it's a fun little spot if you live close by. The approach can be long, tedious, and confusing, but the routes are worth it if you spend the time to find this spot.

The author at Land of Overhangs

Tom Kneiss on "Monster Mash." Atlantis Boulders.
Photo by the author.

Directions: From the upper parking lot on the north side of the dam follow the dirt, gated road across from the lot to the picnic area (same directions as for *Land of Overhangs*). Walk towards the reservoir and down a small path that will bring you to the west end of the *Land of Overhangs*. Walk east while following the entire *Land of Overhangs* outcrop via a narrow path. After reaching the end of the *Land of Overhangs* cliffband, follow a faint trail farther east and down towards the water. The trail will get steep and narrow into a few pines. Be careful not to wander off any of the steep ledges.

If you stayed on the trail, you will end up at the *Learning to Fly* boulder problem and the shore. This is a low roof at ground level just of the trail. The rock continues farther east along the river that feeds the reservoir. Do not go this way. Walk back west, backtracking towards the dam while following the shore. You will come to a bolted wall within 10 minutes walk of reaching the shore. You can also access the cliff by walking south at the immediate end of the *Land of Overhangs* (east end of the cliff). You will be above the cliff. It is difficult to locate the correct section of rock if you access the cliff this way. Look for some Hemlock trees and cautiously descend (you may want to rope up) to a low tier in the rock. Be careful not to fall off the cliff below.

1. John's Route 5.10a R
FA: R. Holzman, T. Knneiss
Named for John Croom, a local outdoor enthusiast. Climb the left side of the wall over a small overhang.

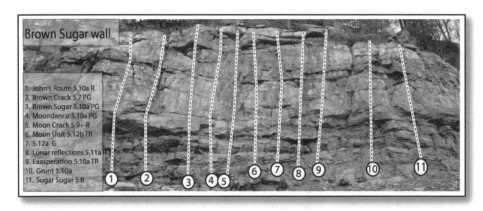

Brown Sugar wall

1. John's Route 5.10a R
2. Brown Crack 5.7 PG
3. Brown Sugar 5.10a PG
4. Moondance 5.10a PG
5. Moon Crack 5.9+ R
6. Moon Unit 5.12b TR
7. 5.12a G
8. Lunar reflections 5.11a R
9. Exasperation 5.10a TR
10. Grunt 5.10a
11. Sugar Sugar 5.8

2. Unnamed 5.7
Climb into the crack.

3. Brown Sugar 5.10a PG
FA: R. Holzman, R. Ross
Follow two bolts and gear to the top.

4. Moondance 5.10a PG
FA: R. Holzman, N. Morell, R. Lukas
Be careful around the large, loose flake at the beginning. Follow two bolts and gear right of the previous climb.

5. Moon Crack 5.9+ R
FA: N. Morell, R. Holzman, T. Kneiss
Small Stoppers are very helpful on this route. Climb the crack immediately right of the previous route.

6. Moon Unit 5.12b TR
FA: R. Holzman, N. Morell
Climb the hardest possible area right of the crack and over a bulge.

7. 5.12a PG
FA: J. Forte, R. Holzman
The face right of the previous climb past bolts.

8. Lunar Reflections 5.11a R
FA: N. Morell, R. Holzman
Climb the faint crack on the right side of the wall.

9. Exasperation 5.10a TR
FA: R. Holzman
Climb the face just right of the crack.

Tom Kneiss soloing, circa "97. RH photo.

128

10. Grunt 5.10a R/X
Climb the nice face past a bulge.

11. Sugar Sugar 5.8 X
Climb the end of the outcrop.

Tangerine Dream Area

This small sub-section of the main *Ancient Crag* cliff. It offers 6 short toprope routes and a small cluster of 6 boulders. The approach is a bit overgrown, but the rock quality is excellent. The main attraction here is *Tangerine Dream*, a short but stout 5.13a. Also, *Fire Starter* 5.10c is not to be missed.

Directions: This area is located on the north shore of the reservoir just before the *Ancient Crag*. You can see the boulders of this area from the other side of the dam by looking left of the highest point of rock. You will see a large cluster of boulders that are much better quality than they appear from the other side of the reservoir. To access this area, park at the one/two-car pull-off at the large bend in the road just after passing under the cement tower on the north side of the reservoir. You can also park at the main lot above the reservoir and walk down to this lower lot. You can only fit two cars at the pull-off so walking from the main lot is a better option. Walk over the guardrail near the sharp curve and trudge through the waist-high blueberry bushes, then diagonal down and left until you reach the shore. The boulders are a short distance along the shore, just past a large rock-drainage.

1. Waterfowl 5.8+ PG
FA: R. Holzman
Maneuver into a nice crack that breaches the left side of this short wall.

2. Fire Starter 5.10c R/X
FA: R. Holzman
Right of *Waterfowl* is a nice arete near a deep V-notch. Boulder across the V-notch and pull out under the roof to large buckets above the lip. Follow up the arete to top out.

3. The V 5.9+ PG
FA: N. Morell
Grunt up the large V-notch.

4. Tangerine Dream 5.13a R/X
FA: R. Holzman
Technical moves struggle past two opposing seams on beautiful, orange-colored rock.

Ryan Lukas on "Radio Flyer" at
City of Boulders. RH photo.

5. 5.10b R
FA: N. Morell
Balance moves lead up a short crack just right of the previous route.

6. 5.10a R
FA: R. Holzman
Climb the thin face next to the previous climb.

Other Nearby Areas

The Devils Elbow

Located about 8 miles downstream from the dam on the Lehigh River, this small sandstone cliff offers a few short routes in the 5.4 to 5.11 range. The rock is poor quality and unclean. A few boulder problems like *Devil's Tennis Elbow* V2 and *River Rat* V0 exist here.

The City of Boulders

I discovered this wealth of bouldering in the early '90s. This area has massive boulders that dwarf the size of the boulders at the *Atlantis Area*. From a distance, the area looks, literally, like a city of boulders. Enormous house-sized boulders in all shapes and sizes cover the shoreline as far as the eye can see. The rock here is the same quality rock as *Atlantis* but with five times the amount of boulders and better problems. Unfortunately, this area is posted with no-trespassing signs and the approach is quite lengthy and cumbersome. For these reasons I have excluded this area from this book. Classic problems here include *The World's fastest Car* V4, *River-bottom Nightmare Band* V3, *Potato Masher* V2, *Jess's Route* V1, *Nighthawk* V8, *Radio Flyer* V0, *Marble Mantle* V6, *figure Four Traverse* V4, and many, many others. Problems in the V8 to V11 range have been developed here also. More information about this amazing spot will be available in the future on www. paclimbing.com.

Cube Boulder Area
This is a collection of a few boulders on the southwest side of the top of the dam just below the road. Hike a few hundred feet in the woods to find these boulders.

Ryan Lukas. Atlantis Boulders. Photo by the author.

Tom Kneiss developing a new problem at City of Boulders. Some of the mass quantity of boulders can be seen in the background. RH photo.

131

6. Mocanaqua (Main Wall)

Area Beta

Location
Just outside of Mocanaqua, PA.

Type of Climbs
Bolted, trad, cracks, but mostly face. Thin conglomerate edges. One of the best spots in PA!

Additional Info
Good area for top roping but can be crowded on weekends.

Main Wall Mocanaqua

The Mocanaqua Climbing area, known to the local climbers as "Main Wall" or "Moc Wall", is arguably one of the best areas to climb in Pennsylvania. The first impression this area leaves on climbers is a memorable one. The steep, daunting wall that looms over the approach trail imprints a lasting image on the mind of any climber. From this trail, the cliff's expanse seems blank and featureless, leaving one wondering how it may be possible to scale this glassy void. However, upon closer inspection, the trademark sharp edges and thin crystals begin to reveal themselves, leaving climbers fumbling with anticipation.

This spectacular cliff is 80' high and contains routes that range from 5.4 to 5.13a. The climbs here are popular with beginners and experts alike. Although many of the climbs are bolted, a small rack is recommended for placing gear between the bolts on most routes. The "Main Wall" is located in a deeply-forested grove; this forest-canopy provides adequate shade for climbing on hot summer days. Despite the fact that the summer is pleasant, climbing in the winter months can be quite unpleasant.

This area is sometimes crowded on weekends. Other days, you may be the only climber at the cliffs. If you do venture out on a busy weekend, the area is small; you may have to wait to find an available climb.

If you like to boulder, be sure to check out the nearby Boulder Garden. This area offers some of the best bouldering in the East!

History

Climbers first visited the Mocanaqua Climbing Area sometime in the 1960's. *Beginners Crack* and *Pizza Crack* were climbed during this time. Not long after Jeff Clovis and the Miscavages climbed and developed routes here. However, it was not until the late 1970s and early 1980s that a renaissance of development took place at the Main Wall. During this time, Albert Pisaneschi, Bob D' Antonio, and George Peterson, developed all the bolted climbs and many of the difficult trad climbs. They were also accountable for introducing top-notch climbers like Hugh Herr, Rich Romano, and Alison Osius to the area. During the early "90s Nick Morell and myself added several difficult new lines like *Sea of Glass* a challenging 5.13.

Area Description: "Moc Wall" offers some of the best quality trad and sport climbing in Pennsylvania. Expect to find 5.4 to 5.13a climbing on rock ranging from 40' to 80'high.

Geology: Pottsville conglomerate and quartzite. Similar to The Gunk's.

Location: Northeastern Pennsylvania, about 15 miles south of Wilkes-Barre.

Camping: Ricketts Glen State Park. To reserve a campsite call 888-PA-PARKS, 7 a.m. to 5 p.m. Monday to Saturday, The Park is located on State Route 487, 10 miles north of Mocanaqua, in the town of Red Rock.
Council Cup Campground. 212 Ruckle Road, Wapwallopen, PA. 570-379-2566

Climbing Season: The best time to climb in Mocanaqua is from late March to November. Sometimes the summer months can be humid and sticky, with abundant thunderstorms. Climbers frequent this area in the winter months if a warm day arises; however, nearby Paradise Rock gets a fair share of sunshine in the winter.

Access and Restrictions: In 1996 the Blue Coal Company turned over the land and cliffs to The Earth Conservancy. The Earth Conservancy recognizes and permits rock climbing on their property. The Access Fund and local climbers organize cleanups and events here on a regular basis. Please do your part to keep this area clean and maintain the healthy relationship with the present landowner. To participate in the annual cleanup, contact the local climbing shop.

Safety Concerns: Although the rock is very solid at this area, there are many loose rocks on the large ledges above the cliff. Please be mindful not to dislodge any harmful rocks when lowering from the top or setting up topropes.

Descent: The Descent from most climbs can easily be achieved by using the trails at either the east or west end of the cliff. Rappel stations are located above *Pizza Crack* and *Beginners Crack*.

Nearby Mountain Shops, Guide Services, and Gyms: The nearest climbing shop is Top of the slope and its located in Wilkes-Barre on Main Avenue near the downtown. This shop has virtually any supply a climber could need. This shop offers the only guide service in the area. Wilkes Rocks is a great climbing gym that is also located on Main Avenue in downtown Wilkes-Barre.

Emergency Services: The nearest phone is located at Jackson's Store on Route 22 in downtown Mocanaqua. Dial 911 for emergency assistance. The nearest hospital is in Wilkes-Barre.

Services: Downtown Mocanaqua has a small supermarket located on Route 11 near the blinking light. Snacks, drinks, and groceries can be purchased there. The nearest gas station is located six miles north in the town of Tilbury. All services are available in the town of Wilkes-Barre.

Nearby Climbing areas: Paradise Rock, The Library, Squirrel Rock, and a million other areas are located a few miles away.

Directions from Berwick: Drive north on Route 11. Turn right onto State Route 239, just before the car dealership, and drive over the bridge that spans the Susquehanna River. Continue through the small town of Mocanaqua. Shortly after a ninety-degree left turn you will see a cemetery to your left. Go straight, veering from Route 239, and follow SR 3004 exactly 1 mile from the cemetery, until you reach a hidden parking lot off in a wooded area on your left. Park here. The rock is slightly visible from the parking area. An obvious trail leads to *Pizza Crack* at the center of the cliff.

Directions from Wilkes-Barre: Drive south on Route 11. Turn left onto the bridge that crosses the Susquehanna River. Follow the directions above to the rock.

Main Wall Left

The first few routes are located at the extreme left side of the wall. There is a two-bolt anchor above the first few routes.

1. The Blue Comet 5.10d TR

FA: R. Holzman, N. Morell

Begin at the left end of the cliff 10' feet left of *Stardust*. Climb low-angle rock to a small ceiling. Pull the ceiling and continue to the top.

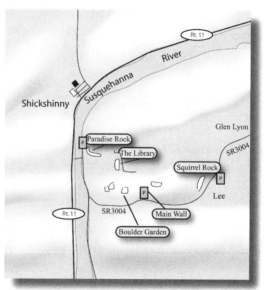

2. Stardust 5.10b G

FA: A. Pisaneschi

This climb gets its name from the silty residue found on its holds. Climb over a bulge, passing a bolt 10' up and continue past 2 more bolts (crux) to finish.

3. Meatball 5.10a R

FA: A. Pisaneschi

Climb to the obvious ceiling with a bolt on it 10' up. Continue straight to the top.

4. Guido 5.8+ PG/R

FA: A. Pisaneschi

Climb the face between the crack and *Meatball*.

5. Beginners Crack 5.4 PG

FA: A. Pisaneschi

This is the obvious left-facing corner/crack to the right of *Stardust*. Climb the corner to the top of a flake and move left and up to a two-bolt anchor.

Var. 1: 5.8 Climb straight up to the crack at the top.

6. Bullseye 5.7 PG

FA: A. Pisaneschi

40' right of *Beginners Crack*, past a broken section of cliff, there is crack set back behind the base trail. Climb this crack to an alcove, then pull a small ceiling and continue to the top.

7. Unnamed 5.9 G
FA: A. Pisaneschi
Follow 2 bolts at the left end of the ledge.

8. Iodine 5.11a PG
FA: A. Pisaneschi
Climb the thin crack and seam just right of the previous route.

9. No Name Crack 5.11d G
FA: A. Pisaneschi
A very difficult and sustained route. Climb the obvious crack. Use medium-sized cams.

10. Mercury 5.11d R
FA: B. D' Antonio, A. Pisaneschi
Climb the bolted line a few feet right of the previous route.

Unnamed 5.13+
FA: R. Holzman
TR the pebble covered wall.

11. Corner Crack 5.7 G
This is the crack at the far right end of the ledge

12. Corner Pocket 5.10a
FA: A. Pisaneschi
Begin on the ground near a diagonal crack that moves up and left. Climb bolts on the corner of the wall near the ledge that contains the previous climbs.

13. Over the Top V4
This classic boulder problem is located a few feet left of *Razors Edge*. Begin by standing on a pointy block on the base trail with your hands on two small crimps. Pull yourself onto the rock and crank up to a slanting crack. Downclimb the crack.

14. Razor Blade 5.10d PG
FA: A. Pisaneschi, Dave Miscavage
Muscle your way up a thin vertical seam to a bolt (crux). Make difficult moves past 3 more bolts and reach the top.

15. Sea of Glass 5.13a
FA. R. Holzman
Near a tree and block on the ground, boulder thin, glassy moves to a mono-digit pocket and a closed vertical seam. Find better holds above and follow these to a crack. Use the finger crack to gain the top.

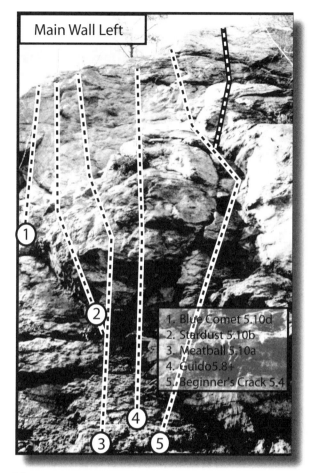

Main Wall Left

1. Blue Comet 5.10d
2. Stardust 5.10b
3. Meatball 5.10a
4. Guido 5.8+
5. Beginner's Crack 5.4

16. Happy Hooker A2
FA: A. Pisaneschi, R. Romano, J. Nonamaker
Use hooks to aid the wall just right of the previous route.

17. Walk on the Wild Side 5.10d
FA: A. Pisaneschi
Climb *Double Wave* to a ledge at the second bolt, or move out left from the first bolt and climb the steep rock to a bolt 50' above the ledge (you will move left passing *Membrane* to reach this line). Continue to the top. A more direct variation can be done left of *Double Wave*.

18. Membrane 5.12d
FA: A. Pisaneschi
Start on *Double Wave* and move left after the second bolt and follow two more bolts above to the top.

19. Double Wave 5.10c G
(4 bolts) Follow the bolted line left of *Pizza Crack*. At the second bolt move right to

a bulge and follow two more bolts straight up to the top. Walk left to the rappel on *Pizza Crack*.

20. Pizza Crack 5.6 PG

FA: A. Pisaneschi, D. Miscavage

This climb follows the obvious crack that starts where the approach trail meets the rock. The crack resembles a pizza pie. Ascend the crack to a hidden piton and climb a flake to a large ledge. From the ledge move left, then up to a fixed anchor.

21. Easy Dreamin' 5.9+ G

FA: T. Hancock

Follow the bolted line right of *Pizza Crack*, until it is possible to merge with the previous route after the fourth bolt. Bring small cams.

Var. 1: Direct Finish 5.11a

FA: A. Pisaneschi

From the regular line at the third bolt, continue up and right to fixed gear and follow the direct line straight to the top.

Bob D'Antonio on the first ascent of Mercury, 1988. Photo courtesy Bob D.

22. Tumor 5.12a PG

FA. A. Pisaneschi

Easier if tall. Make bouldery moves to a ledge and a bolt 15' right of the previous route. Fire through the crux at the first bolt, then move right to a small pine and continue to the top.

23. Whale Back Crack 5.8

FA: G. Peterson, a. Pisaneschi

Climb the zigzagging crack right of *Tumor*. Finish up an obvious off-width corner up high near the top.

24. S.O.B. 510a PG

Start on *Whale Back Crack* and branch off at the top at the off-width corner to a direct line straight up.

25. Manure Pile 5.9+ PG R

FA: A. Pisaneschi

Originally done as a solo ascent. 10' right of *Zig Zag Crack*, stick clip or brave your way to a bolt 15' up. Follow bolts to the top.

26. New Hampshire Crack 5.9 R

FA: Steve Hare

Walk past the right end of the cliff, a few-hundred feet, until a smaller cliff appears. This climb follows the obvious crack in the center of the face.

27. S.O.B. Crack 5.10d

Climb the crack right of *New Hampshire Crack*. Angle up and right following to a finish out right.

28. The Purple Butterfly 5.11c R

FA: N. Morell, R. Holzman

Climb the right side of the bulge just right of *New Hampshire Crack*. Essentially start on the crack out right and move left from the crack at a bulge. Power over the direct bulge to finish.

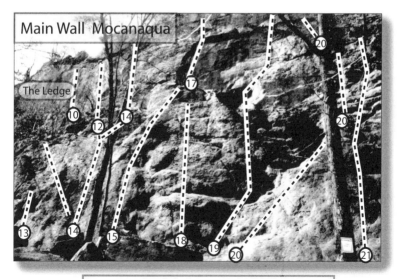

10. Mercury 5.11d	17. Walk on W.S. 5.11+
12. Corner Pocket 5.10a	18. Membrane 5.12d
13. Over the Top V4	19. Double Wave 5.10c
14. Razor Blade 5.10d	20. Pizza crack 5.6
15. Sea of Glass 5.13a	21. Easy Dreamin' 5.9+

29. George's Traverse V4

FA: G. Peterson

Traverse the short wall that contains the previous two routes. Traverse from left to right.

Bob D'Antonio leading a classic at Moc Wall.
Photo courtesy Bob D.

Main Wall Mocanaqua

20. Pizza Crack 5.6
21. Easy Dreamin' 5.9+
22. Tumor 5.12a
23. Whaleback 5.8

141

7. Mocanaqua Boulder Garden

Area Beta

Location
Adjacent to Moc Wall.

Type of Area
Hundreds of boulder problems. Some of the best bouldering anywhere.

Other Info
Not a well-known area until the publication of this book. Limited parking and trails need improvement.

Mocanaqua Bouldering

The bouldering in the Mocanaqua region is supreme. The quality of rock is unrivaled with any other in the state. The rock resembles the best quality stone found at The Gunk's but with smooth, marble-like stone in spots. This bouldering dreamscape offers a playground for the modern rock jock.

Numerous areas encompass a widespread region of rock. I have chosen to include a small portion of the more accessible spots in Mocanaqua. Many, many more areas exist in the region but are relatively difficult to find. If you like smooth, sexy conglomerate, "Moc" hits the spot.

The Boulder Garden

One of the best-quality spots for bouldering and one of the easiest to access. A two minute walk off the main road leads to large cube-shaped boulders with an array of exciting and diverse problems. This place can be overgrown in the summer but still offers great problems close to the road. Should you decide to hunt for some of the other boulders farther into the gardens interior, you will find a difficult hike through deep brush. I recommend staying near the main road that runs to the Main Wall. The best boulders and best problems are here anyway.

History: This area was originally explored and developed by Albert Pisaneschi, George Peterson, and Bob D'Antonio. In the mid to late '80s, this group developed numerous

143

classic problems up to V7 in "The Garden". At this time, most of the obvious lines on the largest boulders were developed. Albert Pisaneschi was one of the most influential and significant developers during these years. Albert developed an incredible amount of classic problems on the obvious boulders scattered throughout the area.

Bob D'Antonio was also very active at "The Garden" during this time. He established many true classics throughout the woodland and at nearby Hawk Rock.

From 1990 on, Nick Morell and I developed a great deal of problems at this area. We were amongst the first to establish a significant amount of sit-start problems here. Numerous classic, difficult grade problems were added at this time. Later Tom Keneiss and Ryan Lukas were also active at this area. Mike Pezzuto, Judy Rakowski, Dave Grabinski, Steve Salemi, The Lichtner's and a new crew of talented locals have been active in recent years mining out eliminates and exciting new lines.

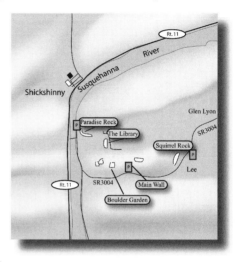

Directions: This area is located 1 mile west of *Main Wall* (*Moc Wall*), in Mocanaqua. You can see the boulders north of the road when driving from the town of Mocanaqua, just before you reach the main cliff. You can park at *Moc Wall* and hike a faint trail that parallels the main road and leads to the boulders, or park at a small pull-off three-fourths of a mile before the *Main wall* crag. Be sure to park far enough off the main road. Do not "bandit park" on the roadside. Use only the small pull-off or walk from the *Main Wall* lot.

Introduction Boulder
This boulder is located at the far east end of the boulder garden. It is the closest boulder to the Moc Wall climbing area. You can see this boulder from the road if you look close enough. A faint trail leads to it.

1. Little Roof V0-
Climb the roof on the backside of the boulder. Several variations exist.

2. East Side V0
Climb the east side of the boulder. Several problems can be done at the same grade as well as a long traverse.

3. Unnamed V0+
Climb the downhill arete.

4. Revolver V5
SDS on the short face just left of the downhill-right corner and move into a horizontal and a gaston. Gain the top out.

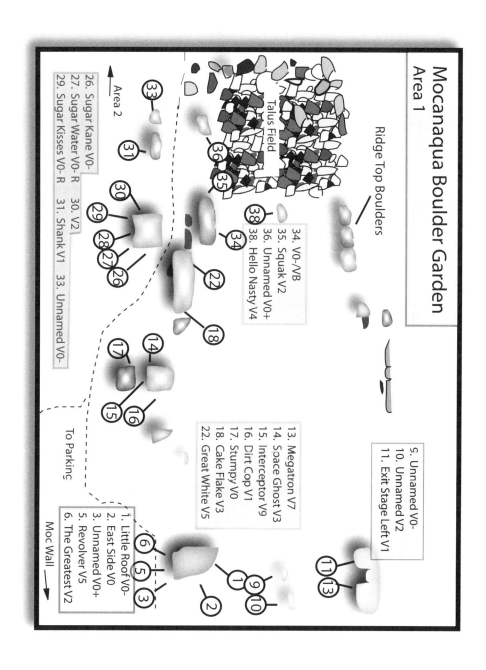

Mocanaqua Boulder Garden
Area 1

Area 2

Ridge Top Boulders

Talus Field

26. Sugar Kane V0-
27. Sugar Water V0- R
29. Sugar Kisses V0- R
30. V2
31. Shank V1 33. Unnamed V0-

34. V0-/VB
35. Squak V2
36. Unnamed V0+
38. Hello Nasty V4

13. Megatron V7
14. Space Ghost V3
15. Interceptor V9
16. Dirt Cop V1
17. Stumpy V0
18. Cake Flake V3
22. Great White V5

9. Unnamed V0-
10. Unnamed V2
11. Exit Stage Left V1

1. Little Roof V0-
2. East Side V0
3. Unnamed V0+
5. Revolver V5
6. The Greatest V2

To Parking

Moc Wall

145

5. Unnamed V1
Fun moves pass the face next to the previous problem.

6. The Greatest V2
SDS on the left side of the boulder and climb past a cleft.

7. Unnamed V2
SDS left of the previous problem and traverse the top lip to finish near problem number

8. Unnamed V3
SDS on the previous problem and traverse up and around the right side of the boulder and finish on problem number 1.

9. Unnamed V0-
It is not worth finding this problem. Climb up the hill a few yards past the *Introduction Boulder* and look for two very small boulders in a vegetated section of the hill. Climb the face on the left boulder from a sitting start.

10. Unnamed V2
SDS on the boulder right of the previous boulder and traverse a very sloping section under the lip and top out on the right.

11. Exit stage Left V1
On a long boulder that is somewhat high and above the previous problem, climb the left corner that sticks out from an alcove.

12. Unnamed V0+
Climb out of the alcove.

13. Megatron V7
Climb into the shallow, sloping, left-facing corner and move right to an exciting top out.

14. Space Ghost V3
Balance moves barndoor up the left arete of this boulder.

15. Interceptor V9
Climb the very technical orange-colored face right of the arete.

16. Dirt Cop V1
Climb the small face to the right of and around the corner from the previous route.

17. Stumpy V0
Located on the boulder behind the previous routes find the small arete and pit; then climb the corner.

The Great White Boulder
This boulder is the next sizable boulder along the boulder field. It is long and has a cave under it. Its most distinguishable feature is the beautiful white-colored arete on the boulders

left side.

18. Piece of Cake Flake V3
Start near a tree at the right side of the boulder and climb a seam and edges to the top.

19. Spanking the Whale V3
Climb the right-center of the long side of the boulder above a cave.

20. Extraordinaire V7
Same problem as above but with a sit start.

21. Hogwinked V1
Avoid the tree to ascend the face left of the previous route.

22. White Arete (a.k.a. Great White) V5
One of the best problems in the state! Climb the beautiful, white arete.

23. Whitey V9
Technical moves follow the steep crimps left of *White Arete*.

Nick Morell bouldering.
RH photo.

24. The Slant V5
Climb the face just left of the previous climb.

The Sugar Cube
This is the large, white, cube-shaped boulder downhill from *The Slant*.

25. Unnamed V0-
Ascend the uphill side of the boulder.

26. Sugar Kane V0-
This one will put a great taste in your mouth. Run up the sweet face on the east side of the cube.

27. Sugar Water V0- R
On the south face of the boulder climb the rightmost problem.

28. Sugar Daddy V0- R
Climb the center of the boulder

29. Sugar Kisses V0- R
Smootch the left/downhill face of the boulder all the way to the top.

30. Unnamed V2
Climb the west side of the boulder near the downhill arete.

Satellite Boulder
Directly across from the west face of the *Sugar Cube*, you will see a small rectangular boulder.

31. Shank V1
SDS and climb crimps near the corner.

32. Shag V2
SDS and climb the sharp crimps left of the previous route.

33. Unnamed V0-
On the boulder behind the *Satellite Boulder* there is an easy face. Climb it.

Unnamed Boulder
This boulder is above and left of the previous outcrop of rocks.

34. Unnamed V0-/VB
SDS and climb the northeast face on this boulder.

35. Squak V2
SDS and traverse up the west corner.

36. Unnamed V0+
SDS and climb the boulder directly behind *Squak*.

37. Glory Traverse V1
SDS and traverse the right side of the boulder.

38. Hello Nasty V4
SDS and climb the center of the boulder

39. Unnamed Traverse V1
SDS and traverse the left side of the boulder. AV2 variation can be done by traversing up the left side and down the right side.

40. About Face V2
Difficult to locate. West of *Shank* there is a long, low boulder. Go to the boulders south corner; SDS and climb the face/corner.

Ridge Top Boulders
By bushwhacking straight up from *The Lump Boulder*, you will come to a short, somewhat-high outcrop of rock with a few dirty problems on it. If you continue straight up from here you will see a long boulder in the talus. Continue to slog up the talus and you will end up in the center of a wall with a few problems. You can also access this point by locating a white post across from the large pit on the old dirt road that winds above the boulders from the Mocanaqua climbing area parking lot. Walk downhill and right from the white post. The problems here range from VB to V2. There is also a V0, V1, and V3 highball on a large,

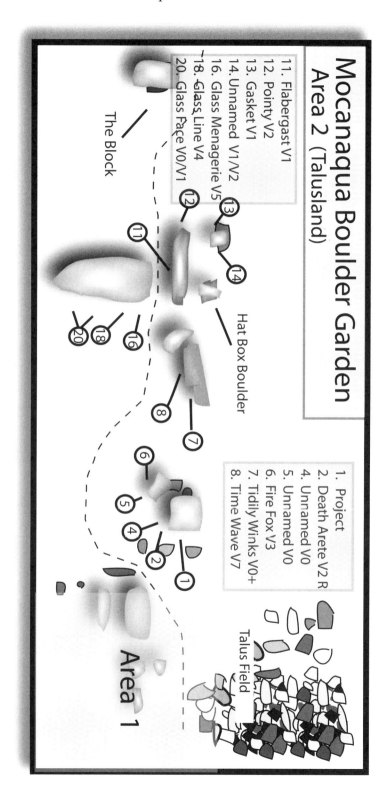

Mocanaqua Boulder Garden
Area 2 (Talusland)

11. Flabergast V1
12. Pointy V2
13. Gasket V1
14. Unnamed V1/V2
16. Glass Menagerie V5
18. Glass Line V4
20. Glass Face V0/V1

The Block

Hat Box Boulder

1. Project
2. Death Arete V2 R
4. Unnamed V0
5. Unnamed V0
6. Fire Fox V3
7. Tidily Winks V0+
8. Time Wave V7

Talus Field

Area 1

square, perched boulder just west of the main rock cluster.

Talusland Area

This area is the second major bouldering section in the large boulder garden. It is nestled between some pine trees and a large talus field that borders its west end.

The Perched Overhang

From the previous boulder, walk across some talus and you will immediately see a large overhang perched above another boulder. There are a few worthwhile problems on the south and east faces of the boulder as well as the small boulder next to it.

1. Project

SDS and climb thin edges on the east face of the boulder.

2. Death Arete V2 R

Climb the arete.

3. Unnamed V1

Climb the face left of the arete

4. Unnamed V0

Nice moves follow good holds left of the previous route.

5. Unnamed V0

This problem is the first problem on the small, detached boulder, left of *The Perched Overhang*. Start with hands below a hole in the rock and go to a crack.

6. Fire Fox V3

SDS in a low horizontal left of the previous route and fire up to holds above.

The Wave

This boulder is just west of the previous boulder. It is very steep and has a large, blank scoop-feature, creating a wavelike wall.

7. Tidily Winks V0+

SDS and climb the cleft in the rock at the right side of *The Wave*.

8. Time Wave V7

Start on two crimps at head level and fly up left to a big hold and a very exciting top out.

9. The Green Room V8

Start from the same crimps and move right.

10. Project

SDS to the previous two problems. Do either or both problems; really two projects.

Pumba Boulder

This is the long boulder just left of *The Wave*. It is perched on rocks and is not very high.

11. Flabbergast V1
SDS in a pocket and climb the center of the boulder where it is perched.

12. Pointy V2
SDS at the left side of the boulder.

13. Gasket V1
Above the previous problem is a rectangular face perched over a pit. Climb the left corner of the perched rock.

14. Unnamed V1/V2
Climb the right side of the same boulder as the previous route.

Gigantor
This is the long boulder that continues downhill, directly across from the *Pumba Boulder*. Many excellent problems exist here.

15. Unnamed V0-
Easy climbing follows the uphill face of this boulder.

16. Glass Menagerie V5
SDS and climb the arete just left of the previous problem.

17. Wax Feet V4
Same problem as above, but starting low on a pinch.

18. Glass Line V4
Delicate moves scale the face a few inches left of the arete.

19. Smearing FateV4
Climb the face a few inches left of the previous problem.

20. Glass Face V0/V1
Several problems have been done to the left of and downhill of the previous problems. They vary in difficulty and are located on the face, downhill from the previous problems.

The Block
From the top corner of the previous boulder, look west you will see a large block out in the talus. A few easy problems have been done on it.

Area 3
This area is located about 5 - 10 minutes walk west along the talus field. Keep low at the bottom of the talus and you will run into the next series of boulders. This spot can also be accessed by following the approach trail from the first pull-off.

Speckled Boulder
This is the low, long boulder you first come to when following the approach trail from the roadside pull-off or when hiking in from *Talusland*.

1. Unnamed V0-
SDS and climb the northeast side of the boulder.

2. Unnamed V0-
Climb the rightmost route on the downhill side of the boulder.

3. Slope Shelf V2
From a sit start, climb to a sloping shelf just left of the previous route.

4. Elf Wad V3
SDS just left of the previous problem.

5. Unnamed VB
The crack at the left side of the boulder.

6. Boulder Traverse V1
Traverse the boulder.

Ryan Lukas enjoying one of the best boulders in the East! Photo by the author.

7. Unnamed V1
Start below a big shelf on the boulder
that attaches to the previous boulder on its left side. Fire up to the top of the boulder after gaining the shelf.

8. Huggys V4
A sit-down-start variation of the previous route that hugs the belly underneath to gain the shelf.

9. Huggys Traverse V4
Traverse in to the previous route.

Marble Head
This is the massive boulder with the very steep, blank face on the downhill side. The thin seam on the downhill side remains a project but appears to be doable in the V12 range.

10. Unnamed VB
Climb the crack at the far northwest end of the boulder.

11. Marble Head V1
Climb the marble-like face next to the previous route.

12. The Tailsman V0
Ascend the easy corner/crack to the right of *Marble Head*.

13. Wingman V3
This is an eliminate problem of the previous route that uses only the arete.

14. Unnamed V6
SDS and crank up the left corner of the downhill face of this boulder.

15. Unnamed V0-
SDS and move left up the southwest corner of the boulder.

16. The Scoop V0-
Climb up the center of the scoop. Harder if you go straight up to the point.

17. Unnamed V0+/V1
Can be easier or harder depending on how you climb it. SDS and fire up the arete left of the previous route.

18. One Move Wonder V0-
SDS and climb the northeast side of the boulder.

19. One Move Blunder V2
On the boulder behind the previous problem there is a short problem that ascends the arete from a SDS.

The Toasted Marshmallow
This boulder is the huge marshmallow-shaped boulder above the previous problem. Its downhill face is the color of a toasted marshmallow.

20. Project
Climb out of the pit at the right end of this boulder.

21. Post Tostie V2 R
Climb the right corner of this giant rock and slant up and left.

22. Tootsie V1 R/X
Climb the center of the boulder. Many variations exist to the right and left at virtually the same grade.

23. Unnamed V1 R
Climb the northwest face.

24. Short and Swift V5
Two hard climbs exist on the small face on the boulder above the previous climb.

25. Pittance Pit V5
The hard face directly left of the previous climb when looking at it from uphill.

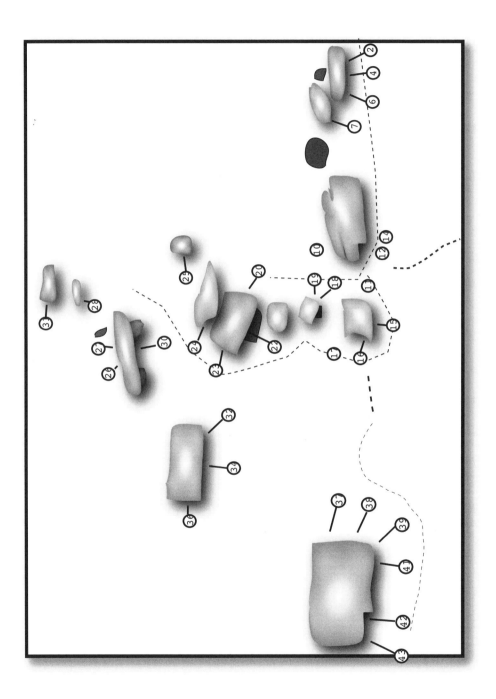

Perched boulder

This boulder is the long, rod-shaped boulder perched on top two boulders at its right and left sides. It has a cave under its downhill side.

26. Unnamed V0-

Looking at the boulder from uphill, climb the right side of the boulder.

27. Rhubarb V1

Climb the center of the uphill face.

28. Sweat V2

Ascend the bulge at the left side of the boulder.

29. Humble V1

Ascend the corner left of the previous route.

30. Middle of Nowhere V4

Climb the downhill face of the boulder directly across from the previous climb.

31. Middle of SomewhereV5

SDS and climb the somewhat-loose arete on the boulder above the previous climb.

Pebble Cube

This is the nice-sized rectangular boulder west of *The Marshmallow*. Several classic lines exist on this boulder.

32. Unnamed V0+/V1 R

Dance up pebbles on the downhill-right side of this boulder.

33. Boob Tube V1 R/X

Climb up just left of the previous route.

34. Pebble Pull V2 R/X

Climb past small pebbles at the left center of the boulder.

35. Unnamed V5

The left arete of the boulder.

36. Unnamed V1 R

An all time classic. Climb the beautiful but technical white-colored face on the boulders left end.

Dream Boulder

Walk west through the woods a few hundred paces and you will come to a beautiful square-shaped boulder. This is probably the nicest boulder at "Moc", and one of the nicest in the East! You can also access this boulder by parking near the pull-off on the road and hiking past the religious area.

37. Hard and Thin V4
Climb the right side of the east face of the boulder. Hard and thin.

38. Unnamed V5
Balance up the thin face left of the previous route.

39. Unnamed V1
Climb the downhill corner of the boulder.

40. Unnamed V3
Climb the downhill face past ledges.

41. Unnamed V4
Pull off small crimps to gain ledges in the center of the boulder.

42. The Big Chill V7
SDS and climb out of the small right side of the small roof at the downhill-left side of the boulder. Gain a faint crack and top out above.

43. Split Second V7
Gain the sloping left side of the overhang and dyno to the lip. Pull the difficult top out.

Bob D'Antonio cranking on the Dream boulder, circa 1980s. Photo courtesy Bob D'Antonio.

8. Paradise Rock

Area Beta

Location
Downtown Mocanaqua, overlooking the Susquehanna river.

Type of Climbing
Steep and difficult mixed bolt/trad.

Other Info
Do not attempt to set up topropes from above. This is a lead-ground-up area.

Paradise Rock

Climbers either love or hate *Paradise Rock*; however, I feel it offers some of the most impressive routes in the state. Climbers who love the area do so because it is a challenging area with steep, technical routes. Personally I love this spot and rate it as one of the best in Pennsylvania. I guess the big overhangs and vibrant-colored rock bring me back time and time again.

This 65'-high crag is perched above the Susquehanna River in a dramatic fashion that wraps around the hillside. Bright orange, yellow, and gray hues saturate the cliff and give it its characteristic, painted appearance. The only drawback to this unique tapestry is the coal seepage that runs down from above. This runoff coats the rock with slick varnish, which accounts for a challenging climbing experience—and sets the stage for what many consider "sandbagged routes". Yes, you know you're in Pennsylvania when coal seepage is the defining character of the cliff. Don't let this Pennsylvania oddity discourage you. All of the climbs here are on 4-star quality rock with similar texture to The Gunk's.

The walls of *Paradise Rock* were once much higher until regional coal mining buried a significant portion of the cliff. A sister area to *Paradise* named *The Sun Bowl* or *Coal Bowl* is now virtually covered in coal. Some routes still exist at *The Sun Bowl*, but most are dangerous to climb due to old bolts and decaying rock. Work is being done to replace some of the bolts here. Some of the routes here are the most impressive and difficult in the region, if not the state.

Expect to find about 35 routes here that range from 5.4 to 5.12d. Most of the climbs are in the 5.10 and up range with semi-bolted faces. Since gear is abundant in many areas of the cliff, bolts on most climbs are only to supplement gear. A common mistake first-time climbers make at *Paradise* is to assume the area is a sport crag because of the many bolts. Please note that many of the climbs here should be done with trad gear. *The Library* is only a few minutes walk away and offers many bolted sport routes if that is your preference. It is also extremely important to note that it is extremely dangerous to attempt setting up topropes at this area. The steep coal slopes above the climbs are loose and extremely hazardous. Attempting to set topropes at this area from above can result in severe injury or death! *Paradise Rock* is a lead crag only.

History

The first recorded climbers to climb at *Paradise* were Albert Pisaneschi and George Peterson. In the mid '80s, the two pioneered several trad leads and many solos of the cliff which are now bolted. Al was the most prolific climber here doing a great deal of the routes free-solo. Al was a true hard man of the region for several decades. Jeff Clovis was also active during this time. Bob D'Antonio added several very difficult lines at Paradise Rock during the late-80s. A hard 5.12 put up by Bob was a local test-peice for many years. Bob's amazing talents yielded another truly hard line *New Generation*, a blindingly difficult 5.12c that to this day has seen few repeats.

Many other local climbers were regular fixtures at this crag throughout the 90s. Marty Molitoris was one such climber who was extremely talented and made short work of many local classics. Nick Morell, Ryan Lucas, Tom Kneiss, and others brought high standards to the area during this time. I came up with a 5.13 on the far right of the wall that can easily be toproped and makes for challanging climbing.

General Location: 15 miles south of Wilkes-Barre and 15 miles north of Berwick, overlooking the town of Mocanaqua, above the Susquehanna River.

Area Overview: 35 routes ranging from 5.4 to 5.12d. Some trad but mostly partially bolted (trad/bolt) mixed routes. A handful of boulder problems on the cliff.

Geology: Pottsville Conglomerate. Very solid rock similar to Shawangunk Conglomerate but with orange and grey hues. Some areas have large deposits of black varnish from coal runoff above, but the rock is incredibly solid and clean.

Access Concerns and Restrictions: The land here is owned by The Earth Conservancy. Following talks with The Access Fund and the local climbing shop, climbing is acknowledged and permitted. A large parking area was constructed in recent years, so refrain from attempting to drive to the crag via the old dirt road. Cars have been locked in behind the gate after it is closed in the early afternoon. Please be courteous to other land users and local residents and keep noise to a reasonable level for nearby homes.

Hazards: Please do not attempt to set a toprope up by climbing the coal field above the cliff. The slope is incredibly hazardous and loose! All routes at this area must be done as a lead to set a toprope. Several near-death experiences have been had attempting toprope setups from above the cliff. A helmet is advisable on certain climbs.

Typical Weather and Climbing Season: Without question, it rains a lot in this part of the state. Some attribute this to hairy gnomes who live in caves in the coal hills and work at co-gen plants that belch coal refuse into the atmosphere by the ton. Either way, it rains a lot in summer. Summer is typically hot and humid with afternoon showers. Due to sun baking the rock, summer is often a difficult time to climb here—the nearby *Library* is recommended and offers cool summer climbing. On the contrary, winter months can, at times, provide adequate temperatures due to the cliff's exposure to the sun. Fall and spring are most ideal.

Directions: From Wilkes-Barre, take Route 11 south to the town of Schickshinny. From Berwick, take Route 11 north to Schickshinney. At the Chevrolet dealer at the south end of town, find a bridge that crosses the Susquehanna River. Cross the bridge into the town of Mocanaqua. 100' after the bridge, take the first left, just before going under the railroad-overpass. Follow this road 1 block until it ends at the sewer plant near a large parking lot for hikers and climbers.

Cross the railroad tracks and walk right about 100' until you see a dirt road on the left that goes into the woods and slightly parallels the railroad. Walk on this road a few-hundred feet, and you will see a faint path on the left that is very easy to miss (if you miss it, you can hike up the first dirt ATV road on the left). Hike up this narrow steep path that winds along the dirt pit you can see from the parking lot. Be very careful not to get too close to the dirt pit as the sides are very loose! The path will come out at a dirt road that winds back down to the sewer plant. At one time you could drive your car to here, but this is not allowed anymore. The gate to the road is locked at the end of the day and radioactive coal-mutants come and steal your gear if you are stuck here past dark. Actually, it may have been a guy named Joe who works at the sewer plant; either way don't drive past the gate. Turn right on the dirt road, and you will come to the first few climbs just after reaching the road from the approach trail.

Main Area

This is the highest section of the cliff. It has large overhangs above. Two-bolt anchors can be spotted from the ground for most routes.

1. Tracer 5.11a PG

FA: Jeff Klovis

The first lead-climb done at Paradise. Start atop a block at the far left end of the *Main Area*. Climb up to a thin crack in a left-facing corner (small gear) to a bolt near the end of the corner. Pull up over the bolt at a small ceiling and go straight up to another bolt up high in a small corner/ bulge. Climb to another bulge (bolt) and continue to a fixed-anchor above.

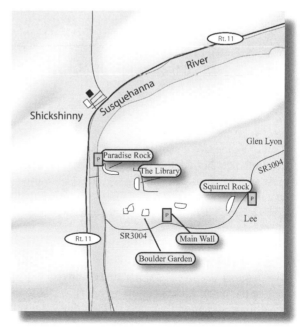

2. Ledge Traverse 5.11b PG

FA: A. Pisaneschi

Play connect-the-bolts by climbing from *Tracer* to *Roofin Madness*. Bring small to medium cams to supplement the bolts.

3. Direct Drive 5.11a PG

FA: Al Pisaneschi

Climb past two bolts to another bolt at a small ceiling capped by a very large overhang. Move into the overhang and clip another bolt, then pull the exciting crux exiting the ceiling and gain the communal anchor above.

Var. 1: (Climb 3a on topo) Direct Direct Drive 5.11b PG

FA: A. Pisaneschi

A direct variation pulls over the lone bolt next to the regular route.

4. New Generation 5.12c PG

FA: John Peterson, FFA: A. Pisaneschi, G. Peterson, B. D'Antonio

Work up to a bolt, then up to the right end of a two-tiered ceiling. Move over the first ceiling to some bad fixed pitons; make cruxy moves to the second ceiling at a bolt (difficult clip). Grunt through the crux and move slightly right to another bolt and an anchor.

5. Cyclops 5.9+ PG

FA: A. Pisaneschi

Bring your largest cam for this one. Climb the large off-width crack right of *New Generation*.

Var. 1: 5.10c Move out over a bolt from the regular line.

6. I-Beam 5.10b G

FA: A. Pisaneschi

Cruise up to the first crux, between two bolts, and 15' up. Move past good gear placements to a steep section of rock and another crux at the third bolt. Move out of an alcove (bolt), and cruise to the top.

7. Astro Protection 5.12d PG

FA: B. D'Antonio, A. Pisaneschi

Climb to a bolt at a bulge 10' up. Muscle to another bolt then to a ledge. Pass a ceiling on the left and make thrilling, difficult moves to the top.

Main Area Right

This is the right side of the big wall. Several two-bolt anchors are on top of most of the climbs.

8. Chicken Legs 5.10a PG

FA: A. Pisaneschi

Left of a pine tree a short pseudo-flake leads to a bolt at 10'. From the first bolt, continue to climb past horizontals until you reach a ceiling that is passed on its left. Immediately pass another ceiling to gain a position under a large overhang. Pull through this overhang at a large weakness, just right of the *Cyclops* off-width, and angle towards a small, scraggly tree at the lip. Continue to the anchor above.

9. Roof of Madness 5.10c PG

FA: A. Pisaneschi

Begin directly in front of a pine and climb to a bolt above a bulge (optional cam placement before the bolt). Continue through horizontals to the left side of a ceiling, then the right side of a ceiling, until you are under a flake that splits through the center of a large roof.

Paradise Rock Main Area

1. Tracer 5.11a
3. Direct Drive 5.11a
3a. Dir Dir. Drive 5.11b

4. New Generation 5.12c
5. Cyclops 5.9+
6. I-Beam 5.10b

Pull the crux overhang (med cam/ bolt) and continue to make challenging moves to the anchor.

10. Unnamed 5.10b PG
FA: A. Pisaneschi
Slightly right of a pine tree follow a thin crack that weaves right to a bolt at 20'. Pull over a bulge at the bolt (crux) and continue up and right until it is possible to exit to the right under a large overhang. Climb up to an anchor.

11. Tricks 5.9+ PG
FA: A. Pisaneschi, Dave Pareott
Easier if tall. Boulder up the glassy face just right of the previous route to a bolt following good gear placements to another bolt at a thin, vertical seam. Make a long move (crux) and climb up and right to the anchor.

12. Broken Finger 5.7 G
FA: A. Pisaneschi, G. Peterson
Boulder up a face to a blocky ledge that leads to a small left-facing corner with a bolt. Climb past the corner (crux) to the anchor.

13. Black Beard 5.8 G
FA: A. Pisaneschi, G. Peterson
Pillage the thin crack at a slick, left-facing, orange-colored corner. Step right at the top of the corner then move up and left to a bolt (Crux). From the crux climb up to the anchor used for the previous few routes.

14. White Water 5.7 PG/R
FA: G. Peterson, A. Pisaneschi
This route was recently retro-bolted but the bolts were soon removed. A few feet right of *Black Beard*, splash into a short crack to a horizontal and step right and up to a good ledge. Drift past a slight runout (Crux), up a slabby face, then rest out the calm waters to the anchor above.

15. Beginners Delight 5.3/5.6 PG
Several easy lead climbs have been done to the right of *White Water*. The difficulty ranges from 5.3 to 5.6 depending on what line you choose. This is a popular spot to introduce beginners to *Paradise Rock*.

Mirror Wall
This is the smooth, blank-looking wall just past *Beginners Delight*. The right side of this wall wraps around to the right near *Agent Orange* and continues towards the *Rambo Wall*. There is an anchor to rappel above *Mirror Image* that is shared by *Fine Line*. *Agent Orange* shares a two-bolt anchor with *Mayday* and *Fear Factor*.

16. Mirror Image 5.10a/d PG
FA: A. Pisaneschi
3 bolts, small gear. Climb the dark-colored face 75' right of the *Beginners Delight Wall* near a small gully. Gain a high bolt (gear before this) and top out (bolt) on a small ledge. Either continue past another bolt at a ceiling/bulge (5.10d), or move left and escape via easier terrain. Be careful not to dislodge loose coal when topping out on the small ledge that is midway through the climb.

17. Fine Line 5.10a/d PG
FA: A. Pisaneschi
One bolt and gear bring you to the top of this classic line. Climb through horizontals to a thin, vertical crack in yellow-colored rock to a bolt at the top of this short wall. Finish the same as the previous route.

18. Agent Orange 5.12d PG/R
FA: Bob D'Antonio, A. Pisaneschi
Two bolts, small/medium gear. One of the best 5.12s in Pennsylvania. This route sees very few ascents. Some stick clip the first bolt but with a good spot the landing is reasonable. Begin this classic at a thin, rising crack where the climb *Fear Factor* starts. Traverse up and left to a bolt, then make cruxy, technical face-moves over yellowish-orange colored rock to another bolt and the anchor.

19. Mayday 5.10a G
FA: A. Pisaneschi
Boulder halfway in from the previous route to a bolt between *Agent Orange* and *Fear Factor*. Climb up to an anchor.

20. Fear Factor 5.9 G
FA: A. Pisaneschi
Originally done as a boulder problem. Begin this route directly in front of some birch trees

Paradise Rock Main Area Right

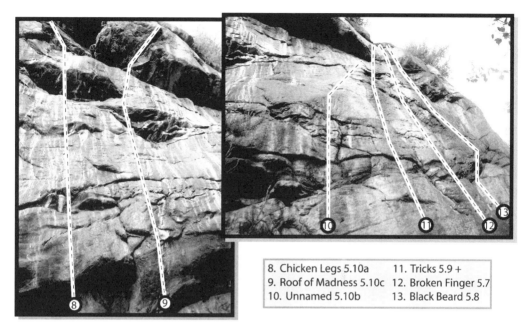

8. Chicken Legs 5.10a	11. Tricks 5.9 +
9. Roof of Madness 5.10c	12. Broken Finger 5.7
10. Unnamed 5.10b	13. Black Beard 5.8

at the left side of a small ceiling that is at head level. Climb a thin seam (optional gear) to a bolt, then past a horizontal, then move left to the communal anchor.

21. Silver Streak V1
The small ceiling near the previous route contains two classic boulder problems worth doing. Just right of *Fear Factor* pull the center of a small ceiling. Descend off the right-hand side of the ceiling near a green streak.

22. Green streak V0
Another longtime area classic. Pull the ceiling just right of *Silver Streak*.

Rambo Wall
This is the black-colored wall with two cracks on its left side, and a steep, overhanging wall on its right side where it passes around a corner. Al Pisaneschi originally did these routes as free solos; although, he considers them boulder problems. Whatever way you look at them, it's an impressive achievement.

23. Introduction 5.6 PG
FA: A. Pisaneschi
Climb the leftmost crack to a tree.

24. Mixed Up 5.7 PG
FA: A. Pisaneschi

Climb a crack to a bolt.

25. A Bolted Problem 5.9 PG
FA: A. Pisaneschi
This route, like the rest of the routs on this wall, was originally done as a boulder problem. Climb a black-colored face right of *Mixed Up* to a bolt. Continue to the top.

26. Rambo 5.11a PG
FA: A. Pisaneschi
This route was originally done as a boulder problem, also. Follow a corner to a bolt with a horizontal capped by a ceiling. Move to another bolt, then into a shallow corner, then on up to the top.

27. Rambo Direct 5.11c PG
FA: B. D' Antonio, G. Peterson
Start slightly right of *Rambo* under a bolt and a small ceiling. Fly to a horizontal under the ceiling then move left to join the *Rambo* regular route.

28. 5.13a Incomplete
Climb the roof just right of *Rambo*.

Bob D on the first ascent of "Agent Orange." Photo courtesy of Bob D' Antonio.

Hickory Wall
This is the last section of the cliff. Several worthy climbs exist here. All the routes on this section of the cliff were done as boulder problems. Note: Excellent boulder problems up to the grade of V9 have been done on the small, overhanging walls, just of the ground at this end of the cliff.

29. Pine 5.10a PG
FA: A. Pisaneschi
The leftmost route on the short wall left of the arete.

30. Maple 5.9+ PG
FA: A. Pisaneschi
Climb the center face.

31. Hickory 5.10d PG
Climb the fantastic arete right of *Maple*.

32. Oak 5.10a PG
Climb ledges to a small ceiling with a bolt around the corner from *Maple*. The face to the left of this route has been climbed on gear at 5.10 also. The face next to this route can be done at the same grade.

33. Unnamed 5.7 PG/R
FA: A. Pisaneschi, G. Peterson
Run up the nice slab to the right of *Oak*.

34. Ebb Tide 5.13a
Climb the center of the giant roof.

35. Oranguhang 5.11d
FA: A. Pisaneschi
Climb the right side of the large overhang at the right end of the cliff.

36. Coal Cushion 5.10a X
Climb the unprotected roof with pockets under it.

37. The Arete V3 R
This is the beautiful arete at the end of the cliff.

38. The Grand Traverse V5/ V8
Depending on what lines you traverse, the grade varies substantially. This is a boulder problem worth mentioning. Traverse the entire length of the Paradise cliff. Start at the *Main Area* and finish at the opposite end of the cliff.

Bob D'Antonio on Rambo Direct.
Photo courtesy Bob D.

Paradise   Rambo Wall

23. Introduction 5.6	26. Rambo 5.11a
24. Mixed Up 5.7	27. Rambo Direct 5.11c
25. A Bolted Problem 5.9	28. 5.13a

Hickory Wall

29. Pine 5.10a
30. Maple 5.9+
31. Hickory 5.10d

Oak

32. Oak 5.10a
33. Unnamed 5.7

Oranguhang

34. Unnamed 5.7   36.. Unnamed 5.13a
35. Unnamed 5.6   37. Oranguhang 5.11d

The Coal Bowl (a.k.a. the Sun Bowl)

This is the impressively steep wall around the corner from the last climbs at Paradise Rock. It has been a long time since many of these climbs have seen ascents—like since the first ascent for instance. Many amazing climbs were put up here. If this area had some more travel, this would be as popular as the other nearby crags.

Note: The bolts here are old and may be dangerous. Please use caution when climbing here. Setting up a toprope from above here is as dangerous as wearing red in the Crip's section of Compton.

1. Al's Crack 5.9+ R
FA: A. Pisaneschi
Climb the first crack you see at the entrance to the bowl.

2. Coal Bowl Crack A2
FA: A. Pisaneschi
This one hasn't gone free yet despite many attempts. Hugh Herr even tried to free this climb but was unsuccessful. Try to climb or aid the finger crack in the long roof just off the ground.

3. Working Man 5.11c PG/R
FA: A. Pisaneschi
Climb the first bolted line over steep rock.

4. Golden Slumbers 5.12b/c PG/R
FA: A. Pisaneschi
Climb the bolted line past gold-colored rock.

5. Coal Crack 5.12a/b R
Climb the difficult crack.

6. Welcome to the Strip'ens 5.12b/c PG/R
FA: A. Pisaneschi
Climb the next bolted route down the line.

7. Emphazema 5.11d PG/R
FA: A. Pisaneschi
Climb the last bolted route in the bowl.

*Bob D'Antonio leading at the Coal
Bowl. Photo courtesy Bob D.*

9. The Library

Area Beta

Location
Near Paradise Rock and the town of Mocanaqua.

Type of Climbing
Fantastic sport routes and a few good crack climbs on an amazing conglomerate block.

Other Info
Very cool in the summer.

The Library

I defiantly rate this area very high on my scale of areas to visit. Nestled in a grove of pines, the setting at this crag is spectacular—aside of the swath of coal hills, of course.

The Library is a unique and popular climbing destination for the climbers who actually know about this place. The location of this spectacular area has been kept secret amongst local climbers. Climbers have heard rumors about a fabulous sport climbing area nestled between the steep walls of the trademark crevice this area is famed for. For years, The Library has beckoned climbers to locate its mysterious whereabouts and taste its characteristic difficult routes. The Library is one of Pennsylvania's best-kept secrets.

Regional coal mining uncovered the passage that resembles a book stack at The Library. When climbers first saw this resemblance, they quickly named this area The Library. Although it was a blessing that mining uncovered this rock climbing gem, areas like Paradise Rock and surrounding areas were once much higher before they became partially-engulfed in anthracite. Perhaps the biggest upset of wide-spread mining is the area identical to The Library, that is presently resting under 80'of coal. This doppelganger was considered the best climbing spot in the region until it was put to rest in an anthracite tomb.

Although the difficulty of the climbs range from 5.7 to 5.13a, the majority of the routes at The Library are 5.10 and above. Even though this is mostly a sport climbing area, many classic trad-routes can be found here, too.

Retro-bolting seems to be a new trend at this area. Please note that although routes are void of bolts, doesn't mean they haven't had first ascents. Many of the climbs at this spot have been climbed trad or soloed. The steep vertical walls at The Library wisp cool air through their enchanting passages making this area irresistible on hot summer days. This draws the area to stay moist after rainstorms taking several days to dry. On days like these nearby Paradise Rock can be a …well, a paradise.

Bob D'Antonio on the first ascent of "Flamer." Photo courtesy of Bob D.

Descent: Occasionally climbers mention that there are only a few descent options at the Library. This statement is far from true. Descents can be easily achieved via the following options: Rappel stations are fixed above the following climbs; *Mantle Route*, *Nuclear Arms*, *The Arete*, *War and Peace*, *Nose Drops*, and *Corn Flake Crack*. The pine tree above *KB* makes an excellent rappel tree, also. Many people often descend the *Descent Route*, a 5.4 climb at the west end of the freestanding block. It is recommended that you climb this route first and familiarize yourself with the climbing it to assure it is within your comfort level. Please note that many of the rappel anchors are placed over the lip of the cliff. They were established this way because many of the routes are short and their topouts are quite exciting. Should anchors need to be replaced in the future, please remember that placing anchors over the lip was the intent of the first ascentionist. All anchors should be placed over the lip. If you want to replace anchors, put them past the topout.

History

During the late 1980s, George Peterson, Bob D'Antonio, and Al Pisaneschi began toying with the thin cracks at this area. Shortly after ticking off classics like *Stairway to Heaven*, *Cornflake Crack*, and several other trad routes, the potential for cutting-edge sport routes was realized. Surprisingly some of the routes that are bolted today were done trad or soloed. *Nuclear Arms* is a prime example of this. Essentially, Al, Bob, and George are the original developers of The Library. All of the original lines were established by them. Jeff Clovis was also very active at this time as well.

One summer in the late-80's, Bob D. and George Peterson introduced Alison Osius to The Library. Hugh Herr and Rich Romano also frequented this spot during this time as well as Mike McGill.

The Library

Nick Morell, Bob Barrett, Ryan Lukas, Tom Kneiss, and myself established other classic routes in the mid-90's at The Library.

I would like to note that the route *War and Peace* was first toproped by myself and Nick Morell. We both quickly sent the route. We started to bolt the climb and never had the chance to finish it. A climber finished bolting the line before we got back to complete it but I am unsure if it was ever lead clean by this climber before I was able to lead the route. Because of this, the annotation of first ascent after the climb refers to the first ascent done when Nick Morell and I originally discovered the line and toproped it, hence doing the first ascent toprope. I think it's pretty uncool to steal a route off someone who is obviously bolting it anyway; regardless, someone else may have the FFA.

Geology: Pottsville Conglomerate, quite unique but similar to Gunk's rock, without horizontals.

Directions: From Paradise Rock (see directions for Paradise Rock), walk to the far end of the Paradise cliff and you will see a large free-standing boulder across the coal field. This is The Library. Walk across the coal field, going down a steep hill, and this will bring you to the front wall of The Library.

The Main Block

When entering The Library, *The Main Block* is the obvious 45'-high block that is detached from the main cliff. The routes begin on the front side (this is the opposite side from the library-like passage) and continue around onto the opposing backside. Due to the overhanging nature of the front side, the majority of routes on it are rated 5.11 and up. Rap anchors are located on top of *Nuclear Arms*, *Corn Flake Crack*, and *Mantle Route*. The easiest way to the top of *The Main Block* is by climbing *Corn Flake Crack* or *The Descent Route*.

1. Wax Arete 5.11d PG
FA: R. Holzman
Climb the left arete near a tree, passing bolts. This climb was lead but a bolt still needs to be added. The tree is very cumbersome to pass but I didn't have the heart to remove it.

2. Darling Dainty Feet 5.11c PG
FA: A. Pisaneschi, J. Nonamaker, G. Peterson.
Climb past three bolts on the very short face at the entrance to The Library. There is a two-bolt anchor above.

3. Nose Drops 5.12a PG
FA: Bob D'Antonio, Albert Pisaneschi
This climb takes the prominent arete seen when first arriving at The Library. Be mindful of the sharp boulders below the first clip. Clip a bolt at a bulge 7'right of a beautiful arete. Move left to the arete, continue past three more bolts and top out.
Var. 1: Up Your Nose 5.12 c R
FA: R. Holzman
Boulder directly up the arete to join the regular version of the route.

4. Unnamed 5.12d PG
Climb the steep bolted line right of *Nose Drops*.

5. Nuclear Arms 5.12d G or R

FA: Bob D'Antonio, A. Pisaneschi

Make bouldery moves past a stud (R rating) or begin on the slightly safer previous (G rating) route and move right to a bolt just right of the previous route. Continue up and right past three more bolts and a drilled pocket at the crux. Without using the drilled pocket the route is 5.13a/b.

6. Phazers on Stun 5.10d PG

FA : D. Miscavage, G. Peterson, A. Pisaneschi

Originally done on gear and rated 5.9! This climb is the fourth bolted climb from the left. Step off the right edge of talus blocks to a bolt. Follow a thin crack on small gear to another bolt. Climb the crack to the arete above.

7. Unnamed 5.12c PG

FA: A. Puseneschi, J. Clovis

A technical sustained route. Five feet right of the previous route climb a shallow corner to a bolt 10 feet up. Continue past horizontals to a cruxy move at the second bolt. Pass one more bolt before topping out.

8. Colonl Red 5.12d G

FA: A. Pisaneschi

Two feet left of the large chimney a boulder problem start leads past two bolts. After the second bolt, continue up the corner and face to one more bolt and the top.

9. Urine Over Your Head 5.8 G

FA: D. Miscavage, A. Pisaneschi

Wizz up the fantastic finger crack just right of the previous route and at the end of the big chimney. Stepping over to the chimney makes the route 5.3.

10. The Chimney 5.5 PG

Climb the obvious chimney.

11. Cahones 5.11a PG

FA: A. Pisaneschi

Climb the smooth face just right of the big chimney to a bolt under a small ceiling. Follow two more bolts up the sharp-edged arete. Bring small to medium gear for the anchor at the top. Using the corner at the start drops the grade.

12. Unknown 5.12a PG

Boulder up to a bolt 10 feet off the ground. A big move at the second bolt leads to a nice exit-crack. Small and medium gear is helpful to lead this route.

13. Mantle Route 5.11d PG

FA: A. Pisaneschi, D. Miscavage

Mixed gear and bolts lead to a powerful mantle just before the ballsy topout. There is an old Rappel anchor at the top.

14. Tales from the Crimpt 5.11c X

FA: R. Holzman, T. Kneiss

Best to TR this one. The original line starts just right of a vertical crack and climbs over crimps to a shelf at graffiti. From this position climb over a bolt to a good horizontal and the top.

15. Unnamed 5.10a TR
A few feet right of *Tales*, climb the face and bulge.

16. Unnamed 5.4 R
Climb the gritty corner next to a large chimney.

17. Descent Route 5.3 G
This route is commonly used to descend from the top of *The Main Block*. It is recommended to climb this route first and familiarize yourself with the climb before downclimbing it. Scramble up a small offwidth crack with some trees growing out of it.

18. Leave it to Beaves 5.10a
FA: Christa Messick, Scott Messick

Begin as low as possible sitting in a pit and climb past two bolts. The route is 5.9 from a standing start.

19. Book of Four Words 5.11c PG
FA: R. Holzman

Climb the arete next to the chimney past bolts and gear.

20. Easy Day for a Layback 5.10a G
FA: R. Holzman

This route was originally done as a free solo and later retrobolted by an unknown climber. Two routes were bolted and crammed so close you could clip both routes from the same stance. On of these superfluous lines was removed due to its redundancy. Climb the route just right of the big chimney.

21. Lavwelle Latte 5.8 G
FA: B. Barrett, R. Holzman, N. Morell

The name is French for The Milky Way. This route got its name from the milky rock/chalk residue left after drilling the first ascent. Climb over three bolts to the top.

22. The Murky Way 5.10a/b TR
FA: R. Holzman, N. Morell

Climb the face between *Lavwelle* and *Flamer*.

23. Flamer 5.11a G
FA: Bob D'Antonio, G. Peterson

Between two trees this spectacular face climb follows four bolts.

Var. 1: 5.10a G
Move out right at the crux just after the first bolt, then rejoin the regular line slightly before reaching the small ceiling.

24. Great Expectations 5.10a G

FA: R. Holzman, N. Morell, B. D' Antonio

10' right of *Flamer*, boulder a slick section of rock to a bolt 12-feet up. Follow two more bolts to a cruxy move at the last bolt (optional gear placement after bolt). Follow a plum line from the last bolt to the top.

25. Brass Monkey 5.8 X

FA: R. Holzman

Mostly done on toprope. Climb the face between *Great Expectations* and the corner.

26. 5.10b G

FA: M. Cichon

Some people lead out left of the arete which is an easier variation but the original line hugs the arete to the top. Climb the arete to an anchor above.

27. Easy Keyhole 5.5 G

Squirm up the obvious chimney.

28. Grey Face Left 5.9 X

The start is bouldery but the top is easy. Climb over a bulge just right of the large chimney and follow the left side of the face above to an easy top out.

Christa Messick leading at the Library. Photo by the author.

29. Grey Face 5.9 G

FA: A. Pusaneschi

Climb over a bulge just right of the previous route and follow the left side of the face above to an easy top out. This route was originally done as a solo until it was bolted by local climbers. Either way it makes a good solo or lead.

30. Corn Flake Crack 5.7 G

Climb the obvious crack. There is a fixed anchor above.

31. Warm Up Route 5.6 G

This route was originally done as highball boulder problem then was later bolted. Climb the mellow face at the right end of the wall ten feet right of *Corn Flake*.

32. Hour of Darkness 5.11b G
FA: M. Cichon, R. Holzman
Most climbers find this route low quality because it is often dirty and wet. If you get it on a dry day, it's actually a fun route. Crank over grimy holds past two bolts and small gear.

33. Pine Line 5.11d G
FA: N. Morell, G. Peterson, R. Holzman
Climb the face at the leftmost part of the back wall of The Library.

34. K.B. 5.11d G
FA: Bob D, G. Peterson, A. Pisaneschi
Named in memory of Kevin Bein, one of the countries most prolific climbers, who died on the Matterhorn. Climb the route right of *Pine Line*.

35. Sad, Sloppy, Worthless, and Weak 5.10a G
FA: Bob D, G. Peterson, A. Pisaneschi
Climb to a bolt at a shallow, left-facing corner and step up and right to a ledge. Move back left past two more bolts.

36. The Bitch is Back 5.10a/b G
Climb the bolted route to the right of the previous route. The route that is squeezed next to this line is 5.10 also.

37. Stairway to Heaven 5.9 R
Trickey to protect. Climb the crack to the right of *The Bitch*. Often dirty but a great climb nonetheless.

38. Thunderstud 5.12c PG
FA: B. D'Antonio, G. Peterson
Named for the type of bolt used during the first ascent. Climb past four bolts to the top. The crux is at the small undercling at the top of the flake.

39. War and Peace 5.13a PG
FA: R. Holzman, N. Morell
A sustained difficult line. Follow the bolted line right of *Thunderstud*.

40. Coal Shaker 5.13c/d TR
FA: R. Holzman
Climb the blank face right of *War and Peace*.

41. Unnamed 5.11a PG
Make technical moves past three bolts, then easier climbing leads to a nice top out.

42. Pod Head 5.10d R
Right of the previous route there are two thin cracks. Climb the leftmost crack.

43. Ryan's Crack 5.10b R
FRA: R. Lukas

177

Climb the rightmost of two cracks.

44. The Knotty Pine 5.10b X
FA: R. Holzman
Climb the face right of the previous route. Best done as a short toprope.

45. Unknown 5.10b PG
FA: R. Holzman, N. Morell FFA: Unknown
I toproped this line in the early '90s but someone recently bolted it. Climb past bolts on the steep face outside and left of The Library and just off the road.

46. The Steep 5.12b PG
I started originally bolted this route, came back one day and found it removed. Someone later rebolted it again, moved my original anchor then the bolts were once again chopped by someone. I added bolts in again. If you go to climb it, it may or may not have bolts. Someone has also decided to squeeze a route in inches from this line. The finishing hold was also crowbared off of the route which may now make the route significantly easier since it was originally 5.13a. Climb the right most route on this wall.

Bouldering at The Library
Some of the finest boulder problems in the region lie on the right-end block that makes up The Library. To locate these problems, simply walk to the right end of the outside wall just right of the chimney near the route *Tales from the Crimpt*.

A. Nuclear Eyes V4 R
One of the best problems in Northeast PA! Start on edges directly in front of a hemlock and fire to two distinct pockets about 10' up. Top out.

B. White Flash V3 R
A few inches right of *Nuclear Eyes*, climb to small finger pockets and top out.

C. KamakazeeV3 R
In front of an oak tree climb to a shallow horizontal and the top.

D. Coal Cracker V8
SDS just right of the previous route, move up on thin edges to a sidepull 10' up. Continue up the corner near the face. A stand start makes the route V2.

E. Unnamed V0
SDS and climb the corner over big ledges.

F. Breaker Boys V1
From a sit start climb a small overhanging block between the previous route and a crack to the right.

G. Unnamed V0+
Follow over a bulge to a crack and escape out a notch. A sit down start adds length but not difficulty.

H. Nick's Problem V4
From a sitting start climb up to and over the small ceiling at the right side of the face.

I. Unnamed V0+
The arete right of the previous route.

Other Boulders
Great bouldering exists in "The Room" behind The Library (southwest side). The large cave beyond this hosts some excellent boulder problems. Al Pisaneschi was the first to develop many problems here. Later Nick Morell and myself added a dozen excellent problems here to the grade of V8 and many problems along the ridge like *The Tempest*. Mike Pezzuto added an excellent sit start to a problem that pulls the steep arete over two mono pockets and the regular line called *Third Base*. The stand-start goes at V9; the sit-start V10.

If you walk the ridge between The Library and Boulder Garden/ Main Wall areas there are a great deal of amazing problems

Bob D'Antonio leading "Thunderstud." Photo courtesy D'Antonio collection.

that were developed over the years by Al Pisaneschi, George Peterson, Nick Morell, and myself. About one hundred boulder problems, some as hard as V10, can be found here. If you venture to some of the bouldering on the ridge between The Library and main wall areas, I highly recommend locating a boulder problem called *The Tempest* V8. This problem is on a lone boulder downhill from the cave at the back of *The Library*. Only a few minutes walk from the back end of The Library, the problem is downhill and near a back road in Mocanaqua with some homes nearby. The problem sit starts the overhanging white bulge on the north-facing face. For more information about the great bouldering near here visit   www.paclimbing.com.

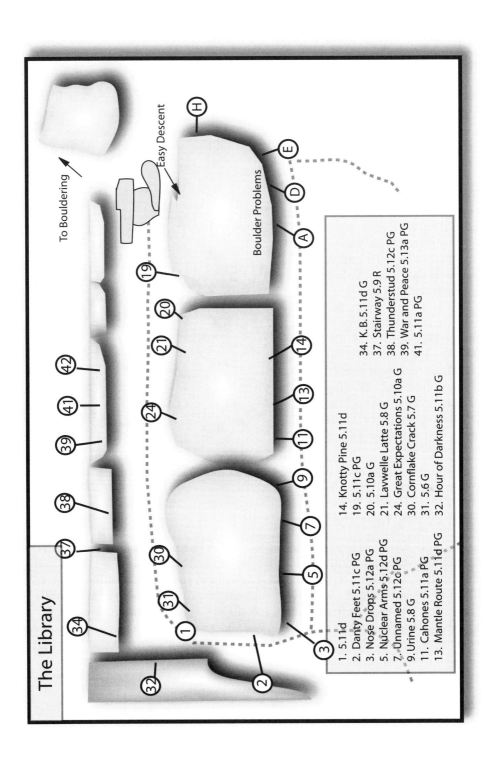

The Library

To Bouldering

Easy Descent

Boulder Problems

1. 5.11d
2. Danty Feet 5.11c PG
3. Nose Drops 5.12a PG
5. Nuclear Arms 5.12d PG
7. Unnamed 5.12c PG
9. Urine 5.8 G
11. Cahones 5.11a PG
13. Mantle Route 5.11d PG
14. Knotty Pine 5.11d
19. 5.11c PG
20. 5.10a G
21. Lavwelle Latte 5.8 G
24. Great Expectations 5.10a G
30. Cornflake Crack 5.7 G
31. 5.6 G
32. Hour of Darkness 5.11b G
34. K. B. 5.11d G
37. Stairway 5.9 R
38. Thunderstud 5.12c PG
39. War and Peace 5.13a PG
41. 5.11a PG

Scott Messick leading "Lavwelle Latte." Photo by the author.

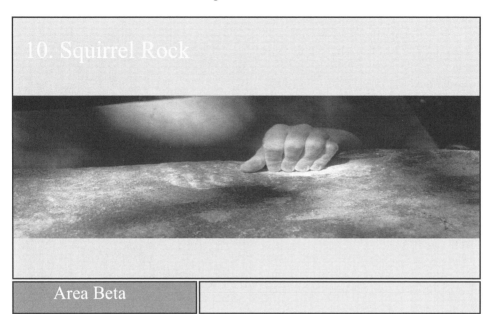

Area Beta

Location
Glen Lyon, PA.

Type of Climbing
Sport climbing and bouldering.

Other Beta
Very nice sandstone area with lots of boulders. Only a few sport routes and the cliff is short.

Squirrel Rock

Long regarded as one of Mocanaqua's "secret crags", Squirrel Rock offers unique sandstone that is uncharacteristic to this region. The rock here somewhat resembles the well known Pennsylvania diabase abundant at Governor's Stables, Haycock Mountain, and Mount Gretna; however, the rock is sandstone. Squirrel rock offers rock slightly similar to these diabase icons but with a mix of firm sandstone.

Short, bolted sport routes, soft landings, enormous boulders, and a quiet, secluded setting are some positive aspects about this area. The routes vary from 30' to 50' high and range from 5.7 to 5.12c.

The bouldering here is also a popular attraction and in recent years has seen a lot of activity and a few bouldering competitions. At least 30 high-quality boulders lie scattered under the forest canopy with problems ranging from V0- to V8. Perhaps the most impressive feature here is a monolith called *The Titanic*. This 40' high boulder, that is the size of a three-bedroom house, is one of the largest sandstone boulders in the state.

Area local Dave Grabinski recently put a lot of effort into cleaning many of the older boulder problems here and established a fair amount of new problems as well. Due to his cleaning efforts, this area went from a C grade area to an A+ bouldering destination.

History: George Peterson, Albert Pisaneschi, Bob D'Antonio, Rich Romano, and Bob Perna were the first to establish climbing here in the late 1980s. During this time period, they established classics like *Unnamed Crack* 5.9+, *Hurricane of Change* 5.12c, and the other classic lines. They also established a few classic boulder problems at this area during this time.

In the early '90s Nick Morell and I were the first to establish a significant amount of boulder problems on the fantastic boulders in the area. Nick and I established several dozen area classics that stemmed into the V8 range, and I came up with two problems in the V10/V11 range. The sit start to *Gandy Dancer* is one example. A great deal of bouldering was established but went untouched for many years.

Tom Kneiss, Ryan Lukas, Rub Muti, and Marty Molitoris were also active bouldering here in the '90s.

During the past few years, great efforts went into climbing and cleaning many of the old lines and establishing new and eliminate lines. Dave Grabinski, Mike Pezzuto, Judy Racowski, Matt and Marty Lichtner, and Steven Salemi have established many new and eliminate lines a this area. Thinks to their great efforts in trail construction and lots of cleaning this area is now a stellar bouldering spot. Steve Salemi also established a sit start to an old problem called *Coal Cracker*. The new sit start is called *Rebel* V11, and is a truly hard line. Another great new line was added in the last year by Harrisburg climber Travis Gault. It is called *Pegasus* and goes at V8.

Bob D'Antonio on the first ascent of "Young Americans'"
Photo courtesy of Bob D.

General Location: A five minute walk behind the cemetery in Glenn Lyon.

Ownership: The Earth Conservancy

Access and Considerations: The Earth Conservancy recognizes and permits climbing on their property. The only major consideration when climbing at *Squirrel Rock* is the parking situation. The parking lot is owned by a church in Glenn Lyon. Please give the utmost respect to anyone working or visiting the cemetery. Abide by any restrictions that may arise from the cemetery and present cordial and friendly greetings to anyone you meet while parking--this includes spirits of the netherworld--this way the healthy relationship may continue.

Hazards: Be aware of loose rock and snakes. A major hazard here is open mine subsidence's (underground areas that have collapsed due to mining). When hiking around near the cliff and boulders you will notice large pits around the area. These are old mine shafts and they are extremely hazardous. Be alert when hiking around and leave the area before dark to avoid walking into these giant pits. Every few years in the anthracite region, a notable mine subsidence occurs. Please keep alert and stay a few hundred feet from the mine openings. You never know when one may cave in. Falling blindly into an endless abyss can ruin anyone's day at the crag—what can I say; typical PA.

Geology: Crossbed sandstone and iron-rock mix.

Squirrel Rock

Nearby Areas: Moc wall, Paradise Rock, The Library, Turkey Rock, Sandblaster Crag, and many, many others.

Directions: From interstate 81 south of Wilkes-Barre take the exit for State Route 29 North (South Cross Valley Expressway) via exit 164 towards US RT-11. Get off the second exit (exit 2 towards Alden) and make a left off the exit onto Middle Road. Drive on this road to the town of Glenn Lyon; a very small town a few blocks long. After the second main strip in Glenn Lyon, you will come to a 90-degree turn in (the road now becomes Main Street) that leads to a cemetery on both sides of the road. Pass the cemetery on both sides of the road and park just beyond the fence on the left-hand side of the road at a small parking area. Please park discreetly and leave room for cars to get by.

From here, walk across the road you drove in on to the north side of the paved road (opposite side of the side you parked on) and walk into a dirt road that parallels the cemetery. Follow this dirt road about 100' to a split that goes left or straight. Follow the left-hand split up a small, gradual incline that parallels the paved road you drove in on. A few-hundred feet before the crest of the incline you will see a faint trail on your right. Follow this a few-hundred feet to a path that walks down into the cliff and *Box Boulder*.

A. Box Boulder

This is the box-shaped boulder you see as soon as you walk down to the cliff on the main trail. It is located near the base of *Unnamed Crack*.

1. Wintergreen V3

The best problem at its grade here. The first ascent was done sans crashpad and in sneakers. From a sitting start in the center of the small face under the overhang, climb to the Buddha-like formation and reach out to a hold in the center of the overhang that is just over the lip. Pull over the center of the boulder.

2. Coco Puffs V2

Climb the right side of the roof.

3. The Green Staircase V2 R

Just right of *Coco Puffs* climb the slightly overhanging, green-colored ledges.

4. Footfall V0+

Climb the ledges a few feet right of the previous route.

5. Unnamed Crack 5.9+ PG

Pumpy and sustained. Climb the overhanging hand crack on the overhanging wall that is located on the cliff just above the *Box Boulder*.

B. Slab Boulder

Just past the *Box Boulder* on the boulder trail this is the second boulder you come to. It has a slab on its downhill side.

6. Beer and Coca-Cola V4

SDS on the left side of the boulder with hands on a rail and climb up over the bulge.

7. Slabtacular V0+

Climb the slab at its smooth center 4' right of the previous route. A few variations have been done to the right and left at the same grade.

8. Squirrelly Slab V2

A few inches right of the large crack that splits the boulder, climb up the face using small edges to mantle onto the slab above.

Var. 1: V6 Do the above problem from a sitting start.

C. The Sphere

This boulder is the very small, sphere-shaped boulder just past the *Slab Boulder*. The sphere-shaped boulder is perched on top another boulder and appears to be toppling off.

9. Apple Pie V0-

Climb the left corner from a SDS.

10. The Sphere Traverse V5

SDS on the boulders left side and climb the lip of the perched boulder to its right end and top out.

M. Lictner and Dave Grabinski on "Wintergreen." Photo by the author.

11. Recluse Crack V4

SDS on the left side of the boulder and follow the crack under the perched boulder to top out at the far right side of the boulder.

12. How About them Apples V5

SDS under the center of the sphere at a crack and top out.

D. The Coliseum

Follow the boulder trail to this cluster of boulders visible downhill about 300' from *The Sphere*.

13. Unnamed Arete V0-

On the outside-left-hand boulder of the formation, directly across from the *Titanic Boulder*, climb the obvious arete.

14. Squirrel Master V6/V7

Where the two boulders of this formation meet there is a passage you can walk through to get to the inside. Start on the right side of the notch/passage and climb a thin seam at head-

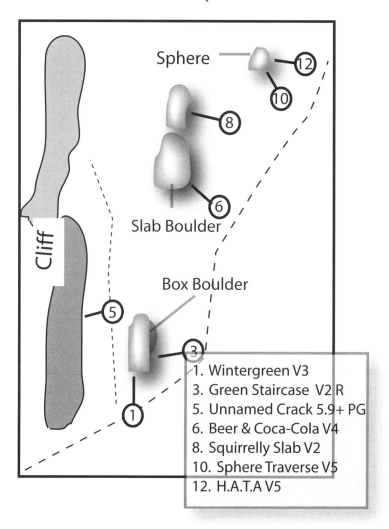

Sphere

Slab Boulder

Cliff

Box Boulder

1. Wintergreen V3
3. Green Staircase V2 R
5. Unnamed Crack 5.9+ PG
6. Beer & Coca-Cola V4
8. Squirrelly Slab V2
10. Sphere Traverse V5
12. H.A.T.A V5

level. Top out in the center of the boulder where the seam ends.

15. Squirrel Nuts V0-
Climb the edges left of the passage at the start of the previous problem.

16. The Matador V5
SDS on a jug at the right side of the passage/notch and climb over the bulge.

17. Bull Rider V5
Start the same as for *Matador* and traverse into *Bucked* and top out.

18. Bucked V4
SDS on sidepulls on the corner a few feet right of *Matador* and grunt up the corner.

19. Slick Willy VB
Climb the easy face just around the corner from *Bucked*.

20. Unnamed/Unrated
Climb the face and seam just right of *Slick Willy*.

21. Fearin Smearin V2
Climb the face and corner in front of a small tree just right of the previous route.

22. Hawaii Five-O V3
Climb the corner just right of the split in the two boulders.

23. Torture Chamber V4
Pull over thin crimps on the face just right of *Hawaii*.

24. Swamp Thing V3/V4
This problem was flooded in a swamp that sometimes forms in this outcrop. Climb the leftmost boulder on the inside of the *Coliseum* outcrop via the nice arete on the boulders left side. SDS on crimps and fly up the corner.

25. Gandy Dancer V4
From a standing start on sharp, small edges a few inches right of the previous route, crimp and fly to a jug near the lip and top out. The sit start goes at V11.

26. Coal Cracker V7
Start this problem a few inches right of the previous route by placing your right finger in a very small pocket and you r left hand on a crimp. Power your way off the ground and crank to a hold just under the lip. Top out. A SDS was recently sent by Steve Salemi. It goes at V11 and is called *Rebel*.

27. Unnamed V5
SDS and climb the overhanging sidepull/arete at the large crack in the boulder a few feet right of the previous route.

28. Mutiny V4
SDS on the previous route and climb up and over the large crack, then up the crimps on the face.

29. Mud Hole V2
Start in the right side of the notch/passage that splits the two boulders inside the *Collesium* formation and climb up and over the bulge.

30. Unnamed V0-
Run up the easy face right of the previous route without using the large crack a few inches to the right.

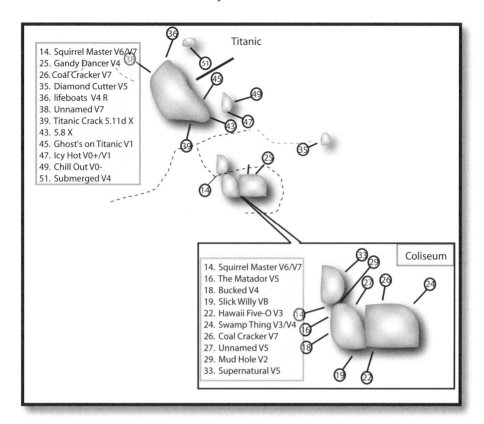

14. Squirrel Master V6/V7
25. Gandy Dancer V4
26. Coal Cracker V7
35. Diamond Cutter V5
36. lifeboats V4 R
38. Unnamed V7
39. Titanic Crack 5.11d X
43. 5.8 X
45. Ghost's on Titanic V1
47. Icy Hot V0+/V1
49. Chill Out V0-
51. Submerged V4

Titanic

Coliseum

14. Squirrel Master V6/V7
16. The Matador V5
18. Bucked V4
19. Slick Willy VB
22. Hawaii Five-O V3
24. Swamp Thing V3/V4
26. Coal Cracker V7
27. Unnamed V5
29. Mud Hole V2
33. Supernatural V5

31. Unnamed V0-
Just past the large crack, climb the face past a big ledge.

32. Unnamed V4
Climb sloping crimps.

33. Supernatural V5
The same problem number 32, but from a SDS.

E. The Diamond
Locate this boulder by walking straight back from *The Coliseum*. After about two minutes of walking you will come to a small diamond-shaped boulder, standing alone in the woods, near a pine tree.

34. Diamond in the Rough V1
SDS and climb the slanting rail to the point of the diamond-like boulder.

35. Diamond Cutter V5
SDS on the right-hand side of the boulder and make contrived moves to gain the sloping top and edges just before the lip. Move left and top out.

F. The Titanic
This is the unbelievable, enormous, three-story-high boulder next to *The Coliseum*.

36. Lifeboats on the Titanic V4 R
Quite possibly the best problem of its grade on this type of Pennsylvania sandstone. On the back side (lowest side) of this massive boulder, climb the overhanging prow on the boulders left-rear side. SDS and climb to a surprising top out.

37. Roast Beef V6 R
Jump to a sidepull and the corner about 10' up on the *Lifeboats* route, and continue to finish on the previous problem.

38. Unnamed V8 R
Climb the face just right of *Lifeboats*.

39. Titanic Crack a.k.a. 5.11d X
A local climber fell from the top of this route when trying to solo it a few years ago. Surprisingly he left without a scratch. Climb the 40'-high crack that splits an overhang at the boulders highest point.

40. Titanic Traverse V3
Pumpy and sustained. Traverse a horizontal at chest level starting at the 5.11d and continuing past brittle rock in the beginning, then continue to the corner near *The Iceberg* boulder. From there you can top out (Var. 1), or continue on a horizontal until you reach the backside of the boulder. Top out near where the horizontal ends near the boulders back side.
Var.1: Traverse to the corner of *The Titanic* boulder near *The Iceberg* boulder and climb up the corner to a ledge (V2); finish here or top out (V2) X.

41. Survivor V4
Start at the right end of a sloping shelf near the right-front side of *The Titanic* and traverse left to a shallow corner about 55' from where you started. Climb up this corner and finish about 15' up.

42. Project
Start the same as *Survivor* and traverse past the corner to a bulge a few inches past the corner. Try to pull up and over this bulge.

43. 5.8 X
Climb the rounded corner across from *The Iceberg*.

44. Tom's Problem V2
Start on the right-hand side of the shelf and climb to a thin, vertical seam. Shoot up to the ledge above. Finish here by traversing out right.

45. Ghost's of the Titanic V1
Around the right-hand side of this gigantic boulder and across from *The Iceberg* there are a series of horizontals; one low, one high. Climb up and over these.

46. Descent 5th Class
Located between *Ghost's* and *Lifeboats* are a series of easy ledges and a tree that are easy to climb to set top ropes or descend the boulder.

G. The Iceberg
This is the 12'-high clump of rock a few feet right of *The Titanic's* front side.

47. Icy Hot V0+/V1
Climb the center face of the boulder. This problem was a little easier until a giant hold broke off.

48. The Big Chill V0
Start on a big hold down low and climb the right corner of the boulder.

49. Chill Out V0-
Run up the slab around the right-side corner from the previous climb.

50. Dinty Moore V0-
Cruise up the left-side face and slab a few feet left of *Icy Hot*.

Bob D'Antonio on the first ascent of Hurricane of Change, April, 89. Photo courtesy of Bob D.

H. Alvin Boulder
Alvin was the submersible that found the Titanic. This boulder is the small overhanging boulder with loose flakes (located behind *The Iceberg* and right of *Lifeboats*).

51. Submerged V4
SDS and climb the left-center of the overhanging face.

52. The Training Grounds
This is a cluster of cube-shaped boulders at the base of the cliff near the *Three Pisans* route. You can easily walk to it by walking south along the cliff from *Unnamed Crack* or simply walking the faint trail up to the cliff from *The Titanic*.

53. Easy Scoop VB
Looking at the rock and cliff from below, climb the sloping corner/scoop formation on the downhill side of the leftmost boulder.

54. Easy Up V0-
Cruise up the face left of a small tree before a split passage on the boulder and climb to the right of the previous boulder that *Easy Scoop* is on.

55. Battalion V4
SDS under a small roof that is right of the previous problem, and climb over the roof on slopers.

56. Unnamed V0
Walk in the passage behind this boulder and climb the right-hand side of the boulder in the passage.

57. Crimpfest V1/V2
Just left of the tree climb up on crimps to the top. Several variations have been done making the problem easier or harder.

58. Unnamed V0-
Climb the face a few inches left of the previous route. To make it harder don't use the corner.

59. Steel Skin V5
SDS on the left side of the boulder directly behind the *Crimpfest* problem and traverse right a few feet to a bulge. Pull over the bulge and top out.

60. When the Nines Roll Over V2
Climb the face and corner a few feet right of the previous route. To make the problem more challenging, don't use the right corner.

61. Unnamed V0
A few easy problems can be done on the face opposite the cliff.

62. Unnamed V2/V5
Climb the nice arete on the cliff and top out through the notch above. A sit down start increases the grade to V5.

63. Lichen It V4
Climb the slab a few feet right of the previous problem.

64. Wafer Face V0+
Climb the loose wafer of orange-colored-rock to a great top out over the small roof above.

65. Short but Sweet V0
Hard to find. Locate a small boulder with a nice overhanging face that is 7'-high on its downhill side. The boulder is down and left from the *Training Grounds* area. SDS and climb the center of the face to the point above. Top out.

66. Cracked Slab Boulder V0-
This boulder is farther south along the cliff. It has a slab on its downhill side that has horizontal and vertical cracks.

67. Slabtagious V0-
Climb over a bulge at the slab's left side.

Squirrel Rock Climbing Routes
Several bolted climbs can be found on the short cliff that surrounds this area.

1. Unnamed Crack 5.9+ PG
Climb the overhanging crack the *Wintergreen* boulder problem.

2. Young Americans 5.11c/d PG
FA: Bob D' Antonio
Climb the bolted face.

3. Hurricane of Change 5.12d PG
FA: B. D'Antonio
Climb the line of bolts over the arete.

4. Three Pisans and a Gambler 5.11a PG
FA: B. Perna, B. D' Antonio, N. Morell
Climb the newest line of bolts.

5. 5.10d
Climb the bolts past amazing pockets at the far right end of the cliff.

6. Squirrel Nest 5.11d TR
Climb the route around the corner from under a roof, and then continue up to large horizontals above. Watch out for squirrels at the top.

Pegasus V8
Above and right of the routes is a nice boulder problem under a roof. SDS low, and under the roof and climb out to a nice top out.

11. Emmaus Bouldering Area

Area Beta

Location
10 minutes from downtown Allentown.

Type of Climbing
A dozen boulders that are perfect for bouldering. The boulders look and feel like granite.

Other Info
Two other areas are just down the road.

Emmaus Bouldering Area

Large, round boulders with granite-like quality that are screaming to be climbed on, is the main attraction of this area. Although there are only about 10 boulders at this area, they are all excellent quality and contain numerous, classic problems. What this area lacks in quantity, it makes up for in quality. Some of the best boulder problems in Eastern Pennsylvania can be found on the large boulders that dot the landscape of Emmaus. It looks like someone took boulders from Joshua Tree and dumped them in the woods near Allentown.

Most of the boulders at this area are somewhat high and have very exciting problems on them. For this reason, climbers repeatedly visit this area regardless of the lack of boulders. Located minutes from downtown Allentown, this has become a popular and easily accessible spot.

A land preservation group named The Wildlands Conservancy now owns the land where this area is located. They have deemed this area an open space for multi purpose recreational use. The area is now shared by mountain biker's, climbers, and day-hikers. A few minutes walk up a well broken trail will bring you to this deeply wooded spot.

This area is well worth an afternoon visit. If there is not enough rock to satisfy you, nearby Bauer's Rock and the Patriot Boulders are only minutes away.

Expect to find 10 boulders ranging from a few feet to 15' high. There are over 44 established problems here ranging from V0- to V8. If you are traveling through Allentown or live nearby, I highly recommend this area for a visit.

Access Concerns and Restrictions: The Wildlands Conservancy owns the land. As a result of talks with The Access Fund, bouldering is a recognized activity on the property. Please respect the land, pack out any trash, and do your part to keep the area clean.

History

In 1981 Sally Rezadich, an outdoor enthusiast had introduced Darryl Roth to the amazing boulders in Emmaus. Darryl was an original developer of nearby Stony Ridge, and went on to develop an incredible amount of routes in Colorado where he now lives. It is not unlikely to see him featured in old editions of *Climbing Magazine*.

Darryl was the first recorded climber to discover the potential at Emmaus. From 1981 to 1983 Darryl, along with Kim Steiner, and Mark Leyominster, established most of the obvious lines at Emmaus. Some of Daryl's established routes include *Maximuman* V5, *Leafy* V3, *Launch Pad* V4, *Twitch* V1, *Yvly* V2, *Ultra Friction* V5 and many other of the original problems and eliminates.

It was nearly 10 years later that any significant development took place at this area. In 1993, Karen Vantine, Dave Pfurr, Mark Ronca, and myself discovered further potential at these boulders.

Karen Vantine developed some classic problems like *Urine Escape Hatch* V4, *Breast Flop* V4, and the *Curious George Start* V3/V4 to *Yvly* and a classic V8.

Dave Pfurr was a regular fixture at the boulders for a long time. Dave developed many eliminates to existing problems and several notable first ascents. He was a local guru-- and still is--for over a decade. Dave and myself were featured on a Television Show that showcased the bouldering at Emmaus.

I was lucky enough to have come up with and developed a few lines at Emamus also. Some lines include: *Indiana Jones* V1, *Zoom* V4, *Pitt Stop* V5, *Manly Traverse* V6 and a few other problems in the V7/V8 range.

Obe Carrion, a local from the Allentown area, also added *Obe's Problem* V6, originally done as a toprope in his early days of climbing.

Directions

From the toll plaza at the Allentown exit of I-476 (NE Extension of the PA Turnpike), merge onto US-22 east, via exit 56, toward PA-309/I-78 East. Merge onto PA-309 south towards Quakertown. Follow PA-309 about1.6 mi and merge onto I-78 East/PA-309 South. Follow this road for 3.5 mi to Exit 57 (Lehigh Street south ramp). Take exit 57 and make a right off the exit ramp onto Lehigh Street.

Follow Lehigh Street for .3 mi and turn left onto 31st Street near the Dunkin Doughnuts. Follow 31st Street over the rail road tracks for .2 mi and turn right onto Emmaus Avenue.

Follow Emmaus Ave. for .5 mi. Just past the Commix Hotel, you will see Alpine Street on the left. Turn left onto Alpine Street and go two blocks to a dead end. Park at the lot or near the gate at the roads dead end. Do not block the gate. Park here and walk past the gate and follow the trail .3mi uphill, veering left at the first trail-break, to the second of two bridges. At the bridge you will see the trail break up and right to a steep bank across the stream. Follow up the bank towards the steep, rock-strewn hill ahead and you will see the rock at the top of the hill. The approach should take 10-15 minutes.

A. Golf Ball Boulder

This is the large boulder perched high atop the hill, and the first boulder you come to when hiking to the boulders. Most of the problems are high and dangerous.

1. Indiana Jones V1 R

Looking at this boulder from the bottom, climb the left side of the boulder. Begin near a fallen tree and climb the arete and face.

2. Unnamed V2 X

You may want to toprope this one. From atop a sub-boulder climb the crimpy face just right of the previous problem. The crux is at an awkward rail at mid-height.

3. Pitt Stop V5

Start in a pit around the back-right-hand side of this boulder. Pull out of the pit and climb nice crimps to an interesting top out.

B. Blob Rock

This boulder is a large blob of rock located beneath the *Castle Boulder*. Most of the routes are on the downhill side.

Jess Holzman cranking an area classic.

4. Unnamed V0-

Step up the center of a slabby face on the *Blob Rock* using only your feet. Looking uphill, this is the left-hand slab of this boulder.

5. Smearcase V0

Traverse the entire slab, starting on the right and finishing after an obvious flake. The trick to this problem is to only use your feet to do the problem. Use of the knees, hands, chin, or other extremities is considered off route.

6. Maximuman V5

A difficult, sustained, and technical problem. Traverse low holds and a horizontal at the bottom of the boulder from left to right. Start just left of the *Grunt Dihedral*.

7. Girly Traverse V6

Cruxy and sustained. Begin this traverse on chest-level holds at the left end of the downhill side of the *Blob Rock*. Continue past the large off-width crack, drop very low to a sharp rail that leads to the traverse finish, and pull around the right end of the boulder to top out on *The Blob*. Not such a girly problem after all.

8. Manly Traverse V6

Start this problem deep in the cave at the beginning of *Urine Escape Hatch*. Climb that

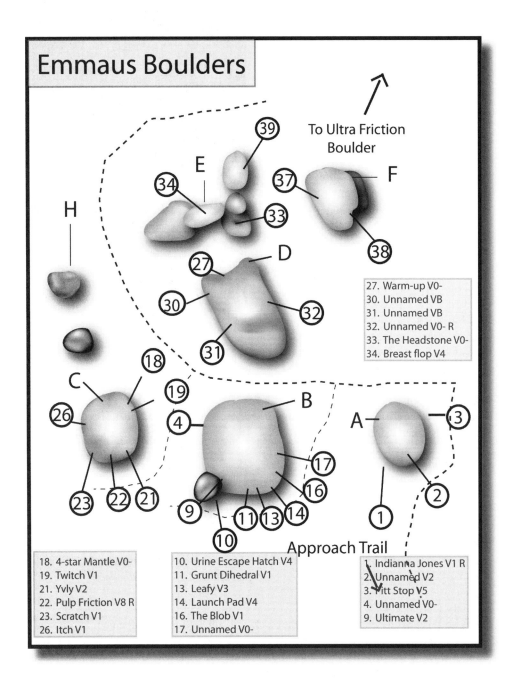

Emmaus Boulders

39

E

34

H

37

F

33

27

D

30

32

31

18

C

19

26

4

B

A

3

17

23 22 21

16

2

9

1

11 13 14

10

Approach Trail

To Ultra Friction Boulder

38

27. Warm-up V0-
30. Unnamed VB
31. Unnamed VB
32. Unnamed V0- R
33. The Headstone V0-
34. Breast flop V4

18. 4-star Mantle V0-
19. Twitch V1
21. Yvly V2
22. Pulp Friction V8 R
23. Scratch V1
26. Itch V1

10. Urine Escape Hatch V4
11. Grunt Dihedral V1
13. Leafy V3
14. Launch Pad V4
16. The Blob V1
17. Unnamed V0-

1. Indianna Jones V1 R
2. Unnamed V2
3. Pitt Stop V5
4. Unnamed V0-
9. Ultimate V2

problem past its crux to nice crimps at head level, and follow the *Girly Traverse* route to its finish and continue around the corner onto and up the V0- slab.

9. Ultimate Boulder Problem V2
A sit start at the left side of the downhill side of this boulder leads to tricky face moves up high. Start as deep in the cave as you can and move to an edge and finger pocket above a shelf.

10. Urine Escape Hatch V4
Start left of the previous problem and deep in the cave. Keep your feet off the ground and climb the overhanging face; then move slightly right to nice crimps above.

11. Grunt Dihedral V1
Ascend the dirty, awkward crack/dihedral.

12. Zoom V4
Climb sidepulls a few inches left of *Leafy*. Zoom over nice edges and the fun top out. Holds on *Leafy* are off route.

13. Leafy V3
A small tree nicknamed Leafy once grew out of the crux hold on this classic. One of the best problems in the region. A must do. Start on an edge with your right hand and a sidepull for your left and dyno high and right to a bucket. It's not over yet; bring your feet up to the bucket then do an exciting but easy top out.
Var. 1: V8 SDS to the previous problem.

14. Launch Pad V4
Pull up on small edges just above head level on the downhill-right side of this boulder. Gain a bucket and continue to the top.

15. Unnamed V6
SDS and climb the steep face up to *Launch Pad*. Finish on *Launch Pad*.

16. The Blob V1
Climb the right corner of the boulder from a low start.

17. Unnamed V0-
Climb the smooth slab around the right corner of the steep face. Easier variations have been done to the right.

C. Main Boulder (A.K.A the Joshua Tree Boulder)
Left of the previous boulder is a large, round boulder named the *Main Boulder*. The name of this boulder originated because it is large and has a lot of quality problems on it. It looks like someone took this boulder from Joshua Tree and dropped it at Emmaus.

18. Four-star Mantle V0-
Climb a short face and mantle the top of the boulder.

19. Twitch V1

A great problem with an exciting crux. Start with your hands on a small flake at the base of an obvious crack. Work up into a finger-lock in the crack then stand up to top out. Topping out is the crux.

20. Unnamed V0+

Inches left of the previous problem is a good rail a few feet off the ground. Start on this rail and pull up over the sloping top of this great boulder (crux).

21. Yvly V2

Pronounced why-va-lee. Crimp a good sidepull and pry to a rail. Intricate moves lead up and left to a fun top out near this boulders highest point.

Dave Pfurr, the mayor of Emmaus, cruising "Yvly."
Photo by the author.

Var. 1: Curious George Start V3/V4

SDS to this problem.

22. Pulp Friction V8 R

A powerful highball problem that climbs the highest section of this large boulder. Begin on two crimpy sidepulls working technical moves to gain a sloping edge above. Next, grab a sidepull to the left and climb up on good holds to the top.

23. Snatch V1

Jump to a flake at the right of an overhanging face (crux) and continue over the top.

24. ScratchV0

Jump from the ground to a hidden bucket and the beginning of a shallow crack in the center of an overhanging face. Work the crack to the summit.

25. Dave's Variation V2

Do the same problem as above without lunging for the opening holds.

26. Itch V1

Climb the painful finger-crack left of the previous problem.

D. Castle Boulder

This is the large, rectangular boulder in the center of the surrounding boulders. Often

Jess Holzman on "Grunt Dihedral."

mistaken for the *Main Boulder*. All of the problems on this boulder are easy but well worth doing. A great warm up spot. Descend off the low front end or downclimb the corner left of the first route.

27. Warm up V0-
Climb the face just left of an obvious crack without touching the corner to the left.

28. Easy Crack V0-
On the backside of this boulder is an obvious crack. Climb it.

29. Graffiti Face V0-
A great warm up. Make fun moves up the center of the face right of the crack.

30. Unnamed VB
Hug the arete a few feet right of the previous problem and slightly right of a block on the ground.
Var. 1: VB
Climb out right from the problem just mentioned.

31. Unnamed VB
Climb a faint crack

32. Unnamed V0- R
Start on a face and gain the arete above while keeping your feet off the large block to the right where the boulder makes a big ledge. Top out where the arete ends.

E. Cave-like Boulder
Directly behind the *Castle Boulder* is an egg-shaped boulder atop a pseudo cave. Some low-quality problems have been done here.

33. The Headstone V0-
Climb the face at the rightmost side of this formation using only the face for holds. Climbing straight to the top on the smallest holds available is the most enjoyable way to do this problem.

34. Breast Flop V4
Traverse the egg-shaped boulder from right to left on an obvious horizontal. Pull up over the boulder at the end of the traverse. See if you can guess how this problem got its name. Some holds have broken possibly changing the grade.

F. Perched Boulder
Just right of the *Cavelike Boulder* is a large boulder resting atop a much smaller block.

36. Unnamed V2
Begin at the start of *Your Mind* and traverse left then up. Finish with an easy top out.

37. Your Mind V1
Climb the center of the left side of the boulder. The crux is topping out.

38. Obe's Problem V6 TR or R/X
Climb the steep, perched side of the boulder.

39. Unnamed V1
On the boulder across from the *Perched Boulder*, climb the center of the face near a small, vertical flake.

G. Ultra Friction Boulder
Following the trail, this boulder is a few minutes walk uphill and right of the *Main Boulder*. This is the boulder farthest right in the woods. Quality friction problems can be found on this boulder.

40. Unnamed V0+
Use slopers to climb the left corner of this boulder, climb out to an incut sidepull, then straight up to the top.

41. Awakening V3
Center of the boulder from a low start.

42. Climb OnV1
Start on a gaston just above head level and crank to a big sidepull. A fun top out ends this fine problem.

43. Brief Introduction V0-
Climb the arete

44. Ultra Friction V5
Climb the blank face on the right side of this boulder.

G. Miscellaneous Boulders
Several other problems have been established on smaller, more obscure boulders at Emmaus. Some of the most common routes exist on the small boulders above the *Main Boulder*. Area local Tim Bonner also established some interesting boulders on the trail farther west of the main boulders. They're easier to find during winter when the trees are bare. Walk right on the trail rather than left when it splits coming from the parking lot. When you come across a stream that crosses the trail, cross the stream and head up left towards the hill. You will see a good practice slab and other boulders up on the hill. These are not as nice as the Main Area, but fun if you want to explore a little.

Jason Olshenske on "Yvly." Photo by Gus Gruner.

12. Bauers Rock Bouldering Area

Area Beta

Location
10 minutes from downtown Allentown.

Type of Climbing
A little over a dozen boulders.

Other Info
The problems are great, but the boulders are covered in graffiti.

Bauer's Rock

Shards of glass and layers of graffiti dissuade most climbers from frequenting Bauer's Rock. I admit that upon my first visit, I was a little appalled by the appearance of the area; however, a hard session of bouldering slanted my negative views of the rocks. Delicate face moves, desperate dynos, and tricky problem solving suddenly made the place significantly more enjoyable.

Bauer's Rock is also known as Big Rock Park and White Trash Rocks. Whatever you choose to call this area, you'll find about two dozen boulders and more than 60 established lines. The problems range from V0- to V8. In a nutshell, the problems are good; the place looks bad. Due to the demeaning appearance of Bauer's Rock, efforts were made to restore this bouldering area to a more natural state. Cleanups were held in years past, but little headway has been made. The unfortunate reality is that the area has more graffiti than a Harlem A-Train from the 1970s.

I knew a climber who witnessed a miscreant tagging a boulder with paint one evening. The climber was so appalled by this act that he packed up his crash pad, quietly left the boulders, and decided to relieved his colon on said tagger's automobile. Save from revengeful defecation, you can do your part by packing out trash and respecting the area. If you can get past the lack of aesthetics at this area, Bauer's Rock can be well worth your visit.

Rock Climbing and Bouldering Pennsylvania

It is important to note that there are many good boulders scattered around the nearby woods and within a mile radius of the main area. If you hunt around you will find some interesting problems. An old PMA (Pennsylvania Mountaineering Association) member used to have parties at his nearby house that hosts amazing boulders adjacent it. He no longer lives there but the boulders still rest a stones throw away from the new tenant's living room.

History

Area local Keith Uhl began to develop Bauer's Rock in the late '70s. At this time a few bolts were placed to protect highballs such as *Two Dollar Tour* V3 and *Monkey Puzzle* V0-R. These climbs were done as lead ascents then later repeated by Keith without a rope. These were some of the first true boulder problems established at Bauer's Rock. Mark Termini and Scott Wagstaf were also active during this time.

In the 1980s Darryl Roth became active at Bauer's Rock establishing problems such as *The Wrath of Roth* and other hard problems on *The Doors Boulder* (named for Doors graffiti on the boulder). Darryl Roth was very active at Bauer's during the '80s. He sent many classic lines and numerous eliminates. Kim Stiner was around for some notable contributions to the area as well as Jeff Ellison who established *Jeff's Arete* V7, a challenging but often overlooked classic.

During the '90s Bauer's Rock fell into a state of obscurity, seeing few climbers cling to its paint skinned boulders. One ambitious climber who *was* active during this time was Karen Vantine. Karen climbed a great deal of problems at Bauer's and nearby Emmaus Boulders. Also in the '90s, Dave Pfurr, of Emmaus fame, was an active climber at Bauer's. Dave came up with some great eliminates and classic problems. I was also active in developing a handful of problems like *Graffiti Artist* V5, *Naughty by Nature* V3, *Post Modern Problem* V6, and some notable problems in the V7 range.

In present times, the sport of bouldering is undertaking a large growth and so is Bauer's Rock. Hard corps locals toy with endless eliminate-problems and variations of existing classics at every outing. Recent new lines have been put up by Aaron Love, Dave Lloyd, Mike Pezzuto, Judy Racosky and other local climbers.

Geology: Ordovician carbonate with a feel between Diabase with some granitelike features—also paint.

Directions

From the junction of 4th street and Emmaus Avenue in southern Allentown (Mountainville) take State Route 145 south and follow the hill to a crest. At the light make a left onto East Rock Road. Follow the road slightly less than one mile and you will see a parking area on the right with a gate. There used to be a sign here that said Big Rock Park. Walk past the gate and down the road until you come to a fenced-in area with a large tower behind it. Walk the trail on the left side of the fence and continue straight back to the rock. From the parking lot to the boulders should take no more than 5 minutes of walking.

The first area you come to is the main bouldering spot. Obvious graffiti marks the *Graffiti Pile Left* (on your left) and the *Pump Monster* boulder perched on ledges on the right. The *Incredible Hunk* boulder is located way off to the right as well as three smaller satellite boulders (*Dish*, *Lost*, and *Doors* boulders). The *Paleface* and *Homer's* boulders are located straight downhill from the *Graffiti Pile*.

206

A. Graffiti Pile Left

This is the pile of boulders you can see when you are standing at the top of the outcrop after walking in on the approach trail. Looking downhill, these boulders are on your left-hand side. Several warm ups can be done here as well as a few challenging classics.

1. Monkey Business V0-

When you walk in this is the first boulder on your left. From a standing start pull up on crimps in the center of a short face and top out.
Var. 1: Graffiti Artist V5 Do the same problem from a sitting start, beginning on low crimps out right.

2. Paintastrophe V1

Climb the face right of the previous route without using the crack or stepping onto the boulder on the right. Finish at the highest point of the boulder.

3. Cave Climb VB

Climb up and out of the cave via a crack where two boulders meet.

4. Pitfall V0

Find your way out of the pit that is hidden in the boulder pile above the cave.

5. Graffiti Crack VB

Climb either of the two cracks or between them.

6. Hidden Problem V1

SDS on jugs and gain a smooth arete and climb it to the top.
Var. 1: Hidden Escape V1 From a sit start climb the previous problem and move out left.

7. Two-Dollar Tour V3

Before the advent of the crash pad this problem was done by Keith Uhl as a very short lead route. This route was quite possibly the shortest

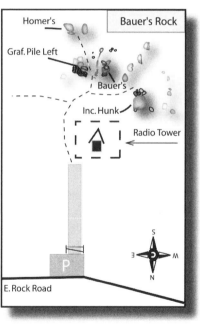

lead route in the world. Keith did the route shortly after this as a regular boulder problem (unroped) and was going to remove the bolt; however, this bolt is one of climbing's historical landmarks and I'm glad to see that it was left in.

Climb the sloping bulge directly over a heavily-rusted bolt. A sit start was also done to the problem at V4.
Var. 1: Post Modern Problem V6 Sloping holds and long reaches make for an exciting problem. SDS on the corner and make a long move out left to a hidden hold around the corner. Finish above.

8. Jam Crack V1

207

Start low and jam the crack just right of *Two-Dollar* Tour.

Var. 1: Poki Arete V5 SDS in the crack and move right to the arete.

9. Dyno-Mite V1

Do a fantastic dyno around the corner on the short face, right of the previous climb.

10. Unnamed V2

SDS on small crimps and then pull over a bulge to a dirty top out.

B. Bauer's Rock (Lower Tier)

This is the wall directly across from *Graffiti Pile Left*. It is the lower tier of rock with a ledge above and large boulders (*Pump Monster Boulder*) perched above. The routes are labeled from left to right.

11. The Grimearete V1

Start right of *Acid Drop* and climb the arete on the right side of the lower tier of this outcrop.

12. Acid Drop V8

SDS on the overhanging face with a peace symbol—or whatever is painted on it this week—and make a huge dyno to an exciting top out.

13. Hoover V0-

Use crimps to crank up the left side of a short, steep wall. Using the broken corner to the left is considered off route.

14. Pile Driver VB

Skum up the broken corner right of *Acid Drop*.

C. Pump Monster Boulder

This boulder is actually a grouping of boulders located on a ledge above the previous problems. The grouping has a large overhang on its downhill side and an amazing overhanging wall on its west side. Old bolts can be found on top the *Pump Monster* route/ problem. Use caution when using these. They are quite old.

15. The Escape Club V0

Easy moves lead out the left side of a roof to a tricky face.

16. Jelly Bean Roof V2

This problem was originally done as an aid route. Use a thin seam to lunge to a lip in the center of an overhang. Pull over it and top out.

17. Jaws of Doom V0-

Climb out the crack at the right side of the roof.

18. The Morrell V0-

A Morrell is a type of mushroom (non-hallucinogenic). A small patch of them used to grow under this problem. From a SDS climb the small boulder that touches the right side of the

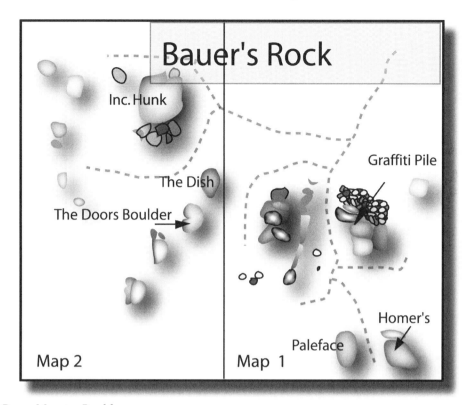

Pump Monster Boulder.

19. Hangman V2- R

A high problem with scary top moves. Climb the left side of the overhang.

20. Brass Bowl V0- R

From the *Jaws of Doom* roof, walk left to gain the backside of the outcrop. Look up to spot a high, extremely overhanging wall (*Pump Monster*) perched on a ledge. *Brass Bowl* climbs the small face to the right of the big overhanging wall.

21. Power Hitter V0-

Start the same as for *Brass Bowl* but instead of going straight up the face, move left before a bulge and traverse left across the face.

22. Power Hitter Direct V0

Start a little bit left of *Power Hitter* and climb a crack/flake to join *Power Hitter* at the top out.

23. Pump Monster V3 X

High, steep, and really dangerous. There are old anchor bolts on top if you prefer to TR this one; I strongly recommend a TR. Climb the center of the severely overhanging face left of *Power Hitter*.

D. Paleface Boulder

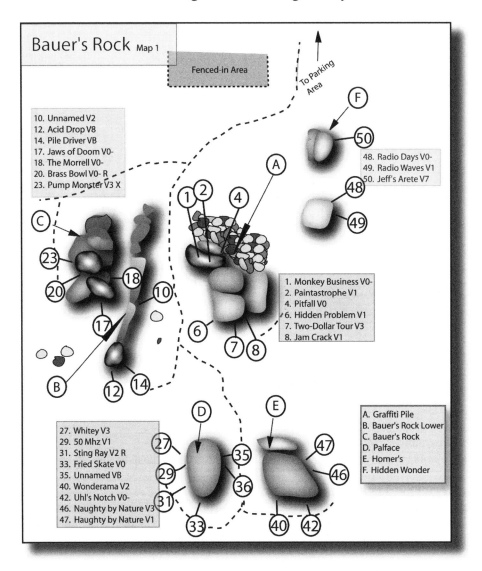

Bauer's Rock Map 1

Fenced-in Area

To Parking Area

F

10. Unnamed V2
12. Acid Drop V8
14. Pile Driver VB
17. Jaws of Doom V0-
18. The Morrell V0-
20. Brass Bowl V0- R
23. Pump Monster V3 X

48. Radio Days V0-
49. Radio Waves V1
50. Jeff's Arete V7

1. Monkey Business V0-
2. Paintastrophe V1
4. Pitfall V0
6. Hidden Problem V1
7. Two-Dollar Tour V3
8. Jam Crack V1

A. Graffiti Pile
B. Bauer's Rock Lower
C. Bauer's Rock
D. Palface
E. Homer's
F. Hidden Wonder

27. Whitey V3
29. 50 Mhz V1
31. Sting Ray V2 R
33. Fried Skate V0
35. Unnamed VB
40. Wonderama V2
42. Uhl's Notch V0-
46. Naughty by Nature V3
47. Haughty by Nature V1

Named for its clean, pale-looking face. You can access this boulder by walking straight down a faint trail that starts at the bottom of *Graffiti Pile* and leads downhill a few minutes walk. You'll come to a low-profile boulder on the left called *Homers Boulder*, and the *Paleface Boulder* on the right. These two boulders are the cleanest and best quality boulders here.

27. Whitey V3
Climb the center of a small face using crimps and a seam on the left side of the northwest face of this boulder.

28. Daryl's Crack V0-
Climb the nice crack just right of the previous route.

29. 50 MHz V1
Without using the corner, climb past slanting cracks two feet right of *Daryl's Crack*.

30. Zigzag Crack VB
Fire up this beautiful zigzag crack.

31. Sting Ray Petting Zoo V2 R
At the right side of the *Paleface Boulder*, climb up a right-slanting ramp and move straight up over a bulge. Using the corner of the boulder makes this problem easier.

32. Unnamed V0
Climb the easy section of rock right of the previous problem.

33. Fried Skate V0
This climb is on the low-angle face around the corner from *Sting Ray*. From a sitting start climb over a bulge to slab and then climb the easy slab to the top.

Joe Forte cruising an area classic. Photo by a Manasseh Franklin.

34. Unnamed V0-
SDS and climb the face right of the previous climb.

35. Unnamed VB
Climb the right side of the boulder.

36. Wanderlust V0+
Begin on number 35 and traverse left using a horizontal crack. Continue to traverse the crack and top out where the crack reaches the top of the boulder.

37. Unnamed V0-
Climb the face.

38. Unnamed V0-
Climb the easy face next to the previous route.

39.Unnamed V0-
The easy face right of the previous problem.

211

E. Homers Boulder

This boulder is the large boulder directly across from the *Paleface Boulder*. Some excellent problems are located on the boulder's downhill side.

Manasseh Franklin climbing at Bauer's. Photo by Joe Forte.

40. Wonderama V2

Climb the left-downhill corner of the boulder by using the corner and face just left of the arete.

41. Unnamed V1

Delicate moves let you travel over the thin face in the center of the boulder.

42. Uhl's Notch V0-

Begin to the right of a big V-notch at the roof section of this boulder. Balance up the face to a big horizontal and then traverse left squirming through the notch.

43. Unnamed V0

Start the same as the previous route, but instead of climbing through the notch continue to traverse left, until it is possible to top out where the horizontal meets the left side of the roof.

44. Unnamed

Begin by climbing problem number 43 until you are left of the notch and pull directly over the center of the roof.

45. Unnamed V2

Climb the section of rock right of the previous problem.

46. Naughty by Nature V3

From a SDS, begin on a small face just left of an arete. Traverse right and around the arete to a jug. Dyno up to a good hold and top out.

47. Haughty by Nature V1

Crank on positive holds just right of the previous problem. The right corner is off route.

F. Hidden Wonder Boulder

This boulder is located off left in the woods, before you reach the main Bauers Rock outcrop. It is a square boulder that is hard to find.

48. Radio Days V0-
Climb the arete.

49. Radio Waves V1
From a low start climb the center of the face.

50. Jeff's Arete V7
A true achievement for the 1980s. Climb the hidden arete from a sit start. This problem is located on a boulder hidden low in the woods near the *Hidden Wonder Boulder*.

A. The Incredible Hunk Boulder (a.k.a. The Brain Boulder)

This very large boulder is tricky to find in the summer because it is blocked by vegetation. It is easier to find in winter. To locate this boulder, stop just before Bauer's Rock and walk off to your right on a faint trail. After three minutes you should see a very large boulder with a low roof on the uphill side, and a slab on the downhill-right (west) side.

1. Cock Ring V0
Start on the leftmost side of this boulder and behind a boulder on the ground. Begin on holds left of the small dihedral and hand traverse right over a short, steep wall. Top out at the right side. A few variations can be done pulling up the steep wall.

2. Pinkie and the Brain V1
Crouch start on the jutting knob of rock near a large boulder on the ground and grunt up over it.

3. The Prow VB or V1
This is a stand start to the previous problem.

4. Ring Grip V1
Climb the crack/corner at the left side of the low roof and right of the previous climb.

5. Time Traveler VB
Start at the previous problem and step right above the roof. Traverse a ramp to the top.

6. Aruf Roof V2
At the center of the roof, use a cheatstone or grab the lip of the roof and climb up and right to the top.

7. Escapade V7
SDS and climb edges under the roof just right of the peace sign. Pull the roof and top out. One of the best problems here.

8. Nerve Ending VB
Climb the right side of the overhang from a standing start.

9. Lobes VB
Climb the left side of the greenish-colored slab.

10. Monkey Puzzle V0- R
Using small flakes and knobs climb the center of the steep slab near prehistoric bolts.

11. Impossible Dream V2 R
Climb the right-hand side of the slab using vertical faults.

12. Alpine Route V0-
Around and right from the previous route, climb up without using the large rock to step on.

B. The Dish
This boulder is a small boulder with a steep side located directly below and west of the *Pump Monster* face.

13. The Dish V1
Climb the center of the boulder. Several variations of the boulder have been done at slightly harder and easier grades.

Joe Forte, "Uhl's Notch," photo by Manasseh Franklin.

C. The Doors Boulder
This is the next small, rod-shaped boulder below and slightly to the side of *The Dish*.

14. The Wrath of Roth V4
One of the best problems of its grade at this area. From a low start move off thin crimps at the left side of the boulder.

15. Unnamed V2
Climb the center of the boulder.

16. The End V3
Climb the right arete from a sit start. Some easier variations exist to the right.

D. Lost Boulder
This boulder is located at the farthest, west end of the hill. Walk downhill a bit from *The Doors Boulder* and you will see a faint trace of rock where the hill slopes down to the west. This boulder's overhanging face is hidden and easy to miss. Slightly below the boulder is a building from a radio complex.

17. Aerodynamics V7
SDS and climb the small, left-side face of the boulder, and move right to top out at the smooth corner.

18. Up Your Nose V8
SDS on the nose of rock just right of *Aerodynamics*.

19. Orange Munge V5
SDS in the center of the overhanging face near loose, sharp edges.

E. Miscellaneous Boulders V0-/V1
Several small boulders lie scattered around the previous boulders. Problems are short and range from V0- to V1.

Other Bauer's Rock Boulders

At least 10 other established boulders lie scattered throughout the hillside. Many problems in the V0 to V6 range have been done on these boulders. The better boulders are downhill and facing Quakertown. Most are tricky to find, that's why they aren't included.

Problems in the V10 range exist on some boulders within a 5 mile radius of Bauer's. Unfortunately, the boulders are highly access sensitive.

A nearby area called the Patriot Boulders was developed by Keith Uhl and myself. Darryl Roth was also active at this area. The area only has a few problems but they are high and fun. The area is in downtown Allentown near the railroad and the river off Constitution. Information about this area can be found on www.paclimbing.com in the near future.

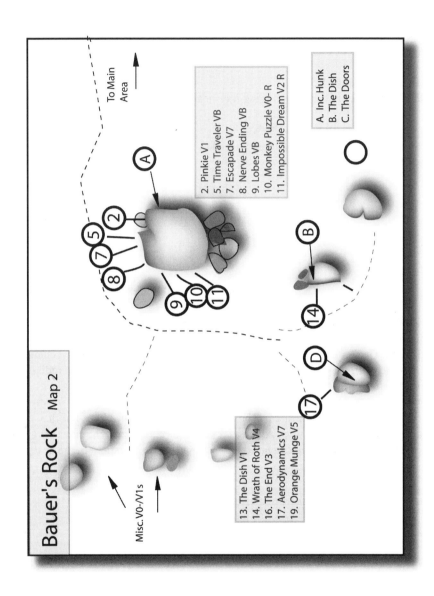

Bauer's Rock   Map 2

To Main Area

Misc. V0-/V1s

2. Pinkie V1
5. Time Traveler VB
7. Escapade V7
8. Nerve Ending VB
9. Lobes VB
10. Monkey Puzzle V0- R
11. Impossible Dream V2 R

A. Inc. Hunk
B. The Dish
C. The Doors

13. The Dish V1
14. Wrath of Roth V4
16. The End V3
17. Aerodynamics V7
19. Orange Munge V5

13. Haycock Mountain Bouldering Area

G. Filippini

Area Beta

Location
Lake Nockimixon State Park near Quakertown.

Type of Climbing
The most popular diabase bouldering area anyplace.

Other Info
Bring a pad. Summer can be a horrendous time to climb here.

Haycock Mountain

Haycock Mountain offers a tremendous amount of bouldering on Triassic Diabase, a unique type of rock found almost exclusively in this fortunate part of the world. Southeastern Pennsylvania is blessed to host this fabulous rock type. This rock type is found almost exclusively in "The Diabase Belt" that runs from southern New Jersey to South-central Pennsylvania. South Africa is the only other part of the world this rock type is found in. This is a pretty big claim for Pennsylvania due to the modern Diabase craze sweeping the East.

This rock has recently become more and more popular due to its unique qualities and knack for yielding difficult problems. Because of this, Haycock Mountian has become one of the most popular bouldering destinations in the state. Due to its geographical location near several major metropolitan locations, this climbing area has become a popular destination for climbers all around the tri-state area and Southeastern Pennsylvania.

Perhaps, the greatest lure to the mountain is the incredible amount of boulders around the mountain. The vast amount of quality stone in the area still yields a good amount of potential for new boulder problems. Several hundred problems lie nestled throughout the deeply-forested woodland. Problems ranging from V0- to V12 make this area diverse enough to challenge virtually any level climber: problems hard enough for the seasoned hard man, yet easy enough for novice climbers to have a very enjoyable outing as well.

This diverse Mecca of rock offers smoothly-sculpted boulders varying in height from a few feet to 20' tall. These intriguing sculptures have finely-molded scoops, fins, aretes,

217

bulges, and other amazing features. One look at these unique geologic features, and you can't help but think that this area was meant for bouldering. After spying the next outcrop in the distance, you'll wonder what unique treasure waits in the distance.

The vast network of trails on the mountain can be a bit confusing. Due to this problem, it is recommended for first-time climbers to hook up with a local or knowledgeable climber for a tour of the boulder fields. Most local climbers are excited to help newer climbers to the area. Due to the scattered nature of the boulders, I have made every attempt to make the most detailed maps for the area that I was capable of. Hopefully, it will be useful to Haycock first-timers. Particularly in the summertime, trails can be quite confusing to navigate due to large amounts of vegetation.

One deterrent can be the landings. Although many problems can be found with good, flat landings, large amounts of talus are abundant under many of the boulders. For this reason a crash pad, even two, will be a valuable asset to have on the mountain.

This guide offers a select amount of problems found on the mountain. There are so many boulder problems on the mountain that it would go well beyond the scope of this book to include all the problems at the area—unless the thought of carrying a three-ring binder to the rocks appeals to you. I tried to include the more popular areas and the best problems. By no means are these all the good problems on the mountain. This book will get you to the more popular areas and give you an idea of some of the classics.

Should you plan to visit Haycock on a regular basis, I highly recommend purchasing Char Fetterolf's *Bouldering on Haycock Mountian*. Char's guide is an excellent in-depth guide that is regularly updated.

This area can be classified as one of the more highly traveled, popular areas to climb in Pennsylvania. For these reasons, great problems can be found at almost every area on the mountain. When you visit here, allow yourself the opportunity to come more than once. This will allow the time to accurately get a feel for what the bouldering here is all about. If you love to boulder, visit this area. The rock quality here is four-star. You would be more likely to find a new problem before a lose hold. A playground of modern bouldering *Haycock* will not disappoint any level climber.

History

Much of the rock on Haycock mountain was pioneered by Pete Cody. Some of the earliest documented climbing on the mountain was by Ed Vansteinwick. In the late '70s, Ed put up several lines near the top of the mountain. Pete Cody later became active and added many of the original classics. Bob D'Antonio and other Philadelphia climbers along with climbers from the Northeast like Nick Morell, Ryan Lukas, and myself were introduced to the area. A fair amount of new problems up to V7 were established during this time.

During the '90s climbers like Mark Ronca, Pete Zeigenfuss, Dave Lloyd and many others added lines into the V9 range. Shortly after this, an incredible amount of climbers began to frequent the mountain. Char Feterolf was perhaps the most active adding perhaps more lines than any other climber. His problems extend well into the V12 range.

Haycock Mountain

Geology: Triassic Diabase.

Access and Restrictions: Haycock Mountain is located on State Gamelands property just outside the border of Lake Nockamixon State Park.

Hazards and Dangers: Crash pads, water, and other items are recommended but two necessities are a fresh layer of skin and forearms full of strength. If you are not used to Diabase, it is abrasive to the skin. Perhaps the most threatening hazard on the mountain is hunters. It is a little known fact that there are more people in the woods with guns the first day of hunting season than there were in the entire Vietnam War. Wear orange during hunting season!

Many landings at Haycock are hazardous. A crash pad is recommended when climbing on the mountain. Also, remember to bring plenty of water or other hydrating fluids since many of the boulders are a long hike from the car. Pay close attention to retracing your footsteps if you venture far into the reaches of the mountain as trails are not always well marked. If you're not familiar with the mountain, it's easy to get lost.

Tics and Poison-ivy are prevalent on the mountain. Snakes and spiders can also be a nuisance here. I was once bit by a poisonous spider that swelled my leg like a balloon. Wear repellant or visit here during winter—it's easer to find the boulders in winter too.

The area can be busy on weekends. Hungry crowds visit each weekend looking to fill their appetite for Diabase testpieces.

Camping: Camping is not permitted on the mountain. Here are two options for pay-camping: Tinicum Campground, Bucks County Parks and Recreation Department, located off route 32 (River Road), Erwinna, PA (215) 757-0571 Deer Run Campground, Bucks County Parks and Recreation Department, Cafferty Road, Point Pleasant, PA (215) 757-0571 A Youth Hostel is located at the south end of the park: 215-536-8749 Cabins can be rented at the park: 888-PA-PARKS

Season: The prime season to climb on the mountain is September to May. The fall and winter offer excellent conditions for friction on the slopy rock; however, keep in mind that winter temperatures can drop below zero. Summer is a popular time but humid conditions, moist, damp rock, bugs, Poison-ivy, and dense vegetation dissuade many climbers at this time. Many climbs are a grade harder in the humid summer conditions.

Directions

From the north: From Quakertown head south on State Route 313 until you reach State Route 563. Turn (left) north on Route 563 and follow signs for Lake Nockamixon State Park. Follow Route 563 for 6.5 miles, and turn left on Top Rock Trail, a small paved road. If you reach the blinking light at the junction of 563 and 412, you went 1 mile too far. Follow Top Rock Trail Road approximately .5 mile to a fair-sized gravel parking area on the left. A trail starts at the top end of the parking lot left of the gate. Walk 10-15 minutes up this trail, veering left at a boulder (*Trail-split Boulder*) for Areas 1-7 (not including Area 2) or right for Area 2.

Area 1/Map 1
Teddy Bear Area

This area encompasses a group of boulders just off the trail, about 10-15 minutes walk from the parking lot. It is the first major series of boulders you come to when walking the trail from the parking lot. The area starts at a small boulder just off the trail (*The Bubbler*) and continues to *The Teddy Bear Boulder*, a large boulder off to the right of the main trail.

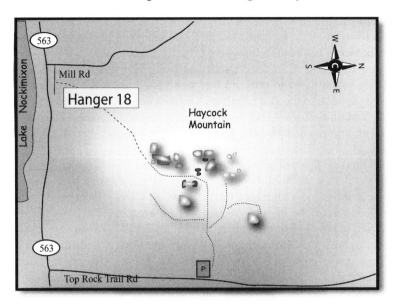

Several smaller satellite boulders can be found in this area as well. The *Tri-Force Boulder* is the most notable of these satellite boulders. The V10 problem *Peligro* can be found on this boulder.

Approach Boulders
When hiking in, after 10 minutes of walking, you will reach a boulder where two trails fork off to the right and left. The problems start about two minutes walk from here and continue on the small hard to locate boulders from here all the way to the *Fun Boulder*.

1. The Bubbler V6
A few minutes walk past the *Trail Split Boulder*, take the left split and find a small, 6'- high boulder off the right side of the trail, just past a large open area of trees. The boulder has an overhanging corner and face on the opposite side of the side the trail is on. Sit start and climb this side.

A. The Fun Boulder
This boulder is only a few paces past the previous boulder. It has a large scoop-like slab and is located right off the trail.

2. Dave's Problem V1
Climb the detached boulder just left of the scoop-like slab. Sit start.

3. Fun Boulder Problem VB
Climb the left side of the slab.

4. Slope Book V0-
Climb the shallow openbook feature in the center of the slab.

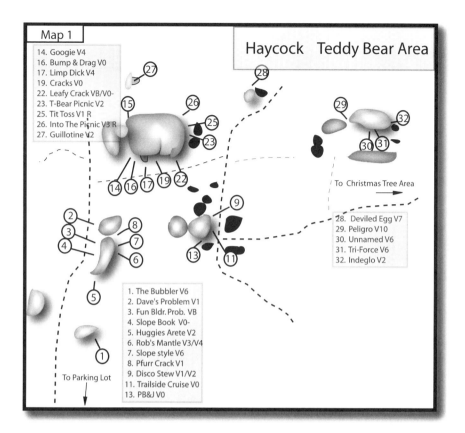

Map 1

14. Googie V4
16. Bump & Drag V0
17. Limp Dick V4
19. Cracks V0
22. Leafy Crack VB/V0-
23. T-Bear Picnic V2
25. Tit Toss V1 R
26. Into The Picnic V3 R
27. Guillotine V2

Haycock   Teddy Bear Area

To Christmas Tree Area

28. Deviled Egg V7
29. Peligro V10
30. Unnamed V6
31. Tri-Force V6
32. Indeglo V2

1. The Bubbler V6
2. Dave's Problem V1
3. Fun Bldr. Prob. VB
4. Slope Book V0-
5. Huggies Arete V2
6. Rob's Mantle V3/V4
7. Slope style V6
8. Pfurr Crack V1
9. Disco Stew V1/V2
11. Trailside Cruise V0
13. PB&J V0

To Parking Lot

5. Huggies Arete V2
SDS and climb the overhanging, smooth back-side corner just right of the previous route.

6. Rob's Mantle V4
SDS on broken edges three feet right of *Huggies*. Next, climb up to and over a mantle at head-level.

7. Slope Style V6
Climb the face right of *Rob's Mantle*. The large crack to the right is off route.

8. Pfurr Crack V1
Climb the large crack and corner at the right end and backside of *The Fun Boulder*.

B. The Picnic Rock
Looking uphill from *The Fun Boulder*, walk directly to your right a few paces through the woods and you will run into *The Picnic Rock*. It is located on the Blue Trail.

9. Disco Stew V1/V2
Looking to the left off the Blue Trail, this is the rightmost arete.

10. Trailside Triumph V0-
Climb the left face that touches the arete of *Disco Stew*.

11. Trailside Cruise V0
Inches left of the previous climb, cruise up rock over a bulge between *Disco Stew* and *Air*.

12. Air VB
Climb the left side of the face over horizontal cracks.

13. PB and J V0
Climb the downhill, smooth, and bulging corner near a rock behind the corner.

B. Teddy Bear Boulder
This boulder is directly uphill and slightly left of *Picnic Rock*. It is a large boulder and is only a few paces uphill from both the *Picnic* and *Fun* boulders.

14. Googie V4
Looking at the boulder, climb the sloping-left corner near a boxed-out section. Traverse the corner back into the rear and top out.

15. Jeff's Route V1/V6
Doing this route without a fist jam (originally done this way) increases the grade to a V6. Climb out from underneath a rock leaning against the back face and climb up and right to mantle on a ledge.

16. Bump and Drag V0
SDS and climb the right side of the back corner of this boulder. Other variations of this problem have been done at the same grade.

17. Limp Dick V4
Not recommended for some men and may frighten some women. This climb starts by jumping to the phallic-looking protrusion in the left center of this boulder. From here climb up and right to top out at a seam 5' back.

18. Flying Matilda V5
Sidewalls are off. Start under the previous climb at an undercling and climb up and over the big knob.

19. Cracks V0
There are two cracks just right of the previous problems. They can be climbed individually, separate, or in between the two at the same grade.

20. Slender Crack V0+
A few inches right of the previous two cracks is another crack that goes at a slightly harder grade.

21. Squeeze Job V1
Climb the easy face near the crack. Using the crack is off route.

22. Leafy Crack V0-/VB
Near the right-hand corner of the boulder, climb the vegetated crack up onto the face above.

23. Teddy Bear Picnic V2
Climb the beautiful, overhanging crack in the center of this boulder.

24. Show Me Yours V4 R
Begin a few feet right of *Teddy Bear Picnic* and go up to a crimpy rail and then the top.

25. Tit Toss V1 R
Start down low on the right side of the overhanging face of *The Teddy Bear Boulder* and climb to two crimps. Fire for the top.

26. Into the Picnic V3 R
Start on *Tit Toss* and climb left to merge with *Teddy Bear Picnic*.

27. The Guillotine V2
This is a small feature of rock a few feet behind *The Teddy Bear Boulder* near the Red Trail. SDS and climb the feature of rock a few feet off the ground that looks like a blade. The boulders on the sides are off route.

28. The Deviled Egg V7
A few paces up and right from *Into the Picnic* you will come to a small, 7'-high egg-shaped boulder with another small boulder connected to its right side. Squeeze the egg and avoid using the boulder on the right. Using the boulder on the right drops the grade to V6.

C. Tri-Force Boulder (A.K.A.) The Amphitheatre
Looking uphill at *The Teddy Bear Boulder*, this boulder is directly right of *T.B.* Walk across the Blue Trail and there is a faint trail that leads to it. If you walk more than one minute you went too far. The boulder is a long, rounded boulder with a nice landing and an insignificant, long boulder directly across from it.

29. Peligro V10
A blindingly hard classic that was first done by Chris Redmond. Start under the left alcove of the boulder with your left hand in a good crack and your right stretched out to a small crimp and fire to gain the sloping top.

30. Unnamed V6
Climb the center of the boulder over rounded, sloping rock at a vertical fault.

31. Little Secret (A.K.A.) the Tri-Force V6
As hard and grueling as it looks. Start in a shallow dihedral at the boulders right side (contrived standing start) and traverse left past vertical flakes almost to *Peligro* and top out on the slab.

32. Indeglo V2
SDS in a shallow dish at the right end of the boulder with feet on/under a small overhang. Slap up and left in a shallow dish-area. The boulders on the ground are off.

33. Easy Versant V0+
This problem starts near the previous problem and climbs straight up the dish. Basically an easier variation of the previous problem.

D. Classical Boulder
This boulder is located directly behind *The Deviled Egg* and can be tricky to find.

34. Mozart on His Way to Prague V4 R
Traverse the left side of the boulder while following a crack.

35. Novella V1
Climb the right side of the slab.

Area 2 (Not Mapped)
Lower Blue Trail and Yellow Trail Areas
This small area is located to the right of and below the above area (Area 1). To find the boulders mentioned below, walk right at the square boulder (*Trail-split* Boulder) that splits the trail coming from the parking lot. If you make a left at this boulder you will end up at Area 1. If you make a right you will end up at Area 2.

1. Slap Happy V3
From the trail split (10-15 minutes walk from the parking lot) go right. Walk another 5-10 minutes up the Blue Trail and you will see a small boulder in the woods off the left of the trail (quite difficult to locate). SDS and gain two slots and fire up over the bulge. The crack at the left is off route.

2. Humpty Hump V3
This problem is very difficult to locate. Off to the right and in the woods is a thin, high boulder with a rounded downhill side. Hump the two smooth aretes to the top.

3. Alien Head V0-
SDS and climb the boulder off to the right of the Blue Trail a short ways past *Slap Happy*. It looks like the head of an alien and is quite easy to locate. The problem goes up the side of the boulder that you can't see from the trail.

4. Chiba V4
Walking through the woods past *Alien Head*, this is the next boulder you will come to. Begin low on an incut that is slightly above a right facing protrusion, and climb up and left.

5. Sleeping Puppy V1
This problem is on a boulder that can be found by taking a faint trail uphill a few-hundred feet after starting on the Yellow Trail. It can also be reached by walking away from the

Blue Trail at *The Amphitheatre*. Hold each side of the ear-like formations on both sides of this boulder and run up the top out.

6. Domino Boulder
Located past *Sleeping Puppy*, follow another bad trail uphill, and a short walk will lead to this boulder. Walk uphill and slightly right from *Sleeping Puppy*.

7. Unnamed Arete V2
Easier if tall. Climb up the downhill arete.

8. The Float V2
Climb the face just right of the previous climb.

9. Jale V4
SDS and climb out from under a roof to the arete.

Area 3/Map 2
Summit Area Lower
This area is a collection of boulders located just below the summit of the mountain. Many boulders can be found to the left and right of the trail here. To find this area, simply walk uphill from *Teddy Bear* on the main trail and you will run into *The Pit Overhang* and *Mac Boulder*.

A. The Pit Overhang
About two minutes uphill and right of *The Teddy Bear Boulder* is an overhang/boulder perched above a pit.

1. Pit Crack V0+
Start in the crack under the pit and climb it.

2. Pit Bull V3
Gain the lip of the large boulder capped above the pit and hump over the top.

3. Humpty Dumpty V1
Locate this boulder by stumbling up a faint trail on the back-right end of *The Teddy Bear Boulder*. Climb the short face near a tree.

4. Unnamed V0-
Climb the arete next to the previous problem.

5. Some Other Time V0
Climb the left side of the arete on the boulder left of *Humpty Dumpty*.

D. Mac Boulder
This boulder is located on the Red Trail above *The Teddy Bear Boulder*, and slightly right of and below *The Airplane Tail Boulder*.

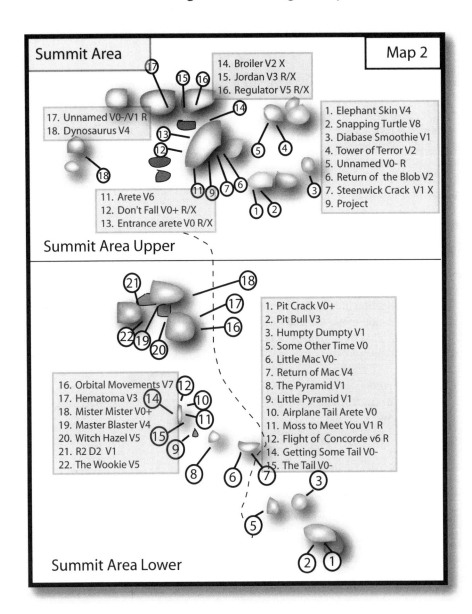

Summit Area

Map 2

14. Broiler V2 X
15. Jordan V3 R/X
16. Regulator V5 R/X

17. Unnamed V0-/V1 R
18. Dynosaurus V4

1. Elephant Skin V4
2. Snapping Turtle V8
3. Diabase Smoothie V1
4. Tower of Terror V2
5. Unnamed V0- R
6. Return of the Blob V2
7. Steenwick Crack V1 X
9. Project

11. Arete V6
12. Don't Fall V0+ R/X
13. Entrance arete V0 R/X

Summit Area Upper

1. Pit Crack V0+
2. Pit Bull V3
3. Humpty Dumpty V1
5. Some Other Time V0
6. Little Mac V0-
7. Return of Mac V4
8. The Pyramid V1
9. Little Pyramid V1
10. Airplane Tail Arete V0
11. Moss to Meet You V1 R
12. Flight of Concorde v6 R
14. Getting Some Tail V0-
15. The Tail V0-

16. Orbital Movements V7
17. Hematoma V3
18. Mister Mister V0+
19. Master Blaster V4
20. Witch Hazel V5
21. R2 D2 V1
22. The Wookie V5

Summit Area Lower

6. Little Mac V0-

Begin on the undercling in the center of the face and top out.

7. Return of Mac V4

Start at the left corner of the boulder, and traverse the lip past underclings by using the top and other holds. Finish at the right end of the boulder.

8. The Pyramid VB/V0-

Between *Teddy Bear* and *Airplane Tail* there is a pyramid-shaped boulder with an easy finger crack (V0-), and an easy slab (VB).

9. Little Pyramid V1
Climb the crack on a small boulder just left of *The Pyramid.*

G. The Airplane Tail
Located one minute up the main trail from *Teddy Bear.* From the left side of *The Teddy Bear Boulder*, walk up the trail until you see a boulder on the left side of the trail that looks like the tail of an airplane. It is across and left from *Return of Mac.*

10. Airplane Tail Arete V0
Looking at the boulder from the main trail climb the right arete.

11. Moss to Meet You V1 R
Climb the center of the slab just left of the arete. The left side of the boulder is off route.
Var. 1: Dink Variation V5 SDS the same problem.

12. Flight of the Concorde V6 R
Start in the pit just around the corner from A*irplane Tail Arete* and climb the left arete of the boulder to the peak.

13. Air France V2
From a low start climb the arete right of *Flight.*

14. Getting Some Tail V0
From a sit start climb the slab on the backside of the tail.

15. The Tail V0-
On the side of the boulder nearest the trail, SDS on the left side of the tail and climb up and right across the tail.

H. Wookie Boulders
This is the group of boulders on the way to *Top Rock.* They consist of three large boulders (not all are visible from the trail) just off the left side of the trail, shortly after the *Airplane Tail.*

16. Atomic Mushroom V7
Delicately balance up the bulge and slab at the left side of this boulder.

17. Hematoma V3
Climb the vertical seam at the right side of the slab.

18. Mister Mister V0+
Climb the blunt, bulging prow.

19. Master Blaster V4
In the pit behind the previous problem, sit start at a crack and throw high to eventually gain the top.

20. Witch Hazel V5

This problem is on the boulder behind the previous problem. Using the rock at the base of the overhang, climb the corner from an undercling.

21. R2-D2 V1

Start in a dihedral and move right.

22. The Wookie V5

Start in the same dihedral as for the previous problem and move left. Top out on the slab above.

Area 4/Map 2
The Summit Area Upper

This is the large clump of boulders at the summit of Haycock Mountain. You can find this area by walking uphill past Area 3. When you see a giant boulder (*Van Steenwick Boulder*) with two high cracks on it, you know you are in the right spot.

A. The Turtle

This boulder is a long, flat rock perched above boulders 100' from *Van Steenwick Crack*.

Dave Pfurr. Photo by the author.

1. Elephant Skin V4

Pull up over the left side of the boulder from a low start, to a grunting top out.

2. Snapping Turtle V8

Traverse the lip of the boulder from *Turtle Crack*. Move left to top out at the left end on the slab's top.

3. Diabase Smoothie V1

SDS and climb the right arete on the boulder that is 30' right of *The Turtle*.

4. The Tower of Terror V2 R

Located between the *Summit Boulders* and the *Van Steenwick Boulder* is a small, high boulder in some talus. It has a crack on its downhill side and a nice arete on its right side. Climb the right arete.

5. Unnamed V0- R

Climb the crack left of the arete.

6. Return of the Blob V2
At the right end of the very high boulder with two highball cracks (*Ed's Crack* and *Van Steenwick Crack*) is a blob-shaped boulder. Begin in a sloping, horizontal crack in the alcove between the boulders, and climb out right onto the slab, and up to top out.

C. Top Rock Lower Boulders
These are the two long, high boulders just below and left of the *Summit Boulders* and *Tower of Terror*.

7. Van Steenwick Crack V1 X
Climb the high finger crack at the right end of this enormous boulder. Top out through block above.

8. Ed's Crack V0 X
The wider crack left of *Van Steenwick's*.

9. Project
Climb the high, blank face left of the previous climb.

10. Unnamed V0- R/X
The corner left of the project line. Move up over big holds.

11. The Arete V6
Climb the arete from a sit start.

12. Don't Fall Please V0+ R/X
The mellow crack around the corner from the previous climb and on the left side of the left wall near the big boulder near the corridor. How's that for a run-on sentence?

13. Entrance Arete V0 R/X
Left of the crack there is an arete at the entrance of the long trench on the backside of this boulder. Climb it.

14. The Broiler V2 X
Looking in the trench from the outside, this climb starts in the alcove on the right-hand wall and climbs a diagonal crack to a slab and a high, dangerous top out.

15. Jordan V3 R/X
Looking in the trench, this climb is on the left-hand wall at the left side. Climb the arete and lunge for a big hold. Continue to the top.

16. The Regulator V5 R/X
Start 15' right of *Jordan*, under a boulder perched at the top of the trench, and climb left on crimps until it's possible to gain the big hold on *Jordan*. Follow *Jordan* to the end.

17. Unnamed V0-/V1 R/X
Left of *Jordan* are a few cracks and face climbs capped by small ceilings above. Several problems have been done here. They vary from V0- to V1, depending on what line you

Jason Olshenske on "Fluffy Clouds." Photo by Jessica Shoemaker.

pick and how you climb it.

D. Dynosarus Boulder
From the previous few problems walk downhill slightly, and a bit right. After passing bad-quality boulders you will see a small boulder with a steep downhill face.
18. Dynosaurus V4
SDS on the left side of the boulder on a big incut, and fly to the top.

E. Summit Boulders
These are the two distinct, large boulders, perched above smaller boulders. They are at the crest of the mountain and overlook the talus below. They are up and 75' behind the *Van Steenwick Boulder*.

9. The Squeeze V0-
Start on the downhill side of the boulder sitting on the small slab at the left end of the leftmost boulder. Climb up and into the groove between the two boulders and squeeze up the gap.

20. The Watchtower V1 R
Start right of the previous problem and climb up to the blade of rock on the right-hand side of the two formations that make *The Summit Boulders*. Move out onto the face near a rock and continue to the top.

21. Summit Pit V3 R
A nice climb with a burly top out. Start on the backside of the summit boulder outcrop and climb up and out of the obvious pit.

22. Unnamed Arete V0 R
Climb the back arete near the *Summit Pit*.

23. The Blob V0-
Climb the right side of the boulder adjacent to *Summit Pit*. This is the small boulder left of the formation when looking at the formation from the backside.

24. The Shard
This is the boulder slightly behind and left of the summit formation when looking at it from the backside. The arete goes at V2; the face goes at V1.

Area 5/Map 3
Christmas Tree Area
This area is located 5 minutes walk on the Yellow Trail from the Blue Trail and *Picnic Rock*.

A. Bullet Hole Boulder
Located approximately 5 minutes walk up the Yellow Trail (the trail that splits off the Blue Trail at *Picnic Rock* and goes right). It is touching the left side of the Yellow Trail and has built holes shot into it and a dot painted on it near the trail.

1. Bullet Arete V0-
SDS on the right arete of the boulder right of the *Bullet Hole* problem.

2. Bullet Hole V1/V2
The problem is V1 if done using the holds on the face, V2 if you skip them. Climb the center of the boulder.

B. Jumbly Boulders
A short way past *The Bullet Hole Boulder*, two boulders with an insignificant boulder between them have some nice problems on them.

3. Unnamed V0-
Climb the corner next to the trail on the leftmost of the two main boulders.

4. Mumbly Pegs V3
Climb the face near the tree on the trail on the rightmost of the two main boulders.

5. Jumbly Corner V1
Cruise up past a big, blocky hold on the left corner of this boulder.

6. Unnamed V0-
Run up the center of the face left of *Jumbly*.

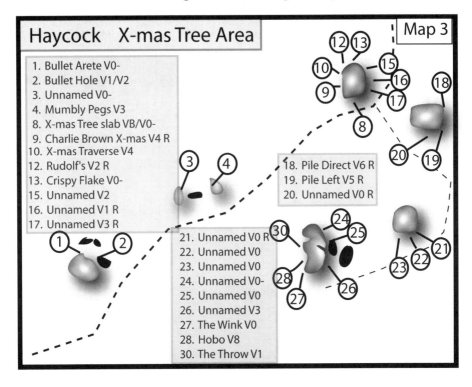

Haycock   X-mas Tree Area

Map 3

1. Bullet Arete V0-
2. Bullet Hole V1/V2
3. Unnamed V0-
4. Mumbly Pegs V3
8. X-mas Tree slab VB/V0-
9. Charlie Brown X-mas V4 R
10. X-mas Traverse V4
12. Rudolf's V2 R
13. Crispy Flake V0-
15. Unnamed V2
16. Unnamed V1 R
17. Unnamed V3 R

18. Pile Direct V6 R
19. Pile Left V5 R
20. Unnamed V0 R

21. Unnamed V0 R
22. Unnamed V0
23. Unnamed V0
24. Unnamed V0-
25. Unnamed V0
26. Unnamed V3
27. The Wink V0
28. Hobo V8
30. The Throw V1

7. Unnamed V0+

Make your way up the easy corner left of the previous problem.

C. The Christmas Tree

This is the large, triangular-shaped boulder with a greenish-colored face. It is located right on the Yellow Trail just past the *Jumbly Boulders*.

8. Christmas Tree Slab VB/V0-

Run up the slab on the short side of the boulder that touches the trail. Easier or harder depending on where you climb it.

Var. 1: V1 Climb the right arete onto the slab a few inches around the corner from the slab route mentioned above.

9. Charlie Brown Christmas V4 R

Climb the blank, center face of the highest part of this boulder past fractures.

10. Christmas Tree Traverse V4

Start on the crack on the left side of the high, triangular face and traverse it up right, and on to the slab around the right corner near the trail.

11. Quanza V2 R

Climb the bulging, shallow corner just left of *Charlie Brown*.

12. Rudolph's Chalked up Nose V2 R
Inches left of the previous problem and just before a small tree climb the shallow corner.

13. Crispy Flake V0-
SDS off a flake on the ground and climb up.

14. Descent VB
The easy climb left of *Crispy* can be used to descend this boulder. I recommend you climb up the problem first.

15. Unnamed V2
On the boulders right side (opposite side of *Charlie Brown*) climb the rightmost corner.

16. Unnamed V1 R
Climb the left center of this boulder 20' left of the previous climb.

17. Unnamed V3 R
Begin at the left side of this boulder, left of the previous climb, and traverse up and high to the right and then top out onto the slab.

D. The Pile
From *The Christmas Tree*, a trail cuts downhill and veers back towards the Blue Trail. This boulder is located just past where this trail shoots off the main trail. The boulder is high on most sides and very high on its back/hidden side. It is a fairly chossy/dirty boulder. It is seldom climbed.

18. Pile Direct V6 R
Begin standing in a horizontal on the right side of the greenish-colored, overhanging face on the backside of this boulder. Climb to the top.

19. Pile Left V5 R
Begin the same as the previous problem and climb up and left.

20. Unnamed V0 R
Climb the left corner of the overhanging face and top out via a finger jam out right.

21. Unnamed V0 R
Climb the face left of and around the corner from the previous problems. You can see the long face from the trail. Climb its center.

E. Green Carpet
Follow the trail downhill and slightly right from *The Pile* and you will see an easy slab touching the trail on the right-hand side. Basically, the next large boulder, two minutes walk downhill from the previous boulder.

24. Unnamed V0-
Climb out of the cave on the top side of the right side of the boulder.

25. Unnamed V0
Climb the grungy crack at the center of the boulder.

26. Unnamed V3
Climb the downhill side of the boulder near the trail.

27. The Wink V0
On the left side of the boulder, right of the tree.

28. Hobo V8
SDS in the alcove at the boulders right-center and climb on thin holds out left to a high, sloping hold.

29. The Opus V9
Same as the previous problem but when you reach the high, sloping hold, continue to an edge out left to get the top.

30. The Throw V1
Climb the tiers in the prow from a low start at the alcoves left side.

31. Pipeline V6
Begin on *The Throw* and traverse out left on a seam.

Area 6/Map 4
Top Rock Area
This is a collection of boulders on the summit of the mountain and left of the *Summit Area*.

A. Top Rock Area
This is the large boulder capped by a triangular-shaped boulder. The formation is behind and a bit right of *Dynosarus*, and left and across from the *Van Steenwick Boulder*.

1. Original Route V1 R
One of the first routes done at Haycock. Climb the left-hand side of the large main boulder. Move right along the roof to a crack and top out.

2. Blood Drop V3
Follow the slanting crack around the corner and left of *Original Route*.

3. Unnamed V4 R
Start at the left end of the boulder and gain the roof. Climb a thin horizontal under the roof-cap.

4. Project
Pull the center of the roof.

B. Pinnacle Rock
This is the boulder off the right end of the main *Top Rock Boulder*.

234

5. Pinnacle V0
Climb the backside of the pinnacle directly behind *The Alcove*.

6. Pinnacle Arete V1
Climb the obvious arete right of the previous problem.

7. The Hop V0
The arete is off. Looking at the formation from downhill, this is the left side of the boulder. Use holds from a ledge to gain the top.

8. Mantable V0+
Looking at the boulder from downhill this is the right side of the boulder, SDS and climb to a block/mantle and top out.

9. The Alcove
Small passage directly behind *Pinnacle* and right of the main *Top Rock* boulder.

10. Mighty Mouse V3
Climb through the big, obvious roof on the right side of the passage.

Photo courtesy of Gino Filippini

11. Hidy-Ho V2
Climb the center of the face on the left-hand side of the passage.

12. The Chimney that Time Forgot V0
From the back of *The Alcove*, take a left and you will see a chimney. Climb it.

C. The Trench
On the backside-left of the *Top Rock* formation is a long trench with a few problems in it.

13. Loose Goose V1
Looking at the back of the trench, this is the right side with a broken flake near its top. SDS on crimps and climb past loose rock.

14. Crack V1
Climb the easy crack across from the previous problem.

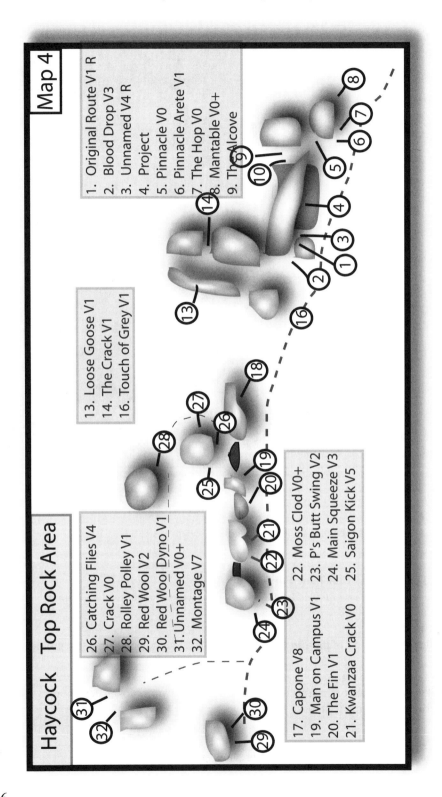

Map 4

Haycock   Top Rock Area

1. Original Route V1 R
2. Blood Drop V3
3. Unnamed V4 R
4. Project
5. Pinnacle V0
6. Pinnacle Arete V1
7. The Hop V0
8. Mantable V0+
9. The Alcove

13. Loose Goose V1
14. The Crack V1
16. Touch of Grey V1

17. Capone V8
19. Man on Campus V1
20. The Fin V1
21. Kwanzaa Crack V0

22. Moss Clod V0+
23. P's Butt Swing V2
24. Main Squeeze V3
25. Saigon Kick V5

26. Catching Flies V4
27. Crack V0
28. Rolley Polley V1
29. Red Wool V2
30. Red Wool Dyno V1
31. Unnamed V0+
32. Montage V7

15. V2

Climb the arete right of the crack. The crack is off route.

16. Touch of Grey V1

Left of the overhang near the large *Top Rock* boulder, move up a seam to the top of the rock.

D. Slope Wall

Left of the *Top Rock* formation is a sloping boulder that is long.

17. Capone V8

Start at the right end of the boulder near a shallow, small dihedral and traverse the sloping rail under the lip to top out near a tree out left. A variation of this problem can be done starting at the left end of the boulder and traversing right.

18. Unnamed V2

Climb the finish of *Capone*.

E. The Glass Wall

The long boulder just left of *The Slope Wall*.

19. Man on Campus V1

Between the *Slope Wall* and *Glass Wall* is a small roof. Start at the right side. SDS and campus to the left and top out.

20. The Fin V1

Near a tree at the right side of the main *Glass Wall* formation, climb the obvious prow.

21. Kwanzaa Crack V0

Climb the flaring seam left of the previous problem.

22. Moss Clod V0+

SDS and climb the flake left of *Kwanzaa*.

23. Pete's Butt Swing V2

Left of the previous problem, start on two incuts and fly to the top.

24. Main Squeeze V3

Start on a bulge left of the previous problem and move right to an edge.
Var. 1: V7 SDS of the same problem.

F. Callous Boulder

Overhanging, small boulder above *Glass Wall*.

25. Saigon Kick V5

SDS on the left arete of the boulder.
Var. 1: Funky Butt Love V5 SDS on left corner and a good hold at right and fire to the top.

26. Catching Flies V4
Climb the center face.

27. Crack V0
Around the back of the boulder is a crack. Climb it.

G. Blob Boulder
Behind the *Callous Boulder* is a blob of rock with a few problems on it.

28. Rolley Polley V1
SDS and climb rolls on the front side of the boulder.

H. Red Wool boulder
Left of and slightly downhill from *Glass Wall*. Bushwhack a bit and find this dirty, small, vertical wall that is about 10' high.

29. Red Wool V2
Start on a sidepull in the middle of the boulder and climb up.

30. Red Wool Dyno V1
SDS on arete right of *Red Wool* and dyno.

31. Unnamed V0+
Climb the backside of the boulder

32. Montage V7
On the left side of the boulder is a passage with a thin seam on its right side. Climb this from a SDS.

33. Unnamed V6
Climb the arete on the boulder behind the previous problem from a low start.

Area 7 (Not Mapped)
The *Tall and Dirty Dome* and *James Brown* areas are located off a faint trail farther past the previous problems. There are no maps for these areas.

A. Tall Dirty Dome
Walking farther left of *Red Wool*, you will pass small talus and choss boulders. After these, the next high boulder is the *Tall Dirty Dome*. It is a pile of dirty choss. Most of the problems here are not worth the walk.

1. Unnamed V3
Walking past the high, dirty dome and you will come to two satellite boulders with rounded corners. SDS and climb the farthest arete.

2. Ridding the Elaphant V7
Straddle the prow with a dish out right and climb up.

3. Unnamed V0-
Climb the easy face.

James Brown Area
Difficult to find and not worth wading the sea of vegetation between the other areas and these low-quality boulders. Continue past *Dirty Dome* and you will find a group of boulders within a few minutes walk.

4. Escapeism V0
Climb the left side of the face to a horizontal with a loose block in it.

5. Funky President V0
Right of the previous route.

6. Cup of Tea V4
SDS and climb an arete out of a pit. Overhanging and hard.

Area 8/Map 5
Gateway Area
Locate this area by walking on a side trail from *The Fun Boulder* or a side trail near *The Teddy Bear Boulder*.

A. The Gateway Boulders
This area and these boulders can be found by walking left through the woods on a faint trail near *The Teddy Bear Boulder*. It is the next distinctive series of boulders you will reach.

1. Lip Service V0-
SDS and climb the left lip of the small boulder.

2. Unnamed V0-
Climb right of the previous problem.

3. Unnamed V0-
Climb the easy face.

4. Throwing Oranges at the Eskimos V3
The arete across from *Nightmere Arete*. Sit start and climb up.

5. Unnamed V0-
Climb the flake around the corner and up the wall to the left of *Throwing Oranges*.

6. Empty Words V2
Climb the face on the boulder directly across from the previous problem.

7. Jesus Calls for War a.k.a. The Nightmare Arete V7 R
Climb the beautiful, clean arete on the downhill side of the boulder.

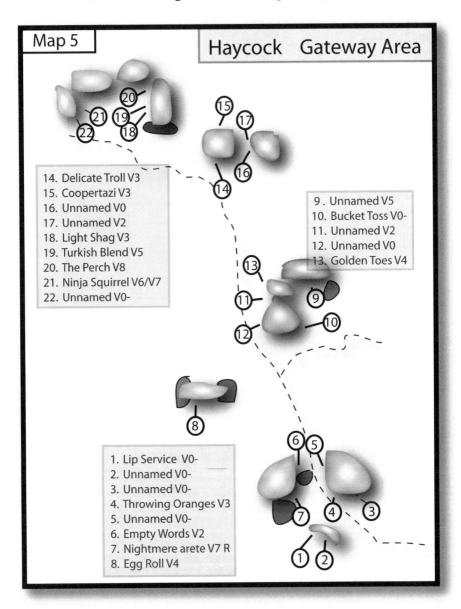

8. The Egg Roll V4

Begin low on an undercling and climb up the roof. The boulder below is on route for the start of this problem.

Golden Toes Boulders

This group of three boulders is located a few minutes walk uphill and slightly left of *The Gateway Area*. You can also walk to *The Wookie* by walking right for a few minutes.

9. Unnamed V5
This boulder is the long boulder at the top of the group. SDS on sidepulls and finish out left.

10. Bucket Toss V0-
Climb the arete downhill from the previous problem.

11. Unnamed V2
Climb the face from a sloping hold that is up from and left of the arete.

12. Unnamed V0
Climb the arete left of *Bucket Toss*, on the other side of the boulder.

Turkish Blend Area
This spot consists of a small group of boulders nestled together with excellent problems. Walk directly uphill from *The Golden Toes Boulders* and these are the next significant boulders.

13. Golden Toes V4
Climb the face left of number 11 without using the arete.

14. Delicate Troll V3
Begin at the bottom end of the leftmost of two boulders and traverse the sloping lip

15. Coopertazi V3
On the top side of this boulder start on slopers on a low rail and gain the top. A V4 SDS can be done to this problem.

16. Unnamed V0
SDS on the right side of the boulder, right of the previous problem.

17. Unnamed V2
Climb the problem left of the previous problem.

18. Light Shag V3
On the boulder left of the previous few problems there is a low roof. Start low under the right side of the roof and climb up.

19. Turkish Blend V5
Start low and in the same spot as the previous problem. Move up and slightly left to a sloper and the top lip.

20. The Perch V8
Start on the left side of the boulder and move up and left to top out.

21. Ninja Squirrel V6/V7
Without using the corner, climb the thin face on the boulder directly across from *Turkish Blend*.

Matty McGovern bouldering at Haycock. Jessica Shoemaker photo.

22. Unnamed V0-
SDS and climb the corner of *Ninja Squirrel*.

Other Haycock Mountain Boulders
Hundreds of boulders that are not mentioned in this book can be found around the mountain. Below I list a few that are close to the areas featured in this guidebook.

The Empire State Boulder
Above and right of the Blue Trail, and just below and right of the *Summit Area* you can find this boulder.

1. King Dong V2
Traverse across a face from the right to reach the left side of the boulder.

2. Flaming Moe V4 R
The problem is technical and the top out burly. The arete is off route. Climb the left face

of the boulder.

3. O.D.B. V0
Climb the big flake on the left arete.

Lonely Boulder
This boulder can be found by following a faint trail uphill from *Jumbly Boulders*.

4 Blueberry V3
Begin left of a crack and merge to climb the crack.
Var. 1 V0 Climb the large holds left of this problem.

5. Delusional V8
SDS on the obvious, difficult looking arete, and climb up it to escape.

Other Nearby Areas
Hanger 18
Hanger 18 is probably the best and closest spot to the main Haycock boulders—it's actually on the south side of Haycock Mountain. A great deal of quality problems can be found here. For a free mini-guide, check out www.paclimbing.com.

Directions: This spot can be accessed by either walking past the *Caves Area* for about 15-20 minutes or parking off Kinzler Road. To park off Kinzler Road, drive on 563 and turn right on Harrisburg School Road (not far from Top Rock Trail Road). Turn right on Kinzler Road and continue to a stop sign after the road becomes gravel. Go straight at the stop sign (road becomes paved again) and follow the road to an overpass and a very small lot just past the overpass. If this lot is full, continue farther down the road to park. Do not overcrowd this lot!

Kings Road
Quality Diabase can be found off Kings Road near the Boy Scout camp. For directions to this spot, ask local climbers.

The Cabbage Patch
Karen Vantine and Jeff Gagliano developed some large, high, and hard problems at this interesting Diabase area. Various climbers from the Philadelphia vicinity also developed some lines V10 and harder. This area is smaller, but more concentrated than Haycock. For more information, contact local climbers.

14. Ralph Stover State Park (High Rocks)

Area Beta

Location
Just north of Philly.

Type of Climbing
Sport, trad, and toprope.

Other Info
A very popular area but not a destination.

Ralph Stover State Park

I wouldn't brag about the quality of *High Rocks* or "Stover" as locals call it, but this small crag has become one of the most popular cliffs in Pennsylvania—mostly due to its proximity to the Philadelphia metropolitan. Mostly a trad and top-rope area, this crag is host to over 100 routes that range in difficulty from 5.0 to 5.12d. Also, a few good boulder problems exist at the base of the cliff.

From a geologist's standpoint, the rock here is a Brunswick Shale; from a climbers standpoint, it's a slick-slab-enthusiasts paradise. The polished shale adds a distinctive quality creating delicate faces on a mirror-clean surface—you can just about see your face in the slabs face. If you don't like micro-edged faces, crack-climbs are abundant here also. A few nice roofs can be found here also; *Neanderthal* 5.8+ is a climb that is not to be missed.

If you do one climb here make it *Phone Booth* 5.10. This climb holds a trademark feature that put Stover on the map—escape from "the phone booth", and you'll know why. Despite the rumors of loose rock and dirty climbs—which are true—I highly recommend this area if you live near Southeastern Pennsylvania or Western New Jersey. The climbs are excellent if not interesting, and you can work on your delicate, balancy moves because of the polished surfaces.

History

High Rocks holds one of the oldest histories of Pennsylvania climbing. In 1750, Joseph Doan and Moses Doan, the "Eagle Spy", whose efforts had resulted in defeat of Washington's arm on Long Island, climbed a gully to escape a militia.

Joe Walsh was the first recorded rock climber to climb at the cliff in the 1930s; he is also noted for discovering the cliff for climbing potential. In the mid-1950s, Roland Machold and George Austin established one of the first 5.8 routes in the East. This route (*Orangutan*) is a classic to this day.

Around the same time, Lou Lutz, one of the primary developers and founders of nearby *Livzey Rock*, began developing routes at Stover with Bob Chambers. These climbers, clearly ahead of their time, had established many trad routes that were quite prolific.

Neanderthal 5.8+ was a prime example of this. It was first sent in 1957 and hadn't been repeated for half a decade. The legendary Ritner Walling, known for his first ascents in the Tetons and the Northeast, lived in nearby Philadelphia. This climber was, without doubt, a highly influential climber of his time—and one of the most colorful climbers I've ever met.

In the late '70s and early '80s, Tom Moffat, Bill Shaniman, Tom Stryker, Mel Hamel, and in the mid-80s, Colin Lantz were active at the crag. Colin was noted for establishing difficult boulder problems and bringing the grade of 5.13 to the crag.

During the 1990s, Dean Hernandez and Michael Flood were active developing several very difficult bolt-protected routes as well as other classic climbs at Stover. A climbers coalition for the area was also formed during this time and was headed by Michael Flood. Many great accomplishments were achieved at Stover: trail maintenance, erosion projects and control, a Port-a-Potty, bolt and anchor replacement, and an access newsletter.

The '90s also yielded development from Mark Ronca, a prolific climber who developed many routes in Eastern Pennsylvania and New Jersey (primarily in the DWG).

Access and Ownership: The crag is located in Ralph Stover State Park. The park acknowledges and permits climbing. Please maintain a healthy relationship with the park so climbing will be allowed in the future.

Guidebooks for This Area: More comprehensive books for this area have been published in the past. The first guide for Stover was known by locals as the "Green Guide". It was published around 1974 by Peter Kolman and Kirby Ellis. Tom Stryker also published *Red Rock: A Climber's History and Guide to High Rocks*. I highly recommend this guide due to Tom's intimate knowledge of the cliffs. In 1992, Doug Reilley published *Rock Climbs of the Tohickon Gorge: A Climbers Guide to High Rocks*. Doug's guide is the most extensive guidebook available to the area, and I highly recommend purchasing it if you frequent this area. Paul Nick also published a guidebook for the crag that is currently available. If you plan to climb here a lot, I recommend any of these books.

Geology: Brunswick Shale; slick and quite polished from decades of use.

General Description: Well over 100 routes, not including routes at nearby crags that are part of the same ridge, with grades ranging from 5.0 to 5.12d. The rock is 30 to 125'high.

Location: 10 miles north of New Hope.

In Case of Emergency: Dial 911.

Area Hazards: Due to the nature of the cliffs, shale can be somewhat loose and slick. Wear a helmet! Several gullies are subject to major erosion problems so it is recommended to refrain from using them; they can be dangerous. Many of the trees on top tend to be unstable. Use several trees or bolt anchors when building toprope anchors. Due to the nature of the soil, many trees don't have a lot rooting them in.

Directions: From Pennsylvania 611, find Route 413 south. Drive less that one mile to the small town of Pipersville, and turn left onto Dark Hollow Road. After driving over Tohickon Creek, continue about one mile and turn right onto State Park Road. After one-half mile turn left onto Tory Road. Park in the lot a few hundred feet further. The rock is located a few yards down the trail on the opposite side of the road as the lot. This will bring you to the top of the cliff and vista. Follow the trail that branches right and it will bring you to the base of the rock and the *Practice Face* (following the left branch takes you along the cliff-top). Please stay on marked trails due to erosion problems.

The Practice Face: This is the short 35' face at the very left side of the cliff. You can find it by following the descent trail that starts at the right side of a detached fence. The trail winds down to the west end of the cliffs. Three good warmups exist here and topropes are easy to set up. This is also a very crowded spot on weekends. The best way to access the top to set up ropes is by cautiously walking down ledges from above the face. **Note:** Please do not use the gully behind the *Practice Face*. Erosion problems exist and the gully is dangerous.

1. Orvie 5.8+ TR
FA: Unknown
Named for a patch of graffiti with the name Orvie (now not highly visible). Start around the left face of the *Practice Face* wall, in the center of the short west-wall. Climb the center of the face, keeping off the corner to the right, pass a good ledge and head for a prominent notch at the top.

Photo courtesy of Gino Filippini

2. Orvie Direct 5.9+ TR
FA: Unknown, Mid-'80s
Hump the blunt arete along sharp stone on the left wall of the rock. The route is 5.10a if you off-route the obvious layback just above the ledge that is halfway up the climb.

3. Triple Overhang 5.7 PG/R
FA: M. Cohen, Mid-'60s
Start this climb on the left side of *The Practice Face* and a few feet left of a large tree. Climb up past horizontal seams to a faint notch at the top. A 5.8 variation can be toproped to the right.

4. Ivy Leaf 5.4 PG
FA: J. Walsh, '30s
Climb the obvious crack just right of the previous climb. Veer slightly left near the top.

A. Finger in the Dike 5.6
Climb the face right of the previous route.

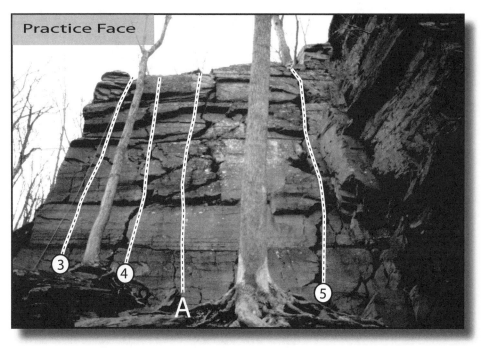

5. Practice Climb 5.2 G
FA: J. Walsh,'30s
This is the large crack at the right side of the wall.

The Neolithic Wall
This wall is the next wall past *The Practice Face*. The large ceiling in its center has challenging climbs. You can set topropes above by walking along a ledge (*The Neolithic Ledge*) from atop *The Practice Face*.

6. Unnamed 5.4 PG
Start on the right side of the corner on the left edge of *The Neolithic Wall* and climb 50' to a bolted anchor on the ledge above.

7. Unnamed 5.6 PG
Climb the crack just right of the previous climb (crux) to a small ceiling and notch above. There is a piton at the ceiling.
Var. 1: 5.5 PG Climbing the crack just right of the regular route makes the climb a bit easier.

B. Stopper Ceiling 5.10d TR
Climb the difficult face left of *Neanderthal*.

C. Neanderthal 5.8+ PG
FA: M.G. Block, Gordon Dickson
Climb the nice crack and ugly offwidth. A very popular climb.

248

Neolithic Wall

Great Buttress

This is the highest section of the cliff. It is located a few hundred feet past *The Neolithic Wall*.

8. Tales from the Crypt 5.10a PG

FA: M. Hamel, T. Stryker 1979

Follow three bolts near a tree to a bolted belay above and rappel.

9. Dean's List 5.9 or 5.11a PG

FA: Dean Hernandez

Gear is recommended to supplement the bolts on this climb. Follow four bolts right of *Tales*. If you avoid the arete the route is 5.11. Using the arete makes it 5.9.

The Hawk's Nest

A short way past the previous area find a few large overhangs just off the ground. There is a large gully to the left that can be used to descend climbs in this area.

10. Ripper Traverse V2/V4

Depending on what line you take the grade varies. Traverse the *Hawk's Nest* wall starting at the large gully on the left and finishing at *Hawk's Nest* 35' later.

11. Welcome to Stover 5.10d PG

FA: T. Stryker

Pull over the center of two ceilings and pass two bolts.

12. Foot Free and Fancy Loose 5.7+ PG

FA: T. Tiers, R. Wolfe

Near a big tree, climb a left-facing corner and climb out the right side of the roof above. Belay at the two-bolt anchor above.

13. Hawk's Nest 5.6 PG

FA: G. Austin, R. Machold
Climb the openbook above the ground (crux) to a ceiling. Move left and up to a corner and another ceiling, then left to a two-bolt belay. You can climb a second pitch up loose rock to the top by moving right around a ceiling and following a chimney to the top (pitch two is not recommended).

14. Marty Broke It V7

Named for Marty Trumbore who broke a hold that increased the grade significantly. Climb the steep overhanging face right of the previous route. Easier if tall.

Obnoxious Partner Buttress

This is the rightmost end of the cliff. Two large buttresses lie separated by a large chimney.

15. Obnoxious Partner 5.8+ G

Climb the obvious, 50'-high crack on the left side of the buttress.

Phone Booth Buttress

At the far right end of the cliff a steep overhanging buttress can be found. Around the right corner of this outcrop is a small face known as *The Far Face*. The buttress gets its name for a phone-booth-sized void located high in the steep rock.

16. Called on Account of Pain 5.11d TR

FA: B. Ramanowicx, M. Barnhart
Begin on the left side of the steep wall at the chimney. Move up and right following steep rock. Climb the overhanging wall over steep crimps to the top. A 5.12 variation starts

directly below the steep wall.

17. Phone Booth 5.10a R
FA: P. Cravens
Climb steep overhanging rock to the "phone booth". Climb out of the booth and escape out right to climb the corner to the top.

18. Far Face 5.7 PG/R
Climb the left side of this clean, short face to a flake. Continue up the left side of the face passing horizontals and faults and move onto the top.

19. Far Face Direct 5.8+ R/X
Climb the center of the 50' face.

20. Far face Corner 5.4 PG
Climb up right into the right corner of the face.

Other Eastern Pennsylvania Areas

Scranton Wilkes-Barre

The Wilkes-Barre Scranton area has a great deal of some of the best climbing in the state and some of the best rock in the Mid Atlantic. Over 100 areas are scattered throughout the hillsides between Mocanaqua and Carbondale. Due to access issues I have chosen not to publicize these areas. The Rim, The Trenches, Morgan Ridge, The Edge, Hawk Rock, Standing Pillar, Muro De Sachmo, Turkey Rock, Sandblaster Crag, The Theatre, Tilbury, The Sanctuary, The Penitentiary, and many other areas have numerous documented climbs and boulder problems. These areas were developed by George Peterson, Al Pusaneschi, Bob D'Antonio, Bob Murray, myself, Nick Morell, Tom Kneiss, Ryan Lukas, Rob Mutti, and several other climbers. Route names and topos may be available in the future at www.paclimbing.com.

The Flatirons

This is a small bouldering area that I developed with Tom Kneiss. It can be seen from I-80 between Tamaqua and Delano. Several boulders a few feet high lie on top of a mountain behind the small village of Lofty, PA. The boulders are located above the railroad tracks and extend to the notch that goes down to Tamaqua. Problems range from V0- to V7.

Centralia

In 1990 I discovered and developed a great deal of bouldering in the Centralia region. At least 5 areas have fantastic bouldering and hundreds of problems. The rock is a nice conglomerate like the Gunk's. Problems up to V10 exist in the region. Myself and Tom Kneiss also added some excellent roped climbs. I plan to add some topos to www. paclimbing.com in the future.

The Castle

Joe Forte and myself developed an interesting crag in coal country in the middle of Schukill county. Joe was very active cleaning routes and placing anchors and making the crag a great destination. Maybe someday if access permits this area will be made more public.

Wolf Rocks

A prominent vista along the Appalachian Trail, Wolf Rocks offers pleasant views of the Pocono Mountains. Because of its long approach and lack of problems, Wolf Rocks is not a popular area. The overhanging nature of this short cliff makes it a somewhat interesting place to boulder, but the 40-minute hike, although flat and easy going, discourage most from visiting this spot. If you live nearby and like out of the way places, you can keep yourself busy here for a few hours. If you don't live in the immediate area, Wolf Rocks is not worth checking out.

Rock Type: Conglomerate similar to The Gunk's but softer in texture.

Directions: From Stroudsburg, follow State Route 191 south up steep hills until cresting the top of the mountain at Fox Gap. This will be the final summit on Route 191 before you start going back down the other side of the mountain. You will see a parking area on your right with an Appalachian Trail sign-post. Park in this lot and follow the white-blazed Appalachian Trail approximately one and a half miles to the Wolf Rocks outcrop.

Classic Routes: *Knife Arete* V2, *Randy's Overhang* V0+ R, *Rockin Roof* V1 R/X, *Short Slop* V6, *Expander* V7.

Birdsboro

One of the more popular sport climbing areas in the state. This area has recently seen a great deal of bolting activity and increase in number of sport routes. Each year a local activist committee holds a clean-up day and social event. Although the quality of some of the climbs at this area is questionable, a great deal of the routes here are excellent. I decided not to include this area in the guide because of the underlying access issues of the past. Since things have been going great access-wise, I plan to include Birdsboro in the next edition of this book. Future info will be available at www.paclimbing.com.

Central Pennsylvania

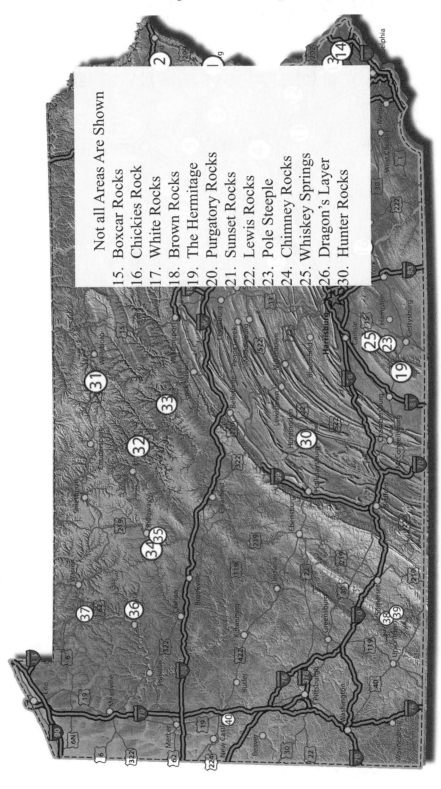

Not all Areas Are Shown

15. Boxcar Rocks
16. Chickies Rock
17. White Rocks
18. Brown Rocks
19. The Hermitage
20. Purgatory Rocks
21. Sunset Rocks
22. Lewis Rocks
23. Pole Steeple
24. Chimney Rocks
25. Whiskey Springs
26. Dragon's Layer
30. Hunter Rocks

15. Boxcar Rocks

Area Beta

Location
On the mountain above Tower City, PA.

Type of Climbing
Sport, trad, and bouldering on a 3 mile wall of rock.

Other Info
Some of the most intriguing geology in the East.

Boxcar Rocks (the Chinese Wall)

A very impressive rock formation that is distinct and unique, Boxcar Rocks is a collection of large conglomerate blocks that dominate the forest in a train-like formation. This geologic wonder has dozens of boulder problems and routes, on the front and back walls of this unusual cliff-band. The outcrop gives the illusion of a colossal stone train streaming through the forest, high above Tower City.

The area is coined both Boxcar Rocks and The Chinese Wall for two reasons: First, the rocks form massive boulders (some 80' tall) that resemble boxcars of a train; second, this outcrop looks like a giant wall, that goes on for a great distance like The Great Wall of China.

The rock is 10' high at its lowest point and 80' at its highest. Many of the face routes are littered with baseball-sized cobbles, adding to the aesthetic nature of the cliff. Four-star cracks and large boulders are some of the highlights you can expect to find; the quiet mountain setting also brings an added allure.

In 2007, an Adopt-A-Crag event was held at this area. A relationship was made with the Pennsylvania State Game Commission, and a stewardship was planned between the land manager and climbers. A new trail was also constructed around the cliff. In recent years graffiti has become a problem at this once pristine area. Although the Game Commission has been regularly patrolling the area for vandals (fines in excess of $1,000 dollars were recently administered), problems still persist. Hopefully, climbers will remain proactive and continue this land stewardship.

Note: Take it upon yourself to inspect all fixed top-anchors. In the past, hangers have been removed and meddled with. Although no serious damage has been noted, it is advised that you thoroughly inspect all anchors. The main concern, is that a great deal of miscreant locals can regularly be found frolicking along the top of the cliff, beer can in one hand, Chesterfield in the other. Usually these locals are pleasant—who isn't when they've downed a few gallons of Genesee and shot off enough ammo to supply a small arms dealer—but it's the spray-paint-toting kids who look like they walked out of a Marilyn Manson video, and carry a copy of *Helter Skelter* in their back pocket that worry me. All new anchors have been placed a modest distance under the lip of the crag. This was done so experienced climbers will be comfortable enough to reach the anchors but Metallica-attired beer-swilling teens won't. Use caution when attempting to gain access to these anchors and parts or the outcrop. Don't be afraid to rope up if necessary.

This section lists boulder problems and routes. Routes are identified on the topo maps by numbers and boulder problems by letters. This is done to differentiate boulder problems from routes on the topo maps. A few boulder problems on the *Whale Formation* are listed by numbers because they can be done as starts to the routes above them.

Geology: Pottsville Conglomerate.

Emergency Info: Dial 911.

Location: 3 miles above Tower City.

General Overview: 80'-high cliff with about 70 routes: 10 sport, 20 trad, and 40 toprope. About 200 boulder problems exist here (100 are documented in this section).

Recommended Rack: Quickdraws, mixed-size cams, nuts, a crash pad for bouldering.

Access Issues and Restrictions: The area is owned and managed by PA State Game Commission. Climbing is allowed. Respect the land, pack out trash, and report vandalism to the local police. Camping is prohibited in State Gamelands.

Area Hazards: Snakes and poison ivy. Please inspect all top anchors. In recent years anchors have been painted and meddled with!

Nearby Areas: Several other areas not featured in this guide lie nearby. The Dark Corridor, a massive black-colored conglomerate quarry is the closest. The Castle, a popular sport area, is 15 miles away. Several good bouldering areas lie east and west of the main formation. If you hike the ridge east, rock is abundant for miles. If you cross Goldmine road and venture into the woods you will find a long expanse of unclean, undeveloped rock.

History

The first climbers to visit Boxcar Rocks were Curt and Margie Harler, and members of the Pennsylvania Mountaineering Association in the 1970s and early '80s. During this time, routes like *Moby Neil* 5.6, *Russel's Ruin* 5.5, *Curt's Crack* 5.7, *Margie's Curves* 5.7, and all the obvious crack climbs were established.

In the '90's Lukas Wolfe and Ryan Lukas were active developing several dozen boulder problems and routes at Boxcar Rocks. Ryan Lukas, Rob Mutti, and I were also active at this time developing dozens of routes and boulder problems. Ryan Lukas developed boulder problems in *The Trench*, on the main wall, and several trad lines on the overhang past *The Spade* boulder. Ryan also was involved with me in developing the first bolted route (*Autumn's Child* 5.10a) at Boxcar along with me.

I added over one-hundred boulder problems to the area and several trad lines. Many of the blank faces and some now-bolted routes were done by me as solo routes and scary run-out trad. I was also active developing many of the bolted lines at the area

In the late-90s, Nick Morell, Dave Pfurr, Tom Kneiss, and Randy Ross were active at the area. Dave Pfurr established a few worthwhile boulder problems. *One Man's Thimble* V1 is one of his most classic lines. Randy Ross later added a variation that exits the problems high mantle, and continues to finish on *Moby Neil's* frightfully high top out 65' above. This problem is seldom repeated. Also during this time period, Nick Morell added several highball and challenging boulder problems. Tom Kneiss added a few nice eliminate problems on *The White Fang*, as well as a classic trad line called *Kneissiology* 5.6.

In recent years, Joe Forte has been active replacing many older bolt anchors and developing several bolted climbs. Joe did the first ascent of *Snap Crackle Plop* 5.10b, and was active bolting several other routes at the area. Scott and Christa Messick were also active in developing bolted climbs with me like *Door to December* 5.10b. Jess Holzman was active establishing routes like *Birthday Girl* 5.7 and was along with myself establishing many classic lines on the cliff since 2000.

Although many of the routes have now been bolted, this area is not, and should never become a heavily bolted area. As of today, there are very few lines left to be bolted and I strongly feel that the area should be preserved and not grid-bolted like so many other areas in Pennsylvania, just so someone can squeeze another line in. Contact local climbers if you plan on establishing any routes here to determine if the route may have already been done on gear or as a solo. Boxcar should remain a natural setting, aside from the spray paint that is.

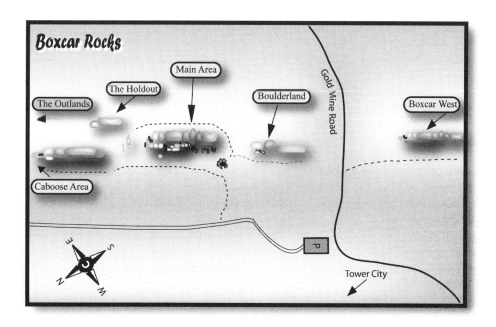

Directions

From Tower City, drive Goldmine Road south and climb the steep mountain. Goldmine road will crest the mountain, high above Tower City. Continue south on Goldmine to the third parking area on the left. There will be a State Game Lands lot and a gate at the back of the wooded lot. Park here and follow the dirt road behind the gate. Walk slightly less than one mile and take the first right. This will be a small trail in a wooded grove of pines. Follow this to a large campfire area and the rock. The giant whale formation is the first outcrop you will see. You can access this by walking to the right of the campfire and locating a set of stone stairs.

Whale Wall Bouldering Area
This area is located just under and left of the giant whale formation. Several fun warm-up problems can be done here. Problems on the *White Fang* should not be missed.

The White Fang Boulder
This is the fanglike boulder that comes to a sharp point. It is located just below *Moby Neil*.

A. Fang Traverse V1
On the downhill side of the fang, start at the very left side on the corner (SDS) and a small pebble, and traverse on a pebbly horizontal; then pull up over the right side to finish.

B. Toothache V1
Traverse in or begin at the center of the fang, reach to the sharp lip above, and gain the point above. End by standing on the other side of the formation.

C. White Fang V0-
SDS and climb the left edge of the fang, topping out over a sharp point.

D. Tom's Dyno V4
SDS and climb to the pebble-rail, then dyno the point at the left center of the boulder.

E. Cavity Creep V5
An eliminate version of the previous problem that uses a micro-pinch pebble in the blank face.

The Piano
A few feet left of the White Fang boulder is a small gritty boulder with some problems on its downhill side.

F. Steinway V0-
Traverse the top of this small boulder.

G. Maestro V0-
Start low and pull over the small roof at the center of this boulder.

Nick Morell on the "White Fang " boulder, circa late-90s. Photo by the author.

The Streaked Boulder
This boulder is just left of the previous few routes and has green streaks on its downhill side.

H. Arete Eliminate V0-
Dance up the pebbles on the right side of the boulder. The arete is out.

I. Green Streaks V0-
Make your way to the top between the two green streaks just left of the previous route.

J. Unnamed VB
Climb the face just right of the tree.

K. Streak Traverse V2
Avoiding the large horizontal, traverse on pebbles at mid-height, navigating through or around a tree, until it is possible to plop over the left side of the boulder.

Pebbles Boulder
The next boulder left of the previous boulder.

L. Pebble Prancer V2

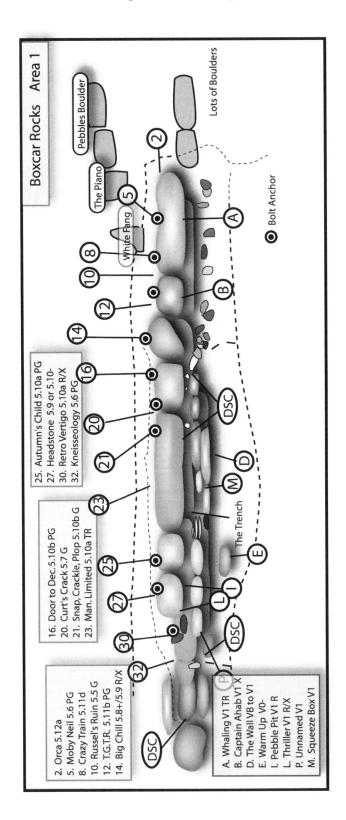

Boxcar Rocks   Area 1

Pebbles Boulder

The Piano

Lots of Boulders

White Fang

Bolt Anchor

The Trench

25. Autumn's Child 5.10a PG
27. Headstone 5.9 or 5.10-
30. Retro Vertigo 5.10a R/X
32. Kneisseology 5.6 PG

16. Door to Dec. 5.10b PG
20. Curt's Crack 5.7 G
21. Snap, Crackle, Plop 5.10b G
23. Man. Limited 5.10a TR

2. Orca 5.12a
5. Moby Neil 5.6 PG
8. Crazy Train 5.11d
10. Russel's Ruin 5.5 G
12. T.G.T.R. 5.11b PG
14. Big Chill 5.8+/5.9 R/X

A. Whaling V1 TR
B. Captain Ahab V1 X
D. The Wall VB to V1
E. Warm Up V0-
I. Pebble Pit V1 R
L. Thriller V1 R/X
P. Unnamed V1
M. Squeeze Box V1

Begin on pebbles at the right-downhill side of this boulder and dance over the top. The arete is off route.

M. Pebble Charmer V2

Climb the slightly overhanging face just left of a tree. Short but sweet.

N. Flaky Flake V2

Start with both hands on a hallow flake and top out. A lot of climbing for a seemingly short route.

O. Dancing on the Lion's Back V7/V8

Traverse the pebble covered face just below the lip, using the lip only when necessary to keep the route reasonably possible.

Routes on the Whale Formation

Just past the small campfire area off the approach trail, you will see a massive boulder perched up high that begins the start of *The Chinese Wall*. This behemoth boulder is called the *Whale Formation* and resembles a giant whale. If you look close enough at "The Whale" you will see its large pebble-filled mouth, and even a black eye perfectly placed in its head. The highball boulder problems (that can be toproped) begin on the north-facing side. The routes at this area begin on the downhill south-facing side. You can access the routes by scrambling down the ledge just right of the *Whale Formation*.

1. V0- R

Prance up the pebbly face left of and around the corner from the start of *Moby Neil*. Begin at the right side of this short rectangular block and head for a small pocket. Mantle the ledge and traverse off left. Can be done as a harder start to *Moby Neil*.

2. Orca 5.12d TR

FA: R. Holzman
Begin this climb by soloing up either *One Mans thimble*, *Welcome to Boxcar*, or the start of *Moby Neil* and climb up and under the back side of the giant whale. Struggle under the Buddha-like belly of the whale until you reach the mouth. Fire up the head to the narrow top.

3. Welcome to Boxcar 5.10 or V0 R

This route is a boulder problem start to *Moby* Neil; however, some do this as just a boulder problem and traverse off left at the top of the square boulder below The Whale. Begin on the small face on the square boulder that supports the giant Whale formation. Climb up the center of the face to a ledge 17 feet up and move to the *Moby Neil* corner (this is the obvious flake that goes to the summit just right of the whale head). Instead of climbing into the flake climb slightly left of the flake to the top. There is a fixed anchor at the top.

4. One Mans Thimble V1 R or Very X

One of the best boulder problems in the region and one of the most classic highballs in the East if you decide to brave the bold variation to the top. This problem starts on the arete just right of the previous route. Climb the beautiful, pebble coated arete on the

263

Tom Kneiss on "One Man's Thimble. Photo by the author.

boulder under The Whale's belly. Walk off the ledge (V1 R) or brave the solo up the *Moby Neil* flake to the top (V1 very X).

5. Moby Neil 5.6 PG
Gear is tricky to place and unreliable in a few spots. If you are a competent trad climber this route is PG. Follow the path of least resistance a few feet right of *One Mans Thimble* to a small ledge right of The Whale's belly. Climb off the ledge into and up a pebble-coated flake/ crack to the fixed anchor above.
Var. 1: 5.11d PG Climb the blank face at the beginning and join the flake at the top to finish.

6. Locomotive Breath 5.10c TR
FA: R. Holzman
Climb the face just right of *Moby Neil*.

7. Phoebe Snow 5.11c TR
FA: N. Morell, R. Holzman
This climb begins a few feet right of *Moby Neil* near two horizontals mid-way up. Climb the steep pebble-coated face past two horizontals to a cruxy top section.

8. Crazy Train 5.11d TR
FA: R. Holzman, N. Morell
Climb the face a few feet right of the previous route. The top section is very strenuous and moves past fantastic hand-sized pebbles. There is a two-bolt anchor above.

9. Steam Power 5.10d TR
FA: R. Holzman
Climb the arete, keeping off the crack to the right, just right of the previous climb.

Little wall
This is the very short wall that starts a few feet right of the previous climb. The top section has a short boulder resting above the horizontal that splits this short wall. There is an alcove into which you can crawl through to the north side, at the right side of the wall.

10. Russell's Ruin 5.5 G
Climb the obvious crack just right of the previous climb.

11. Cobblestoned 5.11d TR
FA: J. Forte
Climb the left side for this short wall.

12. The Great Train Robbery 5.11b G
FA: R. Holzman, J. Forte
Climb the right side of this short wall passing bolts to a two-bolt anchor above.

13. Throw Momma from a Train 5.8 R/X
FA: R. Holzman
Boulder to the alcove and climb through it to safety on the other side.

14. The Big Chill 5.8+/5.9 R/X
FA: R. Holzman, T. Kneiss
Bring a large gear for your only piece of pro. Some smaller cams can be used for the back section of the overhang. Climb the unprotected face to a roof near the obvious cave/alcove 30' up. Continue over the center of the overhang. If you swing over the hang to the left or right the grade drops to 5.8. Chain anchor above.

15. Conjunctions Junction 5.9 R
FA: R. Holzman
Boulder the green-colored face to the crack at the right side of the overhang.

Locomotive Wall
This is the long stone wall that is a sub-section of the lengthy Boxcar outcrop. It begins just past the jutting overhang (*Big Chill* route). A bolted line (*Door to December*) is the first route of this wall.

16. Door to December 5.10b PG
FA: R. Holzman, J. Lewis, Scott and Christa Messick
3 bolts, large gear, two-bolt anchor. Start on a flake, then step left to a bolt and climb past two more bolts right of the previous climb to a two-bolt anchor above. The crux is above the horizontal. Bring large gear to supplement the bolts at the horizontal.

17. Boxcar Willy 5.10a TR

FA: R. Holzman, J. Lewis
TR the face right of the previous climb

18. Casey Jones 5.10a TR
FA: R. Holzman
Climb the face right of the previous climb.

19. Pebbles and Bam Bam 5.10a TR
FA: Unknown circa 1980s
A visiting climber came up with the excellent name for this previously unnamed route. Climb the nice white-colored face just left of the crack.

20. Curt's Crack 5.7 G
FA: Curt Harler
You may want a large cam for the awkward traverse from the main crack, past the horizontal, to the rightward continuation of the crack. Climb one of the best cracks in Pennsylvania just right of *Pebbles and Bam Bam.*

The Observation Car
Walking on top of this massive boulder has the feel of an observation car on a train. This is the long wall right of the previous climbs.

21. Snap Crackle Plop 5.10a G
FA: J. Forte, R. Holzman
Start at a nice flake and follow the green-colored streak to nice finger pockets after the horizontal.

22. Silver Streak 5.11c TR
FA: R. Holzman, J. Forte
Start a few inches right of the base of the green-colored flake and climb thin pinches left of the black streak, following the white streak to the top.

23. Manhattan Limited 5.10a TR
FA: R. Holzman, R. Lukas
Climb the face near the black streak.

24. Unnamed 5.9 TR
FA: R. Lukas
Climb the nice face past big pebbles, and finish at the top

25. Autumn's Child 5.10a PG
FA: R. Holzman, R. Lukas
The first bolted route at Boxcar. Climb past bolts to the large horizontal above. You can use a large cam in the horizontal or a small stopper in the flake off to the right and above the horizontal to protect the face after the bolts.

26. Margie's Curves Left 5.7 G
FA: Curt and Margie Harler

Climb the leftmost of the two cracks at the right side of the high wall.

27. Headstone 5.9 or 5.10-
FA: R. Holzman, R. Lukas, J. Lewis
Depending on whether you take the right or left side of the headstone feature, the grade varies: right is 5.10-, left is 5.9. The route is easier the higher you brake out of the crack. Climb the crack and stem out onto the face between two cracks and climb straight to the top. There is a two-bolt on the detached block above.

28. Margie's Curves Right 5.6 G
FA: Curt and Margie Harler
The rightmost of the two nice cracks.

29. Vertigo 5.9+ R/X
FA: R. Holzman
Climb the face, on little pro, that is just right of the crack.

30. Retro Vertigo 5.10a R/X
FA: R. Holzman, T. Kneiss
A fun toprope or dicey lead. Climb the center of the face to a ledge. Continue to the top. A fixed anchor used to be on top but only one bolt remains.

31. Birthday Girl 5.7 G
FA: J. Lewis, R .Holzman

Tom Kneiss and Dave Pfurr enjoy a crisp autumn day at Boxcar.

Gear can be used before the first bolt. Climb the face past two bolts. A fantastic warm up and introduction to Boxcar Rocks. See if you can locate the amazing finger-tube.

32. Keneisseiology 5.6 G
FA: T. Kneiss
A great climb. Climb the nice crack a few feet right of the previous problem. Grade varies depending on moisture and how many pebbles break off.

33. 5th class Gully
A few feet right of the previous climb there is a gully that can be utilized to ascend or descend the cliff. A good spot to access the backside of the outcrop or other climbs.

The Freight Yard
This area includes many train-car-shaped boulders that are 50' high and hold some of the best routes in the area.

34. Vagabond 5.11a TR
FA: R. Holzman
Climb the nice, clean, high column of rock to a two bolt anchor above.

35. Roundhouse 5.10 TR
FA: R. Holzman
Climb the route slightly right of the previous.

36. Battery Powered Life 5.10a PG
FA: R. Holzman, J. Forte
Climb past two bolts and move right to a two-bolt anchor.

37. Instant Gratification 5.10a PG
FA: R. Holzman
A great, short route located a few hundred feet past *Battery Powered Life*. Climb past bolts over a technical face to an anchor above.

38. Ambient Endeavors 5.9+ G
FA: R. Holzman, R. Lukas, J. Lewis
Climb past small gear placements and one bolt to a two-bolt anchor above.

Main Area Front Wall
This is the front side of the main area. This is also the side that faces the way you approach the rock and the first visible rock you see when walking in from the parking lot off Goldmine Road. Several nice boulder problems exist on the left side of this wall and in the trench and pit above.

Whale Formation
This is the uphill side of the rock formation that looks like a giant whale.

A. Whaling V1 TR
Toprope the whale formation over a small roof and climb the face above. The grade

varies depending on what path you take to the right or left.

B. Captain Ahab V1 X
Boulder the scary face on the outcrop just left of the previous formation.

C. Descent/Ascent
Left of the "gallery window " (a window-shaped feature that you can crawl into to look onto the other side of the outcrop), you can scramble left into the trench to gain the top of the cliff. This is the easiest area to access the top to set topropes. If stoned teens can do it, you can too.

D. The Wall
Below and left of the previous problems, just off the hiking trail, you can find a nice boulder wall that is green colored. Several problems can be done here varying in grade form VB to V1.

E.   Warm up Boulder Problem V0-
Climb the small, detached boulder at the left end of the *Warm up Wall*.

The Trench
This area is a long trench formed by a series of boulders. This beautiful rock formation is accessed by crawling through the **Descent/Ascent** mentioned above or by simply walking above *The Wall* to walk into this trench. Accessing the cliff-top from this trench is the easiest way to set topropes up.

F. Trench Warfare V0
Climb the pebbled face a few feet left of the **Descent/Ascent** at the right end of the trench. Can be easier depending on what path you take.

G. Trench Mouth V0-
Climb the face a few feet left of *Trench Warfare*. Variations have been done to the right and left at the same grade.

H. Squeeze Box V1
Tricky to find. Locate the split in the rock formation that leads you into the trench from the ledge. This problem starts by crawling down a passage right of the passage that leads into the trench. Climb up on edges. The back wall is off.

I. The Pebble Pit V1 R
Looking at the trench formation from the north, this problem starts on the arete of the last boulder in the trench on the left side. Climb this beautiful arete to its top, avoiding stemming to any other formations or cracks.

J. Ryan's Pebble Traverse V0
Traverse the trench at mid-level up the boulder. Start at the far left of the trench at *Pebble Pit* and finish just past *Trench Warfare* by topping out.

K. Squeeze Play V0+

Ryan Lukas bouldering on an interesting formation at Boxcar.
RH photo.

Climb up the somewhat steep face a few inches left of the beautiful arete.

L. Thriller V1 R/X

A fall from this problem would surely be fatal! Climb the thrilling arete on the boulder that is perched above the anchors for *Retro Vertigo*. This is the arete just right of those anchors. If you fall onto the ledge its R rated. If you weave a bit left and fall you may end up falling down the 80' cliff below! Descend carefully down the chimney near *Pebble Pit*.

M. Squeeze Box V1

Tricky to find. Locate the split in the rock formation that leads you into the trench from the ledge. This problem starts by crawling down a passage right of the passage that leads into the trench. Climb up on edges. The back wall is off.

N. Mr. Clean V0+ R

Climb the brilliant white-colored wall behind *Thriller*. This problem can be climbed anywhere on the wall without affecting the grade. Several variations can be done to the right and left. Be aware that the ledge at your back ends at a 50' drop!

O. Ghost Arete V0+ R

The arete just right of the previous problem.

P. Paintball V1

Climb the left-hand side of the wall on the opposite side of the boulder that the previous two problems are located on. A bit of an eliminate.

Q. Unnamed V0
Climb the face right of the previous problem. Mind the ledge below.

Access Gully
A short access gully is located immediately left of the previous two problems. This is a good spot to access the cliff for topropes.

Train Wreck Wall
This is the next section of the cliff. It gets its name from the jumbled, wrecked-looking sections of rock. It is located just past the access gully that brings you to the top of *Headstone* and *Retro Vertigo/Birthday Girl*.

R. The Fickle Finger of Fate V1
Climb up to and over the finger of rock that protrudes out 15-feet right of *Knob Goblin*. Go directly over the point of the finger to achieve the grade.

1. Knob Goblin V0
Locate this problem on a boulder that juts out over the main rock outcrop a few hundred feet left of *Fickle Finger* and past an easy section of rock. Jump to a knob of rock that protrudes out from a small roof and top out.

Descent Alcove 5th Class
The descent route from the high boulder-ridge left of *Knob Goblin* is located on the ledge behind and left of *Knob Goblin*. It large off-width crack /corner in the boulder.

2. Slabsation V0- R
This problem is the high slab a few feet left of *Knob Goblin*. Several variations of this problem have been done on this slab. All hold the same grade.

3. Pebble Pusher V0 R
Just left of the previous route and left of a small tree growing out of a ledge in the center of this long boulder, climb up to a shallow crack/seam near the boulders top.

4. Power Pebbles V1 R
Climb the face just left of *Pebble Pusher*.

5. Pueblo V1 R
Left of the previous route and just right of *Whistle Crack*, climb the lichen covered face.

6. Whistle Crack V0- R
Sometimes if the wind blows through this crack, you can hear it whistle. In front of a tree a few feet left of *Pueblo*, climb the crack.

7. Whistler V1 R
Prance up the very shallow corner a few feet left of the crack.

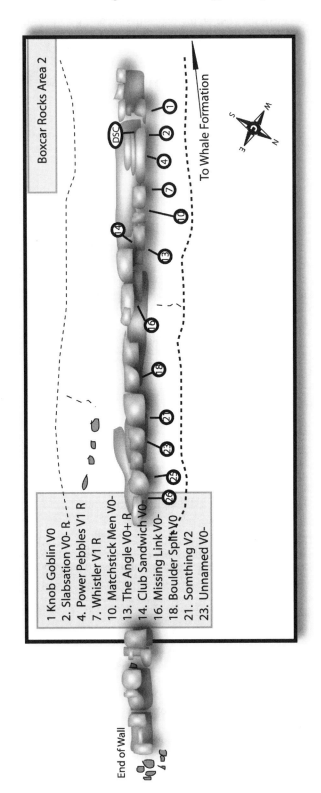

Boxcar Rocks Area 2

To Whale Formation

1 Knob Goblin V0
2. Slabsation V0- R
4. Power Pebbles V1 R
7. Whistler V1 R
10. Matchstick Men V0-
13. The Angle V0+ R
14. Club Sandwich V0-
16. Missing Link V0-
18. Boulder Split V0
21. Somthing V2
23. Unnamed V0-

End of Wall

8. Door Knob V1 R
Find the doorknob-sized pebble in the center of the face of this boulder. Hope the knob doesn't break off, and climb past it.

9. Bed Knobs and Broomsticks V1R
Carefully navigate up the lichen covered face left of the doorknob feature and before the crack.

10. Matchstick Men V0-
Climb the easy crack slightly left of the previous route.

11. Fluke Flake V0
Climb the nice flake just left of the crack.

12. Unnamed V0+ R
At a horizontal, climb the face in the center of this boulder. A variation can be done between this problem and the flake to the right.

13. The Angle V0+ R
Cruise up the low-angle face just left of number 12, then climb to a bulge.

14. Club Sandwich V0-
Just left of the previous route near a tree, climb the shallow corner facing left.

15. Crack VB/V0-
Climb the easy crack left of *Club Sandwich*.

16. The Missing Link V0-
This problem is located on a ledge/bouldering room that is perched high on the backside of this boulder atop the cliff. The problem is on the opposite side of the boulder from all the previous routes. To get to it, climb the easy crack (previous problem) and you will see a pebble-coated face directly right of the crack as you go down the backside of the boulder. Find a missing pebble in the sea of pebbles (hint: just above head level) and climb past it.

17. Ledge Routes VB
On the boulder left of the previous few climbs are some easy problems that can be done.

Descent 5th Class
At the left side of this boulder and above talus where two boulders are split by a large gap, a descent can be achieved on either boulder left or right. There is a fin of rock on the backside of the leftmost boulder.

18. Boulder Split V0
Climb up just left of a tree over a bulge at a horizontal where a large boulder is split horizontally on a ledge.

19. Crack V0-
Climb the crack just left of *Boulder Split*.

Descent 5th Class
You can achieve an easy descent from the outcrop just left of the crack.

20. Unnamed V0-
Climb over the bulges just left of the 5th class descent.

21. Something from Nothing V2

SDS and climb out and right from the alcove/passage that leads to the other side of the outcrop. A little easier variation has been done that moves out left of the passage. For the true V2 variation climb from the SDS, and then out over the left-center of the bulge.

22. Alcove V0-
The easiest line out the obvious alcove.

23. Unnamed V0-
Two problems can be done to the left of the alcove before the crack to the left. Both are quite easy.

24. Crack V0-
The obvious crack left of the previous route.

25. Boulderdash V0-
Climb over the boulder left of the crack.

26. Crack V0
Climb another classic, easy, crack left of the previous route with two boulders perched to the left and right.

27. Unnamed V0's
Some easy problems have been done on the boulder to the left of crack.

28. Beer Daze V0+ R
Climb up the center of the high boulder two boulders across from the easy crack.

Area 3
This is the next area along the cliff. It continues to the end of the outcrop.

1. Unnamed V0+ R
Climb the center of the face.

2. The Narrows V0-/V1

The narrowest point of the ridgeline lies on top the boulder left of the previous boulder and boulder problem. A few very easy problems can be done on this boulder.

3. Unnamed V0

There is a boulder immediately left of *The Narrows* that has a small boulder perched on top its right side; then there is a gap in the ridge and another boulder. Climb the left face of this boulder. A few problems have been done on this boulder at the same grade.

4. The Straddler V1

Straddle the flake on the very narrow boulder just left of the previous route.

5. Unnamed V0-

A few easy problems have been done on the boulder to the left of *The Straddler*.

Caboose Boulder

This is the last boulder on the main ridge, before a large break where the ridge eventually starts up again.

6. Unnamed V0 R

Climb the middle face of the boulder near the arete.

7. Red Caboose V0 R

Climb the arete at the end of "The Caboose".

8. Unnamed V1 R

Climb the high face.

9. Unnamed V1 R

Climb the high face.

10. Sea of Pebbles V6

Traverse entire cliff! Start at any point and circumnavigate all of the rock. There are several cruxes depending on what line you choose to make the traverse.

The Spade

This is the spade-shaped boulder near the campfire area at the far end of the wall. This and the boulder near it are excellent.

The Holdout

This is a hidden wall located just behind (south side of) the campfire area near *The Spade* boulder. Basically walk the cliff to its far east side and the small campfire area. *The Holdout* is hidden from view behind and slightly east of the campfire area, but before *The Overhangs* area.

The Overhangs

A nice section with a few overlapping overhangs exists just past *The Spade* boulder and

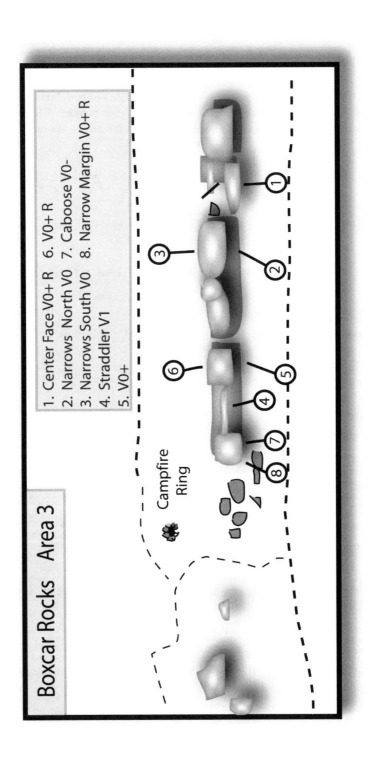

Boxcar Rocks   Area 3

1. Center Face V0+ R   6. V0+ R
2. Narrows North V0   7. Caboose V0-
3. Narrows South V0   8. Narrow Margin V0+ R
4. Straddler V1
5. V0+

Campfire Ring

Dave Pfurr bouldering in the "Pebble Pit." RH photo.

campfire area. Some classic trad routes have been established here by Ryan Lukas.

The Hideout
If you hike past *The Overhangs* you will pass many good boulder problems. If you continue to hike for 15 - 20 minutes, you will eventually come to what appears to be the end of the line. This area is called *The Hideout* (not to be confused with *the Holdout*). Excellent bouldering can be found here in a tranquil setting nestled in pine trees. Some classics here include: *The Ball Route* V0+ R, a mega-classic line that has baseball-sized holds over every inch of the wall; *Hair Club Fro Men* V2, a great SDS problem on a blunt arete; *Silent Lucidity* V4, a thin crimp-line over micro holds. Many other classics can be found here if you brave the long walk from the main areas.

Other Boxcar Rocks Boulders
If you continue past *The Hideout* you will find a break in the ridge. After a bit of hiking, you will come to many free-standing pinnacles. It really isn't worth hiking to these, but they are interesting.

A nice bouldering area can be found between *The Whale Formation* (when you first come in) and Goldmine Road. If come to Boxcar Rocks to boulder, I recommend you check out this area first. A lot of undeveloped rock exists on the west side of Goldmine Road. If you explore this vegetated ridgeline, you are likely to find a lot of unexplored rock, first ascents, and poison ivy.

The most exciting regional treat is an area discovered by the author, Joe Forte, and the Messicks called Heart of Darkness Crag. This high, steep cliff is made of black conglomerate rock. Very little has been developed here.

16. Chickies Rock

Area Beta

Location
Susquehanna River near Columbia.

Type of Climbing
Trad climbing on a high and scenic cliff.

Other Info
Weekends can be crowded.

Chickies Rock

Located on the east bank of the Susquehanna River, Chickies Rock offers breathtaking views of the South Central Pennsylvania landscape. Imagine climbing one of the overhangs on the *Riverview Ledge*; your feet quiver as you glance over your shoulder, staring at the cool waters of the Susquehanna, 100' below. This is the setting that surrounds one of the most popular climbing areas in Pennsylvania. At Chickies, high climbs, multi-pitch routes, and a beautiful setting make a great spot to visit for Pennsylvania climbers.

That being said, a few things detract from this area. The rock quality on the high wall is excellent, but the rest of the area leads a lot to be desired. Grass, moss, and dirt are regular fixtures on all other walls at Chickies. Another deterrent is a serious lack of rock. Over 60 established routes are closely packed at Chickies, but you can't escape the reality that this is a small climbing area.

One thing that makes up for the lack in size is the height of the rock. The highest section tops out at 135', which makes Chickies one of the highest cliffs in this region and one of the highest in the state.

The routes here range from super easy to 5.12+. This is a great spot for beginners and seasoned climbers who want stout trad leads. Topropes are easy to set up at the northwest and southwest ends of the cliff. Make sure you bring a lot of webbing if you are setting up at the south end or high wall section. The north end has a lot of trees and easy walk-ups to set TRs. Many climbers also use the *Riverview Ledge* for toproping. Please note that this requires an experienced climber to set the ropes and you'll need to place gear for the anchor and scramble an exposed ledge. The top of the high wall can be toproped, but you'll need a 60 meter rope to do so. This wall can also get very crowded on weekends.

History

People have climbed at Chickies Rock longer than most areas in Pennsylvania. Unfortunately, a lot of the older history was not well documented. It seems like everyone I talked to said they climbed there, some as far back as the 1960s, but was unwilling to claim any first ascents. It is known that some of the earlier climbers were Curt Harler, Jeff Martin, and members of the Pennsylvania Mountaineering Association. Mike Pantelich developed and named a few routes along with Joe Urkovich and Mike Reaber. Some of these were The Library, Sunday Morning and Witch's Brew. In later years Hans, Tony, and Hugh Herr as well as Barry Rusnock, Jeff Batzer and Eric Horst were active leading some of the more difficult lines at Chickies Rock and developed Space Ace as well as other climbs. Sue Holland wrote a guidebook for Chickies in the 1980s. This book documented the names and grades of all the climbs at Chickies.

Ownership: The cliff is owned by Chickies Rock County Park. They allow and respect climbing. Please do the same.

Geology: Lower Cambrian Chickies Quartzite. Interesting animal borings can be found in sections of the rock. These ancient holes, called Scolithus tubes, can be found at various locations about the cliff.

Access and Restrictions: The park asks that you adopt a leave-no-trace ethic. Bolting and fixed anchors are not permitted. Please keep noise to an appropriate level and conduct yourself in a polite manor if the park officials appear. Remember it is a privilege for the county to allow climbing. Please respect this so that we may continue to climb here for years to come.

Rack: A standard rack will suffice for most routes. Small, medium, and large cams and nuts are standard fare here. Large pro is useful on certain routes.

Hazards: The clifftop at Chickies is a popular destination for vandals, rock trundlers, glass breaking aficionados, and other folks who don't know people are climbing beneath them—or worse, do know. On a few occasions, people have claimed their lives from jumping from the top. Please beware of falling glass, rocks, trees, bodies, etc.

Nearby Areas: Governor's Stables, Michaux State Forest, Pevine Island, Kelly's Run, The Emerald Haven, Atomic Crag, Psychedelic/Sex Wall, Mason Dixon Crag, Safe Harbor, Euro Wall, Star Rock, The Black Wall. Note: Most of these are closed to climbing.

1. Frosted Flake 5.3 PG
Climb the dirt-filled flake and crack near where the hillside meets the left end of the cliff. Climb past a tree to gain a fern-covered, low-angle slab. The climb ends on the ledge.

2. Unnamed 5.9 R
Climb the greenish-colored face between *Frosted* and *Solution*.

3. Solution Crack 5.8+ PG/R
Cruise the nice finger crack to its top.

4. Great Expectations 5.11a X
This is a great climb, but is often dirty. Start 2' right of the finger crack (*Solution Crack*),

Frosted Flake

1. Frosted Flake 5.3 PG
2. Unnamed 5.9 R
3. Solution Crack 5.8+ PG/R
4. Great Expectations 5.11a X
5. By Pass 5.10a X
6. Hit and Run 5.6 G

and climb to a small overhang 14' up. Pull the center of the hang on thin edges and cruise to the ledge above. You can probably protect using the crack, but it is off route.

5. By Pass 5.10a X
Keeping off *Solution Crack*, climb to the right past the ceiling on *Great Expectations* to a shallow corner. Go up this corner to the ledge.

6. Hit and Run 5.6 G
Ascend the small right-facing corner a few feet right of the previous climb to a small pseudo-overhang near its top. Climb through this feature to the ledge above.

7. Northwest Corner 5.4 G
This is the large obvious arete/corner on the far left edge of the Chickies Rock outcrop. Climb the path of least resistance to the top of the greenish-colored corner. Keep on the edge the entire way up.

8. Northwest Buttress 5.8 X
Pull on nice edges at the large corner to gain a crack that starts 10' up. Follow up and slightly right, arching rightward above the *Ivy League* off-width.

9. Ivy League 5.6 G
Best to skip this climb. Climb the gross off-width crack just right of the *Northwest Corner*. This climb is often wet.
Var. 1: Begin in a shallow crack in the gully 6' left of the off-width.
Var. 2: Start at variation 1 and climb straight up and escape out left when the rock gets very steep.
Var. 3: Same as Var. 2, but continue up the steep rock all the way to its top. Stemming to the off-width is off route.

10. Drop Out 5.5 G
Scum up the *Ivy League* off-width and escape right out an undercling-flake at 18'. Move out right on the flake to gain a gully out to the right. The climb ends on the grassy ledge above.

11. Quad-F 5.3 PG
I give this climb a negative four stars. **Pitch 1:** Climb up the crappy gully 10' right of *Ivy* and 12' left of *Thorny* . You can begin this climb on the chossy wall any place you like, then gain the gully at 16' and end at a ledge at 75'. **Pitch 2:** From here, follow the path of least resistance up corners and faces to the top.

12. Thorny Thicket 5.0 PG
Often wet, always dirty. Run up the easy corner 45' left of the cave to a tree. Then cruise the easiest path to the top.

13. Horny Ticket 5.4 PG
Up the face just right of *Thorny*, past a small overhang at 14', then up steep orangish-colored rock to the top.

Chickies Rock
Northwest Buttress

7. Northwest Corner 5.4 G
8. Northwest Buttress 5.8 X
9. Ivy League 5.6 G
10. Drop Out 5.5 G
11. Quad-F 5.3 G

14. Unnamed 5.3
Cruise up the corner to the right of the previous route.

15. Unnamed 5.4
Explore grassy ledges slightly right of the previous climb.

The Cave Area
Just past *Thorny Ticket* you will see a large cave that contains several worthwhile boulder problems. Descend these problems by dropping off the top move or traversing off the ledge above.

16. The Great Escape 5.9+/5.10a R
Climb the dihedral just off the right end of the bouldering cave, then follow a crack that goes out the leftmost portion of the giant roof above.

17. Hard Times 5.10b PG
Find two trees about 8' right of the bouldering cave. From the left edge of the leftmost tree, climb the slimy greenish-colored rock near some flakes to gain the center of the large overhang. Navigate the overhang halfway between the routes to the right and left.

18. Waitin for a Train 5.8+ PG
Pitch 1: Start 20' right of *Hard Times* between two trees. Climb a short, right-facing corner to a large overhang 20' above. Move out left under the overhang, up a small corner, and move out right to a flake. Pull the lip and move left to belay. **Pitch 2**: Move left and up to an obvious corner above. Move right and find the overhang where a crack splits through it. Climb through the roof and up to the summit.

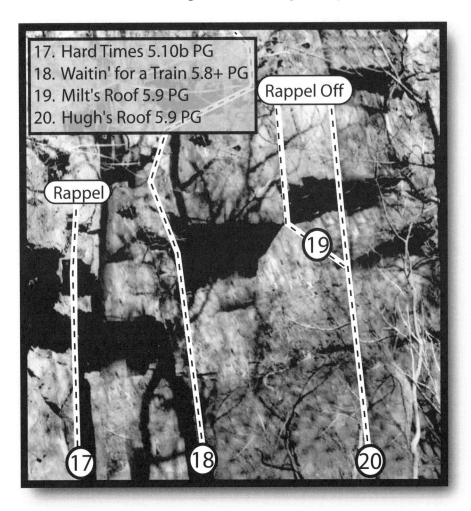

17. Hard Times 5.10b PG
18. Waitin' for a Train 5.8+ PG
19. Milt's Roof 5.9 PG
20. Hugh's Roof 5.9 PG

Rappel Off

Rappel

19. Milt's Roof 5.9 PG
Begin 4' right of the second of two trees that are close together. Climb up and move out left to the roof at a small right-facing corner in the roof. Climb the roof at this corner and continue to another right-facing corner at the roof's right edge. Continue up and right to the ledge above at 75'.

20. Hugh's Roof 5.9 PG
Start the same as *Milt's Roof*, or slightly right of it, and climb up to a small overhang that juts out beneath the main overhang. Climb over this and through a V-notch in the large overhang. Continue to the ledge above.

21. Yo Yo 5.3 G
Easy, dirty, and best left undone. Climb the large gully system a few feet right of the giant overhang. Several variations can be done at the beginning and upper section. The easiest follows grassy sections, past the path of least resistance, to the top.

22. Steppin Out 5.4 PG
Pitch 1: Start the same as *Yo Yo* and cruise to the belay. **Pitch 2:** Move up a corner to pass an overhang, then traverse 10' right "steppin' out" over the overhang. Continue straight up to the top.

23. Orangutan 5.9 PG
Pitch 1: Climb the large *YoYo* corner to the ledge 70' up. **Pitch 2:** Climb up right to a large corner with a roof at the top. Follow a crack to the roof, climb out the roof, then climb the face and corner above.

24. Wild Orangutan 5.10a PG
Pitch 1: Start the same as *Yo Yo* and belay at the communal ledge 70'. **Pitch 2:** Climb up to the roof above (*Orangutan Roof*) and move right to a steep wall. Move around the corner to the summit.

25. Easy Street 5.2 G
Run up easy, unappealing rock just right of the large gully. Continue up the easiest path to the top. Most climbers break the climb into two pitches, midway up, to reduce rope drag.

26. Frigid Face Direct 5.6 PG
Pitch 1: Start at the right end of the overhang 15' right of *Yo Yo*. Climb the shallow left-facing corner and pull around an overhang at its right edge. Belay on ledge above. **Pitch 2:** Go up to and through an overhang then move over ledges to a corner and the top.

27. Frigid Face 5.9 PG
Pitch 1: Climb the crack 6' right of the previous climb to a small grass ledge 12' up at a right-facing corner. Climb the corner to the ledge on top of the overhang. **Pitch 2:** Same as for the previous climb.

28. The Plaque 5.10a R
Pitch 1: Start at a small overhang left of greenish-colored rock at a block. Climb through the overhang and continue up a steep face to a belay ledge at 55'. **Pitch 2:** Run up a corner to a steep face, past ledges, to a corner and the top.

29. Chalk Circle 5.6 PG
Start just right of the previous route and climb a broken crack to a steep face and a belay ledge above at 55'. Climb up ledges and a corner to the top. Can be done in two pitches.

30. Chickies Direct 5.7 PG
Pitch 1: Look to the right of *The Plaque*, and you will see a large overhang with a big corner that leads to this overhang. Climb this slabby corner to the center of the hang. Escape left to pull the left edge of this overhang. **Pitch 2:** Climb an obvious corner to a steep face above, then follow ledges and a corner to the summit (same as for *The Plaque*).

31. Unnamed Roof 5.10a TR
Climb the left-center of the roof slightly right of Chickies Direct.

32. Project

Climb the center of the roof.

33. Too Easy 5.4 G
The name says it all. Start a few feet right of the start to *Chickies Direct* in the woods just before the clearing for the high wall. Climb the face to the chimney and follow this big feature to the top.

34. Witches Brew 5.3 G
A bewitching route that begins at the large clearing this is the leftmost crack that goes up the high wall to a large chimney high above. Get on you're broom and fly up the obvious crack to the *Riverview* ledge-system. At the ledge, spook left into the large, obvious chimney; then brew some moves into the chimney capped by a block. The crux is at the top of the chimney.

35. Kissing Wall 5.5 PG
This climb starts the same as *Witches Brew* and follows the *Witches* crack up to the chimney. From the chimney, step right, approximately 15' under the overhang. Smooch into the right-facing corner; step into the base of the corner; then traverse left to the arete and climb it to the top.

36. Main Street 5.5 PG
Pucker up and follow the *Witches Brew* crack or climb a few feet right of it (slightly harder and less pro) until you are 10' below the *Riverview Ledge*. Traverse right about 10'—or straight if you took the direct variation—to the *Riverview Ledge*.

37. Lester Molester 5.8 R/X
A long time, ago there used to be graffiti painted that said Patty Lester. The graffiti is now gone; start about 10' right of *Witches*, and climb up a slaby face to a horizontal, then to a small ledge that is under the left end of the large *Library* dihedral. Break left and continue up glassy slab to the *Riverview Ledge* at 100'.

38. For Madmen Only 5.7 R
At the shallow right-facing dihedral at orange-black-colored rock, go up and left through shallow cracks/horizontals until you are under the right tip of the large dihedral (*Library* dihedral). From here step right and up into a crack that is midway between the *Library* dihedral out left and the *Snow Flake* arete out right. Climb the crack to the *Riverview Ledge*.

39. The Library 5.5 PG
Read your way up the large, obvious dihedral at the right side of the high wall. Traverse left into another dihedral and climb to a roof; move left, and continue to the giant (*Riverview*) ledge. Walk off the ledge or continue on any of the upper routes off the *Riverview Ledge*.

40. Touch and Go 5.9 R
Between *The Library* and *Snow Flake*, follow technical moves up the nice arete that pull's through an overhang.

41. Snow Flake 5.4 PG

52. Riverview 5.4 PG
53. Inverted V-Overhang 5.10c PG
55. Ape Call 5.8 PG
56. Mike's Roof 5.10a PG

Riverview Ledge

34. Witches Brew 5.3 G	39. The Library 5.5 G
36. Main Street 5.5 PG	40. Touch and Go 5.9 R
37. Lester Molester 5.8 R/X	41. Snow Flake 5.4 PG
38. For Madmen Only 5.7 R	42. The Notch 5.9 PG

Follow *The Library* up the first dihedral and flurry right at its top. Move 5' right along the ledge then continue up to finish.

42. The Notch 5.9 PG
Grunt through the obvious notch between *Snow Flake* and *Sunday Morning*.

43. Sunday Morning 5.4 G
Start at a large, broken, indented section of rock, a few feet right of the previous climb. Climb through steep, blocky features in this broken indentation to a ledge 35' up. Continue to break out right and follow a cleft through easy terrain and grassy ledges to the top.

44. The Lower Undercling 5.8 G
Start the same as for the previous climb. At an overhang in the broken section, traverse left out an undercling below the roof. Continue up the corner above to the *Riverview Ledge*.

45. The Undercling 5.6 G
If you do the previous climb you should do this variation. Start on *Sunday Morning* and follow it past the blocky section to the ledge. Find the higher of two underclings and traverse left to the arete. Follow the thrilling and aesthetic arete to the *Riverview Ledge*.

46. Hollywood 5.7 PG
A truly famous line. Start 10' right of *Sunday Morning* at a glamorous crack and climb it to an overhang with a notch. Climb through the notch to a ledge above. Continue up the middle of the face to the *Riverview Ledge*. Belay here or move right 10' and climb the right side of the face to its top.

47. Train Wreck 5.7 PG
Same route as *Hollywood* but at the top-third of the route, crash slightly left of the *Hollywood* line, and climb up to the top.

48. Shrimp Scampered 5.5 G
Climb the rock 15' right of *Hollywood*; climb an arching curve of rock, and angle left to an overhang and a notch. Pull through this notch and move up to join *Sunday Morning* to the top. From the *Riverview Ledge* follow a corner to the summit.

49. Train Station 5.1 G
Scramble up or down the dirty corner at the right side of the small wall at the south side of the outcrop.

50. Nuts 5.4 PG
Climb the slab on the short, south face of *Chickies Rock*. After the slab, choose a line up some cracks to a small overhang. Pull the overhang at its easiest point.

51. Unnamed 5.5 PG
Move up the blank part of the slab next to *Nuts* and finish on the regular finish mentioned above.

Riverview Ledge Climbs

The next few climbs are located above the giant ledge you can see at the top-third of the high wall at *Chickies*. These climbs can be done by rappelling down to the ledge or more often as a finish to any of the climbs below that lead to this ledge.

52. Riverview 5.4 PG
Start at the left side of the ledge near a corner in the small roof and move left through the overhang to the top while following the easiest path.

53. Inverted V-Overhang 5.10c PG
Start the same as the previous climb; pull through the first overhang, then move left toward a larger overhang pulled at its apex.

54. Space Ace 5.10b PG
This climb is outta this universe. Climb up to the second of two overhangs (same as for the previous two climbs), and pull the right edge of the overhanging V-notch.

55. Ape Call 5.8 PG/R
Start this climb between the right side of the *Riverview Ledge* and the left edge of the massive block that rests atop this ledge. Climb the left side of the overhanging blocks; take a gasp of air, then move right and onto the face.

Scott Messick leading a classic at Chickies. Photo by the author.

56. Mike's Roof 5.10a PG/R
Right of the previous climb, pull a large pointed overhang at a crack and notch. This climb basically pulls the center of the large block through the lip of the big roof between *Ape Call* and *Mike Jr.*

57. Mike Jr. 5.9 PG/R
Difficult to place gear. This climb starts around the right corner of the ledge and overhang (left side of the *Southwest Buttress* near the top section of *Hollywood*). Climb just right of the previous route at a horizontal crack in the roof pulling the right side of the small roof just off the *Riverview Ledge*.

58. The Corner 5.7 PG
Just right of the previous route, follow a corner to the right side of the overhang. Pass this area and climb to the top.

59. Belly-flop 5.5 G
Start at the left side of the *Southwest Buttress* and climb the easy face to a corner and ledge. It is possible to walk the dirt trail at the right side of the buttress and traverse the ledge in

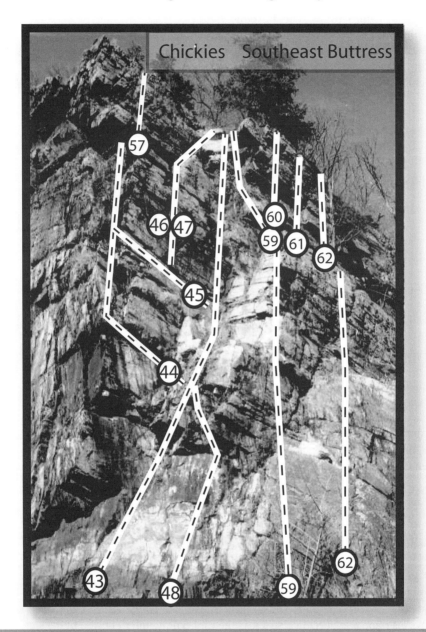

Chickies   Southeast Buttress

43. Sunday Morning 5.4 G
44. Lower Undercling 5.8 G
45. The Undercling 5.6 G
46. Hollywood 5.7 PG
47. Train Wreck 5.7 PG

57. Mike Jr. 5.9 PG/R
59. Belly-flop 5.5 G
60. Paul's Pop Off 5.9 PG
61. Zig 5.4 PG
62. Zag 5.5 PG

also. Flop up the easy, broken-up corner, and escape left around the overhang. There is a big tree above for TRs.

60. Paul's Pop Off 5.9 PG
Start the same as *Belly Flop* and climb to an overhang. Move right to the overhang and pull through it off-routing a block or a stem, left, that reduces the grade considerably.

61. Zig 5.4 PG
Gain the ledge via the dirt trail at the right of the buttress or by climbing the face below. Right of the previous climb, zig over sloping ledges to steeper rock; pass the *Paul's Pop Off* overhang at its right edge, and continue straight to the top.

62. Zag 5.5 PG
Gain the ledge via the dirt trail at the right of the buttress or by climbing the face below. Begin 5' right of the start of *Zig* and *Zig-Zag*, and zag straight up to a bulge/overhang. Move right to a crack and the top. Be careful not to zig or you'll be doing the previous route.

Eric Horst climbing at Chickies circa 1981. Photo courtesy Eric Horst collection

63. Zig-Zag 5.4 G
Right of the *Pauls Pop Off*, follow sloping ledges to steeper rock and break right at the right end of the overhang. Traverse out right at the bottom of a bulge and climb to the top.

Boulder Problems (The Cave)
A unique bouldering cave can be found in the center of the cliff near Milt's Roof. A few good problems are located here. The descents from the problems are done by hanging off the top hold and jumping off. I list only four problems in the cave. Many more exist with eliminates.

A. Standard Undercling Crack V0
SDS and climb the crack at the left side of the cave.

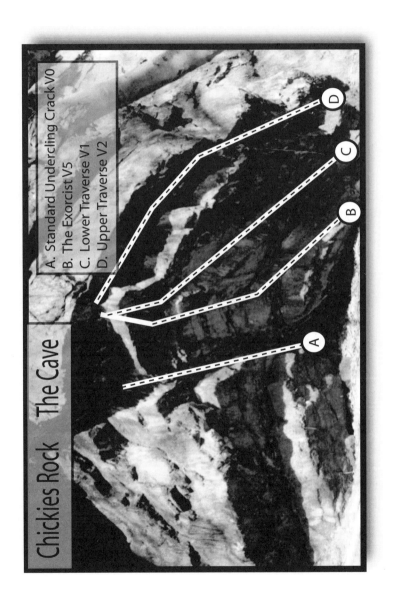

Chickies Rock   The Cave

A. Standard Undercling Crack V0
B. The Exorcist V5
C. Lower Traverse V1
D. Upper Traverse V2

B. The Exorcist V5
SDS and climb the center of the roof.

C. Lower Traverse V1
SDS and climb the lower rail.

D. Upper Traverse V2
SDS and climb the upper rail.

Bouldering on the Pinnacle
From the top of the cliff at it's left side, you can see a large pinnacle off in the woods. Several highball problems can be done on this large boulder.

South Mountain Overview

Predominantly located in Michaux State Forest, the twenty-plus mile South Mountain ridge offers a wealth of climbing opportunities. Located between Chambersburg and Carlisle, the South Mountain ridge is home to two state parks: Caladonia and Pine Grove furnace.

Michaux State Forest encompasses more than 85,000 acres of land. This forest is named after French botanist Andre Michaux who was dispatched by the queen and king of France in 1785 to collect samples for their royal gardens in France. Michaux discovered many new species of plants, flowers, shrubs, and trees during this time—he also discovered the state forest later named after him.

Located within the forest, Pine Grove Furnace and Caledonia State Parks were once the location of the thriving iron furnace industry of the 1700s and 1800s. Timber logging fueled the large stone iron furnaces that were used to create tools, stoves, and even cannonballs that were used in the revolutionary war. One of these massive furnaces still stands at the intersection or routes 30 and 233.

A main point of attraction in this state forest is the famed Appalachian Trail. Twenty-plus miles of this 2,168 mile-long trail are located in Michaux State Forest. One interesting point is that the AT passes by several of the rock outcrops this guidebook covers. These outcrops create beautiful vistas and interesting diversions for hikers along the trail. Some of these outcrops lure day hikers and thrill-seeking locals to scramble along the massive boulders and rock features located throughout the forest.

This section of this book lists 15 climbing and bouldering areas scattered throughout Michaux State Forest. Take note that there are over 21 areas in and near Michaux; I've only listed the more popular ones. Be aware that Michaux has incredibly good climbing spots and incredibly bad climbing spots. I have taken the liberty to map out and go into depth for the better areas but intentionally list brief descriptions of the bad spots. I suppose a popular question to ask is, "Why include the bad spots in a guidebook?" The answer simply is that I wanted local climbers to know about all the climbing possibilities near them.

Most of the spots I include in this section are worth visiting. Areas like the Hermitage, White Rock Acres, Whiskey Springs, Chimney Rocks, Purgatory Rocks, and Pole Steeple are worth checking out. Spots I don't recommend are Wildcat Rocks, Virginia Rocks, Coroners Slab, Sunset Rocks, and Lewis Rock.

For top roping or trad leads, the Hermitage is the best choice. Climbs here cater to all climbers be it novice or expert. Top ropes are easy to set up and a few good leads can be found. A long time ago this area was even featured in *Rock and Ice*. The next best choice for roped climbing is a toss up between White Rocks (Pond Bank), or Pole Steeple. These areas are best suited to the novice climber, but a handful of routes in the 5.9 to 5.11+ range exist for the seasoned climber.

For the bouldering aficionado, Whiskey Springs wins the competition hands down. For decades, this has been the stomping grounds for climbers who live in Harrisburg, Chambersburg, and northern Maryland. It has also drawn world renowned climbers like "hot" Henry Barber, Hugh Herr, Bob Murray, and others. The variety in rock angle, height, and difficulty makes this place just as good for novices as it is for experts.

Ranking in a close comparison is the high-quality conglomerate of Chimney Rocks. Abundant problems up to V11 give this area the prize for having the most difficult problems in this region. Don't miss the thrilling highball's this area is famous for.

South Mountain Overview Map

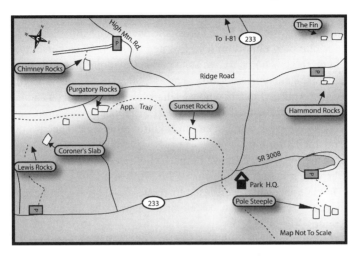

Whether you're a local climber or simply looking for a new place to check out, Michaux State Forest is an excellent choice. Due to the close proximity to Maryland, hope climbers from Maryland will begin to explore the wonders of this region.

In Case of Emergency: Contact a park employee or dial 911. For directions to the nearest hospital, look on bulletin boards or at the park office. If you are in the South end of the park Chambersburg Hospital is the closest. If you are at the North end Carlisle Regional is closer. Chambersburg Hospital is located at 112 North Seventh Street in Chambersburg, PA 17201. The phone number is 717-267-3000. Carlisle Hospital is located at 26 Parker Street in Carlisle, PA. The phone number is 717-249-1212. Please note that a new hospital is being built off the College Street exit off Interstate 81 near Alexander springs Road..

Areas in this Section: Brown Rocks, Chimney Rocks, Coroners Slab, Dead Woman's Hollow Road, Hammond Rocks, The Hermitage, Lewis Rocks, Pole Steeple, Purgatory Rocks, Rattlesnake Rocks, Sunset Rocks, Virginia Rocks, Whiskey Springs, White Rocks, White Rock Acres, Wildcat Rocks.

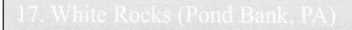

17. White Rocks (Pond Bank, PA)

Area Beta

Location
Pond Bank, Pennsylvania.
There are three other White
Rock areas in PA.

Type of Climbing
Trad routes on clean rock
with nice views.

Other Info
There are 20 nearby areas.

White Rocks

This area has long been regarded as one of the most popular areas in South Central PA. Easy toprope access and excellent trad climbs make this area a fun spot for an afternoon of roped climbing. The outcrop is about 65' high and offers climbing year round due to its sunny exposure—climbing in winter can sometimes be chilly though. The rock here dries quickly after rainstorms. 20 popular routes exist here with a few easy boulder problems scattered around the hillside and cliff. Routes range from 5.3 to 5.10. Most trad climbs here do not protect well, but topropes can be easily set up by walking up the 3rd class gulley at the southeast end of the cliff.

Directions

From I-81 in Chambersburg, take State Route 30 east for approximately 5 miles, until you reach the intersection of routes 30 and 997 at the town of Fayetteville. Make a right and follow Route 997 south a few miles to the small village of Pond Bank. In the center of town you will see a road labeled White Rock Road on the left side of 997. Make a left and follow this road until it turns into a dirt road after about 1 mile. Look for a dirt lot near a water tower. The rock should be visible just above the water tower clearing. A small trail at the north end of the clearing leads up to the rock. The pull-off just north of the water tower lot also leads west to the rock.

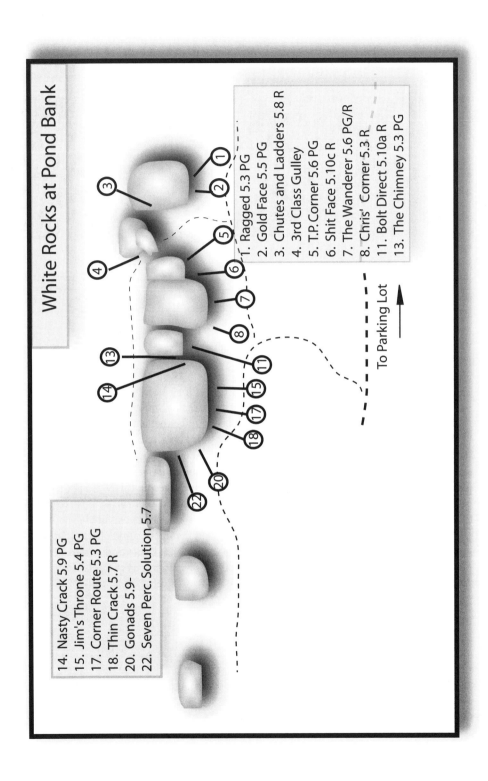

White Rocks at Pond Bank

1. Ragged 5.3 PG
2. Gold Face 5.5 PG
3. Chutes and Ladders 5.8 R
4. 3rd Class Gulley
5. T.P. Corner 5.6 PG
6. Shit Face 5.10c R
7. The Wanderer 5.6 PG/R
8. Chris' Corner 5.3 R
11. Bolt Direct 5.10a R
13. The Chimney 5.3 PG

14. Nasty Crack 5.9 PG
15. Jim's Throne 5.4 PG
17. Corner Route 5.3 PG
18. Thin Crack 5.7 R
20. Gonads 5.9-
22. Seven Perc. Solution 5.7

To Parking Lot

1. Ragged 5.3 PG
Climb the low-angle face at the cliff's right end.

2. Gold Face 5.5 PG
Climb the short gold-colored face on the right side of the 3rd class gulley.

3. Chutes and Ladders 5.8 R
Climb the short, steep wall past very positive holds and rails left of the previous climb. Moving out right or far left near the top drops the grade a bit.

4. 3rd Class Gulley
This is the large gulley at the right end of the cliff. It is used as a downclimb, or to access the top of the cliff.

5. T.P. Corner 5.6 PG
This climb ascends the right side of a corner that is visible on the left wall of the 3rd class gulley.

6. Shit Face 5.10c R
Climb the slab left of the previous climb to a steep wall left of a crack/corner. The crack is off route.

7. The Wanderer 5.6 PG/R
The beginning is a bit tricky to protect but the top has good gear. Climb the easiest path up the face and around the corner from the previous climb.
Var 1: 5.8 R Climb a bit right of the original line, closer to the corner.

8. Chris' Corner 5.3 R
Climb the corner to the left of the previous route, near the gulley/chimney in the center of the cliff.

9. Well Groomed When Pruned 5.4 G
Squeeze the off-width left of the previous route on the right wall of the chimney/gulley.

10. Bolt Right 5.9+ R
Climb the right-hand side of the smooth face at the back end of the gulley to a bolt that is frequently chopped by a miscreant local climber. Climb to the right, past the bolt (Crux), and pull over the bulge above at the right side.

11. Bolt Direct 5.10a R
Climb the center of the smooth face. The right and left corners and face, on both sides, are off route.

12. Bolt Left R 5.7+ R
Climb the left side of the face at the left side of *The Bolt Face*.

13. The Chimney 5.2 PG
Climb the obvious chimney.

14. Nasty Crack 5.9 PG

Jam your way up the nice crack on the left face of the chimney/gulley.

15. Sign of Zorro 5.5 PG

Cruise the easy corner left of the previous route.

16. Jim's Throne 5.4 PG

A route that should not be missed. Run up the easy, low-angle face past large horizontal breaks 10' left of the previous climb.

17. Corner Route 5.3 PG

Climb the large, easy corner that is just right of *Thin Crack*.

18. Thin Crack 5.7 R

Climb onto a nice ledge and gain a thin finger crack with a fun crux at its lower section. Continue straight up past gorgeous, clean rock to the beautiful exposure above.

19. Pine Tree 5.5

Begin below the pine, left of the previous climb, and gain the corner to its top.

20. Gonads 5.9-

Gain a flake and face that is left of and around the corner from the previous route.

21. Reach Around Boo 5.6

Start 10' left of *Gonads* and gain an overhang that is escaped to its right.

22. Seven Percent Solution 5.7

Gain an overhang near the ground and move up to a crack and corner above.

23. Lime Line 5.11a R

Climb the thin, green-colored face right of the crack that leads to the overhang for the previous route. The crack and corner are off route. Using the right corner makes for a nice 5.9 variation.

24. Hangulation 5.10a

Climb the obvious overhang at the far left end of the cliff.

18. Brown Rocks

Area Beta

Location
Adjacent to White Rocks near Pond Bank, PA.

Type of Climbing
A few trad routes or toprope routes.

Other Info
If this area does not provide enough climbing. There are 20 nearby areas.

Brown Rocks

This area is incredibly small with limited routes. The rock quality is great and the routes are enticingly fun, unfortunately the area is rather small. Visiting White Rocks or The Hermitage in conjunction with this area is advised and can make the venture worthwhile. If you live nearby, this can be a fun place to visit; if you live far away, don't waste your time visiting this area.

Should you visit Brown Rocks, expect to find about fifteen routes topping out at 40' in height. The routes range from 5.3 to 512a in difficulty. A few boulders exist with easy problems. Two positive features about this area are the free standing pinnacle and the excellent rock quality. If you don't find this locale interesting, White Rocks is only minutes away, on the other side of the road (see White Rocks section).

Most climbs here are usually toproped. Topropes can easily be set up atop the main cliff by scrambling up the east or west ends of the cliff. A TR can also be set up on top the pinnacle by scrambling up the 3rd class chimney left of the pinnacle. The top accepts small to medium cams and nuts, or semi-long webbing for the large blocks.

Directions

From interstate 81 (Chambersburg State Route 30 Exit), take Route 30 east, approximately 5 miles, until you reach the intersection of Routes 30 and 997 at the town of Fayetteville. Turn right and follow Route 997 south a few miles, to the small village of Pond Bank. In the center of town you will see a road labeled White Rock Road on the left side of Rt. 997. Make a left and follow this road until it turns into a dirt road after 1 mile. Look for a dirt lot near a water tower. *White Rocks* will be partially visible off to your left. If the leaves are off the trees you may sight *Brown Rocks* off of the right side of the road. Park at the dirt lot mentioned above, and locate a dirt road on the right side of the road. Follow this road, passing a small quarry off to the right, and continue straight, until a small trail leads off and left from the road. This trail will occur after about 10 minutes of walking. This will lead to some talus and the rocks located along the ridge. This area is a bit tricky to find the closer you get to it.

1. Big Mama 5.9 R/X

This is the leftmost route on this rock outcrop. It can easily be located as the highest section on the cliff, left of, and slightly behind the pinnacle. The route climbs the center of the face. Using the left corner makes the route a grade easier.

Var. 1: 5.8 R Climb the same route using the left corner.

2. Puppy Love 5.10a R/X

Begin this climb a few feet right of *Big Mama* and climb straight up the steep face.

3. Puppy 5.6 PG

Climb the short face between the previous route and the chimney.

4. Arettissma 5.11a R/X

A saucy little boulder problem. Begin on *North Face Left*, move left onto a beautiful arete, and climb it to the top.

5. The North Face Left 5.10b R

Pop up over a small overhang that connects the third-class gully at the pinnacle's north-facing side. Continue past cruxy moves to gain the top.

6. The North Face 5.9- PG/R

Some prefer to solo this one, but it isn't a bad lead either. Climb the right side of the short, north-facing face, a few feet right of the previous route. Climb this to a small crack that widens near the top.

7. Sundown 5.11d R/X

Climb the front face of the pinnacle to a small overhang 12' up. Pull the left side of the overhang (crux) and continue to the top.

Var. 1: 5.12a Pulling over the center of the hang, while eliminating the corner, makes this route a little harder.

8. Southern Comforts 5.10a R/X

Climb the right hand corner of the pinnacle.

9. Chimneys 5.3

The obvious chimney.

10. Sunshine Superman 5.10a R

Balance up the center of a small face, just right of the chimney.

11. Hopper 5.3

Climb easy rock next to *Sunshine Superman.*

12. Puppy in Heat 5.3

This is the corner, 10' right of a Chimney, at the right side of the outcrop.

19. The Hermitage

Area Beta

Location
South-central Pennsylvania.
Not far from Chambersburg.

Type of Climbing
Trad and toprope. Some bouldering.

Other Info
Can be crowded on weekends.

The Hermitage

The Hermitage, also called Shaffer Rock, is named after the cabin on the Appalachian Trail (Hermitage Cabin). This popular climbing spot offers 32 routes that can be lead- climbed or toproped. The easy access to the top of the cliff makes it easy to set topropes. I recommend a supplement of medium to large-sized gear to accompany the trees that can be slung along the top of the cliff. Bring plenty of webbing and small gear if you plan to set TRs up from atop the pillar. The easiest way to set up climbs on this pillar is to solo or lead a short 5.2 called *Lichen Lizard*.

The routes are short, and top out at about 65', but don't let the lack of height sway you from visiting *Shaffer Rock*; this area is a great place to climb. The excellent rock quality drags climbers from a great distance to climb here. For this reason, the area is one of the most frequented crags in South-central PA. Short, steep walls with delicate crimps and blunt corners characterize the short but eccentric climbs at *Schaffer's*. There may not be a large number of routes here, but all are classic!

Any and all climbs at this spot are worth doing at least once, but the climbs on the detached pillar are must-do. This area can become crowded on weekends; therefore, you may have to wait a while for certain climbs on busy weekends. A limited group of boulders lie below and alongside the cliff. At least 50 problems exist—most can be overlooked— but a few must-do, mega-classics are here for the dedicated bouldering crew.

Location: Approximately 12 miles east of Chambersburg.

General Overview: High quality rock and routes. 32 routes that can be lead or easily toproped. A limited group of boulders lie below and alongside the cliff. Limited bouldering can also be found here. Routes range from 5.2 to 5.13a. Boulder problems from V0- to V7.

Geology: Weaverton Quartzite. Marblelike qualities.

Recommended Rack: Small to medium nuts and cams should suffice. Bring medium to long webbing for TRs. Most cracks take stoppers well. A few off-width routes will require large cams or hexes.

Access Issues and Restrictions: Rock climbing is recognized and allowed here. The only restriction involves guided parties. All guides must register with Micheux State Forest before guiding parties on the land.

Area Hazards: Occasional snakes and rockfall. The rock is quite solid, so the latter is seldom.

Approach Time: 60 seconds.

In Case of Emergency: Contact a park employee or dial 911. For directions to the nearest hospital, look on bulletin boards or at the park office. Chambersburg Hospital is the closest. Chambersburg Hospital is located at 112 North Seventh Street in Chambersburg, PA 17201. The phone number is 717-267-3000.

Nearby Areas: Brown Rocks, Chimney Rocks, Coroners Slab, Dead Woman's Hollow Road, Hammond Rocks, The Hermitage, Lewis Rocks, Pole Steeple, Purgatory Rocks, Rattlesnake Rocks, Sunset Rocks, Virginia Rocks, Whiskey Springs, White Rocks, White Rock Acres, Wildcat Rocks.

History

This area has one of the oldest climbing histories in the state. Since climbing dates back into the 1950s, much of the information has been lost over the years. It is known that an old Dutch/Amish farmer used to hammer pitons into the pillar and climb the obvious routes on the cliff. Older PMA members remember running into this climber and watching him cruise many routes at the cliff. In the 1970s they remember him being "an old Dutch guy" who seemed to have a bunch of the routes dialed. Rick Roundtree has been the most prolific climber at this area. He developed most of the hard routes and pushed climbing here into the 5.10 and up range. Rick is known to have been the local master of this crag for a long time. I added a few hard boulder problems to the area and came up with the bright idea of the 5.13 on the pillar (not been done clean yet).

Directions

From the intersection of State Route 233 and Route 30, take Rt. 233 south 3.5 miles to a stop sign at a pond. Make a left, and follow South Mountain Road (SR2024) east, about 2 miles, until you reach the village of South Mountain. At the far end of town, you will find Old Forge Road on the right. Turn right onto this road and drive approximately 3.5 miles to reach Swift Run Road on your right. The only landmark for this road is that it's the road just after the sign for the Appalachian Trail. The AT crosses Old Forge Road just before you reach Swift Run Road.

Turn right and follow Swift Run Road uphill for about 1 mile and park at the sharp, left

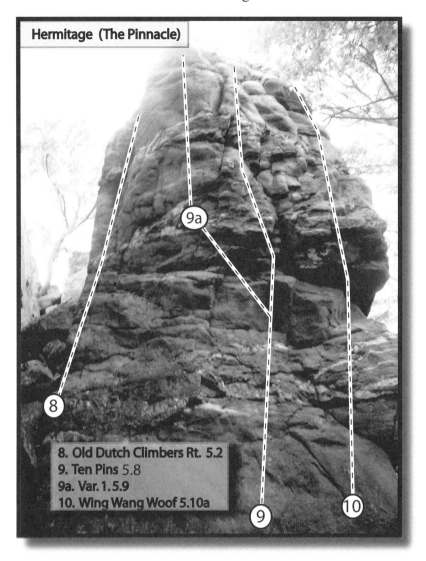

Hermitage (The Pinnacle)

8. Old Dutch Climbers Rt. 5.2
9. Ten Pins 5.8
9a. Var. 1. 5.9
10. Wing Wang Woof 5.10a

90-degree corner. Find a wide trail at the top of the lot and follow the blazes on the trees. The cliff is just a few hundred feet beyond the lot. From the lot, walk left to access a trail that skirts the edge of the cliff. Be careful here; the cliff-edge is high. Be sure to take the easy descent trail at the far edge of the cliff. Many pseudo-trails look like an easy way down but drop off the edge of the cliff. Taking the wrong trail can be dangerous.

The Pinnacle
1. 5.2 G
Climb the easy crack at the right end of the passage, right of *Green Meanies*.

2. Green Meanies 5.9 R
This climb is located in the passage behind the main detached pillar. Looking into the passage climb the right side of the face left of the easy crack. There used to be a green

streak left of the route.

3. 5.11b R
Climb the face between *Green Meanies* and *Wedgies*. Start on a c-shaped hold 10' up, and then follow thin and sloping crimps. The crack is off route.

4. Wedgies 5.8 G
Short but fun. Begin under the overhanging block left for the previous climb, and use a crack to gain the top.

5. Lichen Lizard 5.2 G
A popular ascent/descent route used to set topropes up on the main pillar. Climb a crack right of a small roof on the back side of the pillar. Looking at the back side, this route is on the left.

6. Lichen Left 5.8 PG/R
Climb the face just right of *Lichen Lizard*.

Jess Holzman on "Ten Pins."

7. To My Lichen 5.9 PG/R
Climb nice holds just right of the previous climb on the first ledge of the passage.

8. Old Dutch Climbers Route 5.2 PG
Named for an old Dutch climber that frequented this crag until the early '80s. The man had been climbing *Schaffer's* for decades. Climb a low-angle ramp right of the previous climb.

9. Ten Pins 5.8 PG
At the left-side-face of the detached pinnacle, there is a passage that forms a trench on the back side. This climb ascends the face to the right of the passage. Climb the center of the face over a bulge and cracks. The crux is in the center of the climb at a bulge.
Var. 1. 5.9 R Climb up and slightly left of the main cracks over a bulge/indentation just before the corner.

10. Wing Wang Woof 5.10a R
Start the same as for *Ten Pins*. Just after the start, angle up and right over a small overhang. Continue straight to the top.

11. Marblehead 5.12d R/X
To the right of and around the corner from *Wing Wang*, start left of *Spider Man Direct* at the left side of the front-face of the pinnacle. Move over blank, thin edges and climb straight up and over the smooth bulge above. Continue up the left side of the pillar to the top.

Hermitage (The Pinnacle)

11. Marblehead 5.12d R/X	15. 513a R/X
12. Spider Balls 5.10b R	16. The Bastard 5.11a R
13. Spider Man 5.11a R	17. The Bitch 5.8+ PG/R 18. Leap of Faith 5.7 R

12. Spider Balls 5.10b R

The bouldery crux is near the start, but the whole climb is overhanging and sustained. Start under a small ceiling at the right side of the pillar and go straight up on incuts to a horizontal 18' up. Step into the obvious crack or the face just right (easier), and follow the crack to a small tree; and then gain the top. Two bolt anchor on top.

13. Spider Man 5.11a R

Start the same as for *Spider Balls* before the horizontal; then follow an undercling far out left to join the big horizontal at the left end of the ceiling 18'above. Move right to join the finish of *Spider Balls*.

14. Spider Man Direct 5.12a R

Start under the V-shaped block in the center of the face, or traverse into the V-block and pull over it (crux) to join the *Spider Balls* finish.

15. 5.13a R/X

Move up the right side of the pillar near *Spider Balls* to the perch at the top of the first vertical crack on *Spider Balls*. From here, move up the blank, overhanging right side of the pillar to a vertical, sloping ledge (crux); continue straight to the top.

16. The Bastard 5.11a R

Technical and fun. 2' right of the big gully/chimney, climb the left-hand side of the smooth face to a big pocket. Continue to the top.

17. The Bitch 5.8+ PG/R

Follow a low-angle ramp 12' to a crack, and climb the right side of the face to the top.

18. Leap of Faith 5.7 R

A dyno variation next to the previous route. If you don't make the dyno the route becomes extremely hard.

19. Grungie Face 5.4 PG

The climb is better than it sounds. Climb the face right of *Leap of Faith* and a breach in the rock.

20. Grungie 5.0 G

Squirm up the off-width chimney next to *Grungie Face*.

21. Blazing Saddles 5.6 PG

Challenging for the grade. This beautiful left-facing corner that leads to an overhang near the top is one of the best routes at this area. There is a two bolt anchor above this climb.

22. Lost Religion 5.12a TR

This is a pseudo-eliminate route that climbs the clean, aesthetic wall just right of the *Blazing Saddles* corner. The left corner-wall is off route.

23. In Your Face 5.10c/d X

Climb straight up the amazing, clean arete right of the previous climb.

24. Gary's Variation 5.12c

This variation follows the face, left of the arete, offrouting the large pocket.

25. Crucifixion 5.11a R

From solution holes, climb the corner and face right of *In Your Face*.

26. Yellow Pages 5.8 G

Under a pine tree that is right of the previous climb, move up a small left-facing corner to a ledge where you can traverse under some flakes. From the flakes, move up to the pine tree above.

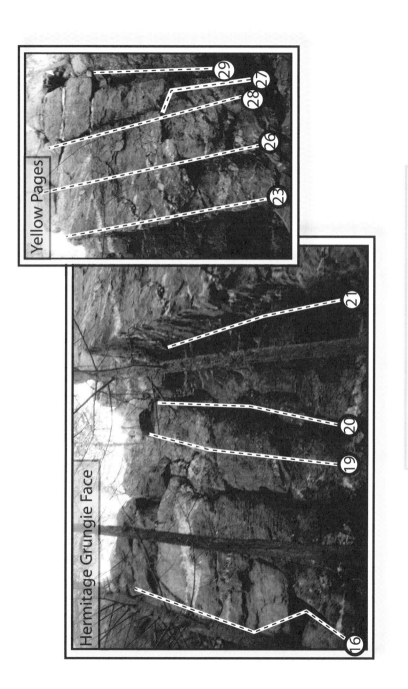

Yellow Pages

Hermitage Grungie Face

16. The Bastard 5.11a R
19. Grungie Face 5.4 PG
20. Grungie 5.0 G
21. Blazing Saddles 5.6 PG
23. In Your Face 5.10 c/d X
26. Yellow Pages 5.8 G
27. Rappel Crack 5.6 G
29. Vision of Stem 5.3 G

27. Rappel Crack 5.6 G
Beginning on the previous climb, gain a small ledge that is traversed left into a small crack; then follow this to the top.

28. Rappel Crack Direct 5.9 G
A few feet right of *Yellow Pages*, start in the center of the face in solution pockets; shoot to a bucket, and gain the ledge above.

29. The Vision of Stem 5.3 G
Climb the obvious left-facing corner at the right end of the cliff.

Christa Messick leading at the Hermitage. RH photo.

20. Purgatory Rocks Bouldering Area

Area Beta

Location
Near Carlisle, Pennsylvania in Michaux State Forest.

Type of Climbing
Some of the best bouldering in the region.

Other Info
A nice area to get away from the crowds.

Purgatory Rocks

High atop a mountain, in a remote part of Micheux State Forest, is a desolate bouldering area named Purgatory Rocks. With isolated surroundings, the name somehow seems appropriate for such an uninhabited area. It's rare to find another climbing party or even remnants of chalk on any of the boulders at this area. A steep, winding road leads to a dark, forested approach trail, secluded on the flanks of South Mountain. Don't let this areas deserted figure dissuade you from visiting Purgatory Rocks; the bouldering is excellent!

Boulders, both large and small, stimulate the landscape near Woodrow Road. The majority of the problems lean toward easier grades, but the problems are some of the nicest in the region. I would consider some of the routes here the best in this part of the state. I recommend visiting this area at least once. Problems range from V0- to V7 with boulders from 3 to 27'high. This spot gives nearby Whiskey Springs stiff competition. I recommend a visit to this spot.

History

Many climbers have visited this area over the years. Old PMA members were the first and Pete Carter has been mentioned to have been an influential climber here and on South Mountain in general. Glen Stoner visited this area as well as Tim garland who was particularly active at nearby Coroner's Slab. Myself and Ryan Lukas developed a large

311

majority of the bouldering at this area and are responsible for a great deal of the harder lines and sit-start problems on both sides of the road. Many problems that have been done both here and in the nearby vicinity are not mentioned in this guide.

Geology: Weaverton Quartzite.

Hazards: The first time I visited this area I stepped on a fat, large, diamondback rattlesnake. This area is infamous for its snake dens – perhaps a little irony for a place named Purgatory Rocks. Be mindful where you step, probe, and top out. Remember: snakes love rocks, and most can easily send V10.

Since this area sees such little climbing activity, many holds can be loose. Watch for large holds that break at the most opportune moments.

Directions

From I-81 near Carlisle, take exit 37 to Rt. 233 south towards Newville.. Drive south on Rt. 233 several miles until you reach the Park Office at Pine Grove Furnace State Park. At the 90-degree bend in Route 233, at the park office, drive 2.5 miles from the park office to reach Woodrow Road on your right. Woodrow Road is a dirt road labeled by a small wooden sign. Drive exactly 1.8 miles through switchbacks, climbing Woodrow Road to its summit. At 1.8 miles, you will see a small parking-patch on your right at the crest of the mountain. Park here, and walk an old road from the parking spot past an undesignated camping area. Bear right at the first Y in the road/trail, and you will see rock to your left within a few minutes of walking.

Area 1

This area can be located by walking down the ridge, past Area 2, until you come to a clearing and a long boulder with long walls stacked next to each other (*Wafer Rock*). Problem number 23 (*Spook Corner*) is actually the first significant boulder problem you'll see when walking to this area from the parking lot.

A. Wafer Rock

When walking in, this is the first cluster of boulders you'll see on the right side of the trail. They're a series of four long boulders stacked next to each other.

1. Pine Slab V0- R

On the first cluster of long boulders stacked next to each other, this is the high slab on the highest side of the boulder. Several variations have been done to the right and left at the same grade.

2. Purgatory V1 R

SDS and climb the west corner, where the slab and narrow flake of the boulder form. Do not stem to the wafer of rock to the right. It's off route.

3. Stuck in Purgatory V0

Jam your body into the off-width crack right of the previous line. Don't get stuck.

4. Horn Haul V4

SDS and climb the overhanging prow right of the previous problem. Start as low as possible and gain a small, sharp edge, then throw around the right corner of the prow to good holds.

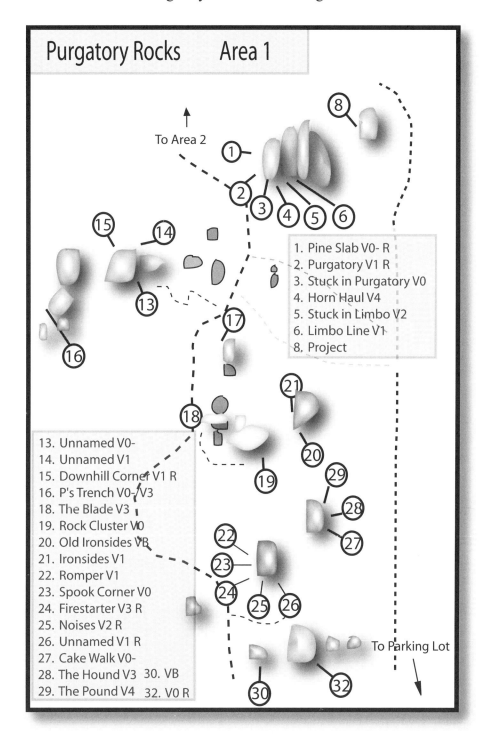

Purgatory Rocks   Area 1

To Area 2

1. Pine Slab V0- R
2. Purgatory V1 R
3. Stuck in Purgatory V0
4. Horn Haul V4
5. Stuck in Limbo V2
6. Limbo Line V1
8. Project

13. Unnamed V0-
14. Unnamed V1
15. Downhill Corner V1 R
16. P's Trench V0-/V3
18. The Blade V3
19. Rock Cluster V0
20. Old Ironsides VB
21. Ironsides V1
22. Romper V1
23. Spook Corner V0
24. Firestarter V3 R
25. Noises V2 R
26. Unnamed V1 R
27. Cake Walk V0-
28. The Hound V3   30. VB
29. The Pound V4   32. V0 R

To Parking Lot

313

Continue straight up to mantle the point above.

5. Stuck in Limbo V2
SDS and climb the short face of the boulder that is around the corner from the prow but is still on the same giant wafer of rock (second giant wafer that forms the packed-together cluster).

6. Limbo Line V1
SDS and climb the center face of the boulder right of the previous wafer.

7. Unnamed V0+
SDS in the corner right of the previous problem, and pull over a small ceiling.

B. Satellite Boulder
This is the square-shaped boulder across from the first cluster of boulders. Several problems in the V0- range have been done here.

8. Project
SDS in an alcove and climb the thin face at the right side of the boulder.

9. Unnamed V7
A few paces downhill and farther up the ridge from the previous problems, you will spy a long boulder with a small cave at its right side. Sit start as low in the cave as possible then climb a difficult flake to its top.

10. Unnamed V0
Climb the steep arete of the boulder directly across the trail.

11. Unnamed V2
At the far right end of the outcrop, there is a boulder perched on a ledge set back to the right of the main outcrop. From a sitting start, climb the arete of the most downhill of two boulders pressed together.

12. Unnamed V1
Climb the somewhat high face a few feet left of the previous problem.

C. Marble Cube
This is a large, smooth rock-cube that can be found by following the trail at the wafer-shaped boulder back toward the parking lot. The trail doubles back toward the parking lot and joins the main approach trail. Follow the trail a few-hundred feet and this boulder is off the right side of the trail. A few square boulders close together make up the group of boulders that surround the main cube.

13. Unnamed V0-
Climb the South face of the boulder.

14. Unnamed V1
This is the corner right of the previous line.

The author bouldering at Purgatory Rocks.

15. Downhill Corner V1 R
Climb the downhill corner.

16. Purgatory's Trench V0-/V3
Several problems, varying in grade, have
been done in the vegetated trench, downhill and right of the main cube.

17. Unnamed V0-
Several very easy problems can be done on a small boulder a few-hundred feet south on
the approach trail.

18. The Blade V3
This is the obvious rock feature that hangs over the trail. Just past the previous problems.
Climb up and over the point. Start low under the blade feature and climb over the center.

19. Rock cluster V0
Climb the backside of the cluster of rock behind the blade-feature. This cluster is semi-
high and has a few lines that can be done at the same grade.

D. Ironsides
This is the large boulder that looks like a small ship's prow. It's located behind the previous
boulder.

20. Old Ironsides VB
SDS and climb the prow.

21. Ironsides V1

Start low and climb the thin face left of the prow to a seam at the top.

22. Romper V1
Climb the overhanging, small face on the small boulder at the backside of the outcrop.

23. Spook Corner V0
Run up easy moves at the highest corner of the boulder to a big jug under the first tier of a roof/prow. Muscle straight up to a good hold and the top.
Var. 1: V0- R Same as the previous route, but move left near the top

24. Fire Starter V3 R
Wild, exciting moves! One of the best problems at this area. Start on the previous problem and climb up to good holds just before the overhanging prow that moves right. Move up into a sidepull, and pull through the flakes that create a notch near the top.

25. Noises in the Forest V2 R
Climb the right side of the boulder at a small arete under the prow, and climb up to a horizontal jug under the roof. Continue left along the horizontal, and top out on problem number 6.

26. Unnamed V1 R
Located on the front side of the boulder..

E. Little Trailside Boulder
This is the small boulder below the previous boulder. It's located on the main trail that takes you to the parking lot.

27. Cake Walk V0-
Climb the left side rail on the boulder.

28. The Hound V3
Start low at the left side of the boulder, and climb up small edges to top out at the center of the boulder.

29. The Pound V4
Climb off an undercling from low in the center of the boulder.

F. Small Unnamed Cluster
A group of three boulders lie near each other off the left side of the trail a short distance after the second cluster of boulders.

30. Unnamed VB
Climb the very easy face just off the left side of the trail and on the first boulder.

31. Unnamed V1
This problem is located on the boulder that is downhill from and behind the boulder on the left side of the hiking trail. Climb the uphill face and right corner.

32. Unnamed V0 R

Fun moves! Walk up the face around the corner and right from the previous problem.

A. Main Area (Area 2)

The Main Area is located midway through the rock escarpment. It contains the *High Rock* boulder, which is the highest boulder at Purgatory Rocks. This area is most easily approached by following the main road past the second Y and walking left when you first see large boulders.

1. Unnamed V0

Many variations can be done on this fun problem. SDS and dyno to the lip.

2. Unnamed V0-

Climb a high face on the far right side of the outcrop.

The author on a short but fun problem.

3. Untouchable V4

Climb the right side of an overhang a few feet left of problem number 2.

4. Intangible V3 R

Climb the overhang slightly left of *Untouchable* to a deep flake at the lip of the hang. Move up to semi-good holds (crux) to the top.

5. Dirty Crack V0- R

Ascend the crack near an overhang.

6. Unnamed V0- R

Cruise the arete next to *Dirty crack*.

7. Unnamed V3

Start on edges a few inches left of the previous problem, and move into a vertical seam. Continue to the top. The corner is off route for this problem.

8. Sharpie V5

In the center of a face that is just inches left of the previous problem, climb sharp edges, avoiding a tempting seam to the right, and gain a good hold up high. Top out.

9. Stumped V0+

In front of a stump, hug a rock column at the left end of this outcrop, and then move right into a fantastic flake. Continue up this to the top.

Rock Climbing and Bouldering Pennsylvania

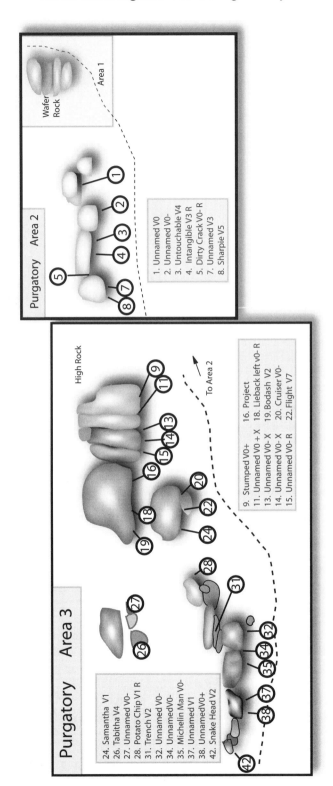

Purgatory Area 1

Wafer Rock

Purgatory Area 2

1. Unnamed V0
2. Unnamed V0-
3. Untouchable V4
4. Intangible V3 R
5. Dirty Crack V0- R
7. Unnamed V3
8. Sharpie V5

Purgatory Area 3

High Rock

To Area 2

9. Stumped V0+
11. Unnamed V0 + X
13. Unnamed V0- X
14. Unnamed V0- X
15. Unnamed V0- R
16. Project
18. Lieback left v0- R
19. Bodash V2
20. Cruiser V0-
22. Flight V7

24. Samantha V1
26. Tabitha V4
27. Unnamed V0-
28. Potato Chip V1 R
31. Trench V2
32. Unnamed V0-
34. Unnamed V0-
35. Michelin Man V0-
37. Unnamed V1
38. Unnamed V0+
42. Snake Head V2

318

Area 3

The high formation of rock with obvious cracks is the start of this area. The area continues to the end of the outcrop along the ridge.

B. High Rock

This is the highest formation at this area. It is easily identified by three distinct cracks that evenly split this large boulder.

10. Purgatory Right V0-

Slightly right of the rightmost crack on this large boulder, climb nice edges to the top.

11. Unnamed V0+ X

One of the best highball problems in the area. This is the rightmost of three cracks. The crux is low at a sidepull, and the top is not to be taken lightly.

12. Unnamed V0+ X

An area classic. Move up on edges and over a bulge to a big move. Merge right with the crack.

13. Unnamed V0- X

Climb the center crack. The bottom is easy, but the top has one balancing move with goods holds if you know where to look.

14. Unnamed V0- X

Run up big ledges between cracks.

15. Unnamed V0- R

A classic at its grade. Cruise this fun crack at the left side of the huge boulder.

C. Hidden Boulder

Well, it's actually not hidden; it's just placed slightly behind and left of the last few problems.

16. Project

Climb the lichen-covered, high face.

17. Layback Right V0- R

Layback a nice flake then cruise to the top.

Var. 1:V0-

Run up the face just right of the flake and rejoin the flake 13' up.

18. Layback Left V0- R

Layback the leftmost of two flakes.

19. Bodash V2

Easier if tall. Start on edges on the left end of this short wall and reach to a horizontal near a notch. Continue up the face a few inches from the corner. Using the corner may drop the grade a little.

D. Edge Boulder

This fabulous boulder is just below the previous boulder. It has amazing deep edges and some of the nicest problems in the region.

20. Cruiser V0-

Step off a small, detached block at the right side of this boulder, and cruise to the top.

21. Unnamed V0-

Climb the face a few inches left of the previous problem through a breach near the top.

22. Flight V7

Sit start just right of the center of the boulder, and pull on tiny holds. Dyno left to a big jug that pulls you sideways.

23. Bewitched V2

One of the best problems at its grade in PA. It doesn't look like there are good holds, but the edges on this face are fabulous. Use amazingly-deep finger buckets to climb the center of this boulder to a jug midway up the problem. Make a big move to gain the top (crux).

24. Samantha V1

Climb edges a few inches left of the previous problem.

25. Unnamed V0-

Climb the short face left of the previous.

26. Tabitha V4

A must-do problem! Above a pile of broken rock 300' left of the *Edge Boulder* you'll find a small boulder. Start on a big horizontal; then fly up to a sidepull and an exciting top out.

27. Unnamed V0-

Prance up the face a few inches right of the previous problem.

E. Potato Chip Boulder

The next climbable boulder on the main trail is located a few yards below and left of the previous few problems. The boulder is perched on a ledge. Its right corner resembles a large potato chip.

28. The Potato Chip V1 R

SDS at the right end of this boulder, fire up to the chip-like feature and continue up and right to top out.

29. Chipper V0- R

Start atop a block and climb through an easy bulge.

30. Unnamed V0-

Scamper up to vertical marks, and then cruise up edges over a bulge.

31. The Trench V2

Begin this problem in a trench at the left side of the *Potato Chip Boulder*. Start on a good horizontal at the far-left side, and follow it to a small arete. Climb this arete to top out.

32. Unnamed V0-
Climb flakes on the boulder below *The Trench*.

33. Unnamed V0-
The arete inches left of the previous problem.

34. Unnamed V0-
Make fun moves to walk up small, slanting seams, left of a big tree.

35. Michelin Man V0-
Begin a low start with your hands on white horizontal ribs that resemble the belly of the Michelin Man. Continue straight up.

36. Edgetibles V1
A classic no matter which way you send it. Climb nice edges in the center of this boulder a few inches left of *Michelin Man*.
Var. 1. V3
A great eliminate. This was the original line before more edges were uncovered under the ancient and ubiquitous dirt/lichen. Start with your left hand on a nice edge at head level, a few inches left of *Michelin*, and fire or dyno to a hold near the top. Top out.

37. Unnamed V1
Use wonderful edges to climb the face a few inches left of *Edgetibles*.

38. Unnamed V0+
Climb up a few inches left of the previous problem.

39. Unnamed V0-
Climb past a breach in the left end of this boulder.

40. Unnamed V0-
Climb out of the small cave on the boulder left of *Edgetibles*.

41. Choss Hound V0
Start on a good horizontal and fire to another higher horizontal. You can use the seam to the right as another variation at the same grade.

42. Snake Head V2
Begin under this boulder that resembles a snake's head. Place your hands on low edges and your feet way under the block that supports the boulder. Fire over the top.

Other Boulders

Many other boulders lie scattered on the south side of Woodrow Road. To find these boulders hike the main trail on the opposite side of Woodrow Road from the above areas. A few minute hike will bring you to the first boulder. One of the nicest boulders is a small, overhanging boulder resting along the trail. Other excellent boulders can be found by walking farther down the trail. If you walk far enough, you'll end up at Lewis Rock. More information about this area can be found at www.paclimbing.com in the near future.

21. Sunset Rocks

Location
Michaux State Forest.

Type of Climbing
Very limited trad, TR, and bouldering. Only a few problems and climbs.

Other Info
Not worth visiting unless you live very close by.

Sunset Rocks

Sunset Rocks is more of a short hike than a place to climb. You will find two, 35' rock sentinels at this area; there are also a handful of boulder problems you can mine-out on a few small boulders at the base of the main rock. A few of the climbs are quite interesting, but unless you live nearby and have visited most of the other climbing spots on South Mountain, I would not bother visiting Sunset Rocks. Sunset Rocks is one of the smallest climbing areas in the region—and probably the world—but the view from atop the rock at sunset is quite worthwhile. Bring long slings for toproping.

History

Not much was ever documented about this area. Older PMA members climbed here and most likely Stan Schoonover. Myself, Jess Holzman, and Mike Rich added some of the hard lines. Not many climbers have visited this spot so history is a bit ambiguous. It is a very small area in a very secluded location.

Directions

From interstate 81, follow State Route 233 south, 12 miles, to the Pine Grove Furnace State Park Headquarters at the junction of Route 233 and SR 3008. Follow 233 south .01miles until you see Shippensburg Road on the right (easy to miss). If you reach the Youth Hostel you drove too far and missed the road. Follow Shippensburg Road 1.3 miles to the end of the road at a lot and a stream. On the left side of Shippensburg Road there is a trail. Follow this trail along an old road to start, then past a field until the trail gets steep and climbs to the summit of the ridge. The rocks are located off and to the left on the sub-trail at the summit. The hike should take about 20 minutes. I strongly recommend grabbing a map at the park headquarters. The maps can be found on the kiosk in front of the park office building.

Sunset Rock Left
From the base of the rock looking up, this outcrop is the leftmost of the two outcrops.

1. Unnamed 5.4

Climb the low-angle left side of this formation.

2. Sunset 5.9+ PG

Climb under a large notch in an overhang in the center of this formation. Grunt through the notch and cruise to the top.

3. Unnamed 5.10 TR

Begin in the gully at the right side of this formation and climb to a point where you can gain a roof 10' up. Move left at the roof and climb an arete to the top.

4. Undercling Madness 5.11a PG/R

One of the best routes at Sunset Rocks. Exciting and sustained climbing. Gain a small overhang near the gully and then crank up loose-feeling underclings to gain the top.

Sunset Rock Right

This is the rightmost of the two rock formations.

5. Sunset Arete 5.9/5.10a R

Depending on where you climb the arete, this route ranges from 5.9 to easy 5.10. This climb is often done as a boulder problem. Begin on the left side of this formation and climb an easy face to the obvious arete. Keep your feet off the boulders in the gully and climb the arete to a long move at the top.

6. Unnamed 5.9- X

Climb a small corner at the left side of the face on this formation. At the end of the small corner, move up and right to gain the top.

7. Sundowner 5.11c X

This is an eliminate route that climbs the center of the rightmost outcrop of rock. Begin a few inches right of a small corner, and climb small holds to a large horizontal near the top. Climb straight up to finish at the rock's highest point. The corner on the left and the crack on the right are off route.

8. Sunset Gun 5.10b TR

Climb a very thin, slanting crack in the center of this rock outcrop. When the crack ends, move straight up to a sloping and cruxy top out.

9. Sunsizzle 5.10a R

Climb the steep face between *Sunset Gun* and *Short Crack*.

10. Short Crack 5.5 R

Run up the short crack at the right end of the rock outcrop.

Moss Slab Boulder

This boulder is located a few feet below the base of the gully that splits the two main rock formations. There are a few fun slab routes on the south face of the boulder. The center of the slab goes at about V0 R; the right side is V0-.

22. Lewis Rock Bouldering Area (Tumbling Run)

Area Beta

Location
Michaux State Forest.

Type of Climbing
Bouldering.

Other Info
Very close to Purgatory Rocks; can be linked with this area and the Coroners Slab. Great bouldering.

Lewis Rock (Tumbling Run)

Lewis Rock is a mere continuation of the ridgeline that lies near two larger formations of rock (Tweekers Hang and Coroners Slab). The boulders, in the height of summer, have as much vegetation as the rain forests of Peru. If you could Napalm the ridgeline, this place would be much more user friendly. The rest of the year this is a fantastic place to boulder. There are a lot of problems and most are excellent!

Safety Concerns and Dangers: Since Lewis Rock is located on a game preserve, hunting is popular here during hunting season. If you want to get shot, this is a great time to climb here. I strongly urge climbers to use caution here during hunting season.

Access and Considerations: This area is owned by the Tumbling Run Game Preserve. It is recommended that you ask permission to climb on their property before visiting.

Directions

From the Pine Grove Furnace Park Headquarters, at the junctions of SR3008 and Route 233, follow Route 233 south, exactly 2.7 miles, to a large parking area on the right shoulder of the road. This area is located at the signs for the Adams/Menallen township lines (signs say Cumberland/ Southampton line if traveling north). Park here and follow the blue-blazed trail about 10 minutes walk. After passing a stream continue uphill following the blazes. Walk on the trail—and stream in places—for 10 to15 minutes. The climbing can be found at the crest of the mountain. Enjoy the excellent views.

The area can also be accessed from the *Purgatory Rocks* parking lot at the top of Woodrow Road (on Woodrow's south side). Simply walk the hiking trail on the opposite side for the road as *Purgatory Rocks*. You will come to the first boulder in a few minutes of walking. I recommend this way of accessing the rock. It is longer, but less intense.

History

This area was climbed by older PMA members but was never a major destination or focul point for development. Cheyenne Wills, Tim Garland, Stan Schoonover, Glen Stoner, and others were climbers who occasionally came to this spot. I was active developing a few problems on the ridgeline and came up with the harder lines (V7ish) at Tweeker's Hang and the two hard lines on the Punisher boulder. Mort Bachler was also active developing lines on this boulder. Most of the bouldering along the ridge was developed by Joel Toretti, Travis Gault, Chet Gross, and a crew of Harrisburg locals in recent years. Thanks to the efforts of these climbers this area has now become a fun destination for this region. Many of the problems and boulders here are clean and appealing.

Streamside Area
This area is located adjacent to the stream at the south tip of the ridge (farthest from Woodrow Road). It is the first rock you come to when coming up the stream/hiking trail.

1. Blade V5
Climb the downhill face over sharp holds to a crack up high.
2. Unnamed V1 X
Climb the high face on the next outcrop along the ridge.

3. Moondance V1 R
Climb up the overhang on the high boulder up from the previous route.

4. Psyco 78
SDS and move into a crack, then out to a pinch, and top out.

5. Unnamed V0-
Climb the nice face left of the crack.

6. V0
Climb the crack that runs up a slab below and left of the previous route.

Lone Boulders
Just north of the previous area, along the hiking trail, there are a few randomly scattered boulders. Several problems have been done on them that range from V0- to V1.

Bank Robbers Cave
This is the fantastic cave located north of the *Lone Boulders*. The best problems at this area are located here.

1. Sloping Dragon V3
On the backside of the boulder just off the trail, climb the face from a standing start.

2. Bank Robbers Cave V8
SDS in the cave behind the previous boulder and climb out the sloping rail to a small dihedral.

3. Dark Crystal V10
SDS at the beginning of the previous problem and move left into small crystals. Climb up the steep face avoiding large holds at the top.

4. Madness to the Method V4
SDS and climb the loose flakes just left of *Dark Crystal*.

5. Gunfighter V5
Climb over the pinch just left of the previous problem.

6. Devil Inside V4
Climb the problem on the backside of the boulder.

7. Dawn's Last Screaming V4
Climb the arete on the next boulder down the trail.

8. Screaming Tranquility V6
Climb the arete left of the previous problem.

Regeneration Area
This area is located across the power line from the *Bank Robbers Cave*. It is the next set of boulders you come to.

1. Toretti's Fin V6
Climb out the cave to an obvious fin out right.

Var. 1: Country Boy Finish V7
Climb the previous problem to the fin and make a big move out right to a sloper at the end.

2. Flip Foot V4
Climb the roof left of *Toretti's Fin*.

3. Toby's Classic V1
Climb the short prow above the previous problem.

4. Unnamed V0
Climb the boulder across from the cave at any point.

Revival Area
The next set of boulders along the hiking trail is called the *Revival Area*.

5. Family Portrait V2
Climb the face on the first boulder at this area.

6. Soul Crusher V5
SDS in the middle of the long boulder off to the side of the trail.

7. Fat Lip V4
SDS on the arete and traverse to the top.

8. Screaming Truth V3
Climb the problem just left of the previous problem.

9. Physical Graffiti V6
SDS in cave and climb into a flake. Move out right to finish.

10. V7
SDS and climb the previous line to the flake. Then throw far out left to the large hole in the rock at a jug.

Generation Area
The next outcrop of rocks.

11. Police Man V2
Of the left-hand side of the trail, on the face hidden from view, climb the first face you see.

12. Clan Elder V2
Climb the problem next to the previous problem.

13. Old School V0
Climb the next boulder along the outcrop at any point.

14. Last Ride V4
SDS and climb the far end of the boulder.

15. Holy Ghost V2
SDS and climb the arete.

16. Common Man V1
Climb the problem next to *Holy Ghost*.

17. Stumped V4
SDS and climb the problem near the stump.

18. Wolfman V5
Climb the problem left of the stump.

19. Freak Parade V3
Climb the prow on the end of the oputcrop.

The Punisher Boulder
Named for how punishing the holds are on this boulder. This boulder is the first good boulder you come to while walking in from the parking area on Woodrow Road. It has a steep face facing the trail.

20. The Punisher V1
SDS and climb the corner

21. Baby Satan V3
SDS and climb the cave near the corner. Basically a SDS of the previous line.

22. Solar Coaster V5
SDS far back in the left of the cave and climb out to and over the corner.

23. Polaroid Millennium V4
SDS and climb over the roof on the left side of the boulder.

Coroner's Slab

This is the very high, massive, 60'-high block set along the ridge. Some excellent boulders can be found around the base of the block. There are only a few routes and most are terribly unclean.

History: The area was named Coroner's Slab by Tim Garland who first discovered the place during a skiing outing during the great blizzard of '93. He climbed here and established most of the lines on the rock. He named it this because it is located across from Grave Ridge. Tim established the first climb here in 1993 with Marc Hilden. The route was done as an onsight lead in a light rain and is called *Chicken Delight*. Two weeks later Tim returned with Steve Simick to establish *Chicken Direct*. Tim later returned to establish *Chicken Pox* with Steve Simick. Tim, at the time, was suffering from Shingles, caused by the dormant Chicken Pox virus. During this outing they established *Chicken Pox*. Tim returned again to establish *Chicken Dog* and *Fried Chicken Corner* with Pete Welker. I was active with Mike Rich—who was not happy being drug 150 miles from Scranton to climb a 60' block in the middle of nowhere—to establish the 5.13a on the far right side of the block. I also established about a dozen boulder problems near the base of the rock.

Directions

Coming from the parking lot on Woodrow Road, this area is located downhill from the *Regeneration Area*, but before the power line. It is located on the downhill side of the ridge. Some climbers hike in from the second road on the left side of Woodrow Road. Hike in along this dirt road that goes off left from Woodrow Road. After about 15 minutes of walking, you will see a clearing. If leaves are off the trees you can see the *Coroner's Slab* up on the hillside. I recommend walking in from The *Purgatory Rocks/ Tumbling Run* main lot on top the ridge. A small trail goes off and down to the *Coroner's Slab*.

You can also access this area by walking the Tunbling Run hiking trail from Rt. 233, and moving up a faint trail near the first clearing you see off right of the stream and heading up and right to the ridge. You need to be close to the rock in the summer to see it.

1. Chicken Direct 5.8
FA: T. Garland, Steve Simick '93 PG/R
Climb the left side of the slab to an overhang at the far left end of the outcrop.

2. Chicken Delight 5.7 PG/R
FA: T. Garland, Marc Hilden ,93
Climb the route just right of *Chicken Direct*.

3. Chicken Pox 5.9+ R

FA: T. Garland, S. Simick

Climb up just right of *Chicken Delight*, and after the base of the expanding flakes, head for the notch in the roof.

4. Chicken Dog 5.10a TR

FA: T. Garland, Pete Welker

Start on the large shelf above the boulder and climb the right-center of the outcrop.

5. Fried Chicken Corner 5.9+ TR

FA: T. Garland, Pete Welker.

Named for how fried Pete's arms trying the first ascent. Climb the right corner of the boulder.

6. Chicken Crack-ette 5.7+ TR

FA: P. Welker, T. Garland

Climb the dirty crack around the right corner of the outcrop.

7. Pennsyltucky Fried Chicken 5.13a TR

FA: R. Holzman, Mike Rich

Start on the steep bouldering wall below the main headwall and climb the hardest section of rock to the ledge. From here, follow the blankest section at the right end of the outcrop while keeping away from the right corner. The crux pulls over underclings and mono-slopers.

Eric Beyeler bouldering at Lewis Rock. RH photo.

Area Beta

Location
Michaux State Forest near Carlisle.

Type of Climbing
Toprope and trad.

Other Info
A very small area with very nice views.

Pole Steeple

Located just above Laurel Lake in Pine Grove Furnace State Park, Pole Steeple is a small rock outcrop with spectacular views from its summit. The cliff is only 65' high and does not have substantial length, but the rock makes up in quality what it lacks in quantity. The unique stone pinnacles—at the cliff's highest point and farther down the ridge—compose the areas thrilling appearance. These quartzite formations create a different appearance than nearby spots with similar rock type. The routes at Pole Steeple are easy to moderate with some limited bouldering at the left end of the ridge and at the main cliff-base. This is a great spot for beginners and is rarely crowded.

Hazards: Despite the high travel of routes at Pole Steeple, there is still a fair amount of loose and brittle rock here. Use caution around anything that looks unstable and wear a helmet. Most of the rock is quite solid, but just because those hollow sounding blocks haven't fallen today, doesn't mean they won't fall tomorrow!

Rock Type: Mount Alto Gray Quartzite, Lower Cambrian Age.

Directions: From the park headquarters of Pine Grove Furnace State Park, take Route 233 south, 2.4 miles to Laurel Lake. Make a 180-degree turn to the right onto Old Rail Bed Road. Follow this road 0.5mi, along the shore of the lake, to a parking area on the right. There will be a sign for the blue-blazed Pole Steeple Trail here. Follow the blue-blazed trail to the formation. The walk should take about ten to fifteen minutes. The walk is mostly uphill but gradual.

Pole Steeple   Overlook Wall

2. White Arete 5.6 G
3. Crack I 5.7 G
4. 5.9+/5.10- R
5. Crack II 5.6 G
6. Crack III 5.7 G

Overlook Wall (Main Face)

This is the vertical wall just right of where the hiking trail meets the cliff. If you search hard enough, cams can be placed for a toprope setup near the edge of the cliff. Otherwise, long slings are needed.

1. Beginners Face 5.4 to 5.5 G

This is the short face to the right of and around the corner from the main wall. It has some nice cracks on it. It faces west near where the trail loops around the back of the outcrop. Several climbs can be done along this wall following cracks, horizontals, and faults. The grades vary from 5.4 to 5.5 (the harder grade travels over steeper terrain).

2. White Arete 5.6 G

On the corner where the west face and main face meet, climb the arete to a crack and small, narrow notch near the top.

3. Crack I 5.7 G

Climb the crack at the right of the face.

4. 5.9+/5.10- R *

This is the ceiling with a block in it between *Crack II and Crack III*. Begin on *Crack II* and climb out right at the blocky ledge. Pull over the center of the first ceiling (crux), then continue over the final ceiling to finish.

5. Crack II 5.6 G ***

This is the most often climbed route at Pole Steeple. Climb the centermost of three cracks over a blocky ledge, then past a pin at the ceiling, and continue straight to the top.

6. Crack III 5.7 G ***

For some, the crux is the off-width; for others, it's the final ceiling. Follow the leftmost of three cracks through a short off-width section, and then finish over the sharp point of rock at the final ceiling. Takes medium to large gear.

The Steeple

This is the large, overhanging, needle of rock, just left of the approach trail.

7. 5.1 – 5.3 G

The face on the left side of the trail, in the gully, has several easy climbs on it that range from 5.1 to 5.3, depending on where you climb on the face.

8. Big Nose 5.6 PG

The obvious overhanging arete on the right edge of The Steeple.

The author on the steeple. Photo by Jess Holzman.

9. Steeple Boulder

This is the large block located below the steeple feature. It has several short boulder problems on it that range from V0- to V1. Most climbers pick one of these problems as the beginning to any of the above climbs.

10. The Steeple 5.8 PG/R **

Start on any one of the problems on *Steeple Boulder* and climb to a big ledge, and then ascend the right side of the overhanging face on *The Steeple*, past a short finger crack, and over small overhangs. Using the arete makes the grade easier.

11. Steeplechase 5.9 PG/R

A genuinely thrilling climb. Glide through bouldery moves of your choice down low, then climb a plum line up the left side of *The Steeple*. The gear is probably not as bad as the rating suggests, but it's rather strenuous to place, and you have to work to find good placements.

The Steeple

10. The Steeple 5.8 PG/R
11. Steeple Chase 5.9 PG/R
12. Steeplejack 5.8/5.9 PG/R

12. Steeplejack 5.8 PG/R
Climb the face between routes 10 and 11.

Short Face:
Between *The Steeple* and *Far Face*, there is a short, but high, wall with a small, tiered ceiling on it.

13. Cute Ceiling 5.7 PG/R
Climb the center of the tiered ceiling. Easier variations can be done at 5.6, either to the right or left of the ceiling.

14. Slab Right 5.3 G	17. Climney 5.2 G
15. Slabtacular 5.6 R	18. 5.7 R
16. Slab Left 5.4 PG	19. 5.9+ R 20. 5.6 R

Far Face
Several easy routes have been done on the long, low-angled face left of the giant steeple. This is a great area for beginners.

14. Slab Right 5.3 G
Skate up the right side of the slab, passing a big crack halfway up.

14. Slabtacular 5.6 R
Start under the center of a small ceiling, 15' off the ground. Boulder over the center of the ceiling and continue straight up past a small ceiling halfway up. The climb has better protection if you veer out right or left a bit.

15. Slab Left 5.4 PG
Start a few feet left of the previous climb and move up the left side of this slab.
Var. 1: 5.5 Start in the left-facing corner and pull out under the lowest of two semi-corners onto the slab. Finish the same as the regular route.
Var. 2: 5.6 Climb up to the second section of the corner capped by a small roof and pull out right onto the slab. Continue to the top.

16. Chimney 5.2 G
Climb the dirty chimney.

17. 5.7 R

Move up to the base of the chimney, and traverse left onto the right-facing face. Move up the face, and use the left arete to gain the top.

18. 5.9+ R

Start under a small ceiling left of the previous route and pull over the ceiling (crux), then make easier moves to the summit.

19. Unnamed 5.6 R

Climb the smooth face immediately left of the previous climb.

The author soloing "Steeple Chase." Photo by Jess Holzman.

24. Chimney Rocks

Area Beta

Location
Near Carlisle.

Type of Climbing
Bouldering.

Other Info
Only a handful of boulders but all the problems are excellent quality. Many nearby areas.

Chimney Rocks

Perhaps one of the best kept secrets in central Pennsylvania, this seldom-visited area offers excellent bouldering on clean rock. Even though there are several other areas named Chimney Rocks in the state—one is even a few miles away in the same state forest—this is *thee* Chimney Rocks.

If you come here, expect to find superb rock quality, high boulders, thrilling problems, unique rock features, and a diverse mix of grades. This area is also noted for moderate-grade highballs, and a small concentration of some of the hardest problems on South Mountain. If the thrilling highballs don't excite you, the rock quality will. Some of the cleanest rock in central Pennsylvania can be found here. The rock somewhat resembles Seneca Rocks conglomerate, but with more colorful tints. If these facets don't lure you here, the 5 minute approach should. If I was forced to come up with one downside for this area, it would be the bad landings on some of the problems. Although many problems here have good landings, a few problems have large blocks placed in less than ideal spots below them.

Many of the free-standing pinnacles here are more op-roped. For this reason I have graded many of the climbs here are done as boulder problems or topropes (both boulder and climbing scale grades are used). Many climbers who frequent this area toprope climbs first, get them wired, and then do them as boulder problems. Many climbers also consider this area a nice spot just for toproping, alone. If you plan on setting up anchors at the top, bring lots of webbing and trad-gear. Many blocks can be slung but a good mix of gear will help. Visit this little spot and you are guaranteed a pleasant day without crowds, in a tranquil setting, with outstanding rock. It truly is a mystery why more climbers don't visit this area.

History

Glen Stoner was the first climber documented that visited this spot extensively. Glen was the most prolific climber to frequent this area and developed the majority of the problems here. Glen has also been the primary land steward for this area and has been involved in maintaining and cleaning the area since the 1980s. I was active at this area adding some difficult sit start problems and developed other problems like Greased Lightning V6, Private Idaho V7 X, Across the Universe V7, Vesper V8, Mission Incredible 5.13 X, and several problems in the V4 to V5 range that have sit starts. In recent years, Travis Gault added a difficult V10/V11 route in recent years at this area also. Many Harrisburg climbers are now developing new hard lines. I would expect to see V12 climbing here soon. It is important to note that many problems are unnamed in this section. This is because I wasonly able to attain some of the correct names from the original developers before going ot print and didn't want to rename anything in this guide. Although many of the original problems were not named I hope to have the correct names for the next addition of the guide.

Directions: From the town of Walnut Bottom (near Carlisle and just of I-81) find route 174. In the center of town, make a right onto T334 (High Mountain Road) and follow it 2.8 miles up the winding hill, until you see a yellow, unmarked gate on the right side of the road. There is a very small parking area here—don't block the gate! Follow the dirt road beyond the gate for less than ¼ mile. There will be a small trail on the left that is very easy to miss. The rock is a few hundred feet off the left side of the trail/road.

Passageway
This is the passage created by a boulder on the left and the high pinnacle that is just off left of the approach trail as soon as you reach the rock.

1. Captain Crunch V0-
Follow the dirty arete on the left side of the boulder.

2. Left Face V0+
Move up the center of the face.

3. Crunchy EliminateV1
Climb the middle face on tiny edges. If you use any big holds you are off route. Kind of an eliminate.

4. Right Face V0-
Climb the right side of the face.

The Chimney Stack
This is the large pinnacle directly in front of the approach trail. The routes are numbered from the left side in the passage to the right side of the pinnacle near where the trail cuts around to the right.

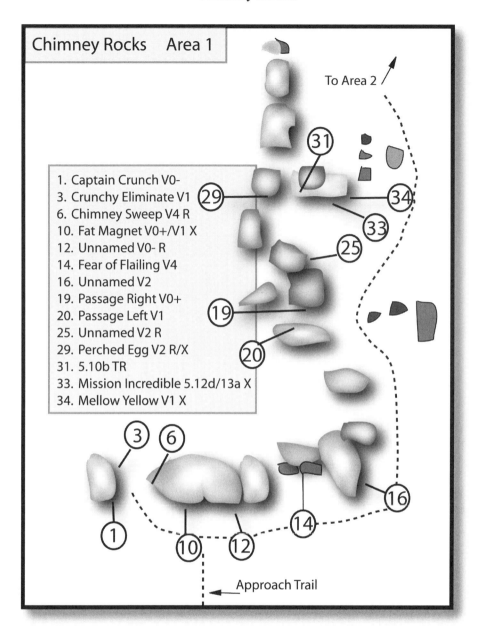

Chimney Rocks   Area 1

To Area 2

1. Captain Crunch V0-
3. Crunchy Eliminate V1
6. Chimney Sweep V4 R
10. Fat Magnet V0+/V1 X
12. Unnamed V0- R
14. Fear of Flailing V4
16. Unnamed V2
19. Passage Right V0+
20. Passage Left V1
25. Unnamed V2 R
29. Perched Egg V2 R/X
31. 5.10b TR
33. Mission Incredible 5.12d/13a X
34. Mellow Yellow V1 X

Approach Trail

5. Unnamed V0-
Climb the left side of the passage on the pinnacle.

6. Chimney Sweep V4 R
This problem follows tiny edges up dark-colored orange rock in the center of the face, right of the previous route.

7. The Flake V0 R
Fun moves lead to a flake that you can follow to the summit.

Scott Messick ready for the next move. Photo by the author.

8. Unnamed V2

SDS and climb up the corner of the giant rock.

9. Unnamed V0+ R/X
Start on the large block and climb the left side of the front-face of *The Chimney*.

10. Fat Magnet V0+/V1 X
One of the best crack boulder problems in the East! Climb the amazing hand and finger crack that runs up the highest point of the boulder.

11. Chimney Direct V3 X
Climb the technical face that is right of the crack.

12. Unnamed V0- R
Follow easy corners at the right end of the boulder to steeper rock above large holds. Follow the easiest path to the top.

13. Unnamed V0 R
Climb up and right of the previous problem.

14. Fear of Flailing V4

From a sit start, deep in the boulder perched atop another boulder at the right side of the chimney outcrop, start low and top out.

15. Campus Man V1
Start on the right, campus the lip of the perched boulder, then top out.

16. Unnamed V2
Climb the small face on the notch/alcove between two boulders right of and around the corner from the pinnacle.

17. Low Ball V1
SDS and climb the clean face just right of the previous route.

18. Unnamed V0-
Climb the easy north-facing face of the next boulder past the previous route.

19. Passage Right V0+
Located in the passage between the two boulders. Look uphill into the passage and climb the first face on the right when coming into the passage.

20. Passage Left V1
SDS and make technical moves on nice crimps on the boulder behind the previous route.

21. Deep Passage V0
SDS and climb the face left of problem number 19.

22. Rock Candy V2
SDS and climb the face that looks like rock candy, just left of *Deep Passage*.

23. Unnamed V0- R
Climb the loose-looking, high face, around the corner to the right of the previous problem. Several variations can be done to the right and left near the same grade.

24. Unnamed V2
SDS and climb the jutting overhang on the downhill side of the boulder that is below the previous problem. This is a small stand-alone boulder; the problem is in the pit below the trail.

25. Unnamed V2 R
Climb the nice face to a very small overhang 10' up. Pull the center of the hang passing edges and awkward sidepulls and top out.

26. Unnamed V1 R
Climb the short face around the corner and right of the previous problem.

27. Drifter V0-
This problem climbs the grey-colored face right of the previous problem. Several variations have been done on this long face including a traverse. All go at a similar

grade.

28. Unnamed V0
Climb the crack at the right side of the long face.

29. Perched Egg V3 R/X
Climb up to and under an egg-shaped boulder perched high above the ground between the main face and the huge detached pillar. Pull out over the scary belly of the egg formation.

30. Unnamed V0+ R
Pull out over steep rock at the left end of the large, detached pillar. Start up on a high ledge.

31. 5.10b TR
Climb the left side of the steep face on the huge, detached pillar.

32. 5.10d TR
Power up the steep left-center of the boulder, to a seam 15' up. Move slightly right to gain the steep center of the pillar. Continue to struggle to the top.

33. Mission Incredible 512d/5.13a X
The grade varies depending on how direct a start you do. Start low on thin crimps in the center of the steep face and gain small finger pockets. Continue up the right-center of the boulder, until it is possible to escape right near the top section of the boulder.

34. Mellow Yellow V1 X
Make fantastic moves up the right corner of the huge pillar.

Area 2
This area is just past a clearing. It is the second grouping of boulders.

Incredible Boulder
The first boulder you come to on this grouping of boulders. The downhill side of the boulder is high and overhanging.

1. Unnamed V0-
SDS and climb the roof on the boulders west side.

2. Unnamed V4
SDS on the left side of the downhill wall and climb up the crack and flakes.

3. Private Idaho V7 X
From a sit start climb the overhanging center face to a long vertical seam.

4. Unnamed V4 R/X
Start the same as the previous route but traverse a horizontal to the right and top out at the right side of the boulder

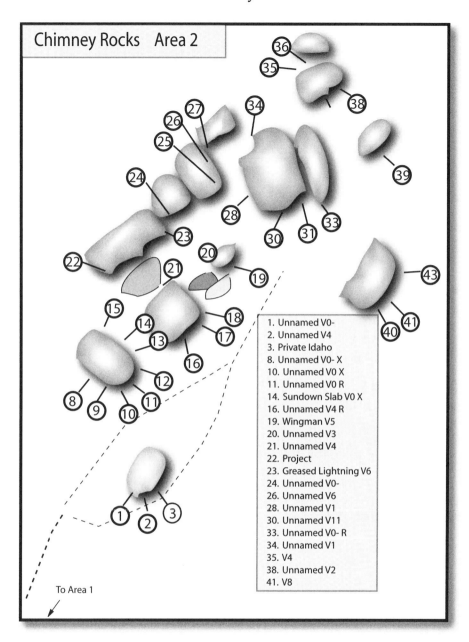

Chimney Rocks   Area 2

1. Unnamed V0-
2. Unnamed V4
3. Private Idaho
8. Unnamed V0- X
10. Unnamed V0 X
11. Unnamed V0 R
14. Sundown Slab V0 X
16. Unnamed V4 R
19. Wingman V5
20. Unnamed V3
21. Unnamed V4
22. Project
23. Greased Lightning V6
24. Unnamed V0-
26. Unnamed V6
28. Unnamed V1
30. Unnamed V11
33. Unnamed V0- R
34. Unnamed V1
35. V4
38. Unnamed V2
41. V8

To Area 1

5. Unnamed V1 R
Climb the right side of the boulders downhill face.

Tower Rock
This is the next boulder past *Incredible Boulder*. It is a high pinnacle.

7. Unnamed V0- R
Climb the left side of the boulders west side

8. Unnamed V0- X
Climb the obvious crack up the center of the face that is right of the previous route.

9. Unnamed V0+ X
Climb the high face right of the previous route.

10. Unnamed V0 X
Climb the center of the downhill face.

11. Unnamed V0 R
Climb the left side of the downhill face.

12. Unnamed V0+ X
Climb over the small overhang 10'up and follow to the top. Several variations can be done pulling over the small overhang.

13. Sundowner V1 X
Often dirty and loose. Climb the left center of the east side of the boulder.

14. Sundown Slab V0 X
Climb the face right of the previous route.

15. Unnamed V0- R
Run up the slab right of the previous route.

16. Unnamed V4 R
SDS and climb the face past small finger pockets and edges to a scary high face and top out.

17. Unnamed V1
The right edge of the downhill face

18. Real as Real V5
Same as the previous but from a sitting start.

19. Wingman V5
Begin sitting in a pit on the boulder perched in talus and pull up keeping your feet locked under the perched boulder and off-routing feet on any other boulders.

20. Unnamed V3
Start in a small pit with a small roof next to the previous problem. SDS under the roof and pull up moving left and off-routing the big holds to the right.
Var 1:V0-
Same problem but use the large holds out right.

21. Unnamed V4
SDS in a pit on the back side of the boulder and pull up the short face.

22. Project

23. Greased Lightning V6
SDS and climb the perfect corner to a big hold above the lip of the ceiling perched above a pit.

24. Unnamed V0-
Climb the easy face right of the previous climb.

25. Unnamed V3
Climb the left side of the face in the narrow passage to the right of *Greased Lightning*.

26. Across the Universe V6/V7
Climb the thin face slightly right of the previous problem.

27. Unnamed V4
Climb the face at the boulders right side keeping off the holds near the crack to the right.
Var 1: V1
Climb the face at the corner/crack right of the previous problem.

28. Unnamed V1
SDS and climb the face on the left side of the boulder near a tree.

29 Project.

30. Project
Start sitting under a roof and make a long move to the lip from heinous holds. Levitate over the roof and top out. The stand start goes at V2. The project feels like it's in the V12 range.

31. Project
Climb the roof right of the previous line.

32. Unnamed V2
Climb the center face in the tight passage on the boulder adjacent to the previous problem. Beware of loose rock.

33. Unnamed V0- R
Climb the loose-looking arete right of the previous problem at the point where this boulder juts out of a passage.

34. Unnamed V1
From a sit start climb a black-colored corner behind the previous route.

35. Delicious V4
On the backside of this boulder climb the right face from a sit start.

36. Delicate and Daunting V5
SDS and climb the steep face left of the previous line.

37. Unnamed V4
SDS and climb the short, steep face on the left side of the boulder.

38. Unnamed V2
SDS and climb the right corner of the boulder that is right of the previous line.

39. Unnamed V1
Climb the boulder from a sit start.

Lonely Boulder
Located below the previous boulder is a small boulder with a steep downhill side.

40. Lonely Overhang V2
Climb out the overhang on good holds on the left side of the boulder.

41. Vesper V8
Climb sharp crimps.

42. Malicious Intent V10
SDS at a block in the right-center of the boulder. Begin on an edge and undercling and work hard moves to the top.

43. Groovin V5
Climb the right arete.

25. Whiskey Springs Bouldering Area

Area Beta

Location
Near Carlisle.

Type of Climbing
Some of the best bouldering in the area.

Other Info
Dragon's Layer is nearby, along the ridge, as well as a few other spots.

Whiskey Springs

Round, gray-colored, grit-textured boulders rest along the Appalachian Trail amid a wooded mountaintop at *Whiskey Springs*. 30 high-quality boulders range in height from a few feet to 25' high and occupy a gorgeous, serene setting. This relaxing environment for which the area is noted makes a quality bouldering destination for climbers in Central Pennsylvania and Northern Maryland. This area is one of the best bouldering spots in the region.

This area is named for a nearby spring that draws clean, pristine waters from underground. It was named Whiskey Springs because a nearby whiskey distillery, that was located in Carlisle, tapped water from the spring to make whiskey nearly 100 years ago. Although this spot is known for fun slab routes, you can expect to find a few good difficult problems as well. Either way a myriad of quality problems and a great atmosphere will occupy your time here. The majority of problems cater to novice and intermediate climbers, but many difficult problems furnish a plethora of worthy problems for any level climber. The high, daring *Flesh Eater* face outfits an amazing route not to be missed by any climber. Although the grade of this problem is not terribly difficult, the commitment and height make it one of the most exciting in the Mid-Atlantic. This spot is never crowded; most days you will find a silent, pleasant bouldering spot. I highly recommend this bouldering area. My advice is to plan enough time to visit this and other nearby South Mountain crags in the same day or weekend. Many are well worth visiting.

History

In the 1960s many of the obvious slab routes and higher faces were climbed by the PCG. During the '70s and early '80s, Tim Garland, Ray Garland, and Cheyenne Wills (founder of the Pennsylvania Mountaineering Association) developed most of the early lines at Whiskey. Climbs like *Platax Traverse* V1, *Arthrictus* V1*, Weber Arete* V0+, *Vulture View* V0-, and *Organ Grinder* V0+ were established during this time. Other climbers who frequented the area were Curt Harler, Doug Gitt, Dave Kilgore, Pete Carter. One of the most noted ascents during this time was the first ascent of *Flesh Eater*: a very steep, high, classic problem that got its name when a climber first attempting it was sliced from falling on the sharp crystals along its fine corner. Glen Stoner was the first person to climb this route unroped. Glen was also a very active developer of the area.

I was active through the area during the '90s developing many challenging sit-start problems like *Harlequin* V4, *Pit and the Pendulum* V8, *Diesel* V5, and about two dozen other problems.

Recently Josh Newman sent *Divide Before Nothingness* V12. It was also repeated by Tim Rose. This is currently one of the hardest problems in central Pennsylvania. Travis Gault also sent a sit start to *Ten High* that goes at V10.

Location: 10 miles south of Carlisle.

General Overview: Excellent bouldering on quality stone. Over 100 problems ranging from VB to V10.

Recommended Rack: A crash pad and slings with a few pieces of gear if you want to TR the *Flesh Eater* Buttress.

Access Issues and Restrictions: The area is located along the Appalachian Trail. Climbing is allowed on the property. Pack out any trash and respect the land.

Area Hazards: Snakes and bad landings.

In Case of Emergency: Contact a park employee or dial 911. For directions to the nearest hospital, look on bulletin boards or at the park office. If you are in the south end of the park, Carlisle Hospital is the closest. Carlisle Hospital is located off Alexander Springs Road in Carlisle, PA. Just off the College Street exit on Interstate 81. The phone number is 717-249-1212.

Nearby Areas: Brown Rocks, Chimney Rocks, Coroners Slab, Dead Woman's Hollow Road, Hammond Rocks, The Hermitage, Lewis Rocks, Pole Steeple, Purgatory Rocks, Rattlesnake Rocks, Sunset Rocks, Virginia Rocks, Whiskey Springs, White Rocks, White Rock Acres, Wildcat Rocks.

Directions

At the junction of State Route 34 and Mill Street (SR 2003), when entering the town of Mount Holly Springs, you will see a Sheetz gas station on the left. Turn east onto Mill Street (SR 2003) that later becomes Park Drive. Drive East 2.2-miles to Petersburg Road. You will pass the Land O' Lakes plant on the left and Flat Glass Products plant on the right. Petersburg Road is the next road after Red Tank Road just past the two plants. Turn right onto Petersburg Road. Note that the road is only labeled on the left branch of Petersburg Road on the left side of SR 2003. Another locator is the sign for the South Mountain

Dragway. Drive 1.4 miles you will reach a stop sign. At this point the road has become Whiskey Springs Road. Follow this road, going straight after the stop sign, past curves, to a parking area on the right at 1.4-miles. Park here and follow the white-blazed Appalachian Trail southwest (same side you park on), up a hill, about 10 minutes walk, to the rock at the hillcrest. Many hiking groups use this spot on weekends. Be aware on weekends the parking pull-offs will only accommodate a few cars. Alternate pull-offs are located farther down the road. Use only designated pull-offs to park.

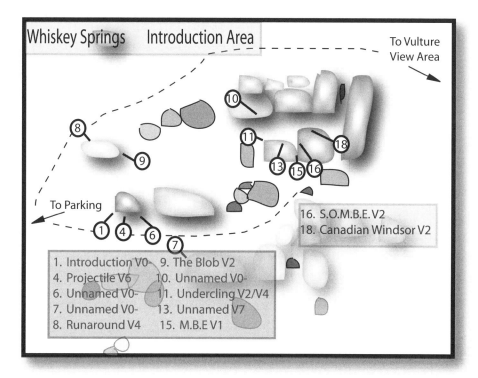

Whiskey Springs   Introduction Area

To Vulture View Area

To Parking

16. S.O.M.B.E. V2
18. Canadian Windsor V2

1. Introduction V0-
4. Projectile V6
6. Unnamed V0-
7. Unnamed V0-
8. Runaround V4
9. The Blob V2
10. Unnamed V0-
11. Undercling V2/V4
13. Unnamed V7
15. M.B.E V1

Introduction Area (Area 1)

When following the white-blazed trail, at the crest of the hill, the trail runs left. Instead of following the trail left, follow a trail straight to some boulders.

A. Welcome to Whiskey Boulder
This is the first sizable boulder on the left of the boulder trail.

1. Introduction V0-
SDS on the left-hand corner of the boulder and climb up.

2. Welcome to Whiskey V1
SDS on a jug at the left side of the boulder and dyno to the lip above. The corner is off route.

3. Grand Illusion V5

351

From a sit start on the big jug in the center of the boulder, move left to a sloping gaston, then up to a nice edge.

4. Projectile V6
Dyno from the big jug in the center of the face to the lip above.

5. Lip Service V2
Start on the same jug as the previous problem, move right to another jug, then fly left to the lip.

6. Unnamed V0-
Climb the crack and jugs on the right side of the *Welcome to Whiskey Boulder*.

7. Unnamed V0-
Climb the arete where the trail passes over big rocks, 100'down from the previous few problems.

B. The Blob
This is the round boulder behind and left of the *Welcome to Whiskey* boulder. If you were to walk the white trail, this boulder is the low, round boulder just right of the trail after if branches off from the hillcrest.

8. Runaround V4
Start near the end of the boulder nearest the trail and traverse the lip. Move low at the overhanging side and top out when you run out of boulder.

9. The Blob V2
SDS as low as possible on the overhanging, somewhat perched end of the boulder, and hump yourself over the top.

C. The Trench
This area consists of a short trench behind and right of the *Welcome Boulder*.

10. Unnamed V0-
Start on good holds, and climb this easy, very short problem.

11. Underling V2 or V4
Start on the corner using underclings, and climb the corner to its top. A sit start makes the problem V4.

12. V6
SDS and climb the face left of the previous climb.

13. Unnamed V7
A difficult problem with exciting moves and a stout top out. Start on smooth underclings and climb the left side of the boulder, just left of the previous route. The large crack to the left is off route.

14. M.B.E Corner V0-

"The Masturbate Edge". Easy moves let you slog up this easy crack next to the previous problem.

15. M.B.E V1

Start on the corner and traverse past the face to the sharp corner. Slap up the corner, avoiding the top.

16. Son of M.B.E (A.K.A. S.O.M.B.E.) V2

This short face is a worthwhile problem that is not to be missed. Small crimps lead to a positive undercling and a long smooth sidepull left of the V0- crack. The easy crack is off.

17. Rock N Rye V3

Climb the corner and face near where a tree meets the corner, left of the previous climb.

18. Canadian Windsor V2

Start by holding the lower of two underclings; move to a horizontal near the top, and climb to the top. The corner is off. If you start on the higher undercling, the grade drops a bit.

19. Bankers Club V5

SDS in the pit and climb over the difficult, strenuous top.

Lower Area (Area 2)

The first boulder of this section can be found just north of (below) *Welcome Boulder*. The boulders in this section extend from below the first boulders at *Whiskey Springs*--over to the *Vulture View* and *Gunk's* boulders.

A. Hidden boulder

Locate this boulder hidden under the trail, north of, and downhill from *Welcome Boulder*.

1. Unnamed V0

From a low start, climb the right corner of the boulder.

2. The Vault V7

Start on the right side of the boulder on a left sidepull and a sharp right-crimp, and shoot left for the top. The corner is off route.

B. Entrance Boulder

Just right of the previous boulder are two boulders that form a passage between them. The boulder on the left of the passage is the *Entrance Boulder*.

3. The Dance V0

A handless ascent if done correctly. Climb the downhill face of this boulder using no hands to scale the slab.

4. The Washboard V0-

Just right of the previous boulder are two boulders that form a passage between them.

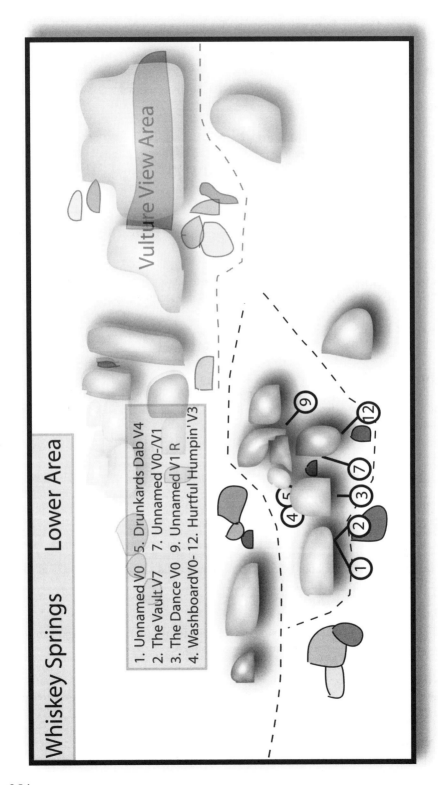

Whiskey Springs   Lower Area

Vulture View Area

1. Unnamed V0
2. The Vault V7
3. The Dance V0
4. Washboard V0-
5. Drunkards Dab V4
7. Unnamed V0-/V1
9. Unnamed V1 R
12. Hurtful Humpin' V3

Looking into the passage from downhill, climb the left wall.

5. Drunkards Dab V4
Start near the point of the boulder that has a rock beneath that supports the boulder. Pull off tiny edges at the lip and crank to a horizontal; then climb the face just left of the previous climb

6. Entrance Boulder Problem V1 R
Climb the center of the green-colored face, near a tree, to the right of and around the corner from the previous climb. Easier variations can be done to the right and left.

7. Unnamed V0/V1
Looking into the passage climb the right face of the right-hand boulder. The center face is V1; using holds on the left makes it V0.

8. The Hump VB
An easy problem following the corner above *Entrance Boulder Problem*. Several variations can be done.

9. Unnamed V1 R
Climb the nice arete via jugs, just right of the previous problem.

10. Cheyenne's Corner V0-
Cruise the nice corner above the arete. Several variations exist off-routing features to increase the difficulty.

11. The Prow V0-
This is the nice prow above the previous problem that starts by pulling the overhang.

12. Hurtful Humpin' V3
SDS with your back on the rock on the ground and slap up horizontals on the overhanging, short downhill face of the boulder, right of *The Prow*.

Area 3
Vulture View Area
This area is notable for the massive boulder (*Vulture View Rock*) and the highest rock here. It is just above the previous area.

A. Vulture View Rock
This is the largest boulder at *Whiskey Springs*. It is in the center of the main outcrop and has a severely overhanging downhill side that has been attempted, but remains a project.

1. Vulture View Traverse V0+
Traverse the backside of the giant boulder.

2. Harlequin V4
Start on holds at head level and hump over the top.
3. Vulture View V0-

Climb the easy crack on the backside of the outcrop.

4. Unnamed V0- R
Climb the right-side-face on the backside of the *Vulture View Rock*.

5. Vulture V0- R
Climb the left-side-face on the back side of the *Vulture View* Rock.

6. Diagonal V0+ X
Climb the crack just left of *Flesh Eater*.

7. Flesh Eater V2 X
This problem is a thrilling highball that is often toproped. Begin by stepping off a block and reaching out to a positive hold on the corner—long stretch for shorter people. Commit to the hold, swing off, and climb the northeast corner of the boulder.

8. Flesh Eater Direct V4 X
Same start as *flesh Eater* but from a lower start on the ground.

9. Jim's Traverse V1/V2
Start on the wall under *Flesh Eater*, and traverse across the wall underneath the overhang above. Several variations can be done, some making the traverse easier.

10. Vulture Crack VB
Climb the easy crack on the west face of the *Flesh Eater* boulder.

11. Hey Vern V0+ R
Climb the left side of the slabby face just right of the crack without using the crack or positive edge to the right. Finish by escaping right and out from under the overhang. You can also escape left by down-climbing the crack.

12. Big Crack VB
Climb the obvious crack on the left side of the west face of the huge boulder.

13. Super Slab V0- R
Climb the slab between *Pebbles* and *Big Crack*. Easier and harder variations exist.

14. Pebbles and Bam Bam V1 R
Right of the previous route is the high center of the slab (most central point). Delicate moves move over green-colored rock on the high-center slab a few feet left of the previous problem.

15. Organ Grinder Direct V0+ R
Prance up the face between *Organ Grinder* and *Pebbles*.

16. Organ Grinder V0+ R
Fall off this one and you'll find out how the climb got its name. Climb up the right side of the slab without stemming onto the crack to the right.

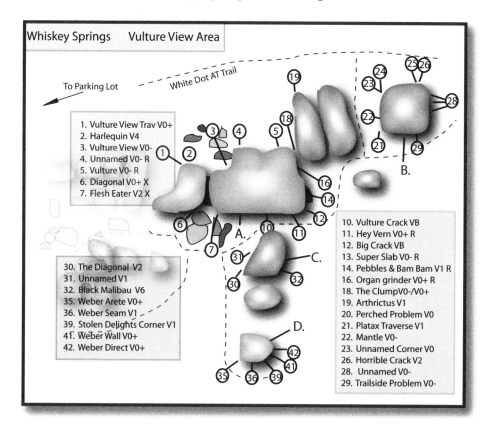

Whiskey Springs | Vulture View Area

To Parking Lot — White Dot AT Trail

1. Vulture View Trav V0+
2. Harlequin V4
3. Vulture View V0-
4. Unnamed V0- R
5. Vulture V0- R
6. Diagonal V0+ X
7. Flesh Eater V2 X

30. The Diagonal V2
31. Unnamed V1
32. Black Malibau V6
35. Weber Arete V0+
36. Weber Seam V1
39. Stolen Delights Corner V1
41. Weber Wall V0+
42. Weber Direct V0+

10. Vulture Crack VB
11. Hey Vern V0+ R
12. Big Crack VB
13. Super Slab V0- R
14. Pebbles & Bam Bam V1 R
16. Organ grinder V0+ R
18. The Clump V0-/V0+
19. Arthrictus V1
20. Perched Problem V0
21. Platax Traverse V1
22. Mantle V0-
23. Unnamed Corner V0
26. Horrible Crack V2
28. Unnamed V0-
29. Trailside Problem V0-

17. Grand Traverse

Traverse the *Vulture View Boulder* and the adjacent boulders without touching the ground. Several variations can be done or several laps.

18. The Clump V0-/V0+

A few easy problems have been done on the boulder adjacent to the previous few problems.

19. Arthrictus V1

Locate this problem by walking behind the *Vulture View Boulder* to its south face. This problem climbs the narrow, downhill face of the boulder that is adjacent to and left of *Vulture View*.

20. Perched Problem V0

Walking down the ridge past the previous problems, climb the downhill face of rock with a boulder perched on top.

B. Platax boulder

This boulder is located slightly west of *Arthrictus*.

21. Platax Living Girdle Traverse V1

Start on the face directly across from *Organ Grinder* and traverse clockwise around the boulder. The original variation ends on the left-leaning crack on the west side of the boulder.

22. Mantle V0-
Climb the easy, east facing side of the boulder.

23. Unnmaed Corner V0
Climb the downhill corner and face

24. Unnamed V5
Below the previous problem on the downhill face of the boulder. Start low and grab the sloping-right lip of the boulder and then climb up. Same problem as the previous but from a sit start.

25. Southwest Corner V1
An area classic. Climb the west facing downhill face and corner of the boulder.

26. Horrible Crack V2
Same problem as the previous, but don't use the corner.

Scott Messick high above Whiskey Springs. Photo by the author.

27. Unnamed V2
Same as number 26, but don't use the crack either.

28. Unnamed V0-
A few problems have been done on the west face of the boulder at easy grades. The left leaning crack is one of them.

29. Trailside Problem V0-
On the front side of this boulder near the trail, climb the right-hand face.

C. Gunk's Boulder
This boulder is the rectangular-shaped, high-quality boulder just below the *Flesh Eater* boulder. A slanting horizontal splits its east side.

30. The Diagonal V2
Start low and right, traverse the nice horizontal up and left and finish at the lip. Top out far to the left.

31.Unnamed V1
Pull over the center of the boulder.

32. Black Malibau V6
SDS and climb sloping holds on the downhill, west face of the boulder near a small pit.

33. Prime Line V0+
SDS on the downhill-east side of the boulder, in a small pit, and climb rails to the top.

34. V6
SDS near the previous problem, and traverse the horizontal across to finish on problem number 32.

D. Stolen Delights Boulder
This boulder is the beautiful, rectangular boulder in the clearing below the *Gunk's Boulder*.

35. Weber Arete A.K.A Glen's Corner V0 +
Downhill from the boulder, climb the left arete (left arete while looking up at the boulder). The face just uphill from this problem goes at the same grade. A variation can be done at V1. It is an eliminate problem.

36. Weber Seam A.K.A Stolen Delights V1
A classic at its grade. Fun layback-moves ascend the beautiful seam on the downhill side of this boulder.

37. Variation V2
Climb the face left of the seam.

38. V2
Climb the face right of the seam.

39. Stolen Delights Corner V1
The corner just right of the previous problem.

40. Unnamed
Traverse the downhill side of the boulder.

41. Weber Wall V0+
The inside corner right of the previous problem.

42. Weber Direct V0+
Pinch the corner right of the corner to top out at the interesting feature above.

43. The Fly V5
This problem is located above and right of the *Stolen Delights Boulder*. It lies just below the trail and a slight bit before the *Trailside Boulder*. Start this problem on the small, downhill face. SDS with right hand on a crimp where the boulder is resting 2' off the ground and

with your left hand on a micro-crimp that has been broken off; your feet should be on the boulder also. Fire to a sloper, match, and fire out left to a horizontal under the lip.

Bolt Boulder Area (Area 4)

After the *Flesh Eater Boulder*, walk down the white-blazed trail approximately 5 minutes walk and you will reach a second outcrop of boulders.

A. Trailside Boulder

After passing the last boulder from *Area 1*, heading west toward *Area 2*, you will see a small, round boulder about 7' tall, off the left-hand side of the trail. Two excellent problems exist on the small, overhanging side.

1. Brass Monkey V4

A lot of climbing for a seemingly short problem. SDS on low edges, crank right to an undercling under a bulge, and continue up. You can use the rounded corner.

2. Segrams 7 V5

One of the best problems at Whiskey. SDS and climb the overhanging face past a series of positive edges in the center of the face.

B. Pap Smear VB

After the previous boulder, you come to a break in the ridge. Walk a short distance and the boulders start up again. The first group you come too will be off right of the white-blazed trail on a splinter trail. This problem climbs the first small boulder you come to. The *Snake Pit* is just past it on the right.

3. Sunset Slab V0-

Three fun slab problems can be done on the long boulder across from the *Snake Pit*. This boulder is between *Pap Smear* and *The Bolt Boulder*.

C. The Snake Pit

Just past the *Easy Boulder* is another grouping of rock. In the grouping and right of the trail in a short rock passage, there is a pit. A few problems exist here.

4. Pit and the Pendulum V8

Looking in the pit, climb the left boulder from a low sit start under the boulder. Move over sharp crimps to a powerful topout.

5. Divide before Nothingness V12

Climb the boulder on the opposite side of pit from *Snake Charmer*.

6. Snake Charmer V0-/V1

A few sit-down-start problems can be done on great holds in the pit if you can crawl into the cave on the backside of the *Snake Pit* near its west side. All are worth doing!

7. Whiskey Roof V5

On the backside of the *Snake Pit* a large boulder forms a pit and a short roof. SDS under the right end and climb great edges under the lip to a stellar top out.

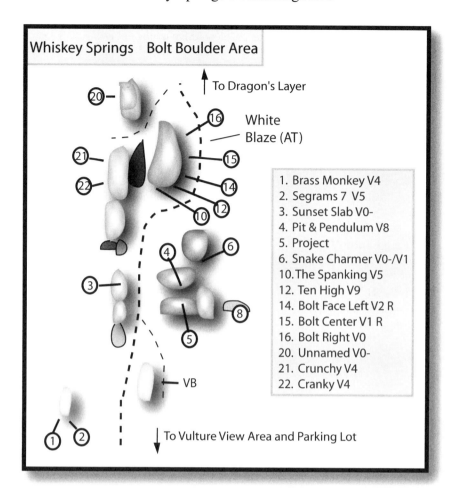

Whiskey Springs Bolt Boulder Area

To Dragon's Layer

White Blaze (AT)

1. Brass Monkey V4
2. Segrams 7 V5
3. Sunset Slab V0-
4. Pit & Pendulum V8
5. Project
6. Snake Charmer V0-/V1
10. The Spanking V5
12. Ten High V9
14. Bolt Face Left V2 R
15. Bolt Center V1 R
16. Bolt Right V0
20. Unnamed V0-
21. Crunchy V4
22. Cranky V4

VB

To Vulture View Area and Parking Lot

8. Sorosis V2

Climb up and over the left side of the roof. An easier variation has been done to the left.

D. Bolt Boulder

This boulder is arguably the best and most unique-looking boulder here. It is the long boulder with an overhanging knob-feature at its front end and a white blaze painted on it. Some of the hardest climbs here are on its face. It is also the last boulder on the outcrop.

9. Leaping Lizards Batman V2 R

Jump the gap from the boulder behind *The Cranking* and gain the good hold of the overhung face up high. Easier than it looks but a bold endeavor nonetheless.

10. The Spanking V5 R

An old area classic that can be a bit awkward. Slap up the left side of the steep face with the trailmarker painted on it. Use the boulder to the left and a kneebar.

11. The Cranking V6 R
A newer, more-pure line up the previous problem. Slap up the left corner and center of the overhanging face.

12. Ten High V9 R
Climb the right corner. The sit start goes at V10.

13. Mo Fro V10/V11 R
Sit start the previous line that does not use the crimps right of the arete.

14. Bolt Face Left V2 R
High and technical. Climb the left side of the long slab on the boulder trail at the boulders highest point.

15. Bolt Face Center V1 R
Delicate moves ascend the center slab.

16. Bolt Face Right V0
A nice problem to end a day of hard bouldering. Easy but very fun climbing passes the right side of the slab.

17. High Bolt Traverse V0+
Climb the face and traverse left without using the good rail at the top.

18. Low bolt Traverse V1
Traverse the slab low.

19. Project
Continue to traverse across the overhung face.

E. Pyramid boulder
This boulder is adjacent to and behind the *Bolt Boulder*. A few problems exist on the downhill face including *Ridge Walk*. A no-hands walk down the boulder.

20. Unnamed V0-
This problem climbs over the bulge on the backside of the boulder.

21. Crunchy V4
Climb the left side of the boulder

22. Cranky V4
Climb the right side of the boulder.

Scott Messick bouldering at Whiskey Springs.

26. Dragon's Layer Bouldering Area

Area Beta

Location
The end of the ridge that Whiskey Springs is on.

Type of Climbing
Bouldering.

Other Info
Can be accessed by Whiskey Springs or another lot (see directions). Not all of the established problems are listed.

Dragon's Layer

This small area is just as nice as Whiskey Springs. The area was first climbed by area local Tim Garland. Tim turned me onto this great spot where I established many problems above the grade of V4. If you climb at Whiskey this area is worth checking out. A lot of secret overhangs lie scattered throughout the nearby hillsides.

Directions

Continue to walk about 10 minutes farther west on the Appalachian Trail and you will run into another series of several boulders. This area is not traveled often, so many of the problems here are unclean. One of the best problems on South Mountain exists here: *Diesel* should not be missed! Another way to access these boulders is to drive T540 (Old Town Road). This is the road that branches off of Petersburg Road, where Petersburg Road becomes Whiskey springs Road. Make a right onto Old Town Road and follow the road about 3 miles to where the white-dot trail (AT) passes across the road. Park here, and follow the trail on the left side of the road to the rock. Please note, this is a very rough road and it is not maintained.

Outrageous Boulder
This boulder can easily be missed. As soon as you see rock when walking from the *Bolt Boulder Area*, walk to the right, downhill, and you will see a free-standing boulder before the main pile of rock. Several great problems exist on this outrageous face.

1. Slope Style V0-
Climb the downhill-right side of the boulder up the sloping lip.

2. Clinch V1
SDS and climb the slanting rail at the boulder right side.

3. Diesel V5
SDS and climb up to small micro-crimps in the center of the face.

365

4. High Octane V6/V7
Climb past pebbles just left of the previous line from a sit start. The climb is V6 or V7 depending on how pure a line you take.

5. Gory Glory V1
SDS and climb up to and across the left corner of the boulder.

6. Unnamed V0-/V1
Several problems have been done on the large cluster past the *Outrageous Boulder*.

7. Project.

8. The Dragon V1
SDS and climb the left wall of the downhill face of this boulder.

9. Enter the Dragon V3
SDS on the detached boulder below the previous problem. Move up and left over the detached block that rises above the pit past white stripes in the rock.

10. Inverted Layback V3
Locate this problem in a boulder hidden from view across from the previous problems. SDS at a rock in a pit and layback across to the lip. Start with your hands and feet matched.
Var. 1: A variation of the previous route follows the same line but without laybacking and off-routing the right wall.

11. Slick Prick V4
SDS on the jutting protrusion of rock attached to the right wall of *Inverted Layback*. SDS and climb the prow.

12. Grey GallopV1 R
Climb the left side of the outcrop perched on a ledge.

13. The White Stripes V0 R
From atop the ledge, climb past the white stripes of quartzite.

14. Unnamed V1 R
Climb out of the large crack right of the previous route.

15. Pile Driver V0+ R
Climb the right side of the outcrop.

16. Stealing Home V3
Climb the downhill-right corner.

17. Unnamed V4
SDS and climb the very short face right of the previous route.

18. Unnamed V0 R

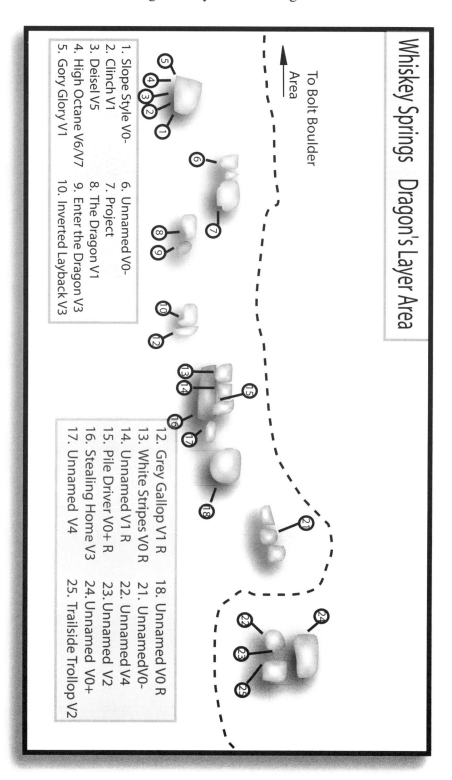

Whiskey Springs   Dragon's Layer Area

To Bolt Boulder
Area

1. Slope Style V0-
2. Clinch V1
3. Deisel V5
4. High Octane V6/V7
5. Gory Glory V1
6. Unnamed V0-
7. Project
8. The Dragon V1
9. Enter the Dragon V3
10. Inverted Layback V3

12. Grey Gallop V1 R
13. White Stripes V0 R
14. Unnamed V1 R
15. Pile Driver V0+ R
16. Stealing Home V3
17. Unnamed V4
18. Unnamed V0 R
21. Unnamed V0-
22. Unnamed V4
23. Unnamed V2
24. Unnamed V0+
25. Trailside Trollop V2

367

Climb the right side of the boulder passing fantastic holds.

19. Unnamed V0- R
Climb the face just right of the previous line.

20. Unnamed V0

21. Unnamed V0-
Several easy problems have been done on this low-quality cluster of rock.

22. Unnamed V4
SDS at the left side of the boulder, and traverse the sloping lip around the right corner to finish by toping out on the roof.

23. Unnamed V2
SDS and climb over the small roof at ground level.

24. Unnamed V0+
Climb the crimpy and sharp face.

25. Trailside Trollop V2
SDS at the left side of the rail, and climb it to top out.

26. Trails End Boulder V0-/V2
A few problems can be done on the perched boulder near the fire pit at the end of the outcrop.

27. Clamshell V6
This boulder is located on the south side of the hill from problem 21. It is a small roof a few feet off the ground, and it is hidden from view from the top of the ridge. Walk downhill a few paces and you will see this roof.

28. The Coffin V5
SDS in a small cave behind problem 26.

29. Dagwood V0
Climb the arete on the small boulder above *Pain Traverse*.

30. Pain Traverse V4
SDS on the overhang hidden below problem 26 and below the hiking trail. Start at the far right corner and work up and left to top out far left.

The Lair
This boulder is located below the previous boulder. It is at the extreme southwest tip of the ridgeline, where the ridgeline starts to go downhill.

31. Crowded House V1
SDS and climb the left side of the boulder.

32. Rob's Traverse V7
SDS on the previous line and traverse the lip of the cave to top out at the far right side.

33. Flash Gordon V4
SDS and climb over the roof at the center of the boulder.

34. Wonderwhirl V7
SDS and climb over the bulging prow under the overhangs right side.

35. Cleaning House V6
SDS in the cave under the boulder below the previous boulder and climb the sloping face above.

36. Tim's Overhang (Project)
If you hike the trail south a few yards, and go left off the trail into the woods, you will see rock. Look for the southwest tip of the ridge and you will find a large overhang with a crack splitting it. This route is still a project, but will go as a TR route in the 5.13 range.

27. Dead Woman Hollow Boulders

Area Beta

Location
Near Lewis Rock.

Type of Climbing
Bouldering.

Other Info
Not worth visiting unless you come from climbing at Lewis Rock.

Dead Woman Hollow Road

This obscure area is named for a nearby road with a rather macabre history. In the 1900s, a woman was killed from a snake bite along this road. The morbid nickname soon stuck. Now the road and bouldering area are named for it. Another equally chilling incident occurred, in more recent times, when two women parked their car at this road to begin a hike along the Appalachian Trail. The two were found murdered a short time after.

If this introduction does not discourage you from visiting this area, the serious lack of rock and heavy cover of vegetation should. With only a few boulders and limited climbing potential, I advise climbers not to go to this area unless you live nearby or are visiting a neighboring area.

Tweekers Hang is the only appealing feature of this area. One look at this high, daunting, overhanging boulder will justify the 15-minute hike. This steep rock feature--which interestingly, looks like a tipped-over billboard--is one of the most awesome boulders in the state. The letdown is that it's the only worthwhile boulder here.

Ownership: Micheux State Forest.

Season: The autumn and spring are the best times of the year to boulder here. Summer is overgrown, and a difficult time to find some of the rock.

Safety and Considerations: First: Note that the main hiking trail from the parking lot is flooded and swampy during and after rain storms. During dry spells this is the quickest way to access the rock, but you may want to consider the alternate approach mentioned in the directions. Second: *Tweekers Hang* is a high boulder, although many boulder it, novice climbers may want to bring a toprope setup for the more daring lines on the boulder.

Directions

From the Pine Grove Furnace Park Headquarters, at the junctions of SR3008 and Route 233, follow Route 233 south, exactly 2.7 miles, to a large parking area on the right shoulder of the road. This area is located at the signs for the Adams/Menallen township lines (signs say Cumberland/ Southampton line if traveling north). Park here and walk the blue-blazed trail for about 10 minutes. After passing a stream, continue uphill, following the blazes. You will see very small boulders off to the left in the woods, midway up a steep hill. Walk this way and you will come to *Tweekers Hang*, a few-hundred feet off the trail. Note: this trail is the same access point for the Tumbling Run Bouldering Area.

The Boulder Problems

When following the approach trail, you will see rock on your left and right, just before the crest of the mountain. There are a few problems on the outcrop to the right, but the main attraction (*Tweekers Hang*) is found by walking left, about 200' before the crest of the mountain. Extremely difficult to spot in summer months, a small boulder will be visible a few-hundred feet off to your left. Walk left off the trail to this boulder. A few problems exist here. *Tweekers Hang* is a few hundred feet past this. If you reach slabby rock near the summit, you went just a bit too far; walk downhill a bit.

Right Side Cluster

These boulders are near the crest and visible to the right side of the trail.

1. Bandido V4

Sit start and climb the right side of the boulder perched on a ledge. This is the rightmost boulder on the ledge. Variations that are easier can be done to the left.

Main Boulder

Just before you reach *Tweekers Hang*, there is a small cluster of boulders stuck together.

2. Slime Traverse V2

At the left end of boulders, traverse right on a horizontal capped by another boulder.

3. Unnamed Edges V0-

The boulder at the right of the cluster of boulders has three nice problems that climb beautiful incut edges to the top.

4. Unnamed V0/V1

The boulder to the right of this cluster has two problems.

5. Worthless Endeavor V0-

The first boulder you come to off the approach trail is very small and has one problem. Sit start and climb up.

Tweekers Hang

This is the large, overhanging wall. It's the highest boulder at this area. Two V0- problems ascend the right end of the wall. The classic line ascends up big jugs slightly right of the center. It was originally rated a 5.4 and is probably only that hard.

Satellite boulder 1

The nice overhanging boulder just past *Tweekers* has a few nice problems on it. A V4 climbs the right side of the boulder up small edges and a flake. A V0- goes up the center of the wall just left of the V4.

Satellite Boulder 2

The next boulder along the ridge is past and slightly above the previous boulders. There is a small roof above the main boulder. A V1 climbs nice edges up the right side of the boulder. A V0- climbs the left side over the hang.

Slab boulder

Just a bit farther down the ridge is a large slab with a few nice, but dirty, problems.

28. Other Areas of Michaux and the Nearby Area.

Area Beta

Many other areas lie scattered throughout the Michaux and Carlisle/Chambersburg region. Here are some other areas that are not as appealing as other bouldering in the region, but I though I would include anyway.

Hammond Rocks

Local graffiti artists and bottle-chucking beer enthusiasts have greatly depreciated the setting of Hammond Rocks. Shallow carpets of glass and a thin skin of paint are abundant on the ground and boulders at this spot. The close proximity to the adjacent mountain road has made this area an accessible and popular party spot

Aside from the festive litter, this area offers a few large boulders 100' from your car. The easy access makes this area an easy visit if you want to check this spot out while visiting nearby Pole Steeple or Chimney Rocks.

Expect to find about 30 established problems that range from V0- to V6. Most of the grades tend to languish at the bottom of the scale but are fun, worthwhile problems nonetheless. The rock varies from a few feet to 25' high, and the quality is quite good. Should you feel like hunting around a bit, other nearby boulders can be found scattered along this ridgeline and mountainside.

The nearby Wafer Wall is a different climbing area with limited potential. However, the rock here is clean and without graffiti. Several interesting problems have been done on this rock spine.

If you live in the nearby area, or just want to check out the rock while visiting other nearby spots, you can keep busy here for a few hours, maybe less. Otherwise, don't bother climbing here. Many other nearby spots are much better.

Directions: Take exit 37 off interstate 81 and drive State Route 233 south towards Newville, approximately 11 miles, to reach Ridge Road (the Pine Grove Furnace State Park headquarters are just at the bottom of the hill from Ridge Road). Turn left and follow Ridge Road, east, about 2 miles, until you see a rock outcrop on the right side of the road. Park here and climb.

The Problems: Little was ever documented about this area. Tim Garland and Cheyenne Wills were amongst the first climbers to boulder here. They were also noted for discovering The Wafer Wall. This area is also called Boxcar Rocks—not to be confused with Boxcar Rocks near Tower City.

The Wafer Wall

Park the same as for Hammond Rocks but walk across Ridge Road and hike on the opposite side as Hammond Rocks. Walk directly north across the road and bushwhack for about 10 minutes. You will see a field on your right. At the back end of the field is a long wall with wafer rock-formations on it. Several problems can be done here.

Rattlesnake Road (Virginia Rocks)

You could climb at Virginia Rocks, but why would you want to? If you are visiting other spots and decide to venture to this area, you will probably still be disappointed. Seriously, if you decide to go to this spot by itself, you will most likely curse me the entire hike out, curse me most of the drive home, and fantasize about burning my car to a smoldering heap while you scratch your chigger-infected legs that night in bed.

Rattlesnake Road, better known as Virginia Rocks, is one of those areas I included just because there is rock there and lots of it's undeveloped. If the place were traveled a bit more, it would host some worthy problems. If you go, the rock is of good quality, but don't—not by any stretch of the imagination—get yourself excited about this spot. If you're looking to develop untapped rock, climb here, but only if you live nearby.

Directions: From interstate 81 near Greencastle, follow State Route16 east, through Waynesboro, to the town of Rouzerville. Continue to follow Route16 a few more miles to the small village of Beartown. Take the unmarked left, off Route16, where Route 16 meets the Appalachian Trail. This will lead into Rattlesnake Road. Follow Rattlesnake Road several miles, until you see an underground pipeline that bisects Rattlesnake Road. The pipeline is the large cut-out that crosses the road. It is covered in grass. Park at the dirt pull-off and walk on the right side (east side) of the pipeline. Walk east until you reach the rock at the crest of the ridge, about 1.4 miles down the pipe line.

White Rock Acres

White Rock Acres, not to be confused with any of the many other *White Rocks* in Pennsylvania, offers high-quality quartzite and conglomerate, with excellent toprope routes. The area is small and quaint with a deeply-wooded mountain setting. The rock is great quality, but it isn't very high: the height ranges from 15' to 40'.

This area caters to beginner and intermediate climbers who benefit from easily accessible toprope setups—and they are abundant here. If you do plan to toprope here, bring a wide range of small and medium gear. A few large pieces and plenty of webbing will also help. Many climbs here are easy to set up via trees or by slinging large blocks. The top is easy to gain by walking to either sides of the small ridgeline.

Lead climbs are also found in moderate quantity here. Most of the climbs are from the 5.3 to 5.8 range with a few slightly harder eliminate routes. Some nice crack climbs are located on the south wall of the first outcrop you see when walking to the area. Due to its shaded location, this area is a nice spot to climb in the summer. The approach is not bad and should only take 10 to 15 minutes of walking, up a gradual incline, with a few steep sections.

If you live nearby, check this area out. It's by no means a major destination, but superior rock and clean, fun climbs make this spot a pleasant day visit for local climbers. A boulder problem the famous Henry Barber put up here is not to be missed.

Directions: From the Getty gas station in the center of town take Front Street south (at the clock tower) passing the pond on its right shore, and make a left onto an unmarked road at the southwest end of the pond. Follow the unmarked road, skirting the south end of the pond over a bridge, and make an immediate right just after your rear tires clear the end of the bridge. You are now on Mountain Road and will pass over another one-lane bridge. Reach a stop sign just after the bridge and railroad tracks. At the stop sign, make a left onto Leidigh Road, and follow it 1.8 miles passing silos for the Land-O-Lakes farm. Just after the farm on the left and the ball field on the left, you will see a road on the right at a stop sign, just before a small bridge. Make a right onto Creek Rd. Creek Rd. follows the creek and branches off left at the sign for White Rock Acres located on the right. At the branch in Creek Road and the White Rock Acres sign, go straight on Kuhn Road. Follow Kuhn Road .07 miles to a sign and yellow gate on the right at a small pull off. Follow blue blazes on the right. The trail is marked to the rocks. The blue blazes will take you uphill about a 10 minute walk to the rock.

Wildcat Rocks

Unless you live in the Carlisle/Chambersburg area, it's best to write this area off your list.

Loose rock, obscene proportions of lichen, and junglelike surroundings are just a few reasons this area is not worth a visit. The only reason I have chosen to include this area is because a large amount of problems at this spot have yet to be developed. Many first ascent opportunities await the brave souls who decide to wade a sea of thorn bushes and poison ivy to claim siege on virgin choss. If you do brave the frivolous journey to this area, here is what you will find: Unique flat-iron-type walls (some up to 30' high), overhanging rock, and incut edges on steep rock. If more people climbed here and the place was a little cleaner, the area would not be as bad as I make it sound.

Established problems range from V0- to V6. Some area classics include *Lichen Revolution* V0+, *Wildcats* V1 X, *Where's Ryan* V1, *Unnamed* V5.

Directions: Take exit 5 off interstate 81 and follow State Route 16 east for 13 miles. Turn left at the storage facility. Turn left onto Chairman Road and follow it downhill 1 mile to rail road tracks at a 90-degree curve and a triangle intersection. Turn left onto Furnace Road and follow this .9/10 of a mile to a yellow gate, tucked away on the left.

29. Safe Harbor

Safe Harbor   (Closed)

Safe Harbor is currently closed to climbing. Although this area has never been officially open to climbing, many climbers have visited this area since the 1980s, and it has become one of the most popular climbing areas in the sate. The large attraction to this area stems from the high quantity of bolted routes. Safe Harbor is one of the most highly bolted areas in the Mid Atlantic. The area was mostly developed by Eric Horst. Climbers like Hugh, Hans, and Tony Herr as well as Grant Horner and Rich Romano were active developing the area in the early years.

Eric Horst has been spearheading the campaign to open Safe Harbor for over a decade. A great deal of progress has been made but the township is afraid the high-tension wires pose a threat to climbers (a ludicrous fear) at this time and are adamant in their plight to keep climbers from Safe Harbor. To help assist the climbing area being open please do not climb at Safe Harbor until the area is open to climbing. Trespassing at Safe harbor can result in fines and trespassing charges,

Eric Horst leading Wonderama. Photo courtesy Eric Horst collection.

378

and can destroy future possibilities of climbing being allowed. Please respect the wishes of the township and local climbers. More information can be obtained by visiting Eric Horst's website www.lancasterclimbing.com.

Notes

30. Hunter Rocks Bouldering Area

Area Beta

Location
Rothrock State Forest, south of State College.

Type of Climbing
Sandstone bouldering. One of the most popular bouldering areas in the state.

Other Info
A very small portion of this area is closed to climbing. Please respect the landowner.

Hunter Rocks

Hunter Rocks is arguably one of the most interesting bouldering destinations in Central Pennsylvania. Huge boulders, abundant with Hueco-like sandstone pockets, can be found nestled throughout the woodland of Rocky Ridge Natural Area. This natural area has one of the most restful settings a bouldering area could hope for: whispering pines, large sandstone sentinels, wavering underbrush, and secluded nooks to lose oneself in.

It's no mystery; Hunter Rocks is a very popular climbing area. Two miles of the boulders lie within Rocky Ridge Natural Area. Climbing is allowed on the property; there is no question about this, rock climbing is allowed at Hunter Rocks on Rocky Ridge Natural Area property—basically this is state game lands and Rothrock State Forest. Areas such as North Ridge Areas, Power Line Right, Power Line Left, Whispering Pines, Beaver Ave, Wave Boulder, and Main Area Right (Hillside Area) are all within the areas open to climbing. In a nutshell, 147 problems at 7 areas mentioned in this guide are open to climbing. That being said, a very small portion of the ridge is closed to climbing—actually it's never been open, but hundreds, maybe thousands of climbers have climbed here over the past four decades. About two acres of rock is located on property that is jointly owned by private owners. Their wishes are that climbers do not trespass on their property. It is unfortunate that some of the most popular problems are on this property, but some of the *best* problems, in my opinion, lie amongst the open side. Many climbers are not aware of the gems hidden within the Rothrock/Rocky Ridge property. For this reason alone, it is worth including this are in this guidebook. With topos, route descriptions, etc., climbers can taste the flavorful problems on the open property. It is my hopes that publishing information will draw climbers to refrain from climbing on closed property and explore the hidden wonders of the open lands.

Hunter Rocks hosts a plethora of wonderment for any level climber. Expect to find hundreds of problems, miles of rock, and one of the most pleasant settings in the state. Problems range from VB to V11. Although there are a good amount of difficult problems here, the areas could definitely benefit from more hard problems. The rock just doesn't yield to more-difficult terrain like the smooth bodies of rock at other parts of the state, but don't let this dissuade you; Hunter Rocks is fantastic!

Many problems here are highball so bring a crash pad. Please respect the land here. Many fragile species of plantlife reside here such as the Putty Root Orchid. Please pack out any trash and keep noise levels to a minimum. Many hikers also use this property, so please share the land appropriately.

Geology: Devonian sandstone.

History

If you climb at Hunter Rocks, you may notice that some of the names of the problems in this guidebook differ from the beta available word-of-mouth. The reason is because no accurate history has ever been preserved for the area. A documented timeline dates back to the late '60s; however, a handful of climbers from the past decade have lacked consideration for Hunter's history. I have tried to rectify this many times to no avail.

This book attempts to document a rich history that dates back several decades and includes many climbers' ascents—some that were legendary and prolific American climbing icons. I feel it's important that previous pioneers are credited for their work in establishing the original problems at this great area. Many climbers like Trudy Healy, Curt Harler, Mug's Stump, Nick Morell, George Morell, Ryan Lukas, Rob Mutti, and many other climbers should be acknowledged for their work and ties to Hunter Rocks. If anyone feels that the dozens of climbers and climbers families I've spent hours on the phone with determining this history are in error, the history is documented finally so feel free to expand upon it. Even though most of us climbed for fun and to claim FA's was laughable, here is a detailed history for the area.

It is important to note that some of the older problems at Hunter Rocks were never named. More recent climbers have come up with some excellent names that have stuck over recent years. Because of this, I have included many of these names or chosen to list the original names supplemented with the more popular, well-known names.

During the 1950s, Hunter Rocks was a popular spot amongst hikers and outdoor enthusiasts. It is no doubt that rock scrambles and easy ascents were filtered out during this time however, the first documented climbers to visit the area were Trudy Healy and Curt Harler in 1968. The two climbers were members of the Penn state Outing Club and had been using topo-quads and geology maps to locate possible climbing areas-- nearby Bellfonte Quarry was discovered by them in this manner and around the same time. Trudy was a well known climber of the era, who devoted much time into starting the Adirondack Mountain Club and co-authoring the first climbing guidebook to the Adirondacks with Fritz Weisner. Although not boulderers per say, it is known that obvious high climbs were toproped by them as well as some obvious high solos like the

Bouldering at Hunter Rocks circa 1990s. Photo by the author.

ones near *The Mojo*, *Healy Wall*, and *Campfire Wall*. Ascents near the power line were also done at this time. Unfortunately, after 40 years, much detail of these ascents have been long forgotten.

The Legendary Mugs Stump grew up not far from Hunter Rocks. Mug's was a legendary alpinist and the only football player at PSU at the time that Joe Paterno told to get a haircut. I was told that several ascents were made by him on the higher outcrops at Hunter's after a visit from living away from home. It is possible Mug's did very little in this part of PA but a friend of mine had climbed with him in the nearby area and other climbers verify that he was active at Hunters and said he would have undoubtably climbed obvious outcrops like *The Stump Wall* and other popular outcrops. Most of the obvious climbs and boulder problems were all sent into the 1980s. Active climbers to visit the area were Mike Pantellich, Dennis King, Carl Hild, Carl Collins, Will Whitel, Neil Gleichman, Dough Gitt, and many other members of Penn State and the outing club. It is known that these climbers developed Classic lines like *Mojo* (later named by other climbers) and most of the high, obvious boulder problems. Hugh Herr was also active in the State College region as well as Eric Horst but are too modest to claim any significant development.

Difficult sit start problems (modern-style bouldering) began at Hunter Rocks in the late '80s and early '90s. Tina Mangeri and a close friend, who subsequently made impressive ascents of Kilimanjaro and Mt. McKinley—and an even more impressive lead-ascent of the 300' road-cut off I-80m near State College--were active with early bouldering in the PSU vicinity. Tina introduced me to the State College climbing scene in the late '80s. This had opened my eyes to the local climbing community and sparked new ideas for development.

During and throughout the '90s, a renaissance of development had taken place at Hunter Rocks. Nick Morell had begun bouldering at the area during this time. Nick was perhaps one of the most talented climbers in the state during this decade—and the most unknown due to his calm and incredibly modest demeanor. Nick began developing numerous hard sit-start problems and eliminates that spanned into the V11 range (although they were originally graded only V9 because Nick was a very modest grader).

Nick, along with George Morell, myself, Ryan Lukas, and Rob Mutti were all very active in developing the existing trails and cleaning hoards of lichen and moss off the boulders (some which were significantly harder until holds had broke). Nick and myself developed and cleaned the problems on *The Sand Egg*, many problems on *The Stump Wall*, *Mojo Area* (named this by later climbers), *Trench Area*, *Lower Area*, most of the problems at the *Power Line Areas*, and dozens of other areas throughout Hunter Rocks. Nick was the main developer of much of the classic problems around Hunter Rocks. Some of his most impressive achievements were his first ascents of problems like *Hemispherical Combustion Chamber* V7 and its V9 variation, *Combustion* V10/V11, *Airy Arete* V3 X, *Moon Unit* V4 R, *Liquid Mind* V6, and dozens of other classics. I developed many classic problems like *Delirium Dive* V4, many of the routes on the *Whispering Pines Boulder* and dozens of problems at other areas and repeated problems like *HEMI* and *Combustion* .

Rob Mutti, Ryan Lukas, Rick Carey, and other climbers were also active during this time developing problems along the ridgeline. Ryan Lukas spent a great deal of time locating and sending many of the isolated extremes of the ridge. Many classic problems were "mined-out" of the ridgeline by Ryan. I remember telling Obe Carrion about Hunter rocks during this time-period and I'm pretty sure he sent some hard lines at the main areas. Ivan Green paid a visit on one occasion and crushed a few hard lines subsequently developing a hard problem along the ridge. Other climbers from the State College area have undoubtedly developed climbs in recent years and a very small amount of rock is still to be developed. Visit this spot and I'm sure you can find some overlooked gems.

Directions

From State College, drive south on state route 26 to the town of Jackson Corner. Just after the town, continue on Rt 26 and locate SR1017 (Martin Gap Road) on the right-hand side of the road. Follow Martin Gap Road. Do not veer left at any of the Y's in the road. Continue until Martin Gap becomes Frew Road. Continue straight and pass under a power line where you can see rock on the ridge to the right. This is the Power Cut area. Park at the pull off just past the power cut for climbing at the Power Cut area. If you wish to continue to the Main Areas, follow Frew Road to a sizable parking area on the right. Follow the trail across a stream on the right side of Frew road to a T-intersection. Continue over this trail and veer left. This trail will take you directly to the *Four-star Boulder*. You can also park at the end of Frew road and follow a trail from the southwest corner of the lot and break right onto the Standing Stone trail. Follow the trail to the right until you reach the climbers trail on the left. Follow this to the *Four-star* Boulder. **Note:** Do not follow the steep eroded trail from the end of Frew Road. This is the old trail that takes you to the closed area. You are trespassing if you follow this trail. It is advised that you park at the main climbers lot before the end d of Frew Road and follow

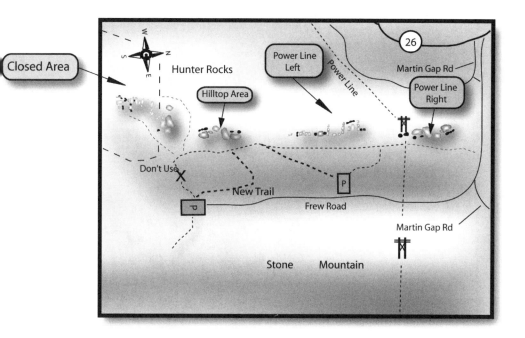

the new trail made by the Standing Stone Trail Club.

Hunter Rocks Main Area (Closed To Climbing)

The most popular climbing at Hunter Rocks is found at this area. High-quality rock with unique qualities unlike any other in Pennsylvania are abundant in this condensed area. Unfortunately, upon request of the landowner, climbing is not permitted on the handful of boulders at this area however, there are hundreds of other quality problems at Hunter's many other areas; please climb anywhere to the right of the Campfire Boulder that extends into Rothrock State Forest. The sole purpose of this section is to provide historic reference to the problems established at this area. Since so many climbers climb or have climbed at this spot, I have decided to include a reference of the great climbs that have been established here.

Campfire Boulder or Campfire Wall
This is the large rectangular boulder (about 18' high) directly in front of you when you come in on the approach trail. There is a fire ring and large flat area in front of it. A cluster of large boulders can be found behind and left of it.

1. Campfire Traverse V0-
Traverse from left to right on the *Campfire Wall*.

2. Welcome to Hunter V2

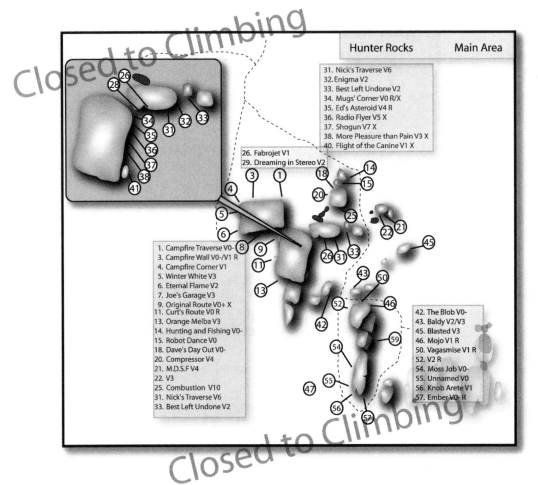

Hunter Rocks   Main Area

31. Nick's Traverse V6
32. Enigma V2
33. Best Left Undone V2
34. Mugs' Corner V0 R/X
35. Ed's Asteroid V4 R
36. Radio Flyer V5 X
37. Shogun V7 X
38. More Pleasure than Pain V3 X
40. Flight of the Canine V1 X

26. Fabrojet V1
29. Dreaming in Stereo V2

1. Campfire Traverse V0-
3. Campfire Wall V0-/V1 R
4. Campfire Corner V1
5. Winter White V3
6. Eternal Flame V2
7. Joe's Garage V3
9. Original Route V0+ X
11. Curt's Route V0 R
13. Orange Melba V3
14. Hunting and Fishing V0-
15. Robot Dance V0
18. Dave's Day Out V0-
20. Compressor V4
21. M.D.S.F V4
22. V3
25. Combustion V10
31. Nick's Traverse V6
33. Best Left Undone V2

42. The Blob V0-
43. Baldy V2/V3
45. Blasted V3
46. Mojo V1 R
50. Vagasmise V1 R
52. V2 R
54. Moss Job V0-
55. Unnamed V0
56. Knob Arete V1
57. Ember V0- R

variation joins and finishes on *Joe's Garage*. It goes at V4.

3. Campfire Wall V0-/V1 R
Several problems have been done from V0- to V1 along the wall near the fire ring.

4. Campfire Corner V1
Assertive moves follow this beautiful corner.

5. Winter White V3
Make interesting moves near a cleft in the rock. Variations to the right and left make the problem easier or harder, depending on what line you pick.

6. Eternal Flame V2
Follow the right side of the rock to the top.

7. Joe's Garage V3
SDS on the low corner and traverse a rail to the center of "the garage" alcove. Continue

to the top from here. A variation moves farther right and tops out. It goes at V4.

8. Garage Door V4
Pull off high holds at the lip and continue over steep rock to the top.
Var. 1: Mental Mechanic V3 A slightly easier variation climbs the wall a few inches right of *Garage Door*.

Healy Wall
The oldest problems at Hunter's have been done on this face. Several problems can be done up the rectangular face that range from VB to V1. Most are highballs.

9. Original Route V0+ X
Climb the left side of the wall over a short overhang.

10. Unnamed V0 R/X
Climb the face between 9 and 11.

11. Curt's Route V0 R
Climb the face right of the previous line.

12. Unnamed Crack V0-
Climb the obvious, easy crack.

13. Orange Melba V3
At the end of the day, sunlight paints the rock a brilliant orange. Climb the beautiful face. A traverse into the climb from the left makes the problem a tad harder.

Entrance Rock
This is the very small boulder located uphill and right, if you branch right just before reaching the *Campfire Boulder*. If you continue downhill from this boulder, you will come to the main area.

14. Hunting and Fishing V0-
SDS and climb the right side of this short boulder.

15. Robot Dance V0
SDS and climb left of the previous problem.

Compressor Boulder
This boulder is located just south of the small *Entrance Rock*.

16. The Green Traverse V0-
Begin sitting on the left side of the boulder and traverse right.

17. Unnamed V0-
Climb the left side of the boulder.

18. Dave's Day Out V0-

Climb the center of the face.

19. Unnamed V0-
Right-side face of the same boulder as the previous problems.

20. Compressor V4
SDS under the roof, around the corner and right of the previous problem.

21. M.D.S.F V4
A vulgar name for a great problem—what can I say, try to guess it. Start in the center of the narrow, overhanging boulder, just off the left side of the trail, coming down from the *Entrance Rock*.

22. Three Martini Lunch V3
Sit start and climb the left side of the boulder. The corner drops the grade slightly and is technically a different problem.

23. Stereophonic V5
Begin at the left side of the wall, traverse past *M.D.S.F.* and top out at the right side of the boulder.

The following two problems are located directly across from *M.D.S.F.*, up in a pit with a steep overhang above. Basically on the downhill side of the *Compressor Boulder*.

24. Pine Arete V1
SDS and climb the right side of the boulder. Often covered in pine needles.

25. Combustion V10/V11
V10 if done a certain way. Start low in the back of the steep overhang and pull small crimps to more crimps at the lip. Continue to the top. This problem was once harder before some holds broke off. Some think this problem is V13--that would be way inflated.

The Sand Egg
One of the most interesting boulders on the ridge, and some of the best problems at Hunter Rocks. This is the egg-shaped boulder between *M.D.S.F*

and the *Stump Wall*.

26. Fabrojet V1
Start in the center of the left side of the boulder and top out. A SDS makes the problem V5.

27. George's Finest Hour V5
SDS in the center of the boulder and top out. Basically the sit start to *Fabrojet*.

28. Delight V4
SDS and climb up the left side of the boulder.

29. Dreaming in Stereo V2
Start at *Fabrojet* and traverse the lip right to top out at the right side of the boulder. A SDS makes the problem V5.

30. Rob's Traverse V7/V8
Begin with a SDS at the left side of the egg and traverse as low as possible under the right side of the boulder until it's possible to top out on *Enigma*. If you start farther left the grade is V8.

31. Nick's Traverse V6
One of the first truly hard lines developed at Hunter's. When it was first cleaned off and climbed, it was remarkably easier. Within a few hours of climbing, so much rock had broken off that the grade had jumped from V4 to V6. The problem is now quite clean and a mega-classic. Traverse from a SDS just right of *George's*, traveling under the boulder, and top out on the far right.

32. Enigma V2
SDS and climb the right side of the boulder.
Var. 1: **V2** Begin a few feet left near the start of *Nick's Traverse* and climb straight up from a sit start.

33. Best Left Undone V2
SDS and climb the very small boulder just off the right tip of *The Egg*.

34. Mugs' Corner V0 R/X
Jaunt up the right side of the high wall.

35. JKSF (a.k.a Ed's Asteroid) V4 X
A nice highball. Basically a dyno that starts on *Radio Flyer*, climbs up right and dynos to the big incut above the nice flake 10' left of *Mugs's corner*.

36. Radio Flyer V5 X
Start on the face 12' left of *Mugs's* and climb up to a nice vertical flake; then move left up small finger pockets to a big incut hold that leads to an exciting top out.

37. Shogun V7 X

Climb the face and shallow cleft left of the previous climb and move out and right over a bulge. A variation goes straight up over the bulge (V8 X).

38. More Pleasure than Pain V3 X
Crimpy and technical. Start the same as the previous route, climb up to the bulge and move slightly left to a good hold at the bulge. Top out onto the low-angle face above.

39. Stump Crack V1 X
One of the oldest lines at Hunter's. Climb the nice crack left of *More Pleasure*.

40. Flight of the Canine V1 X
Traverse from the very left end of the boulder all the way to 6' from the very right end and go straight up to a high, but easy, top out. A few variations a grade harder and a grade easier have been done to the left and right at the finish. Left is harder; right is easier.

41. Cutie V0+
Climb the small roof on the narrow boulder somewhat attached to the main cliff, and left of the high wall.

42. The Blob V0-
Climb the face of the boulder between the previous problem and *Baldy*.

43. Baldy V2/V3
SDS on the sloping left corner of the boulder below *The Mojo Boulder*. Traverse right and top out.

44. Unnamed V0+
Locate a small boulder behind and right of *Baldy*. Climb the obvious face.

45. Blasted V3
Climb the obvious right arete from a sit start.

46. Mojo V1 R
Start on the left face of the boulder and climb/traverse right out the beautiful lip to a point at a weakness and top out. Walk off left.

47. Le Dame Blanche V2 R
SDS at the start to *Mojo* and climb slightly right of the main start; then climb straight up the face above to top out. Walk off left.

48. Vegemite V2 R
Traverse in from the start to *Mojo* and move past the previous problem and top left of the regular top out to *Mojo*.

49. The Hunter V4
Start on problem number 51, instead of moving left into *Mojo*, continue straight up.

50. Vagasmice V1 R

Climb the tight squeeze-chimney in the center of the boulder.

51. The Hunted V2/V3 R
If you climb this with the right beta, the problem is a V2. Start near the beginning of the previous problem and move left into a horizontal traverse. Move past a pocket and gain the *Mojo* finish.

52. The Albatross V2 R
Climb the unappealing right corner of the boulder.

53. Lichenization V0-
Climb dirty rock.

54. Moss JobV0-
Not a very worthwhile climb and often dirty. Climb the face down the hill from the previous problem.

55. Unnamed V0
Climb the face just left of the downhill arete on this rock formation. The problem starts about 200' downhill from the previous problem.

56. Knob Arete V1
Climb the beautiful downhill arete. This is the arete a few-hundred feet downhill from the *Mojo* area.

57. Ember V0- R
Climb the right side of the previous problem.

58. The Throne V0- X
Climb straight to of the large rock formation left of *Mojo*.

59. High Times V1- X
Climb up left of the previous route on nice holds.

The Throne
This is the boulder behind/downhill form the *Mojo* boulder.

1. The Throne V0- X
One of the oldest climbs at this area. Climb the nice corner to the top out high above.

2. High Times V1 X
Start on easy rock and angle up left of *The Throne* to the steeper top with nice pockets.

3. Unnamed V0+ R
This is the boulder downhill from the previous problem. Ascend the face at the north end of the boulder.

4. Ember V0- R

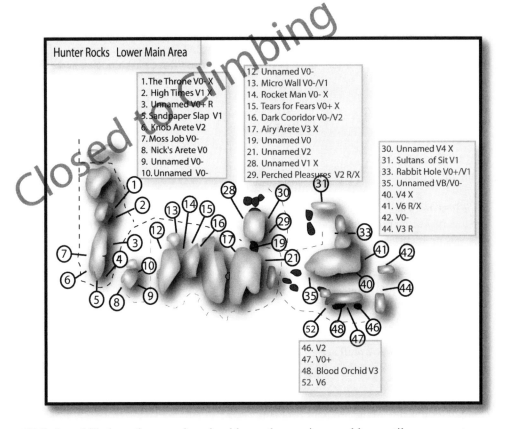

Hunter Rocks Lower Main Area

1. The Throne V0- X
2. High Times V1 X
3. Unnamed V0+ R
5. Sandpaper Slap V1
6. Knob Arete V2
7. Moss Job V0-
8. Nick's Arete V0
9. Unnamed V0-
10. Unnamed V0-

12. Unnamed V0-
13. Micro Wall V0-/V1
14. Rocket Man V0- X
15. Tears for Fears V0+ X
16. Dark Cooridor V0-/V2
17. Airy Arete V3 X
19. Unnamed V0
21. Unnamed V2
28. Unnamed V1 X
29. Perched Pleasures V2 R/X

30. Unnamed V4 X
31. Sultans of Sit V1
33. Rabbit Hole V0+/V1
35. Unnamed VB/V0-
40. V4 X
41. V6 R/X
42. V0-
44. V3 R

46. V2
47. V0+
48. Blood Orchid V3
52. V6

Walk downhill along the same long boulder as the previous problem until you come to a corner at the south tip of the rock. Looking back uphill, this climb takes a line up the rightmost corner of the boulder.

5. Sandpaper SlapV1 R
Climb the center of the short south face of this boulder.

6. Knob Arete V1
Climb the left arete of this small face. A few variations can be done moving left or right at the top. The grades vary slightly harder and slightly easier than the original problem.

7. Moss Job V0-
Climb the green, loose face up the gulley and left of *Knob Arete*.

8. Nick's Arete V0
Climb the nice arete across from the previous problems.

9. Unnamed V0-
Run up the nice face around and right in the gulley from the previous problem.

10. Unnamed V0-

Start at a nice pocket about 30'uphill from the previous route and climb the easy face.

11. Micronauts V0-/V1
Climb this great face climb at the north tip of the gulley above number 10. Several variations can be done including a sit start that makes the problem V1.

12. Unnamed V0-
Directly across the gulley from *Micronauts*, on the corner of the boulder, you'll find this nice climb and easy warm up.

13. Micro Wall V0-/V1
Use fun moves to climb the popular face around the corner and in a trench from problem number 12. Several variations can be done including a sit start that makes the problem V1.

Trench Problems
Several problems can be done left the previous problem. Most are very easy but fun warm ups, or easy problems to spend some time on.

14. Rocket Man V0-X
Looking downhill into the gulley, this problem is on the left side all the way at the back on the left wall. Climb straight up and move left to top out.

15. Tears for Fears V0+ X
Left of the previous route, move past great edges to a big horizontal with a large boulder resting 24' up. Top out straight up. Be aware the top is the trickiest part.

16. The Dark Corridor V0-/V2
Several highball problems can be done in the long, narrow corridor east of the previous area. There is a marginal fixed anchor on top that should be backed up if you wish to TR. Most of the problems are in the V0- to V2 range.

17. Airy Arete V3 X
Big holds under the right end of a big roof lead to a short lip traverse. At the crux climb up and left to one of the best aretes in Central PA. Long, high and exciting. One of the best problems at Hunter Rocks.

18. Moon Unit V4 R
Left of the arete, in a passage between two boulders (between *Airy Arete* and *Scary Arete*), crawl up and right to a hold in the overhang; then move to a crimp and pull over the lip.

19. Unnamed V0
Traverse the horizontal under the roof.

20. Hearts of Space V1
SDS and climb the arete on the left side of the passage. There is a small pine above.

21. Unnamed V2
SDS just left of the arete.

22. Resin Run V1
Several problems in the V1 range exist downhill from the arete. The most obvious follows a run of dark rock.

23. Unnamed V1 R
Climb up the nice obvious seam. Several problems in the V0 range can be done downhill from this problem.

24. Nimble Traverse V3
Traverse from the low, left end of the boulder to the high right end near *Hearts of Space*, or continue farther to top out on *Moon Unit* or *Airy Arete*. The latter two make the grade V4.

Liquid Mind Boulder
This is the small boulder with a very low roof/cave under it. It is across from *Resin Run*.

25. Slopy SlopeV0+
Traverse the lip on the right side of the small roof/boulder and top out at the left end over the hang.

26. Liquid Mind V6
SDS and climb the pinches and awesome crimps under the small roof behind *Resin Run*. Crank over the lip to finish. Several variations have been done making the grade easier and somewhat harder.

The Perched Boulder
This boulder is the high perched rock that is adjacent to *Airy Arete*.

27. Scary Arete V0+/V1 X
Climb up the corner of the boulder across from *Airy Arete*.

28. Unnamed V1 X
Climb the featured left side of the perched boulder above the previous problem.

29. Perched Pleasures V2 R/X
Climb up the right side of the perched boulder and follow a weakness in the boulder.

30. Unnamed V4 X
Up the severe overhang and crack right of the previous route.

Rod Rock
Across from the perched boulder going east, there is a small pit with a small rectangular boulder at the back wall.

31. Sultans of Sit Starts V1

Climb the center of the boulder from a SDS. The top out is the crux.

32. Lip Service V2
Traverse the lip. V4 if you off-route the lip and use only the face holds to traverse.

33. Rabbit Hole V0+/V1
Climb the boulder perched on a ledge above and behind number 32 from a SDS.
Depending on how you do it, it can be V0+ or V1; either way is fun.

Behemoth Boulder
This is the massive boulder below the previous problems.

34. Crumbles to Bumbles V2
Crank one of the nicest problems on this boulder from a SDS at the boulder's left blunt
arete.

35. Unnamed VB/V0-
At the bottom left side of this giant boulder, SDS and run up the nice pockets.

36. V0+/V1 R
Climb up nice pockets right of the previous problem. If you climb up more to the right,
the problem is around V1.

37. V0+ X
An interesting highball. Ascend the nice, shallow, slanting crack toward the middle of
this nice face.

38. Unnamed V5 X
Climb the difficult groove.

39. Steeper than Your Momma V1 X
An easy but intimidating highball. Climb into the huge crack and follow it to the top.
Begin over to the left and traverse to the right to gain the crack.

40. Zen and the Art of Masturbation V4 X
Start in shallow area right of the previous climb and go up to a roof and move right to top
out high above.

41. Masturbatory Frenzy V6 R/X
Around the corner from the previous route on the east face of the boulder. Start low
under the roof around and right of the previous climbs and gain a horizontal under the
roof. Gain an undercling and horn and climb the easier but fragile face above. Easier if
taller.
Var. 1: V1R/X
Start by jumping to the high holds near the lip and continue to the top.

42. Legend V11?
Looking south from the *Behemoth Boulder*, you will see a small boulder with a deep hole

below and slightly above the *CJD Boulder*. Start low at a vertical seam and climb micro holds to the top on the right side of the face. I can't remember how hard the moves are so this grade may be a bit off. A lower start may be possible for a new route as well.

43. Problematic Arete V0-
SDS and climb the left arete.

44. The Problem with Problems V3 R
Start low and climb the crimpy face over the greenish-gray bulge at the top.

45. Crankomat V8
Same problem as 44 but from a lower start.

CJD Boulder
This is the last boulder of the group. It lies on the bottom of the hill below *The Behemoth Boulder*. It's long and somewhat high and is named for a traverse called *CJD*. This problem was claimed to be V13. A consensus by several other climbers is that the route is V11. I myself worked out the crux in a short time and feel the problem is V11. Similarly several other problems claimed to be V11 in the vicinity have been downgraded substantially. Either way, it's a fun problem if you can get past the chossy beginning. Try it yourself and comment on the grade.

46. Unnamed V3 R
Climb the right side of the boulder.

47. Sand castle V0+ R
Climb the center of the boulder through a weakness.

48. Blood Orchid V5 R
Start near the previous problem and dyno to a hold up high.

49. CJD V11
Some feel this is V13, myself and many others disagree. SDS at the very left side of the boulder and don't let your feet touch. Avoid loose feet past V4 moves then milk a rest at the huge bucket midway across; then endure an awesome sloper to a micro-pocket (crux) and continue through V3 climbing to the finish.

50. Toxieo Plasmosis V5/V6
The grade varies depending on what path you take or how many holds have broken this week. Start on CJD's start-holds and traverse to (V0+) and top out.

51. Legionnaires Disease V5
Start with your bum on the boulder left of the stat to (V0+) and climb up to the jug-rest on *CJD* then traverse high, just above the crux holds to *CJD*, and back down to join the regular *CJD* finish. Basically you are going over larger pockets to bypass the *CJD* crux.

52. Zen and the Art of Crash Pad Fabrication V6
SDS and climb the short overhanging face just above and left of the *CJD Boulder.*

Hunter Rocks

Hunter Rocks Hillside Area (Main Area, Right Side)

This spectacular area is located adjacent to and right of *The Main Area* (closed area). This area is open to climbing and is a recommended spot to visit. Four-star classics are abundant here. This spot is easy to locate by walking up the blazed trail from the main parking lot at the dead-end of Frew Road. Just after you summit the hill, break off right, and you will run into *Four-star Boulder*. This boulder is directly across from the campfire ring near *The Main Area (Left)*. This area is a very user-friendly spot because the landings are good, the boulders are not high, it's legal to climb here, and the problems are great.

Four-Star Boulder

This is the first boulder you come to from the approach trail. It's unmistakable due to its overhanging nature. It touches the trail and has a steep face. All the problems on it are, well…four-star.

1. Mr. Grumpers V0-

Named for a local bear cub that lived near by. Climb the left side of the boulder.

2. Graham Cracker Arete V1

Also called *The Incredarete*. SDS and climb the prominent arete on the boulder's left side. A must-do problem that was once a bit crumbly.

3. Traverse V8

SDS on the previous problem and traverse right, past slopers and a deep pocket, to a horizontal. Continue to the right side of the boulder. The original route was done by ascending the mungy gulley/crack at the boulders right side. However, a better variation is to send *Four-Star Arete* to finish.

4. Standard American Ascent V7

Stand start and climb the center face of the boulder over steep terrain to an exciting top out. Several variations have been done. I include just two.

Var. 1: V9 SDS at a deep, small pocket and join the original route.

Var. 2: V8 Start on problem 3 and traverse in and finish on the regular line.

5. Reverse Traverse V9

Same problem as problem number 3, but backwards.

6. Project

Begin on the small pocket and fly out to problem number two and finish on the arete.

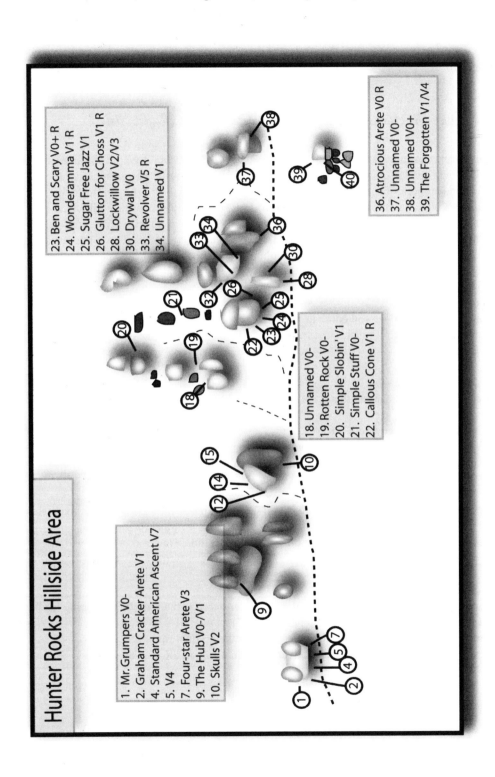

7. Four-star Arete V3
Climb the right arete of this boulder. This problem is also called *Verbing*.

8. Mushroom Tattoo V5
Locate a boulder behind the previous boulder. Walk up the trail to the crest of the ridge and walk down the backside of the ridge until you see belly of rock to hug. SDS and climb the smooth belly of rock.

9. The Hub V0-/V1
Several problems have been done on the ledge of the boulders behind and slightly right of the *Four-Star Boulder*.

The Frat House
The large boulder across from the previous hosts some excellent problems.

10. Skulls V2
SDS and climb the left side of the small boulder below and right of *The Hub*.

11. Spring Cleaning V1
Climb the extremely dirty face right of the previous route.

12. Climbtastic V0+
Climb the pocketed face near the corner.

13. Animal House V0+
Climb the face left of the previous route.

14. Kent Dorfman V0+
Climb up left of the previous route.

15. Forgotten Wonderment V0
Climb the backside of the boulder.

16. Unnamed V1
SDS and climb up next to the previous line.

17. Unnamed V0
SDS and climb next to the previous problem.

Satellite Boulders
The next two problems are located by following the main trail and breaking up and right, walking past the *Ice Cream Scoop*. From the scoop, these problems are on the backside of the two boulders on the left side of the gully.

18. Unnamed V0-
SDS and climb the second boulder back in the group of boulders.

19. Rotted Rock V0-

Dave Pfurr bouldering M.D.S.F.

SDS and climb the boulder closest to the trail.

20. Simple Slobin' V1
Sit start and climb the boulder on the left and down the gully.

21. Simple Stuff V0-
From a sitting start, climb the problem halfway down the gully on the right-hand side.

The Ice Scream Scoop
This is the large boulder alongside the trail that is 18' high. It has a steep downhill side that resembles an ice cream scoop.

22. Callous Cone V1 R
Climb the left-hand face of the boulder.

23. Ben and Scary V0+ R
Begin with a low start at the left corner of the boulder and climb to the top.

24. WonderammaV1 R
Climb large, positive holds at the left side of the overhanging face.

25. Sugar Free Jazz V1
Climb past large horizontals at the right side of the boulder.

26. Glutton for Choss V1 R
SDS and climb the dirty right corner of the large boulder.

The Wall
This boulder is the tall, flat boulder that resembles a wall. It is just past the *Ice Scream Scoop*.

27. The Kitchen Wall V0
Several problems have been done on the side of the wall adjacent to the scoop. The center is the hardest. Problems vary a bit on the easier or harder side depending on what part of the wall you climb.

28. Lockwillow V2/V3
The grade varies depending on where you start. SDS and climb the overhanging side of the boulder right of *The Kitchen Wall*.

29. Willow V1
Move out right from the start of the previous problem.

30. Drywall V0
Climb the east side of the wall.

31. The Ironing Board V0-
Climb the easy right side of the wall.

32. Unnamed V1
From a sit start, climb the left side of the boulder.

33. RevolverV5 R
Traverse the lip of the boulder to gain larger holds at the right side of the boulder near a crack on the face. Climb features on the face to top out.

34. Unnamed V1
Climb the heinous crack.

35. Unnamed V0+ R
Climb the wall between problems 34 and 36.

36. Atrocious Arete V0 R
Climb the easy, but high, tower of rock right of the previous route.

37. Unnamed V0-
Claw your way up the crumbly, loose face in some talus across from the previous problem.

38. Unnamed V0+
SDS and climb this unappealing problem. Eliminates make it as hard as V2.

39. The Forgotten V1/V4
Several problems have been done on the boulder that is off by itself, across and south of

Hunter Rocks

Power Line Area (Right Side)

These are the boulders you can see high on the ridge while driving Frew Road to *The Main Area*. You can see them on the peak of the hill off right of the road under the power line. Many of the best problems at Hunter's are located here. The only drawback is some of the problems are dirty due to infrequent travel. Regardless, I highly recommend climbing here, and with more use the problems will be clean and enjoyable. The views from the ridge are spectacular and many routes are 4-star. The ridge has soft landings and amazing pocketed, round boulders. The area is great for bouldering because unlike the other areas, many great sit starts are abundant on less-high rock. If you want to get away from the crowds in a secluded and tranquil bouldering setting, this is the place for you.

Please note that this guidebook, by no means, lists all the problems at this area. Although it covers a great deal of the classics, numerous other problems have been established here over the past 20 years.

Access and Ownership: Climbing *is* allowed here. The land is state gamelands and part of Rothrock State Forest. Pack out trash; don't overcrowd the parking area; and adopt a low-impact ethic.

Approach: 5 to 10 minutes of gradual uphill walking.

Directions: Park at the small grass lot just after passing under the power line on Frew Road (rock visible on the ridge). Note: if this lot is crowded there is a small pull-off farther down Frew Road. Do not bandit-park on the road or infringe on local flora to park closer to the main lot.

From the lot, walk along an old road at the back side of the lot. Veer up and right to reach the power line and the boulders after about 5 or 10 minutes of walking.

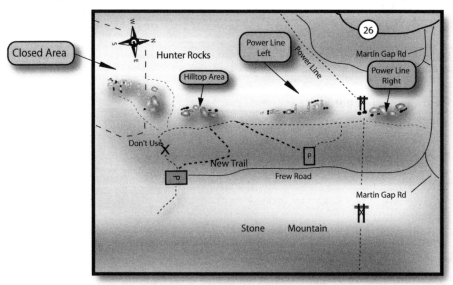

Shock Rocks
These are the two large boulders touching each other under the power line. Many classics exist on them.

1. Shockie V5
SDS and climb the corner of the boulder left of *Magnetic Fields*. Several variations have been done.

2. Magnetic Fields V3/V4
One of the most popular classics at its grade. From a sit start at the left-center of the first boulder to the right of the power line, climb up overhanging rock onto the slab above and top out. A version can be done eliminating some start holds to make the grade V4.

3. Ebb of Reality V3
SDS and climb the face just right of *Magnetic Fields*.

4. Edge of Night V4
Climb the high face near the corner of the two boulders that meet near the dark void of the two boulders.
Var. 1: V4 Traverse in from a sit start on *Shockie* and finish on the regular route.

Electric Boulder
The rightmost of the two boulders touching each other under the power line.

5. Darkness Falls V4 R
Crank up the face just right of the section where the two boulders meet.

6. Dream Theater V3 R
The face between *Sneakie Arete* and *Darkness Falls*. A fun variation traverses from problem number 1 and finishes on this route. It goes at V4.

7. Sneaker Arete (a.k.a Electric Arete) V1 R
Named because it was originally sent in sneakers. A nice highball that eases up a bit near the top. Climb the blunt arete on the boulder that expands out and right from the alcove where two boulders meet. Basically, the blunt arete on the right side of the rightmost of two boulders under the power line.

8. Got TP V2
The big slab for feet is off route. Climb the right-hand corner of the boulder to a sloping top out.
Var. 1: V1
SDS on the corner left of the previous problem and climb the overhanging prow to the top.

Power Trench
This is the trench located behind the two *Shock Rocks*, on the south side of the ridge.

12. Looking Southward V1
Below and left of the previous climbs is a small boulder with a nice left-hand corner. SDS and climb this problem; moving right.

13. Southern Exposure V1
Climb the face right of the previous route from a sit start.

14. Unnamed VB
Climb the wide, dirty crack at the left side of the long boulder in a passage behind the previous two climbs.

15. Unnamed V0
Just right of the previous problem. From a small ledge, climb a faint low crack through a weakness in the rock to the top.

16. Groovin V0
Right of the previous problem, climb a groove. Two variations exist to the right and left of this problem at the same grade.

17. Orange Swirl V1
Climb up the center of the boulder over white/orange-colored rock.

18. Unnamed V0-
Up cracks just right of the previous problem.

The Hallway
Walking back on the north side of the hill (side closest to Frew Road) walk down past unappealing rock to a section with a long trench that goes down the south side of the hill. The long trench that resembles a hallway hosts many exciting problems.

19. Trench Warfare V2
Climb the right-hand corner of the uphill entrance to the trench near a tree. Top out is the crux.

20. Unnamed V0-
Walk down the trench; at the first split on your right, SDS and climb the small face between two boulders.

21. Nick's Dilemma V0+
Climb the right side of the downhill face at the bottom of the trench. The left side of the face is a little easier.
Var. 1: Pick Pocket V0-
Via big pockets, climb the nice corner left of the previous climb.

22. Unnamed V3 R
SDS and climb the steep wall.

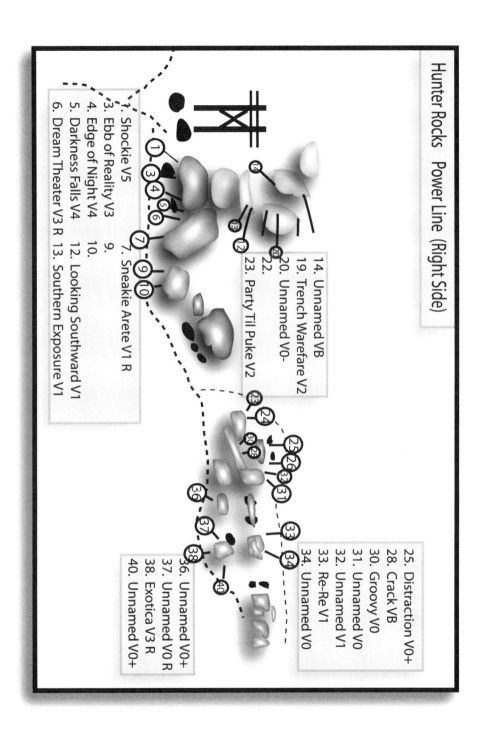

Hunter Rocks   Power Line (Right Side)

1. Shockie V5
3. Ebb of Reality V3
4. Edge of Night V4
5. Darkness Falls V4
6. Dream Theater V3 R

7. Sneakie Arete V1 R
9.
10.
12. Looking Southward V1
13. Southern Exposure V1

14. Unnamed VB
19. Trench Warefare V2
20. Unnamed V0-
22.
23. Party Til Puke V2

25. Distraction V0+
28. Crack VB
30. Groovy V0
31. Unnamed V0
32. Unnamed V1
33. Re-Re V1
34. Unnamed V0

36. Unnamed V0+
37. Unnamed V0 R
38. Exotica V3 R
40. Unnamed V0+

405

Small Unnamed Boulder

This boulder can be found by walking down the blazes from the power line. Just after the past few problems there is a large, unclean boulder to the left of the trail-break, on the left, in the saddle, at the ridge-crest. The next few problems are located on boulders on the south side of the crest, to the right of the orange trail.

23. Party 'Till you Puke V2

The big slab for feet is off. Climb up to a sloping top out from a sitting start.

24. M.Y.L.F V1

SDS at the corner on the left side of the boulder and climb the prow.

25. Distraction V0+

SDS and climb the right side of the boulder . This boulder is just below the previous boulder on the trail.

26. Little Distraction V0+/ V1

SDS and move right along the boulder.

Hidden Alcove

Above the previous two problems is an alcove with a wall at the back that contains a few problems.

27. Unnamed V0-

Climb the wall right of the off-width.

28. Crack VB

Climb the wide crack near the center of the wall.

29. Groovin' the Groove V0

Enter the groove right of the previous problem.

30. Groovy V0

Run up the easy face right of the previous climb.

Mini Boulder

This is the next boulder just past *Distraction* and *Little Distraction*. The back of this boulder touches the wall with the past few problems.

31. Unnamed V0

Climb the cracks at the right side of the boulder.

32. Unnamed V1

Climb the center of the face over white and orange rock.

Unnamed Boulder

The next few problems can be located on the boulder just past the *Table Rock* and downhill of the trail. The boulder has another boulder perched on its top.

Dave Pfurr putting up an area classic, circa late-90s. Photo by the author.

33. Re-Re V1
SDS on the right corner of the boulder and gain the cruxy top.

34. Unnamed V0
SDS and climb the left side of the small boulder perched on the orange trail above the *Exotica* boulder.

35. Road Worrier V2
From a sit start climb the right side of the boulder left of the *Exotica* boulder.

36. Unnamed V0+
SDS just left of the previous route.

Exotica Area
You can get to this area two ways 1.) Walk past the previous problem to a long boulder perched in table-like fashion over two smaller rocks or walk past this and around the next boulder to the north side of the outcrop at the orange trail 2.) Walk past the first few boulders on the orange-blazed trail, past a chossy section of rock, to an overhang at the next good section below the main outcrop. The big overhang is *Exotica*.

37. Neverland V0 R
Climb the right-hand face, left of the overhang, over moss, lichen, and dirt. Not recommended

38. Exotica V3 R
Climb out the center of the roof to an exciting top out.

39. Kung Fu V2 R
Next to the previous problem.

40. Grimly V0+
Climb the right face around the right-hand corner from the *Exotica* roof.

South Terrace Area
Directly above and right of *Exotica*, the orange-blazed trail moves over the crest of the hill. Follow this to the south side of the hill and walk right. This next outcrop hosts the next section of problems.

1. South Terrace V0-
Climb the right side of the first climbable face on the south side of this terrace.

2. Grey Face V0-
Walk left along the outcrop passing the low-quality section to another grey-colored face. Climb the right side.

3. Dirt Cove V0-
Often dirty but worth doing. SDS and climb the left corner of this boulder to a dirty alcove near the top out.

4. Unnamed V0-
Just left of the previous problem is a breach in the outcrop. To the left where the next boulder lies, climb the right-hand face near where it rests on the previous boulder.

5. The Prestige V1/V2
SDS and climb the nice arete at the boulders left end. The large feet at the bottom are off route. A V2 eliminate can be done if you don't use all the pockets at the start.

6. Ugly Face V0-
Around left of the previous route, climb the unappealing face.

7. Incut Glory V1
Directly across the split in the outcrop near a long lichen-covered wall, a large boulder rests. Climb incuts on the left-hand side of the face.

8. Choss Wall V0-
The wall to the left of the previous problem has a few low-quality problems on it.

Unnamed Boulder
Walk to the north side of the saddle. After a dirty boulder, the next climbable boulder has two small problems on it.

9. Unnamed V0+
Climb the left side of the boulder.

10. Sand People V2
Climb the right side of the boulder.

Sand Boulder
The next boulder past the unnamed boulder above.

11. Sand Boulder V0-/V0+
The next boulder along the hill has a few problems on all sides that vary from V0- to V0+.

The Stacks
Walking farther down the ridge, you will see the final outcrop that form large stacks that lie downhill along the south side of the saddle. This outcrop is known as *The Stacks*.

12. Sleaze Stack V2
Climb the uphill corner of this boulder near a tree.

13. Unnamed V0+
Climb just right of the previous climb.

14. Post Modern Sleaze V0-
Climb the uphill face of the second boulder down the passage on the right-hand side of the passage.

15. Unnamed V0+
Ascend the downhill face of the last boulder down the passage.

16. Post Modern Tease V0
Climb the left corner past edges and pockets.

Other Boulders along Rocky Ridge North
Several other individual areas and boulders lie farther along this ridge. Should you decide to hike farther along the trail, you will come to several other areas. Although a good deal of development has taken place at these areas, they also hold a potential for more development. Few climbers visit these spots. For this reason they are not as clean as at the more popular areas. The boulders are a bit of a hike, but host some enticing geologic features.

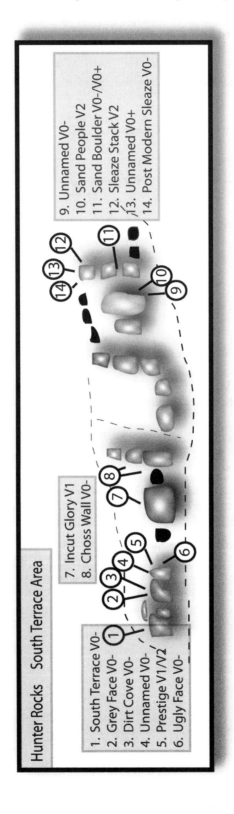

Hunter Rocks   South Terrace Area

9. Unnamed V0-
10. Sand People V2
11. Sand Boulder V0-/V0+
12. Sleaze Stack V2
13. Unnamed V0+
14. Post Modern Sleaze V0-

7. Incut Glory V1
8. Choss Wall V0-

1. South Terrace V0-
2. Grey Face V0-
3. Dirt Cove V0-
4. Unnamed V0-
5. Prestige V1/V2
6. Ugly Face V0-

Hunter Rocks

Many excellent problems lie on the left side of the power line heading towards *The Main Area*. Great landings and short, powerful problems characterize this side of the power line. The problems start directly under the left edge of the power cables. The approach is the same as for the Power line's right side.

Talus Boulders
On the Frew Road side of the power-cut, near where you walk in, there are a few small boulders in the talus with a few problems on them.

1. Talus Food V2
SDS in the small cave left of the power line where two boulders meet in small talus in the field.

2. Short Round V2
SDS and climb over the rounded-bulging corner left of the cave.

3. Mining for Problems V1
Sit start on the corner of the small rod-shaped boulder left of *Short Round*. Traverse in on slopers and continue up.

4. Sand Stop V0
SDS in the cave above talus and between boulders.

5. Sand Top V1
SDS on the corner of the long boulder at the left side of the outcrop.

6. Flop V1
SDS and climb the right side of the last boulder at the beginning of the treeline.

7. Lowery V2
Climb the left side of the same boulder as the previous problem. A V3 eliminate can be done up the boulders center.

8. Project
SDS and climb the low, long roof of the very low boulder above the previous boulders.

Electric Cave
Walk to the top of the power line and look downhill. To your left, there is a low cave with some excellent problems.
9. Visions of Restlessness V0-
SDS on the right wall of the south-facing cave. Looking back uphill, this is the right face.

10. Delirium Dive V4

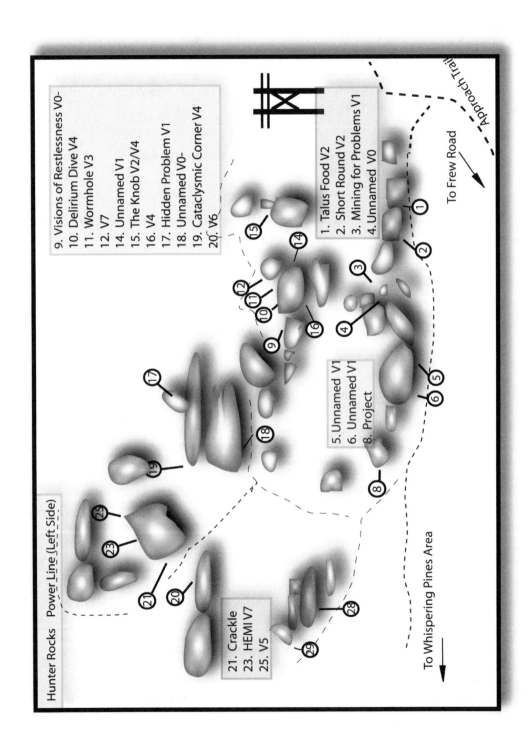

9. Visions of Restlessness V0-
10. Delirium Dive V4
11. Wormhole V3
12. V7
14. Unnamed V1
15. The Knob V2/V4
16. V4
17. Hidden Problem V1
18. Unnamed V0-
19. Cataclysmic Corner V4
20. V6

1. Talus Food V2
2. Short Round V2
3. Mining for Problems V1
4. Unnamed V0

5. Unnamed V1
6. Unnamed V1
8. Project

21. Crackle
23. HEMI V7
25. V5

Hunter Rocks   Power Line (Left Side)

To Frew Road

Approach Trail

To Whispering Pines Area

SDS under the roof's right center with a heel or toehook to make the sit start work. Continue straight up. An easier variation escapes slightly left.

11. Wormhole V3
Climb the crack in the alcove left of the previous problem.

12. Delirium V7
SDS and climb the left-bulging wall, left of the crack. A harder variation goes directly over the bulge, a few inches left.

13. Unnamed V5
SDS and climb the corner just left of the previous problem.

14. Unnamed V1
Going back towards Frew Road, there is another sub-cave in the rock. Several short sit start eliminates have been done here.

15. The Knob V2 or V4
The knob feature to the left goes at V2 or V4, depending on how you do the problem.

Hidden Cave
Under the backside of *Delirium Dive*, basically on the front side of the outcrop, there is a sub-cave that leads back under a breach to *Delirium Dive*.

16. Caveman V4
SDS and begin near where you toehook for the start of *Delirium Dive* and follow micro-crimps to the top. A V3 variation starts slightly left. A V8 eliminate also exists on the micro crimps.

17. Hidden Problem V1
SDS in the alcove under a small boulder attached to the long boulder on the way down *Hemispherical*.

Unworthwhile Pile
This is the long boulder adjacent to the previous problem and just before reaching *Hemispherical*.

18. Unnamed V0-
The uphill wall has several easy problems.

19. Cataclysmic Corner V4
SDS and climb the downhill corner and point. The boulder underneath is off route.

20. Diabolical V6
SDS and climb a small boulder against the trail and above *Hemispherical*.

21. Crackle V1
Climb the crack at the right side of this boulder from a low start.

22. Happily Never After V4

SDS and ascend the right side of the boulder, merging slightly left near the top to avoid the boulder that touches the right side.

23. Hemispherical Combustion Chamber V7 or V9

Hemi for short. An impressive first ascent by Nick Morell in the mid-'90s. SDS in a crack under the center of the steep downhill face of the boulder and move past small crimps to make a long move to a big Hueco. Continue to the sloping top out. Using the pinch and not shooting directly to the large hold in the center makes it V9 (var. called Hunger Artist). Note: A few climbers feel this might be V10.

24. The Stand V4

Stand start the previous problem.

25. Ceribrus V5

SDS and climb the left corner.

Whispering Pines Area

This area is a forested spot at the point of the ridgeline a short way past the previous area.

Pine Point

This is the obvious outcrop right off the trail near pine trees and a large jutting bellylike feature.

1. Belly V2

Begin out right under the big, jutting knob of rock and bearhug out the belly of rock. Top out near the point. The boulders on the sides are off.

2. Unnamed V2

Find the boulder up and left on the ledge above the previous problem. Traverse the boulder from left to right.

3. XpanderV2

Left of and slightly below the previous problem, climb the left side of a boulder up and over a jutting bulge.

4. Talus Problems V0-

A few easy problems can be done on the boulders behind the previous routes.

The Dorms

These are the large, cubed-shaped boulders located off the right side of the trail just past the previous area.

5. Beer Pong V0

The downhill arete of the second boulder in.

6. Lava Lamp V0 R

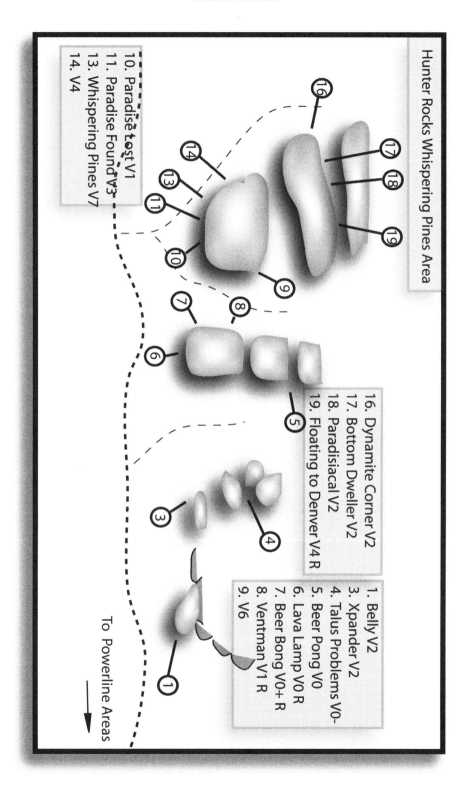

Hunter Rocks Whispering Pines Area

10. Paradise Lost V1
11. Paradise Found V3
13. Whispering Pines V7
14. V4

16. Dynamite Corner V2
17. Bottom Dweller V2
18. Paradisiacal V2
19. Floating to Denver V4 R

1. Belly V2
3. Xpander V2
4. Talus Problems V0-
5. Beer Pong V0
6. Lava Lamp V0 R
7. Beer Bong V0+ R
8. Ventman V1 R
9. V6

To Powerline Areas

The front side of the boulder off the trail.

7. Beer Bong V0+ R
The left face of the boulder near the trail.

8. Ventman V1 R
In the late '80s, Ventman was State College's only homeless man. This problem is praise to him. The problem climbs the face left of the previous.

Paradise Boulder
This is one of the best boulders at Hunter Rocks. Seek it out, and you'll know why.

9. Simply Paradise V6
SDS on the low, sloping-backside corner.

10. Paradise Lost V1
SDS and climb the center of the boulder past obvious features.

11. Paradise Found V3
SDS slightly left of the previous problem and top out this amazingly fun problem.

12. The Hound V0
A climb that barks at you to send it. Start slightly left of and downhill from the previous problem and traverse right and top out near the right side of the boulder.

13. Whispering Pine V7
SDS left of the previous problem and climb to a knob and sloping top. An easier variation moves right near the sloping and strenuous top.

14. Skimpy V4
Easier if you use the left corner. Climb the leftmost problem down on the left side of the boulder near a cleft/corner.

15. Paradise Traverse V5
SDS near number 14 and traverse uphill to top out near problem number 10. A V6 variation tops out near problems 11 and 13.

Bottom Dweller Boulder
This is the large boulder with great problems on its downhill side just below the *Paradise Boulder*. An obscure traverse traverses the downhill face of this boulder. It goes at V8 or V9 depending on what holds you off-route.

16. Dynamite Corner V2
Well, what can I say? It's something else to climb. Ascend the far corner of the boulder.

17. Bottom Dweller V2
Climb the center of the face

18. Paradisiacal V2
Climb up next to the previous problem.

19. Floating to Denver V4 R
Climb the fantastic route at the left side of the boulder.

The Lost Boulder
This boulder is on the south side of the ridge past the previous area. It's very hard to locate but it's the obvious roof/alcove hidden downhill of some other worthless rock off of the main trail.

20. Unnamed V4
SDS way back in the cave and climb out the center. Easier and harder eliminates have been done.

Trailside Rock
This is the long boulder right off the trail above and past *The Lost Boulder*.

21. Unnamed V1
Climb the left side of the rock.

22. The Fins V0 to V4
Two fin-shaped boulders are next along the trail. Problems range from V0- on the first fin to V1 and V4 on the second.

Beaver Ave
This is the large chute that goes downhill past three large, square boulders on the right and two on the left. The avenue-like path that splits them ends at the bottom of the hill.

23. Unnamed V7
One of the best aretes in Central Pennsylvania. SDS and climb the awesome arete on the downhill corner of the first large boulder down the hill.

24. Elephant and Castle V2
The second arete down the hill.

25. Mono Nucleosis V3
SDS and climb past a mono-pocket on the downhill-most arete.

26. Unnamed V5
Walk across a large gulley and find some large, dirty boulders. Walk past these and down the south side of the ridge to find a hidden pit on the downhill side of a square boulder.

The Wave
One of the hardest boulders to find but one of the most interesting at Hunter's. Walk farther south on the ridge until you come to what appears to be the end of the rock escarpments. Look way downhill and you will see faint traces of rock. The obvious perched scoop is the boulder you are looking for.

27. The Wave V5
Somewhat loose but a fantastic problem. Fall off this one and you may splash all the way to the bottom. SDS and climb up the center of the obvious wave/scoop. Brave the high and scary top out. Bring your Clamdiggers and a fresh change of Speedos.

Other Ridgeline Surprises
Between *The Wave* and *The Main Area* other hidden surprises lurk. A few fun but unworthy problems have been established here. Happy hunting.

Photo courtesy of Gino Filippini

31. Blue Ridge Run Rocks

Area Beta

Location
Near Mansfield.

Type of Climbing
Bouldering and roped climbing. Some bolted climbs.

Other Info
This area is a 2 mile hike to the rock.

Blue Ridge Run Rocks

Large boulders with bolted routes in the heart of Tioga State Forest; Blue Ridge Run Rocks is a spectacular area. Even though there are only a few boulders here they are large enough to keep you busy for an afternoon of worthwhile climbing. These large cubes allow excellent climbing on 10' to 40'-high faces. Many of the boulders have bolted routes, but virtually every route has or can be bouldered. A small cliff is located adjacent to the boulders, but the best climbing here is on the massive sandstone blocks.

A small rack is recommended, but you can get by with a few quickdraws and a rope. Many fixed anchors can be found on top of the boulders. If you like highball bouldering, bring a few pads. Landings are good with the exception of a problem or two. Despite the moderately long approach, I recommend a visit to this area.

History

It's important to note that most of the climbs that are bolted at this area were done as boulder problems a long time ago. This has been tolerated because this area is such a remote spot and the original developers live far away. It has also been accepted because the area has become a popular spot for local climbers from the University to safely lead and learn leading. Most of the climbers now visiting this area prefer to lead the boulders rather than do scary highballs. Mike Pantellich was one of the first recorded climbers to actively climb this area. He climbed here in the 1970s. His routes were documented by Curt Harler in a Pennsylvania Mountaineering Association newsletter and the *Climb PA* book put out by them in the 1980s. Tim Toula visited the area when writing *Rock and Road*, the climbing atlas for the United States. I was active developing some harder versions of *Campfire Boulder Problem* as well as some boulder problems and bouldered some of the routes that are now bolted. Nathan Heston has added several bolted lines in recent years. Although some of these were done previously as boulder problems he has developed some excellent new routes and the locals feel he has significantly improved the quality of climbing here.

Geology: Sandstone

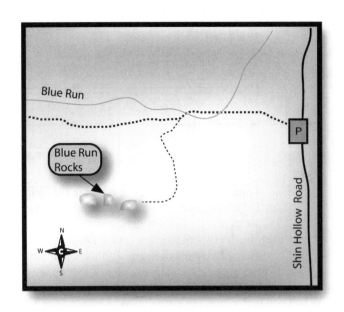

General Overview: Four massive boulders and a small cliff. 47 routes. Some of the routes are bolted but can and have been bouldered.

Ownership: Tioga State Forest.

In case of Emergency: Call 911. Cell phone reception is not good. The nearest emergency services are in Wellsboro.

Directions: Take U.S. Route 6 west for approximately 16 miles. On the right side of the road, you will see the Northwoods Gift Shop (formerly Manhattan Station) and Shin Hollow Road. Turn right onto Shin Hollow Road and follow it north, being careful not to veer off at any forks. At approximately 4 miles, you will see a trailhead on your left for Blue Run Rocks. Park here and begin the 2-mile hike. Follow the red-blazed trail about 30 minutes until you reach a small stream which the trail crosses. Just after the stream is a trail that cuts back to your left, then a second trail that goes directly up a steep hill to the rocks.

A. Campfire Boulder

This is the first boulder you encounter on the approach trail. Several great boulder problems exist here. The easiest descent is off the back or right side. Anchors can be found on top.

1. Campfire Boulder Problem V4 R

Start at the left side of the downhill face and climb up over the center of steep rock. A variation can be done slightly left of the original line at the same grade.

2. Campfire Right V3 R

Climb slightly right of the previous line.

3. All Fired Up V1

Slightly right of the previous problem, fire up the face.

4. Orange Flame V1

A variation just right of the previous line.

5. Warm Up Face V0-/VB

Slightly right of the previous problems is a long face with some easy warm ups.

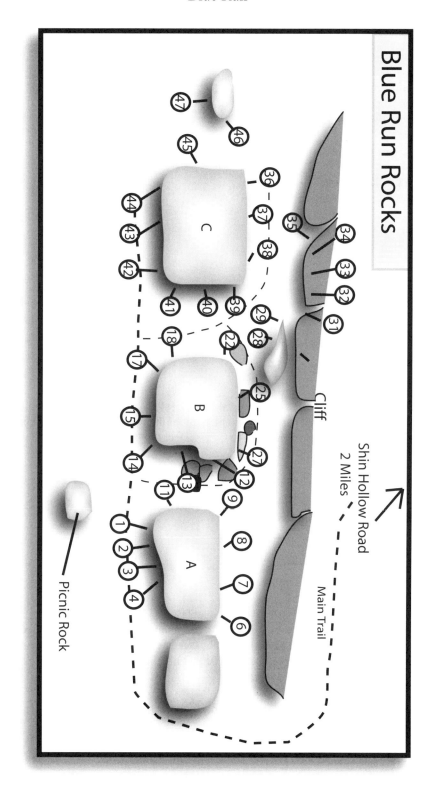

Blue Run Rocks

6. Talus Food V1 R
Climb over an overhang on the backside of this boulder.

7. Seclusion V0-
Cruise the face next to the previous problem. Anchors on top.

8. Cobra V0
Climb the face just right of the previous problem.

9. Echoes in the Forest V0+
Fun moves ascend the clean corner/arete.

10. Ten Kai V1
Climb the left side of the slab.

11. Revolution V2
Climb the right side of slab.

12. La Rocka 5.7
This is one of the first routes to have been climbed at this area. Climb the exciting route near *Revolution*.

B. Tioga Boulder
This boulder is the central-most boulder of the group. Anchors can be found on 5 climbs atop this boulder. Should you prefer to boulder any of the routes on this large stone, I recommend you climb the descent route first. *Crack in the Woods* 5.5 G is the most user-friendly downclimb/descent from this boulder.

13. Gatoraid 5.10b PG
Climb a corner to a roof at an old pin. Pull the roof (crux) and climb the crack above. Originally done as an aid climb.

14. Overhaul 5.10a TR
A few feet left of *Gatoraid*, haul over steep rock. Begin on the left side and move right to a block near the top. Anchors on top.

15. Oasis V1 R
3 bolts and cold shuts. This is a fun, old boulder problem that has been retrobolted. Around the left corner from the previous climb, ascend clean rock past a bulge and continue to the top. A variation can be done using only the arete.

16. Unnamed V0 R
Climb the nice face past nice holds a few feet left of the previous climb. Anchor above.

17. Carnival V2 R
Climb the face just left of the previous climb.

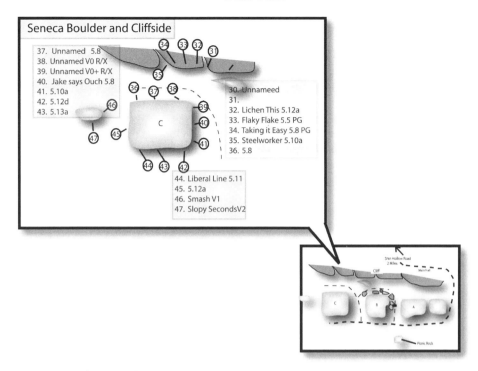

Seneca Boulder and Cliffside

37. Unnamed 5.8
38. Unnamed V0 R/X
39. Unnamed V0+ R/X
40. Jake says Ouch 5.8
41. 5.10a
42. 5.12d
43. 5.13a

30. Unnameed
31.
32. Lichen This 5.12a
33. Flaky Flake 5.5 PG
34. Taking it Easy 5.8 PG
35. Steelworker 5.10a
36. 5.8

44. Liberal Line 5.11
45. 5.12a
46. Smash V1
47. Slopy SecondsV2

18. Plantaginator V3 R
Fun moves ascend the left side of this boulder near the corner.

19. Fern Traverse V1
Traverse the downhill face of the boulder.

20. Power Play 5.11a G
Follow three bolts to chains above.

21. Just another Unknown ClassicV5 R
Hard moves begin at a low horizontal and move straight up the center face of the west side of this boulder.

22. Silent LucidityV0+ R
Climb the arete. Anchor above.

23. Traverse in the WoodsV4
Traverse from left to right on this short wall of the boulder via a horizontal.

24. Sexy Love Passages V5
Same traverse as above but continue past *Power Play* and end at the right.

25. Crack in the Woods 5.5 G
A popular solo or trad climb to set up topropes for other routes on this block. Also an interesting downclimb if you boulder any of the routes on this block.

26. Tree Line 5.5 G
Begin the same as the previous climb and move left into a fault, then climb to the top.

27. Unnamed 5.8
Climb the corner left of the previous route. Anchor on top.

C. Cliffside
The long cliff adjacent to the boulders hosts several good climbs. Most are quite short but fun nonetheless. Four sets of fixed anchors can be found along the top of the cliff.

31. Unnamed 5.6
Climb the face.

32. Lichen This 5.12a
Climb the face to a set of anchors.

33. Flakey Flake 5.5 PG
This easy route climbs the flake and continues to the top.

34. Taking it Easy 5.8 PG
Follow bolts to an anchor above.

35. Steelworker 5.10a G
Climb past three bolts to an anchor.

D. Seneca Boulder
This is the largest boulder of the grouping of boulders. There are 5 sets of anchors on top.

36. Unnamed 5.8
Climb the low-angle face of this boulder.

37. Unnamed 5.8 R
Climb the high face.

38. Unnamed V0 R/X
Climb the high face next to route number 37.

39. Unnamed V0+ R/X
Exciting sequences can be found on the face right of *Jake Says Ouch*.

40. Jake Says Ouch 5.8 G
Fun moves pass bolts in the center of the face.

41. Unnamed 5.10a
Climb the fun route left of *Jake*.

42. Unnamed 5.12d
The face just right of *Step Ladder*.

43. Step Ladder 5.13a TR
Originally an aid line—hence the dowels—that climbs the blankest face at Blue Ridge Run.

44. Liberal Line 5.11
Climb the face left of the blank section of rock.

45. Unnamed 5.12a
Climb the high face to anchors.

46. Smash V1
Climb the right side of the boulder from a SDS.

47. Slopy Seconds V2
SDS and climb the downhill side of the boulder.

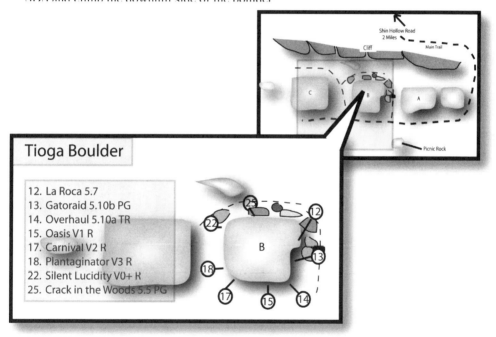

Tioga Boulder

12. La Roca 5.7
13. Gatoraid 5.10b PG
14. Overhaul 5.10a TR
15. Oasis V1 R
17. Carnival V2 R
18. Plantaginator V3 R
22. Silent Lucidity V0+ R
25. Crack in the Woods 5.5 PG

Other Central Pennsylvania Areas

Mount Gretna Bouldering

There is a great deal of diabase bouldering in the Mount Gretna region. Several great areas lie scattered along the hillsides. Dinosaur Rock, Infinity Wall, Parking Lot area, Govoner Dick, The Outlands and many other areas have been developed over the years. The more popular spots are located off of Pinch Road above the village of Mount Gretna. This area was originally climbed in the 1970s by PMA members and Curt Harler. Bob D'Antonio later established problems as hard as V7. I was active in the mid-90s developing Dinosaur Rock and the Parking Lot area and the hardest line on the Infinity Wall.. The true developers that skyrocketed the area into fame and developed the great majority of hard and classic lines were Chet Gross, Joel and Jen Toretti, Erny Coleflesh, Char Fetterolf, Mike Stewart, Mike Decav, Mike Rohler, and a large group of climbers from the Harrisburg area. These climbers made the Gretna region into a well known area and established fantastic problems that outweigh most diabase climbing in the state.

I have chosen to leave out detailed information on Mount Gretna because the rock covers a vast and vegetated area. Also, I want to wait-out any potential access issues. We've spoken to the landowners who are ok with bouldering on the property but things can always change over time. Information about this area is more than abundantly available.

Bob Murray at Govoner Stable
Photo courtesy Bob D'Antonio

Govoner Stable

Arguably the best diabase bouldering in the East can be found at this area. The area was once open to climbing but is now closed. This may change in the future but climbing is not allowed at the present time.

Western Pennsylvania

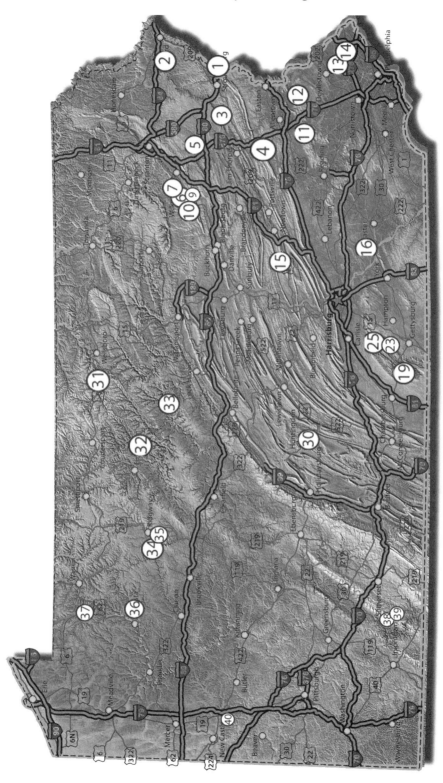

32. Elk State Forest Bouldering Areas

Area Beta

Location
Elk State Forest.

Type of Climbing
Bouldering, some roped at Cliffside area.

Other Info
Many areas lie scattered throughout this state forest. I list a few of the more popular spots.

Elk State Forest

A great deal of good quality rock exists in Elk State Forest. The only problem is, finding it all. Every time I travel through this desolate part of Pennsylvania, I find a new spot. If you were to wander the nearby hills aimlessly, you would certainly find a wealth of untapped rock in this region.

I include brief descriptions of three major areas in Elk. The first area, the Fred Woods Area, is an area I came across in 1997. This area is a great spot in a secluded setting far from civilization. The second and third areas I include, the Boulder Garden, and Cliffside areas, are the most popular—if you can consider an area that is frequented by a handful of climbers popular.

I've left a lot of routes out of this book at these areas. These spots are some of the most adventurous bouldering in the state—even in the East for that matter. If these areas become more popular in years to come I may extend this section of the guidebook; however, since much of the rock is so secluded, I doubt these areas will ever become mainstream destinations. Your best bet is to spend a weekend exploring these natural treasures. They truly are some of the more impressive boulders in the region.

Fred Woods Area

Elk State Forest

Peace, seclusion, and a deeply wooded forest are the highlights of the most well preserved bouldering area in the state. The dark canopy that shrouds grey-colored sandstone blocks reminds us of a more primitive era of humanity. Deep rock passages and stone caverns are what make this area one of the hidden jewels of Pennsylvania bouldering. I don't expect—even with a large circulation guidebook—that many climbers will ever venture into the remoteness of the Fred Woods boulders.

Should you venture here, expect to find a few dozen high-quality boulders with enough problems to keep you busy for a day or two. The grades range from V0- to V8 with a great deal of problems catering to beginner and intermediate climbers. In the past, this area has been used primarily as a bouldering area, but top-ropes can be set up on some of the higher problems in the main passage.

Spring, summer, and fall are the best times to climb here; winter can be brutal. Bring plenty of water and some high energy food. The hike in is flat and easy going but longer than most bouldering approaches (no where near as bad as the Cliffside area nearby).

I list only a handful of problems at this area because this is the kind of spot you need to explore for yourself to fully enjoy the climbing experience this spot has to offer. Have fun and be safe!

History

Hikers had visited the area for a very long time but Jackson Ross was most likely the first climber to come her in the '70s. It is unsure exactly what he climbed here but it was most likely the obvious lines. I found this spot in 1997 and developed a significant amount of problems. In 2000, Joel Toretti and Char Feterolf developed a significant amount of problems as well. Many first ascent possibilities still exist here for the adventurous climber who decides to travel to this hidden gem.

Directions

Take Rt. 555 through Elk State Forest and locate Castle Garden Road on the north side of Rt. 555. Take this uphill until you reach Mason Hill Road. Drive this west a few miles and look for the park trailhead sign for the Fred Woods Trail located on the south (left) side of the road. Walk the trail about 15 minutes to the rock.

Joel Toretti on "New River Dreams." Cliffside area.

1. Entrance Exam V0-
This problem sends the center of the face

on the first boulder you arrive at before entering the main area. It is just off the right side of the Fred Woods Trail. A problem has been done to the left of the main line at the same grade.

2. Unnamed V1
In the small corridor created by the two cube-shaped boulders, directly behind problem number 1, climb the big flake on the left-most boulder in the center of the face.

3. Icehouse V2
Climb the nice corner just left of the previous problem.

4. Ice Arete V5
SDS and send the pretty arete right of the Flake.

5. Unnamed V0
Cruise the unappealing face right of *Ice Arete*.

6. Unnamed V0
The corner right of the previous route.

7. Unnamed V0
The face around the corner from the previous route and on the trail.

8. Wrinkly Face V0+
Climb the face on top a ledge with wrinkle-like patterns and neat pockets in seams.

9. Tranquility Arete V2 R
Climb the awesome, high arete near trees right of where the two giant boulders meet at the right side of this long outcrop.

10. Mecca V3 R/X
Just right of the arete, start on an undercling-pocket and a crimp, pull onto the face and climb the very high section of rock, passing a large, rounded jug that protrudes from the face near the top. Harder starts have been done.

11. Slop Out V1 R/X
The face a few inches right of the previous route.

12. Dirt Factory V0+ R
The dirty crack right of the previous problem.

13. Unnamed V0
Climb the face at any point, right of the dirty crack.

The Passage
This boulder is located on a long passage that is the most distinguishable feature at this area. It has a triangular face that forms a roof and a large tree between the face near the back entrance.

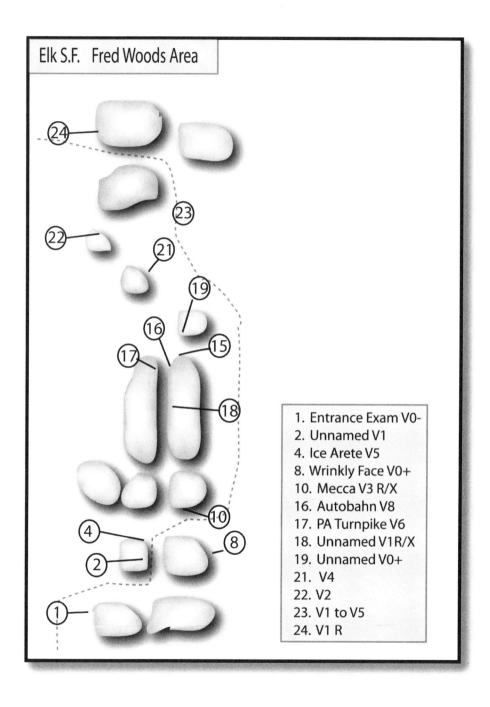

Elk S.F.   Fred Woods Area

1. Entrance Exam V0-
2. Unnamed V1
4. Ice Arete V5
8. Wrinkly Face V0+
10. Mecca V3 R/X
16. Autobahn V8
17. PA Turnpike V6
18. Unnamed V1R/X
19. Unnamed V0+
21. V4
22. V2
23. V1 to V5
24. V1 R

14. Skating on Thin Ice V2 R
SDS and climb the left side of the triangular face.

15. Ice Capades V0 R
SDS under the right lip of the triangular face and climb up and over the roof on good holds. Top out on the low angle face above.

16. Autobahn V8
Named as a take-off on a classic Midwest boulder problem. Traverse the low face on the north side of the passage from left to right. Several variations can be done.

17. The Pennsylvania Turnpike V6
Traverse the obvious horizontal all the way across the long cliff passage's south side. Several variations can be done.

Char working a V10ish problem at Fred Woods. Photo by Joel Toretti.

18. Never After V1 R/X
Climb the seam in the center of the high face of the north side of the passage.

19. Winter Frenzy V0+
SDS on the fantastic horizontals on the boulder directly behind *Ice Capades*. Several variations can be done on this face.

20. Water Clock V2
SDS on the arete and face around the left side of the boulder. Several variations can be done with this problem.

21. Dysplasia V4
Climb the slightly overhanging face off the left side of the trail just past the previous problem.

22. Tick Tock V2

Sit start on the small boulder with flakes just right of the previous problem. This boulder is short with orange-colored rock and loose flakes. Two problems can be done next to each other at the same grade.

23. Unnamed V1 to V5
Several problems have been done on the four-star quality boulder immediately after the previous problem. Grades vary depending on what line you decide to explore on this boulder.

24. Endearment V1 R
This problem is on the backside of the last boulder of the group along the trail. It is located near where the trail continues on to the steep hillside. The problem is near a sizable tree.

Jen Toretti on the "Font Boulder" at Cliffside. Photo by Joel Toretti.

Cliffside and Boulder Garden Areas

An impressive cliff, massive boulders, clean rock, and an approach at the Cliffside area that will evacuate your lungs. What more could you ask for? This area hosts a multitude of huge, cube-shaped boulders littering the landscape below a 40'-high cliff. Little has been developed on the cliff, but that hasn't stopped Robert McBride from pioneering some super-classic trad lines at the Cliffside. The bouldering here is the main attraction. A great deal of development has taken place here that has yielded super-classic-four-star problems.

One of the only drawbacks here is the "Stairmaster" approach to the Cliffside area. Somewhat long and just steep enough to get your heart pumping; expect a 35 to 45 minute hike into the rock. Another drawback is a lack in diversity. Few steep and overhanging problems are located here; however, if you like perfect cube-shaped boulders, this is the place for you.

History

Since a lot of climbers from all over the state have visited this spot in recent years, recorded history is ambiguous—although that hasn't stopped a climber from trying to credit himself for and name many problems here, including problems he hasn't even sent. Regardless of this lack of documentation about recent ascents, a great deal of the original ascents were well documented. The primary, original pioneers of the Cliffside and Boulder Garden areas were Joel Toretti and Chet Gross. These two climbers were the most prolific climbers to visit and develop this area. Thanks to their willingness to share such a quiet and alluring spot, many climbers from all over the state now visit and enjoy this spot. Shortly after them, a crew of climbers from the Harrisburg area began to visit and heavily develop the area. These climbers are, Mike Stewart, Josh Karns, Robert McBride, Josh Newman, Randy Le Force and a crew of devoted Harrisburg locals. Char Fetterolf, of Haycock fame, was also active in the early years as well. I added a few intimidating highballs on the cliff and a few nearby boulders as well.

Although new problems can certainly be done here, it is important to note that the majority of the problems here were sent and not named—climbing here was about fun and just going out climbing. If you've done some sick new line here feel free to name it, but note that most of the obvious lines here were probably sent several years ago by devoted Harrisburg climbers who made this area what it is today.

Directions for Cliffside: Find the Quehanna Highway that runs east/west through Elk State Forest, south of Rt. 555. On the north side of the Quehanna Highway is Red Run Road. Drive this road about two miles downhill. When you reach Sanders Draft look for a giant boulder off to the left in the woods. Park in the small lot across from where you can see the boulder in the woods. Hike the trail on the east side of the road, crossing the stream over a bridge, and continue to follow the trail that parallels the stream. After walking for about 10 – 15 minutes you will see a trail that goes off to the left of the main trail and up a steep hill. Walk directly up the steep hill until you run into the Cliffside Area. You can also bushwack uphill from the parking spot to reach the rock (not recommended).

Directions for the Boulder Garden: Locate a trail off the right side of Red Run Road, and slightly before Sanders Draft (basically before you reach the Cliffside parking spot). Walk the trail on the south side of sanders draft and follow it while paralleling the stream. You will reach the Boulder Garden after about 30 minutes of walking.

It is easier though to follow the Red trail like going to the Cliffside area and continue past the uphill for cliffside. Cross a stream and continue to the ridge past Cliffside. The boulders will be up on your left.

Josh Karns on "Soulshine" at the Cliffside area. Photo by the author.

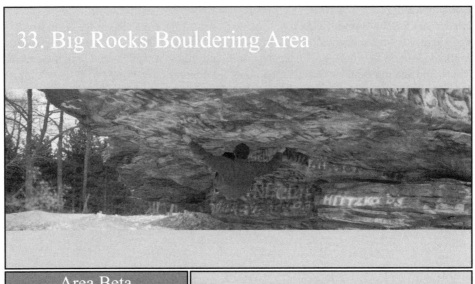

33. Big Rocks Bouldering Area

Area Beta

Location
Near Renovo.

Type of Climbing
Bouldering.

Other Info
A small but nice bouldering area if you live close by.

Big Rocks

Big Rocks is a small collection of boulders located in Sproul State Forest, 9 miles south of Renovo. The boulders range from 10 to 25' high with problems ranging from VB to V8. The rock here is vegetated, graffiti covered, and dirty in many spots. Because this area is not a destination spot, I am only listing a few of the more popular problems that exist here. One big problem with this area is the topouts are extremely vegetated. This is also a very small area with only a handful of good problems. This area would be much better if there was only more rock, the quality of the rock was a little better, and it wasn't covered in graffiti. Some positive qualities about Big Rocks are: fun problems, a tranquil setting, and no crowds. If you live within an hours drive of Big Rocks it is certainly worth the visit, otherwise, don't bother visiting here.

Directions: From Renovo, drive Route 144 south for several miles. On the right side of the road you will see Barney's Ridge road the right. If you end up at a large graffiti-covered boulder just off the left side of the road (*Roadside Graffiti Boulder*), you missed the turn. Drive this road for approximately 1.5 miles and you will see a clearing on the right and some rock off a small side road. Park here. The rock *Main Boulder* is visible from where you walk. Note: In winter, there are occasions when this road is not passable by vehicle. If snowfall is heavy, the road may be closed.

For the *Roadside Graffiti Boulder*, continue on the main road and you will run into it 2 miles past the turn for the main area.

Roadside Graffiti Boulder

You can't miss this one. Several miles South of Renovo, on the left-hand side of the road you will see a boulder with more graffiti on it than a New York subway car. I think every kid in central Pennsylvania has tagged this boulder. Several good problems can be found here—and you can't beet the approach. If not for the graffiti and broken glass, this would be a four-star boulder. Several other boulders with a few problems lie scattered in the nearby surrounding.

1. Warm-Up Traverse V1
SDS at the right side of the boulder and traverse the sloping lip.

2. Roadside Traverse V2
Traverse the horizontal below the top-lip of the overhang.

3. Tornado G-spot V9
Some feel this is V10, it may be but myself and other climbers felt it was more V9, either way it's a fun problem if you live nearby, and like graffiti and glass. SDS under the right side of the roof and climb to thin crimps, then fly out to a huge edge near the lip and top out. I've done the crux three different ways. One way drops the grade, campus moves make the route the hardest of the three ways.

4. Snowball V4
SDS and pull the left side of the roof.

5. Blunderkindt V4
One of the best problems at this area! SDS and traverse the right side of the boulder, going high at the lip of the roof, and top out by pulling around the corner and ending over the finish of *Tornado*.

6. Unnamed V3
SDS on the small boulder off to the right of the graffiti boulder. Climb the very short face.

Main Area

This is the main outcrop of cliff and boulders off the road. The best boulder here is the *Main Boulder*. Most of the other outcrops offer only marginal problems. Groups often come to the cliff section and sometimes set topropes here. The wall is quite short for toproping though.

Main Boulder

This is the large rectangular boulder just past the parking area. It has a low roof at its top end. Several variations of the roof have been done, most are V1 – V2. There is a V4 eliminate that moves to the point in the ledge system, then to a large point in the overhang. This is the hardest variation other than *Lynn*.

1. The 5.9 Bucket Route V0+
Pull the right side of the roof on big holds.

2. Double Heel Hook Problem V2

Also called *The Bar Gash*. SDS in the center of the roof and climb out to the lip. Pull the lip and top out.

3. Lynn V8

This route has drawn much controversy by myself and several other climbers. Originally rated V11, this route was downgraded to V8. Climb the left side of the roof, from a SDS.

4. The Green Streak V7/V8

Another controversial route that was originally rated V10, then downgraded. Some think the grade is V8, but I think it's no harder than V7. Climb to a good horizontal and gain a crimp with a sidepull attached to it in the center of the face just left of *Lynn*. Shoot for a big sloper. Move out right or continue straight up to top out.

5. Entrance Exam V1

Climb up to and past a nice pocket left of *The Green Streak*. Two variations exist climbing with your left hand or right hand in the pocket, then moving up. The first variation is a V0+, the second V1.

6. Unnamed V0-

Climb the left side of the wall.

7. Ego-land V4

Traverse the low face on thin holds on the boulder behind the *Main Boulder*.

The author cranking "Tornado G-Spot."

Other Boulders

A lot of easy and moderate problems can be found in the cluster behind the main problems. Some fun highballs can be done here as well—I've even seen a few climbers top-rope here on occasion.   A very nice boulder can be seen while driving Rt. 144 back to Renovo. Several good problems can be done on this overhanging clamshell. *Renovoation* is perhaps the most famous.

33. Indian Rocks

Area Beta

Location
Ridgway, Pennsylvania.

Type of Climbing
Sport, trad, and bouldering on some of the nicest sandstone in the East.

Other Beta
Not too far from NY state. Worth a visit to a secluded spot with New Riveresque sandstone.

Indian Rocks

Some of the largest boulders in the state—or the Mid-Atlantic for that matter—can be found at *Indian Rocks*. Some of the boulders here are larger than the buildings in downtown Ridgway. Gargantuan monoliths dominate the open forest atop the quiet mountainside where these boulders are located. Just over a dozen boulders with flat landings devoid of rocks can be found here. The smaller boulders are around 20' high, but the larger ones soar near 40' at their highest point.

A few of the larger, higher boulders have some bolted sport routes on them. Although some of these lines have been bouldered in the past, many of the routes have been bolted making for excellent lead routes.

Virtually any route or boulder problem at this area is a classic. The route *Slopeapotimus* has rock quality that can rival routes at the New River Gorge. The bulletproof, clean sandstone here bears remarkable resemblance to West Virginia stone. The rock on *The Little Chief* boulder resembles some stone you might expect to find at Red Rocks.

If there is not enough stone to keep you busy, nearby *Lions Den* has larger boulders than *Indian Rocks*—which is saying a lot. Many lesser-size boulders can be found along the ridge near Garocii Quarry above *Indian Rocks*. The nearby region boasts several quality bouldering spots as well.

History

Area locals Hal Beimel, Todd Beimel, Paul Danday, and John Shippling are the primary developers of this area. Since 1995, this group of climbers has frequented the area and established many classic trad and sport routes as well as boulder problems. Some of their first ascent achievements include *Slopeapotimus* 5.10d, *The Tomahawk* 5.11b, *Last of the Mohicans* 5.6+, *Two Right Feet* 5.10a, *Colorado Corner* 5.10c, and many others. Hal Beimel and Paul Danday were large developers of this spot. The two created trails, cleaned boulders, developed routes, and made Indian Rocks into the fantastic area it is today. If not for their efforts, this area would just be another chunk of rock in the Pennsylvania woodlands.

Also, in the late '90s Rob Ginieczki, mountain biking guru from the Philadelphia and prolific Pennsylvania ice climber, discovered these magnificent boulders and was active in development. While exploring bouldering potential in the region,

I came across the fantastic rock formations here and elsewhere on the mountain while hiking in 1997. I developed about two dozen boulder problems, many of them highballs and some into the V7 range, and two bolted lines in 2007.

Ryan Lucas, Jess Lewis, Larry Felton, Scott and Christa Messick, Mike Stewart, and Dave Case were also active on the mountain in more recent years developing new lines.

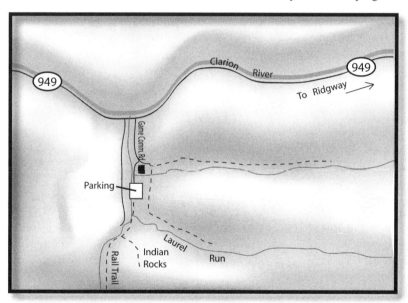

Directions

From downtown Ridgway, find State Route 949 and head west toward Portland Mills. Drive 7.5 miles to Game commission Road on your left. This is very easy to drive past. If you drive over Toby Creek, you went a few hundred feet too far.

Drive 200 yards down Game Commission Road and make a right onto a dirt rood that passes the Game Commission buildings and goes down near Toby Creek. Park at the lot at the rail-trail. From here, walk the rail-trail road south, following the Toby Creek about .75 mile to a faint trail on the left. This trail will be viable shortly after you reach a steep hillside. Do not take the first faint trail you see on the hillside. It is a well-beaten trail you will be looking for. There used to be an old trail marker, but beavers routinely eat the signpost.

Follow the hiking trail uphill about 10 minutes. When you see large boulders, site a faint trail that breaks uphill near a large round boulder on the trail. The main outcrop of boulders will be visible a few minutes after walking up this trail.

Location: 10 miles west of Ridgway.

General Overview: Over a dozen giant boulders ranging from 20 to 40' tall.

Approach: 15 minutes of mostly easy walking with one gradual hill.

Geology: Sandstone

Recommended Rack: Half a dozen draws, small to medium gear, slings for topropes (although most climbs have chains) or a crash pad if you like to solo.

Mike Stewart on "Vanilla Cream." Photo by the author.

Access Issues and Restrictions: The boulders are located on Pennsylvania State Game Lands, Allegheny National Forest.

Area Hazards: Wear bright colors during hunting season due to hunting traffic.

In Case of Emergency: Call 911.

Hillside Boulder

This boulder is the first boulder you come to. It is perched on the hill where the main trail continues up and right, and the bouldering area trail branches off left.

1. Hillside Attraction V1

On the uphill-most face on the right side, climb the face near a big pocket.

2. Hillside Distraction V0+

Climb the face left of the previous problem.

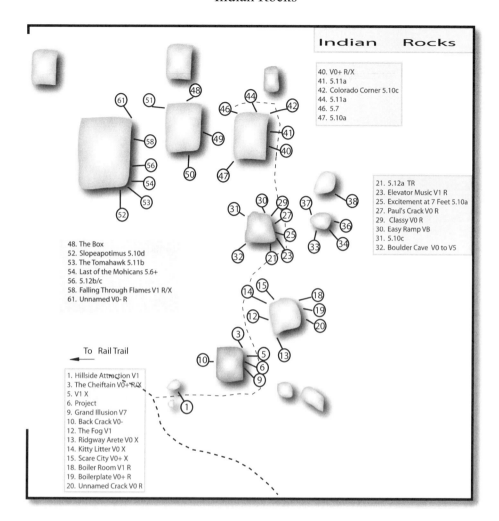

Indian   Rocks

40. V0+ R/X
41. 5.11a
42. Colorado Corner 5.10c
44. 5.11a
46. 5.7
47. 5.10a

21. 5.12a TR
23. Elevator Music V1 R
25. Excitement at 7 Feet 5.10a
27. Paul's Crack V0 R
29. Classy V0 R
30. Easy Ramp VB
31. 5.10c
32. Boulder Cave V0 to V5

48. The Box
52. Slopeapotimus 5.10d
53. The Tomahawk 5.11b
54. Last of the Mohicans 5.6+
56. 5.12b/c
58. Falling Through Flames V1 R/X
61. Unnamed V0- R

To Rail Trail

1. Hillside Attraction V1
3. The Chieftain V0+ R/X
5. V1 X
6. Project
9. Grand Illusion V7
10. Back Crack V0-
12. The Fog V1
13. Ridgway Arete V0 X
14. Kitty Litter V0 X
15. Scare City V0+ X
18. Boiler Room V1 R
19. Boilerplate V0+ R
20. Unnamed Crack V0 R

Trailside Boulder

This boulder is the small, rectangular boulder located just off the trail below the *Hillside Boulder*. Several problems in the V0 range have been done on it.

Chieftain Boulder

After cresting the hill and turning left onto a small side-trail that leads to the main *Indian Rocks* area, this boulder is the most downhill boulder of the group and the first boulder you come to. The boulder is perfectly rectangular and about 20' high.

3. The Chieftain V0+ R/X

One of the best highball boulder problems in the state! Climb past sloping, incut pockets on the uphill-right side/corner of the boulder.

4. The Chief V5

A classic traverse with glassy feet. Start on the previous problem and climb to a horizontal

10' up. Follow the horizontal left to finish at the far-left side of the boulder.

5. V1 X
Climb the face left of *Chieftain*.

6. Project
Climb the center of the face at the boulders highest point.

7. Illusions of Grandeur V4
Start a few feet left of the previous problem and gain the horizontal. Traverse off to the right.

8. The Levitation V6

Start with a pinch and a very small edge and fly up to a horizontal.

9. Grand Illusion V7
Climb the face a few feet left of the previous line to a horizontal. Traverse off right.

10. Back Crack V0-
The easiest way to gain the top of the boulder. Climb the easy crack on the backside (downhill face) of the boulder. Several problems from V0- to V1 can be done both right and left of the crack on the downhill face.

11. Mossy Face V0
From *Back Crack*, walk left and around the corner of the boulder to a short face between the downhill and uphill faces. Climb the center of the face to the top. Several problems can be done on this face from V0- to V0+.

Little Chief Boulder
This is the boulder located diagonal to the *Chieftain* boulder. You can see the high slab from *Chieftain*. Many mega-classic Pennsylvania highballs exist on this boulder. One of the best V1 boulder problems in the East (*Boiler Room*) is on the backside of the boulder. Note: There is no easy descent from this boulder.

12. The Fog V1
Climb the high slab on the downhill side of the boulder.

13. Ridgway Arete V0 X
Climb the arete at the downhill-right side of the boulder.

14. Kitty Litter Arete V0 X
High, dirty, and scary. Climb the arete at the downhill-left side of the boulder.

15. Scare City V0+ X
Climb the very dirty face left of the arete. Several variations have been done between the arete and the tree.

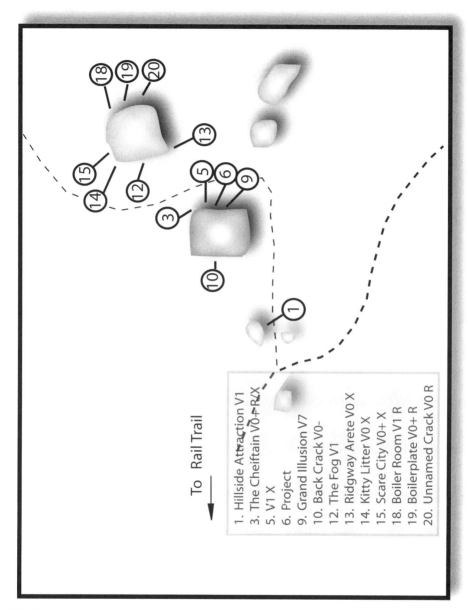

To Rail Trail

1. Hillside Attraction V1
3. The Cheiftain V0+R/X
5. V1 X
6. Project
9. Grand Illusion V7
10. Back Crack V0-
12. The Fog V1
13. Ridgway Arete V0 X
14. Kitty Litter V0 X
15. Scare City V0+ X
18. Boiler Room V1 R
19. Boilerplate V0+ R
20. Unnamed Crack V0 R

16. Tree Line V0-

Climb the unappealing face near the tree. Can be a dangerous but acceptable descent.

17. Dynamite Traverse V2

A fantastic traverse over high-quality rock. Traverse the good, sloping lip on the uphill face of the boulder.

18. Boiler Room V1 R

Climb the right side of the uphill face past amazing incut sandstone plates.

19. Boilerplate V0+ R
Climb up left of the previous problem. The route was originally done as a boulder problem.

20. Unnamed Crack V0+ R
Climb the crack

The Twins
These are two boulders next to each other left of the *Little Chief Boulder*. Several easy problems can be done here. Most range from V0- to V1.

Hilltop Boulder
This boulder is perched on top the hill. You can see it when walking farther into the boulder outcrop. Walk up the hill from the *Little Chief* and *Chieftain* boulders and you will see a large boulder perched on top the hill with a steep face. The easiest descent is on the low-angle ramp on the uphill side.

21. V4 or 5.12a TR
SDS at the corner under an overhanging face and climb past shelves to the top.

Mike Stewart "the Daddy" on the first ascent of an area classic. Photo by the author.

22. V5 or 5.12d TR
An amazing route. Start a few feet left of the original line for the previous problem and fire to a sloping pocket. Continue up to merge with the original line.

23. Elevator Music V1 R
Climb the right side of the downhill arete near the tree. The top out is a bit spooky.

24. Vanilla Cream a.k.a Short Stuff 5.10a G
Follow two bolts up the beautiful face. This is the leftmost of the two bolted lines.

25. Excitement at Seven Feet 5.10a G
The route can be bouldered but is a bit spicy. Follow technical moves past two bolts. The rightmost of the two bolted lines.

26. Pathologic Problem V0 R/X
Climb the face right of the bolts and near the crack.

27. Paul's Crack V0 R

448

Climb the obvious crack.

28. Cruise Control V0 R
The face that is right of the crack hosts an amazing line just right of the crack.

29. Classy V0 R
A must-do problem. Climb the clean face right of the last problem.

30. Easy Ramp VB
A good downclimb from the boulder. This is the mossy face around the corner from the previous route.

31. 5.10c R
Pull over the center of the roof on the backside of the boulder. Watch for loose rock.

32. Boulder Cave V0 to V5
A small cave is located below the roof route on this boulder. Several nice problems that are low to the ground can be found here.

Blob Rock
This is the small—well, small for *Indian Rocks*—boulder across from the *Hilltop Boulder*. It can be seen just across some bushes.

33. Crossfire V4 R
Climb the scary, unclean downhill side of the boulder. Begin on a flake near the ground at a rhododendron bush and climb up into a dirty seam. Continue up this to a frightening top out.

34. Fate Flake V1 R
Climb the loose flake on the backside of this boulder. It's only fate, this flake *will* break.

35. The Blob V0+
Start in the center of the boulder and traverse the rail into the flake then top out.

36. Shelf Life V0+ R
Climb onto the shelf at the right-center of the boulder and follow a flake to the top.

37. Slapshot Arete V0-
SDS and slap up the easy, short, uphill arete.

Beauty Boulder
This perfect boulder is located just behind the previous boulder. It is a small boulder like the previous, with a few nice low-height problems on it.

38. Arresting Behavior V4
SDS and fire up the downhill-right corner, and climb over a steep belly of rock to a finger-pocket at the lip.

Indian Rocks Area 2

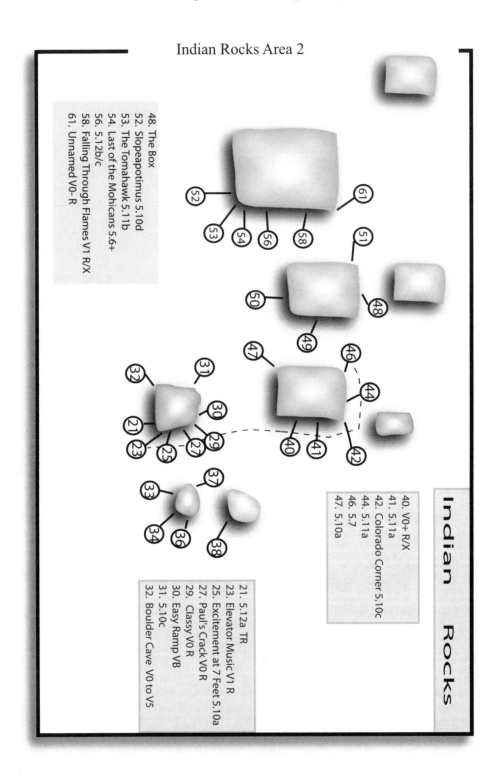

48. The Box
52. Slopeapotimus 5.10d
53. The Tomahawk 5.11b
54. Last of the Mohicans 5.11b
56. 5.12b/c
58. Falling Through Flames V1 R/X
61. Unnamed V0-R

Indian Rocks

40. V0+ R/X
41. 5.11a
42. Colorado Corner 5.10c
44. 5.11a
46. 5.7
47. 5.10a

21. 5.12a TR
23. Elevator Music V1 R
25. Excitement at 7 Feet 5.10a
27. Paul's Crack V0 R
29. Classy V0 R
30. Easy Ramp VB
31. 5.10c
32. Boulder Cave V0 to V5

39. In the Crossfire V5
SDS near the previous line and fire to a sloping shelf and top out near the previous line.

Perfect Boulder (a.k.a. Colorado Boulder)
This boulder is located above the previous boulder. It is large, rectangular in shape, and 35' high. There are bolted climbs on three of the four aretes on this boulder.

40. Unnamed V0+ R/X
On the east face of the boulder this is the highball on the downhill-most side.

41. 5.10c G
Climb the high face just left of *Colorado Corner*. This climb follows tricky moves past a flake.

42. Colorado Corner 5.10c G
Climb the beautiful corner on the east side of the boulder, past bolts to the fixed anchors above.

43. 5.12a TR
Climb the face just right of *Colorado Corner*.

44. 5.11a TR
Follow thin moves after a crack that starts at head level. Break left after the crack and follow thin edges. There are fixed anchors above.

45. Dreamland 5.12d TR
Climb the crack, and break right onto thin edges to gain another crack that leads to the top of the boulder.

46. 5.7 G
Climb the bolted line at the right side of the uphill face on this boulder.

47. 5.10a G
Climb the fantastic downhill corner of this boulder past nice edges and bolts.

Mia's Boulder
This boulder is located above the previous boulder. It is not very high and has some worthwhile problems on the clean face on the east side of the boulder.

The Box
This boulder is located next to and downhill from the previous boulder. It has several easy to moderate highballs on the low angle faces, and a few truly hard lines on the overhanging downhill face.

48. Unnamed V0 R
Climb the easy but high slab on the uphill face of this huge boulder. Many problems at both easier and slightly harder grades have been done on this face.

49. Toumbstone V1 X
Climb the high and scary face on the face around the left corner from the previous problem.

50. Untouchable V5 R
This hasn't been topped out yet due to the mass vegetation above, but it makes a great problem nonetheless. SDS and climb the steep, overhanging face on the downhill side of the boulder. Many variations have been done both on the corner and to the left at similar grades.

51. Easy Side V0-R
The best spot to access the top of the boulder or descend can be found on the short, low side of this boulder.

Christa Messick leading "Slopeapotimus." Photo by the author.

Tomahawk Boulder
This boulder is the highest at this area. It has four bolted routes on it. All are highly recommended and well worth doing. The rock on this boulder is high quality and reminiscent of New River sandstone.

52. Slopeapotimus 5.10d G
Just right of the southeast corner of the boulder near a tree that touches the corner, climb overhanging slopers and incuts past 4 bolts and amazing rock to the top. The anchors above should be backed up.

53. The Tomahawk 5.11b G
Gear can be used at the top after the 3 bolts on this route. Right of the previous route near

a tree and corner, climb the fantastic corner without using the tree or crack to the right—keeping on the face keeps the climb true to the grade. Anchors above.

54. Last of the Mohicans 5.6+ G
Climb the great crack right of *Tomahawlk*.

55. Two Right Feet 5.10a G
Cruise past gorgeous sidepulls and bolts to an anchor above. The crack to the left is off route.

56. 5.12b/c R
Start in a shallow, small, and sloping pocket, and gain a sidepull above. Continue straight up.

57. 5.7 G
Cruise the nice crack right of the previous climb.

58. Falling Through Flames V1R/X
Start a few feet right of the crack and climb past a finger slot to delicate moves above.

59. Smiling with your Mind V0+ R/X
A powerful move takes you off a short flake to good holds above.

60. Solstice V0- R
Climb incuts left of a tree 12' left of the corner.

61. Unnamed V0- R
Climb the corner of the boulder. Bolts were added to this highball.

62. Jasper V5 R/X
Climb the fantastic backside of this boulder over steep rock with beautiful pockets. Many downclimb slightly from the top and drop off to finish this route, rather than endure the unappealing, dangerous top out.

Other Boulders
A great deal of rock can be found on this mountain. I spent quite a bit of time exploring and developing boulders near the main Indian Rocks area, just north of Indian Rocks, and in the nearby vicinity. Some of the best rock is located at the quarry on top of the mountain. Boulders are abundant on the east and west flanks of the quarry, as well as on the backside of the mountain. You can also find some nice boulders with hard problems on the opposite side of Toby Creek near the parking lot. Some boulders are visible from the road on that side. Blue Rocks, an area with epic bouldering, is also located nearby. Spend some time and explore this region, it won't let you down.

35. The Lion's Den

Area Beta

Location
Ridgway, Pennsylvania.

Type of Climbing
Sport, trad, and bouldering.

Other Info
Great spot in a quiet setting.

The Lion's Den

Some of the largest boulders in the East are located at "The Den". Massive sandstone monoliths pop out of the hillside allowing some of the best sandstone climbing in PA. If you visit this spot, you're in for a big surprise. The size of the boulders alone will shock you. The quality of the rock here is excellent. The sandstone here reminds me somewhat of Hunter Rocks, but it is much better quality. The boulders range from a few feet to almost 70' high. There are bolted routes and boulder problems. There are about 40 routes with a lot of room for development. The hike in is a bit grueling but well worth the trip. I recommend bringing a rope and pads. Gear will help in places also but is not necessary. Bring lots of webbing for setting up topropes at the overlook.

History

Hal Beimel and Paul Danday are the original pioneers and developers of this area. They put in all of the original bolted lines and are the true land stewards of the area. Thanks to their efforts and great land stewardship, this area has become a user friendly area. They have also added many fantastic hard climbes like *The Most High*, a mega-classic route that taps into the 5.13 range. Scott Messick, Christa Messick, Jess Lewis, Larry Felton, and I developed many boulder problems and were involved in bolting here also. I also added *Deja "View"* 5.13a.
Location: 6 miles west of Ridgway.

The Lion's Den

General Overview: Over a dozen giant boulders ranging from 20 to 70' tall.

Approach: 15 minutes of mostly easy walking with one steep hill.

Geology: Sandstone

Recommended Rack: Half a dozen draws, small to medium gear, slings for topropes (although most climbs have chains) or a crash pad if you like to solo.

Access Issues and Restrictions: The boulders are located on Pennsylvania State Gamelands,

Area Hazards: Wear bright colors during hunting season due to hunting traffic.

In Case of Emergency: Call 911.

Directions

From downtown Ridgway, find State Route 949 and head west toward Portland Mills. Drive a few miles outside of Ridgway and you will see the Elks Club camp on the left side of the road. Park at a very small pull-off on the right side of the road—do not block any of the gates—and walk past the gate for the Elks Camp. Follow the dirt road to the camp. Behind the south end of the camp there is a trail. Follow this hiking trail about 10 minutes to a bridge. Pass the bridge and site a trail that makes a 90-degree angle to the right from the main trail. Follow this up a steep hill to the rocks.

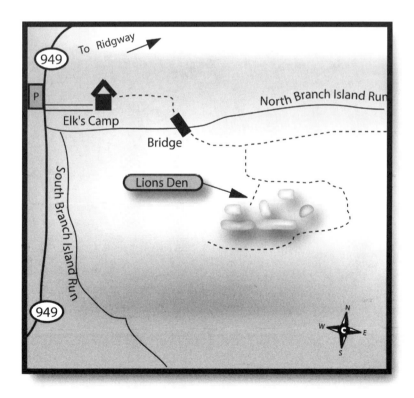

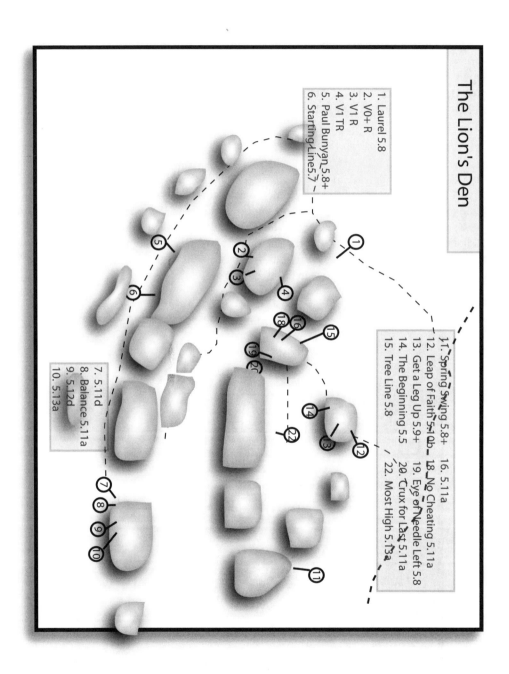

The Lion's Den

1. Laurel 5.8
2. V0+ R
3. V1 R
4. V1 TR
5. Paul Bunyan 5.8+
6. Starting Line 5.7

7. 5.11d
8. Balance 5.11a
9. 5.12d
10. 5.13a

11. Spring Swing 5.8+
12. Leap of Faith 5.10b
13. Get a Leg Up 5.9+
14. The Beginning 5.5
15. Tree Line 5.8
16. 5.11a
18. No Cheating 5.11a
19. Eye of Needle Left 5.8
20. Crux for Last 5.11a
22. Most High 5.13a

1. Laurel 5.8
Traverse right, into a crack, and follow it to the top.

Cave Area
This is the area with a fire ring and large roof that forms a cave under it. Many boulder problems have been done here.

2. Unnamed V0+ R
Climb the face at the left end of the roof.

3. Unnamed V1 R
Climb out under the left side of the roof and pull over the roof at the left side. A variation can be done at a slightly harder grade by moving right and pulling directly out the center.

4. Unnamed V1 TR
Climb the right face of the boulder.

Overlook Wall Left
This is the long, left wall of the scenic overlook. It is high and has a few very nice climbs that can be done on it. Bring long webbing for setting up topropes here.

5. Paul Bunyan 5.8+
Near the center of the wall there is a fallen tree. Start here and climb through a slot in the overhang above.

6. The Starting Line 5.7
Climb up near the cleft in the two faces at the right end of the *Overlook Wall*.

Overlook Wall Right
This is the right outcrop of the overlook. Some of the best quality climbing is located here. A faint trail leads down through bushes at the right side of the rock.

7. 5.11d
Climb the left side of the wall near an arete.

8. Balance 5.11a
Start at the clean, rounded corner, right of the previous climb and climb to a flake and the top.

9. 5.12d
Balance moves leave you standing on a shelf just off the ground 18' right of the previous problem. Snap up to the jug above the ledge and follow the sloping shelf slightly right to a horizontal and a bulging face. Continue up the very blank face using small finger pockets and slopers.

10. Deja "View" 5.13a
Boulder moves climb up to the steep face with nice pockets in it just right of the previous climb. Follow the pockets to the lip of the steep face and fly off the lip using a finger jam

to jump to another pocket a body length above. Continue up the blank face above.

Spring Boulder
Hard to locate, this boulder is nestled between boulders and is identified by a nice corner leading to a roof.

11. Spring Swing 5.8+
Climb the nice crack/corner and traverse left under the roof above.

The Courtyard
This area is a group of boulders that form a circle of the largest boulders here.

12. Leap of Faith 5.10b TR
This is the fantastic overhang with a block below it. The rock is a bit brittle in spots. Climb to the center of the overhang and pull over pockets to the steep face above. Chains are at the top.

Ryan Watts at Lion's Den. RH photo.

13. Get a Leg Up 5.9+ TR
Climb the arete left of *Leap of Faith* and merge with the previous route above.

14. The Beginning 5.5 G
Climb past three bolts on the face around the corner from the arete.

15. Tree Line 5.8+
Climb pockets on the lower end of the boulder.

16. 5.11a
Climb the line of bolts at the upper end of the boulder.

17. Eye of the Needle right 5.7
Follow bolts in the chimney and finish at the anchors to the right on the right-hand boulder.

18. No Cheating 5.11a
Climb the same line as above, but do not stem to the chimney.

19. Eye of the Needle Left 5.8
Climb the chimney and bolts, but move out left and follow bolts to the anchor on the large

left-hand boulder.

20. Save the Crux for Last 5.11a
Climb the steep face to a flake and crack. Chains are above.

21. Project

22. The Most High 5.12d/5.13a
Climb the steep wave feature at the boulders left side. Chains above.

23. Arete 5.11d
Climb the beautiful left arete of the boulder.

Christa Messick at Lion's den.

36. Beartown Rocks Bouldering Area

Area Beta

Location
Northwest Pennsylvania.

Type of Climbing
Bouldering.

Other Info
A nice area with clean sandstone.

Beartown Rocks

Beartown Rocks is an excellent bouldering area. Good landings, massive boulders, and fun problems best sum up this area. Large pockets that speckle the rock create the unique character this spot is known to have. The problems here range from VB to V9. The height of the rock varies from a few feet to 35' high. Most of the problems cater toward the beginner, but the area has a few worthwhile challenging routes and highball problems that are not to be missed. Although this area has been quite established over the years, many problems still await cleaning and first ascents.

This is a quality area; however, a few drawbacks exist. Some of the boulders are very unclean; tourists hiking around can be a slight nuisance—like urinating on you while you climb; and there is a lack of difficult problems. Overall I recommend this area for a visit. If Beartown Rocks doesn't meet your expectations, there are plenty of great areas only a few miles away.

It is also important to note that many of the problems at this area were never named or the names were simply forgotten over the years. Because of this, I have only included names that have seemed to stick over the years, or are descriptive names. For example: Iron Will was first climbed by Bob Value and did not have a name, but the name comes from an obscure eliminate variation that has stuck over the years—a classic like that just begs for a name anyway.

General Description: Sandstone boulders, 6-35' high, some can be toproped. Problems from VB toV9.

Location: Clear Creak State Park, just outside the town of Sigel.

Emergency Services: In the event of an emergency dial 911, contact a park employee 814-752-2368, or the Brookville Hospital at 814-849-2312.

Access and Restrictions: Clear Creek State Park recognizes and permits climbing on their property--they even built an overlook to climb to on one of the boulders. The park asks that climbers respect the land, pack out litter, keep the place clean, limit the use of chalk, refrain from excessive noise, and set a good example for the hikers and tourists.   Climbers are highly visible at this area and set a big impression on onlookers who see climbing as a curious diversion. It is not unlikely for small children to be inspired to solo some of the high boulders after watching a seasoned climber cruise a trade route. Please use sense and judgment toward onlookers (especially children) and keep an eye out for dangerous behavior.

History

Unfortunately, early history for Beartown is a bit ambiguous. Climbers have been to this area as long ago as the 1950s. In the 1960s, members of the Penn State Outing Club climbed a bit on the higher outcrops, mostly toprope, but a few solos were done as well. The first known climber to visit this area was Curt Harler, a pioneer of Pennsylvania climbing. He visited this area for the first time in the late '60s and climbed here occasionally until the early '70s. During this time, he is noted for climbing things like the *Harler Route* and a few obvious problems on that boulder, as well as the overlook and a few problems on the left side of *The Moss Slab*. During the '70s members of the Pittsburgh Outing Club established a few lines here.

In the mid-'70s, at the age of 16, Bob Value of McConnell's Mills fame, developed a great deal of the boulder problems at this area. He established a great deal of the older classics and most of the modern problems here. One of his best claim-to-fames was being urinated of by a drunk tourist while bouldering below the overlook. Carl Samples was also active bouldering here during the 70s and 80s.

In the '80s I found out about Beartown Rocks. Much later, Ryan Lukas and I were noted for developing a few handfuls of problems, some above the grade of V4. Hal Beimel and Paul Danday also developed a good amount of the bouldering here. Many notable ascents were done by them at this area.

Geology: Sandstone Rock City.

Season: March – November.

Directions

From the town of Siegel, drive north on State Route 949, a few miles to the Clear Creek State Park headquarters. About 100' before the headquarters, there is a park road on your right, just after the bridge. Turn right on this road and you will see a sign for Beartown Rocks and the vista. Drive this dirt road, keeping to the right at the split, until you reach a parking area. Park and you will see the rock.

1. Welcome to Beartown V0+

This problem is located on the first good-sized boulder on the left side of the trail coming from the parking lot. SDS and climb the back, left-hand corner of the boulder.

2. Little Wall V0-

Directly across the trail from *Welcome to Beartown* are two boulders that create passage between them. This problem climbs the backside of this boulder. Any part of the face goes at the same grade.

3. Little Arete V0-

Climb the arete to the right of the previous problem. The face in the passage to the right is VB.

4. Unnamed VB

Directly behind the arete (*Little Arete*), climb the arete on the boulder across from problems 2 and 3.

5. Unnamed V0

A few feet left of the arete climb the face up and over a large block that creates a small overhang.

The author bouldering at Beartown. Photo by Ryan Lukas.

6. Unnamed V0-

Climb the face a few feet left of the previous problem.

7. Unnamed V0

Dance up the face to the right of problem number 4.

8. Iron Will V5

Start on a ledge at the left end of the overhang that forms the large cave passage. Begin with hands and feet on the lip of the overhang and traverse right to a top out at the far right side. Don't use the boulder underneath the hang. A variation can be done using only the lip and none of the pockets. This boosts the grade to V6.

9. Tunnel Rat V0+

Begin underneath *Iron Will* and traverse a horizontal under the cave towards the other side. Finish by topping out over the hang. A few variations can be done by topping out farther left.

Beartown Rocks (Main Area)

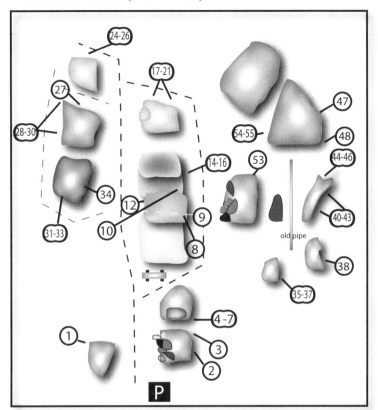

10. Ole Baldy V8/V9
Start with hands on the very blank, sloping face that is right of the cave and the previous problem. Traverse right with feet low and continue to the boulders rightmost edge. Top out at the far right side.

11. Unnamed V0
SDS and climb the face a few feet right of *Ole Baldy* and top out where two boulders rest atop one another.

12. Unnamed V1
Grab holds over the lip of the overhang and top out.

13. Unnamed V0+
SDS in the cave and top out near no. 12.

14. Huggie Bear V2
SDS and climb the overhanging face, to top out at the left edge, where one boulder rests atop another.

15. Bipolar Bear V3
SDS and top out a few feet right of the previous route.

16. Unnamed V2
Climb the overhanging face from a sitting start at the right end of this outcrop.

17. Sandy Overlaps V1/V2
The grade varies depending on what line you take. Climb the overhanging face on the boulder behind the cave outcrop.

18. The Japanese Magician V2
Start around the corner to the right of the previous problem and climb straight to the top.

19. Unnamed V1
SDS and climb the face 2' right of the previous problem.

20. Alaska Pete V1
Climb the right corner of this boulder 4' right of the previous route.

21. Project R/X
Climb the face around the corner from *Alaska Pete* and top out in the center of the overhang.

22. Unnamed V0-
Climb the face to a notch and top out slightly right of the project.

23. Unnamed V0 R
Climb the face 2' right of the previous problem.

24. Unnamed V0+
Directly behind the project is another boulder. Climb the obvious arete directly behind the project.

25. Pocket Route V0-
Climb the face right of number 24 to a big pocket. Finish by topping out through a notch.

26. Unnamed V2 R
Ascend the tricky face over a bulge to top out 2' right of the previous route.

27. Tourist Treat V0 R
An excellent flowing problem. Cruise through buckets and top out. Try not to scare the tourists when you mysteriously pop up over the top.
Var. 1: V0 R Climb the face just right of the regular line.

28. The Ships Prow V3 R
DSD and flow up the beautiful arete that greatly resembles a ships prow. This is much easier from a standing start.

29. Unnamed V0-/V1
A few easy problems have been done to the right of the prow.

30. Pocket Pool V3
Locate a finger pocket about 8' right of the prow. Sit start the beginning and climb from the pocket up to a horizontal, then continue to the top out.
Var. 1: V0- Climb the face anyplace right of this problem.

31 – 33. V0-/V1
The face on the front side of the lookout outcrop can be climbed at a few spots. All are about the same grade.

34. Unnamed VB – V0-
Climb the obvious face.

35-37. Ryan's Boulder V0/V1
This boulder is tricky to find. From the *Cave Outcrop* look towards the parking lot and down to the left. You will see a small boulder. A few sit-start problems exist here. The two easiest are on the arete and left corner. The V1 goes up the center of the face; the rest are V0.

38. Hidden Overhang V0 R
Directly behind problems 35 to 37 you will see an old pipe covered in the ground. Walk over it and you will see a large boulder with one side completely overgrown and covered in dirt. The backside is somewhat high and capped by an overhang. This problem climbs the center of that side.

39. The Loose Goose V0 R
Climb the overhang slightly right of the previous route.

40-41. Friction Slab V0- R
Climb the left side of the giant slab right of the previous two routes.

42. Moss Carpet V0 R
Run up the center of the slab carpeted in moss.

43. Choss Carpet V0 R
Cruise up 2' right of *Moss Carpet.*

44. Intergalactic V4
From a sit start climb the overhanging arete right of the slab side of this boulder.

45. Unnamed V1
Climb the V-notch in the center of the overhanging face from a sit start.

46. Choss Hound V1
Sit start and climb the immensely moss-covered right side of the overhanging face.

47. Descent

48. Brittle Arete V0+ R
Climb the arete left of the descent route.

49. Peanut Brittle V1 R
A tasty classic. 2' right of the arete.

50. Unnamed V0- R
Ascend the face2'left of the arete.

51. Unnamed V0-
2' left of number 50.

52. Mystery Problem
Congratulations. You have come to the route in the guidebook that is the hidden mystery problem. Be the *first* person to e-mail us at www.paclimbing.com and receive a free copy of the guidebook you most likely already have.

53. Unnamed V0-
Climb up 2' left of number 51.

54. Unnamed V0- R
Behind problem number 52 is a high boulder with a large rounded corner. Climb this.

The author on another exciting highball. Photo by Ryan Lukas.

55. Dung Heap V0-R
Climb the corner left of problem number 52.

56. Lichen It V0
Scum your way up left of the arete.

57. Little Rock City Area
To the left of the main outcrops you can see some lesser-height boulders in a field. Some good problems have been done here.

58. Trail Split Boulder V0/V2
Where the trail veers left and splits to go to the *Little Rock City* (this is between the main outcrops and the three very large boulders), there is a small boulder on the trail with a few problems. All are slightly overhanging and make good sit start problems with nice pockets.

Big Boulder 1
Just past the *Trail Split Boulder* you will see three very large boulders. This is the leftmost

of the three. Several highballs can be done on this and all are quite easy.

Big Boulder 2
The next highest in order. A few feet right of the previous large boulder.

59. Bear Claw Arete V0/V2 X
This is the center boulder of the three extremely large boulders. Climb the leftmost arete of the boulder. V2 with sit start; V0 from a standing start.

60. Unnamed V0- R
Climb the face anywhere right of *Bear Claw Arete.*

61. Round-O-Matic V2
Sit start at the rounded feature at the right end of this boulder.

Big Boulder 3
This boulder is the highest of the three and is to the right of the other two. Please note that the descent route from this boulder is achieved by climbing down the *Harler Route* and is at the highest point of this boulder. The route is only 5.4 but can be dangerous.

62. Unnamed V0 X
Climb the high face of this giant boulder anyplace left of the *Harler Route.*

63. Harler Route V0- X
Perhaps one of he oldest lines here. Climb the beautiful and thrilling arete. Very easy but very high. This is also the descent route!

64. Unnamed V0-/V0 X
Climb the face anyplace right of the *Harler Route.*

65. Honeycomb Route V1 X
Climb the nice, pocketed route that is slightly overhanging, on the backside of the giant boulder. This is the leftmost route with golden-colored rock. Note: the routes to the right go at about the same grade and slightly easier.

37. Allegheny National Forest Areas

Area Beta

Location
Northwest Pennsylvania near the New York border.

Type of Rock
Bouldering, Trad, and to-prope.

Other Info
This section includes a few of the many areas in the forest.

General Overview

A wealth of bouldering lies in this national forest near Bradford, Pennsylvania and the New York state border. Much of the bouldering in this part of the state is undeveloped but a small group of locals have gone out of their way to establish a great deal of bouldering. Dana Harrington, Brandon English, and Terry Schreuter have been very active. Bob Value also made many trips to the ANF and was active in this area. Hal Beimel and Paul Danday established some climbs at Rim Rock. I was also active around the ANF and developed some of the boulder problems (mostly near and including Mellow Gold) at Rim Rocks and a 5.13 (Pin Cushion) there. I also discovered Kelly Pines, House Boulder, the Ice Cubes and several other spots not mentioned in this guide. Dana Harrington has discovered several spots with amazing bouldering and some of the best gritstone in Pennsylvania. I recommend checking out flyingnutmuncher.com to see updates on developments throughout the ANF. Dana and his friends have been the most prolific climbers in the ANF along with Terry Schreuter who has developed over 300 routes and boulder problems. The climbing in this part of Pennsylvania is amazing. I highly advise a visit to any of the areas in the ANF.

Rimrock Overlook

Rimrock Overlook

Perched on a mountain vista high above the Kinzua Reservoir, Rimrock Overlook is a gem amongst the Allegheny Mountains. The cliff caters to the more experienced climber, but a few moderate lines can be found. Sharp crystal-pebbles on steep walls are the main attraction here. Routes range from 5.5 to 5.13+ with a broad range of projects for the seasoned hard-man looking for new lines. The bouldering here is amongst the best in the state. Boulders of immense size lie scattered just below the cliff. There are only a handful of established routes, but if you are in the nearby vicinity, I recommend a visit. Please note that only a handful of routes and problems are mentioned in this book. Dozens of other routes and problems have been named and graded here. I only include the most obvious lines.

Ownership: Allegheny National Forest.

Restrictions: Do not toprope off the metal railings at the clifftop. These may look secure but are not. This area is also closed.

Directions: From Warren PA, travel State Highway 59 approximately six miles to the Allegheny River Reservoir. About one mile further, you will cross the reservoir. Continue to drive up the mountain for a little over one mile. The first road on your right after the crest of the hill is a labeled road for Rimrock Overlook. Drive this road to the overlook/cliff.

Partial Area Closure:
The area under the guardrails has recently been closed to climbing. Climb only at areas away from the main overlook.

1. All things are Possible 5.9 R
A bold FA by Hal Beimel. Climb the openbook/crack to the top.

2. Unnamed 5.13a TR
Find minuscule holds on the blank yellow streak right of the crack.

3. Wave Wall
This is the wall that resembles a giant wave cresting over the basetrail. It is the leftmost wall of the main overlook. Several projects wait to be sent on this steep gem.

4. Overlook wall/ Project wall
The rightmost of the two overlook walls.

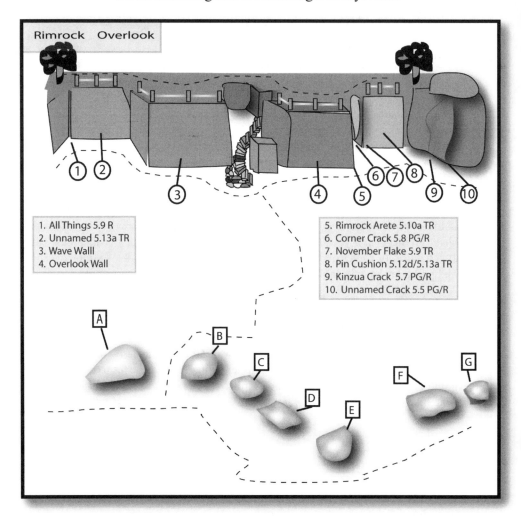

Rimrock   Overlook

1. All Things 5.9 R
2. Unnamed 5.13a TR
3. Wave Walll
4. Overlook Wall

5. Rimrock Arete 5.10a TR
6. Corner Crack 5.8 PG/R
7. November Flake 5.9 TR
8. Pin Cushion 5.12d/5.13a TR
9. Kinzua Crack 5.7 PG/R
10. Unnamed Crack 5.5 PG/R

5. Rimrock Arete 5.10a TR
Climb the beautifully arete on the right side of this wall.

6. Corner Crack 5.8 PG/R
Climb the crack that is set back in the corner to the right of the previous route.

7. November Flake 5.9 TR
Layback the nice flake immediately right of the previous route.

8. Pin Cushion 5.12d/5.13a TR
Depending on where you climb the face this route changes slightly in grade. The 5.13 line moves directly up the center over black-colored rock. Climb the center of the narrow face passing strenuous moves over micro-pinches to end at the railing at the right end of the overlook.

9. Kinzua Crack 5.7 PG/R

If you have very large gear the route is better protected. Climb the leftmost of the two cracks 30' right of *Pin Cushion*.

10. Unnamed Crack 5.5 PG/R

Better protected with large gear. Climb the rightmost of the two cracks.

The Great Pyramid

This is the largest boulder of the group below the cliff. Its downhill side is a massive pyramid shape with a large looming wall above.

Cold Air V2

On the pyramids right-hand wall there is a smaller pyramid feature with a sloping shelf that slants up and right to the end of the boulder. Sit start left, and traverse up right to mantle and move to a notch at the high-right corner of the boulder. Pull onto the mossy slab and right face of the boulder via a crack/notch. Continue to the top or downclimb. Safer variations can be done by traversing until it is comfortable to jump down.

Inca Gold V5

Sit start in the center of the sub-pyramid midway under the traverse of the previous problem. Climb the overhanging face to the sloping lip. You can join the previous problem and topout or downclimb the rail to the start of the previous problem (safer).

Giagantica

The massive boulder right of the previous boulder.

Unnamed V8 X

Climb the rightmost corner of the downhill side of the boulder.

Unnamed V5 X

Climb the downhill-most of several cracks on the right side of the boulder.

Island Boulder

The next boulder of the series. Most of this boulder is moss-covered. There are a few lines on the downhill side that go in the V1 range.

The Cube

The large boulder just below the *Island Boulder*.

Unnamed Boulder

The smaller boulder right of and slightly below *The Cube*.

The Manila Wall V1 R

Climb the sandy-yellow overhang with fun pockets on the uphill corner of this boulder.

Nova V3

Climb pockets on the left/downhill side of the boulder.

Unnamed V7 R

SDS and climb the right side of the boulder a few feet right of where a crack splits the boulder in two. Make fun moves to an incut pocket 9' up and traverse right once you gain the seam under the blank roof. Merge at the top.

Canned Heat V5 R

SDS at the right side of the boulder and climb overhanging pockets to a sloping shelf at a crack with a small corner. Top out in the small corner right of the tree touching the boulder.

Mellow Gold V8

Traverse low pockets from the right side of the boulder to its left side.

Minister Creek

Minister Creek

Certainly worth a visit, Minister Creek is an enchanting, scenic, and unique area hidden in Allegheny's wooded foothills. Steep precipices and an overwhelming amount of boulders can be found along the Minister Creek Hiking Trail. A fair amount of routes and problems have been established, but equal amounts await development. Like other areas throughout the region, intimidating portions of moss plague the boulders. Don't let rock funk scare you from Minister; the climbing is excellent.

Since this area is secluded and little information has ever been documented about this spot, I have chosen to only include directions. Possibly in future additions of this book, I will include a topo. For now, visit the area and enjoy. It is a real adventure.

Directions

Located in Allegheny State Forest. When in Allegheny State Forest, locate the Minister Creek Campground and parking area on PA 666. One half mile from the parking area there is a trailhead on PA 666 (Minister Creek Trail). Hike this trail to the large 80' high boulder overlook for the best climbing. A toprope is advised. Numerous boulders lie scattered throughout the 8 mile trail loop. The best spot is by far the overlook 0.8 mile from PA 666.

Kelly Pines Boulders

Kelly Pines Boulders

Imagine secluded boulders resting among tall timbers, with beds of pine needles for landings. Now envision yourself on massive gritstone blocks, a stones throw from your car, with the only sound for miles being wind wafting through whispering pines. I know this may sound like a fairytale, but this is the setting that surrounds one of Allegheny National Forests best kept secrets.

A dozen boulders rest below tall shafts of red pine inches off Forest Road 131. The boulders are large but can be climbed with reasonable safety. Since myself and Rob Ginieczki are the only climbers known to have climbed here, a lot of the rock is in a virgin state—and I don't mean virgin as in clean and pure, I mean virgin as in dirty and covered in moss. That being said, much of the rock *is* clean and holds an array of steep, technical, and fun problems. If you're in this neck of the woods and looking to do first ascents, this is the spot for you.

Note: The road to access this area is not likely to be maintained during winter months. If your vehicle is not good for winter off-roading, you may be staying here longer than planned.

Directions

From Marienville, take spruce street east. After some houses, Spruce Street turns into a dirt road. It then becomes Forest Road 130. Drive 5miles to the four-way intersection of FR 130 and FR 131. Turn left onto FR 131. Drive approximately 1.7 miles and you will see boulders alongside both sides of the road. Park at the Kelly Pines Campground to access the boulders.

Several massive boulders lie alongside FR 130 also. Drive a short way past the four-way intersection on FR 130 and you will see the boulders.

The Ice Cubes

The Ice Cubes

Located in the heart of Allegheny National Forest, these perfect cube-shaped boulders invite interesting problems on gritstone gems. A few dozen alarmingly symmetric cubes, like ice cubes spilled from a glass, lie scattered down the hillside near Route 219 and Wintergreen Run. There aren't as many boulders here as other nearby Allegheny attractions, but there is enough rock to keep one busy for an afternoon session of hard cranking. And if that doesn't entice you the approach should. You can practically throw your pad from the car to the base of the boulders.

Problems range from V0- to V7. The area was discovered and developed by Scott Messick and myself. There is a great deal of room for new problems. If you happen to be driving by, this spot is a good choice for a few hours on quality stone at one of the forests hidden jewels. Bring a brush since much of the rock is yet untapped.

Directions

From Bradford, find the junction of Routes 59 and 219 (approximately 10 miles south of Bradford). At the village of Timbuck, drive U.S. Route 219 south, about 1.5 miles, and you will see rock off to your left and in the woods. Near the bottom of the hill, on your right, there is a small dirt lot to park at. The boulders are visible on the opposite side of the road (the boulders are on the east side of 219). If you reach the bottom of the hill in the village of Tally Ho, you went too far.

Other Areas

What is mentioned in this guide is just the tip of the iceberg. Bradford hosts several good bouldering spots. Hearts Content has enough boulders for you to boulder, well, to your hearts content. Dana Harrington and Terry Schreuter developed an area called South Slater. Another spot with bolted lines lies beyond Hearts Content. The best rock lies near Pleasant Township Road and parallels the river. This is near Rt. 337 and 62. I recommend checking flyingnutmuncher.com for further info.

38. The Lost Crag

Area Beta

Location
Southwest Pennsylvania.

Type of Climbing
Sport and trad.

Other Info
A great little spot in a beautiful setting.

The Lost Crag

Located in State Gamelands near Dunbar. If these routes were just a bit higher, this area would be a major destination. The rock quality is very good despite some loose rock in places. The main attraction here is the large amount of bolted climbs. If you decide to visit here, I recommend you bring some gear to supplement many of the bolts. A lot of the routes here are mixed bolt/trad routes. If you live in the nearby vicinity, this is a must-visit spot. If you like highball bouldering, bring a pad. Many of the routes here can be done as extreme highballs. The rock is sandstone similar to Coopers Rock in West Virginia. About 75 routes exist here. The massive blocks range from 20 to 40' high.

Directions

Drive south on State Route 119 out of Connellsville (heading towards Uniontown). At the blinking light, make a left onto SR1053 and pass a junkyard on the left while heading towards Dunbar. After reaching the town of Dunbar, make a left at a T intersection and cross Dunbar Creek. Locate the state Gamelands building on your right. Make a right on an easy-to-miss gravel road just before the building. Follow the gravel road and Dunbar Creek on your right. Follow this road almost two miles until you see a very large parking area on the left. Locate a dirt road at the back-right corner of the lot near the gas line. Hike the road about one mile to the crest of a hill. Cross a wooden bridge and just after the bridge locate the first road on the right. Follow this road past an agricultural field until you come to another field on the right. Locate an old logging road at the back-left part of the grass field and follow this past several branches to a sharp turn in the road where it follows the hillside. Walk about 75 yards and look for a faint trail on the right (a stone cairn usually marks this trail). Follow the trail to the crag. The trail leads to *Entrance Block*. Note: The road that parallels Dunbar Creek is sometimes not passable in winter.

The Ocean Block
This is the detached block at the left end of the outcrop. Two short, bolted lines exist here. They are on the uphill side. The top can be accessed via the downhill-right side.

1. Tidal Wave 5.11a

FA: Tim Anderson
(2 bolts and anchor). A short but fun line. Climb the leftmost line of bolts on this block.

2. Tsunami 5.11c
FA: Greg Zamule
(2 bolts and anchor). Climb the bolted line right of *Tidal Wave*.

Crack Wall
This is the leftmost section of cliff. It is composed of a long wall with a detached block just below it. A few good lines can be climbed here.

3. Crack Addict 5.6
A wide crack at the walls right side.

4. Orange Crush 5.10a TR
Climb the corner and face at the blocks right side.

5. Center Crack 5.10
At the right side of the wall, a nice crack splits the center-face of the detached block.

Cave World
This is the next stone feature to the right of the previous few climbs.

6. Campus Corner 5.10d PG
FA: Greg Zamule
Gear is used to supplement the bolts on this climb. Start on the downhill corner and climb to the top.

7. A Flash in the Pan 5.11b
FA: Greg Zamule
(2 bolts). Located to the right of *Campus Corner*, climb the face in the passage.

8. Busy Chopin 5.11a TR
FA: G. Zamule, T. Anderson
An exciting climb on steep rock. Start right of the previous climb under a roof, surmount the roof, and endure an interesting finish.

Tunnel Block
This is the block below *Cave World*. The climbs are located on its downhill side. A rappel is located at the downhill-right side.

9. Slacker 5.6
FA: T. Anderson.
(3 bolts). A great warm up. Run up the easy route passing 3 bolts.

10. Center Crack 5.5 TR
Climb the nice crack just right of the previous route.

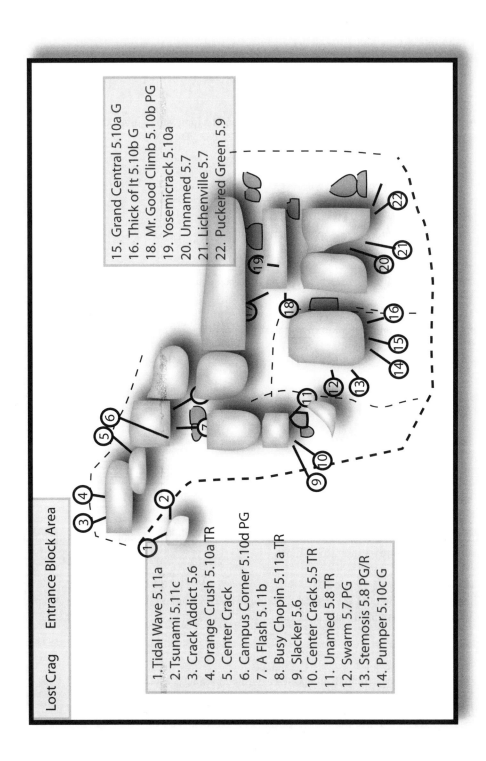

Lost Crag   Entrance Block Area

15. Grand Central 5.10a G
16. Thick of It 5.10b G
18. Mr. Good Climb 5.10b PG
19. Yosemicrack 5.10a
20. Unnamed 5.7
21. Lichenville 5.7
22. Puckered Green 5.9

1. Tidal Wave 5.11a
2. Tsunami 5.11c
3. Crack Addict 5.6
4. Orange Crush 5.10a TR
5. Center Crack
6. Campus Corner 5.10d PG
7. A Flash 5.11b
8. Busy Chopin 5.11a TR
9. Slacker 5.6
10. Center Crack 5.5 TR
11. Unamed 5.8 TR
12. Swarm 5.7 PG
13. Stemosis 5.8 PG/R
14. Pumper 5.10c G

11. Unnamed 5.8+ TR
FA: B. Coblentz
The face just right of the previous route.

Entrance Block
This is the large block located right of where the approach trail meets the rock. It is a good reference point for other climbs. There is a nice roof that caps its downhill-left side. Topropes can be set up via an easy scramble in the right passage of the block.

12. Swarm 5.7 PG
FA: Rick Zinnikas, Jeff Secker
Cruise the nice flake on the right side of the boulder.

13. Stemosis 5.8 PG/R
FA: Tom Kopler, T. Anderson
Ledges lead to an off-width left of the big roof.

14. Pumper 5.10c G
FA: T. Anderson, Matt Johns
4 bolts. Start right of the roof and climb a short corner to steep rock. Follow bolts to the top.

15. Grand Central 5.10a G
FA: T. Anderson, Matt Johns
(4 bolts). Climb four bolts to the right of the previous route to an anchor above.

16. In the Thick of It 5.10b G
FA: T. Anderson, T. Kopler
(3 bolts and shuts). Climb the bulging arete right of *Grand Central*.

Little Yosemite
This is the long block located in the passage behind the *Entrance Block*.

17. Why Bother 5.6 F.A. G. Zamule
Use horizontals to gain a dihedral in the center of the short side of the block in the passage.

18. Mr. Good Climb 5.10b PG
FA: G. Zamule
A fun climb. Climb the downhill arete on this block.

19. Yosemicrack 5.10a
Ascend the finger crack right of the arete on the downhill side of the boulder.

Bulge Block
The rightmost block of the grouping. Several climbs exist on the downhill side and in the passage between the blocks.

20. Unnamed 5.7
FA: B. Coblentz, G. Zamule
Climb the highest line up in the passage between the two blocks.

21. Lichenville 5.7 G
FA: T. Anderson Kevin O' Brien
(4 bolts and shuts). Climb the face in the passage just below the previous route.

22. Puckered Green 5.9
FA: T. Anderson
Begin left of the overhang on the downhill-right side of the boulder and gain a crack. Follow to the dirty and spooky top out.

23. Lucky Charm 5.10a
FA: T. Anderson, T. Kopler
Climb the overhanging-right corner.

S.B.R Block
This is the large block across the clearing from the *Bulge Block*. Several good climbs and boulder problems are found here. Access to the top can be found at the back-left end.

24. Unnamed 5.9
FA: B. Coblentz, G. zamule
Climb the left side of the block on the downhill face.

25. Backscratcher 5.9 R
FA: T. Anderson, Ben Lockard
Start left of a tree and cross over to the right, then climb the face above.

26. Hang on St. Christopher 5.10c G
FA: G. Zamule, B. Coblentz
(2 bolts, gear, shuts). Climb the bulging arete at the right side of the block.

27. Who Needs Pro 5.4 R
Watch for loose rock. Climb the face just right of the corner.

28. Drill Queen 5.4 G
FA: Laura and Norm Reed
(4 bolts). Climb bolts right of the previous route.

29. Tip and Tap 5.10c R
FA: T. Anderson
Ascend the face near the chimney at the top end of the boulder. Moving left after the start drops the grade to 5.8.

30. Preacher Norm 5.10a G
FA: N. Reed
(4 bolts). Begin under the low roof, right of the chimney, and climb the face to the arete

and steep rock above.

31. Long Live the Klingons 5.10a G
FA: G. Zamule, B. Coblentz
(3 bolts, gear). Climb up to the left side of a roof. Continue up the arete to the top.

Chimney Block
This is the next block of the group. There is a large chimney at its side.

32. Chimney Sweep 5.5 R
Climb the face to gain the chimney to the top. The climb starts just right of the chimney.

33. Lame Duck 5.11a G
FA: T. Anderson
(3 bolts). The corridor is off route. Follow bolts right of the chimney.

34. Lumber Jack 5.9 G
FA: T. Anderson
(2 bolts, shuts). Climb the route past two bolts at the right side of the block near the beginning of the passage.

The Corridors
This is the long corridor behind the *Chimney Block*. You can set topropes by an access point at the back-right corner.

35. Beginners Edge 5.10a PG
(2 bolts). Climb the arete at the back-right end of the *Chimney Block*.

36. The Thinker 5.11c TR
FA: T. Anderson
Climb the center face of the back wall of the corridor.

37. Face Value 5.11a TR
FA: T. Anderson
Climb the right side of the wall near the corner making balance moves at the arete.

38. Dyno Sore 5.10d PG
FA: G. Zamuel, B. Coblentz
(1 bolt and gear). Crank under an overhang to an arete above.

39. Climbing on Rainbows 5.10b G
FA: G. Zamule
(3 bolts). Just right of the tree on the *Brutal Block*, climb past three bolts.

40. Mickey Mantle 5.8 PG
FA: B. Williams, G. Zamule
(2 bolts). Run past two bolts in the corridor just right of *Climbing on Rainbows*.

41. Dirty Bird 5.3 PG
Climb the easy face in the long corridor.

42. Into the Light 5.10a G
FA: N. Reed
(3 bolts). Climb the face directly behind *Dirty Bird*.

Brutal Block
This is the large block adjacent to *Chimney Block*.

43. The Matrix 5.10d TR
FA: Norm and Laura Reed
Climb a roof to a corner in the center of the downhill side of the block.

44. Brutal Orangutan 5.12a
Begin on the east face of the boulder next to a steep corner, and climb the arete to a roof and the top.

45. Vini Vidi Vici 5.10a PG
FA : G. Zamule, B. Coblentz
(2 bolts, gear, shuts). Come, see, and try to conquer this one.   Gear will supplement the bolts if you wish. Climb the bolted line right of the previous route.

46. Water Streak 5.10c PG
FA: Norma and Laura Reed
(3 bolts, shuts). Climb past three bolts at green rock next to the previous route.

47. Chip Off the Old Rock 5.10c G
FA: G. Zamule, T. Anderson
(3 bolts). Motor past 3 bolts right of the previous route.

48. Urban Orangutan 5.9 G
FA: B. Williams
(3 bolts, shuts). Move past 3 bolts just right of *Chip*.

49. Cranky old Man (Unrated)
Climb the route near *Urban Orangutan*.

50. Face Up To It 5.10c PG
FA: G. Zamule, T. Anderson
(2 bolts). Located on the long block above the *Brutal Block*, climb past bolts on the narrow face of the boulder.

Short Stack
This is the nice-sized boulder below the *Brutal Block*. A rappel is located on its uphill side.

51. Unnamed 5.10b

FA: B. Coblentz, B. Williams
Climb the nice arete on the uphill left side of the block**.**

52. Reunion 5.11b PG
FA: M. Johns, T. Anderson
(1 bolt, gear, shuts). The top section is a bit cruxy. Climb the center of the face past 1 bolt.

53. Rinse and Whine 5.10c PG
FA: T. Anderson
(1 bolt, gear).   Below the previous route, climb past 1 bolt.

54. Unnamed 5.9
FA: G. Zamule, B. Coblentz
Harder than it looks. Climb the face just below and around the corner from *Rinse and Whine*.

55. Slopers in the Rain 5.8
FA: B. Coblentz, G. Zamule
Climb the route directly right of the unnamed 5.9.

56. Hang on Slopey 5.8 PG
FA: B. Coblentz, G. Zamule
Climb the route just right of the previous route.

57. Slope Stone 5.8 PG
FA: B. Coblentz, N. Reed
The dihedral right of the previous route near the right corner of the block.

58. Psycho Driller 5.7 G
FA: N & L. Reed
(3 bolts). The first climb bolted up the block. Climb the center of the west face of the block.

59. Evil Edge 5.8 G
FA: T. Kopler
(3 bolts). The large ledge to the right is off route. Make fun moves up the top-right edge of the block.

Snip Block
Located at the uppermost-right of the outcrop, this block offers a few short climbs.

60. Corner Route 5.10b G
FA: B. Coblentz, G. Zamule
(3 bolts). Great moves follow an overhanging corner.

61. Snip Snip Snip 5.11b TR
FA: G. Zamule, B. Coblentz, T. Anderson

Move over sharp edges up the center face of the *Snip Block* corridor.

62. Dream the Impossible 5.10c G
FA: G. Zamule, T. Anderson
(3 bolts). Balance your way up the uphill arete.

The Bob Block
The last block of the outcrop offers several good climbs.

63. Horizontal Bop 5.8 PG
FA: B. Coblentz
Climb the lower-left face.

64. Break Away 5.7 TR
FA: B. Coblentz
Diagonal left up the face just above the previous route.

65. The Rock Feels No Pain 5.11a TR
FA: G. Zamule, L. Evans
The face right of the arete.

66. Easier Done Than Said 5.7 PG
 FA: G. Zamule, B. Coblentz
(2 bolts, gear). Climb the uphill arete.

67. Unnamed 5.9 PG
FA: B. Coblentz
(1 bolt, gear). Make exciting moves on the uphill side of the boulder.

68. Crescent Crack 5.7 G
FA: Dough Washabaugh, Curtis Metz
Ascend the obvious crescent-shaped crack.

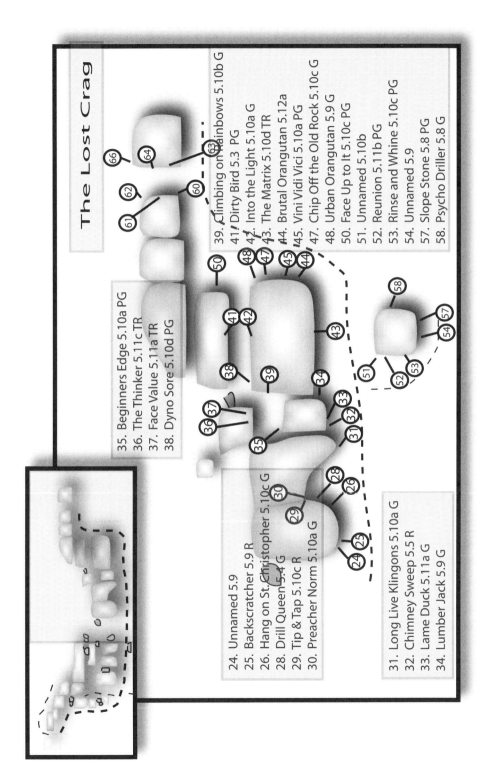

The Lost Crag

24. Unnamed 5.9
25. Backscratcher 5.9 R
26. Hang on St. Christopher 5.10c G
28. Drill Queen 5.4 G
29. Tip & Tap 5.10c R
30. Preacher Norm 5.10a G

31. Long Live Klingons 5.10a G
32. Chimney Sweep 5.5 R
33. Lame Duck 5.11a G
34. Lumber Jack 5.9 G

35. Beginners Edge 5.10a PG
36. The Thinker 5.11c TR
37. Face Value 5.11a TR
38. Dyno Sore 5.10d PG

39. Climbing on Rainbows 5.10b G
41. Dirty Bird 5.3 PG
42. Into the Light 5.10a G
43. The Matrix 5.10d TR
44. Brutal Orangutan 5.12a
45. Vini Vidi Vici 5.10a PG
47. Chip Off the Old Rock 5.10c G
48. Urban Orangutan 5.9 G
50. Face Up to It 5.10c PG
51. Unnamed 5.10b
52. Reunion 5.11b PG
53. Rinse and Whine 5.10c PG
54. Unnamed 5.9
57. Slope Stone 5.8 PG
58. Psycho Driller 5.8 G

39. The Knobs

Area Beta

Location
Near Dunbar.

Type of Climbing
Sport, trad, and bouldering.

Other Info
Very nice area with huge boulders.

The Knobs

Large boulders in a remote mountaintop setting will challenge the most seasoned climber at *The Knobs*. 7 giant boulders and about 12 satellite boulders with some of the finest sandstone in the Mid-Atlantic can be found here. Some of the boulders need a bit of cleaning but the better climbs have 4-star quality faces.

Expect to find about 55 routes/boulder problems that are excellent! Many of the routes here are often done as boulder problems. Should you do decide to boulder any of the routes, be aware they are true highballs and quite dangerous. Several of the smaller satellite boulders have excellent boulder problems of smaller height. Many of the higher boulders have bolted climbs. Although many of these routes were bolted by locals, gear supplements are recommended if you decide to lead any of these. A rack of a few small and medium-sized pieces will be adequate. Many of these routes have been done as boulder problems but make excellent short routes for climbers who prefer safe, fun leads.

The rock quality here should not be overlooked. Bulletproof sandstone with gorgeous edges, small pockets, and deep cracks are trademarks of the area.

Please note the access road to the parking for the crag is sometimes not accessible during winter months. If moderate snow amounts are accumulated, the road may be passable in winter, but during heavy snowfalls, the road may be impassable even to four-wheel drive vehicles.

Location: 6 miles from the town of Dunbar.

General Overview: 20 boulders with 55 routes/problems. 7 of the boulders are in the 30' high range, the rest are 10 to 15 feet high.

Geology: Sandstone

Recommended Rack: Small to medium gear and a few draws. Bring webbing to set up topropes for the routes that do not have chain anchors.

Access Issues and Restrictions: The area is located on Pennsylvania State Game Lands.

Area Hazards: Wear orange during hunting season! The area is a bit of a hike so bring plenty of water for the day.

Approach: A moderate walk—mostly uphill—leads about one and a half miles to the rock. The approach should take a half hour to 45 minuets.

In Case of Emergency: Dial 911.

The Knobs

Directions

Drive south on State Route 119 out of Connellsville (heading towards Uniontown). At the blinking light make a left onto SR1053 and pass a junkyard on the left while heading towards Dunbar. After reaching the town of Dunbar, make a left at a T intersection and cross Dunbar Creek. Locate the state Gamelands building on your right. Make a right on an easy-to-miss gravel road just before the building. Follow the gravel road and Dunbar Creek on you r right. Follow this road almost two miles until you see a very large parking area on the left. Locate a dirt road at the back-right corner of the lot near the gas line. Hike the road about one mile to the crest of a hill. Cross a wooden bridge and just after the bridge locate the second road on the right. Follow the road to a filed. Hike to the back section of the field and find a very overgrown road.   In summer, this road is almost completely unnoticeable. Follow this steep road to the boulders.   Note: The road that parallels Dunbar Creek is sometimes not passable in winter.

40. McConnells Mill State Park

Area Beta

Location
40 miles north of Pittsburgh.

Type of Climbing
Roped climbing and bouldering.

Other Info
I only include a small sampling of this large area.

McConnells Mill State Park

"The Mills", named for an old gristmill that operated on the site until 1928, is a sandstone "rock city". This geologic term refers to the mammoth boulders that form what looks like a city of rock. These sandstone monoliths host a great amount of climbing possibilities.

Over 100 routes and boulder problems have been established at "The Mills". I am only including a select few routes and boulder problems at the main area. I have done this for two reasons: There is not enough room in this guide to accommodate all routes, and Bob Value has already done an excellent guide that I highly recommend buying if you plan to climb here extensively.

History

Many climbers—too many to name for this short route list—were involved from the late '40s to the present. Since I am only giving a select few routes in this book; I am only providing a brief history.

Dr. Ivan Jirak was the first documented climber to visit "The Mills". Dr. Jirak was a pioneer of climbing in Western Pennsylvania and a prominent member of the Pittsburg Explorers Club. He started climbing at "The Mills" in the late '40s. From then on, he and several members of the club, as well as other clubs, developed routes through the 1970s. Climbers such as Bob Value (author of The Mills guidebook), Bill Crick, Keith Bierman, Dough Haver, Nick Ross, Ed Francis, Les Moore, Don French, Ron Walsh, Bob Broughton, and many other climbers were active adding new lines and testpieces at the crag. One of the most prolific ascents was Eric Guerrin's ascent of *Mini Ovest* 5.11d. This climb intimidates climbers to this day. In later years, Rick Thompson, Chris Eckstein, and Rick Zinnakas added some local hard-man lines in the 5.12 range such as *Hanging in Space* 5.12d and *Got the Bosh* 5.12a.

Directions

Follow signs for the mill. When you reach the actual mill, veer left and over a covered bridge. Follow this road up a hill. At the crest of the hill, turn right onto Rim Road. Follow this road about 0.5 mile until you reach a picnic area. Park here. You will be at the top of the cliff. To descend find the obvious large crevasse and descend.

The Sunshine Wall

This area is also called *The Windowpane*. It is the first outcrop you come to when walking down the crevasse trail from above. The routes begin from left to right.

1. Welcome to the Mill 5.12a/b

FA: B. Value '95

At the right end of the wall climb past crimps and follow the steep face.

2. Sunshine 5.9+

Climb the clean face to a corner above.

3. Green Microdots 5.12a

FA: B. Value '83

Begin on the previous route than move right to climb the steep face above.

4. Pocket Route 5.7

15' right of he previous line climb pockets to the top.

5. Mr. Clean 5.10c

FA: B.Value '74

Below a small roof climb the clean face to the top.

Rappel Rock

This wall is located just south of the crevasse.

6. R.O.T.C. Route 5.7+

Climb the obvious chimney in front of the large boulder. The face and crack near the chimney can be climbed at a similar grade.

7. Laid Back 5.10b

FA: B. Value '73

Follow the crack and steep face adjacent to the previous climb.

8. Hanging in Space 5.12b

FA: Chris Eckstein '95

Toproping this route is extremely dangerous if a back-rope is not utilized. Climb a flake off the right end of this boulder and gain an overhanging section of rock. Climb to a notch at the right side of a big roof that is triangular in shape. Pull through the notch and move to the right.

9. Crater Expectations 5.11d

FFA: Rick Zinnakas

Start at the left side of the rock under the large, triangular-shaped roof. Climb to a bulge than move left and continue past tough moves to a ledge. Move right to gain the top.

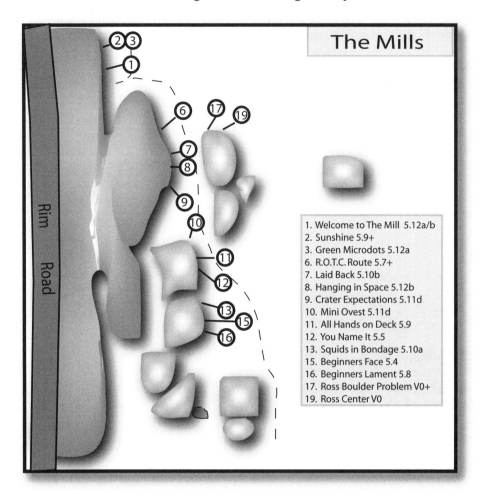

The Mills

1. Welcome to The Mill 5.12a/b
2. Sunshine 5.9+
3. Green Microdots 5.12a
6. R.O.T.C. Route 5.7+
7. Laid Back 5.10b
8. Hanging in Space 5.12b
9. Crater Expectations 5.11d
10. Mini Ovest 5.11d
11. All Hands on Deck 5.9
12. You Name It 5.5
13. Squids in Bondage 5.10a
15. Beginners Face 5.4
16. Beginners Lament 5.8
17. Ross Boulder Problem V0+
19. Ross Center V0

Ships Prow Area

Just past *Rappel Rock* and just past a large chimney a large prow of rock that looks like a ships prow can be found.

10. Mini Ovest (a.k.a. Peter Pan) 5.11d

FA: Eric Guerrin '79

Use a back-rope or groundfall is imminent. Climb the steep, wild prow at the left side of this huge piece of rock.

11. All Hands on Deck 5.9

FA: B.Value '74

Climb the obvious arete left of the previous route.

12. You Name It 5.5

Climb a slab over a roof at the left side of the block.

Beginners' Face

This is the next boulder south of *Ships Prow*.

490

13. Squids in Bondage 5.10a
A "squid" is old climber lingo for "newbie". Climb the rightmost feature on the boulder straight to the top and left of the chimney.

14. The Fast Track 5.10a
Climb flakes to a bulge a few feet right of *Beginners*, then merge with the regular *Beginners Face* to finish.

15. Beginners Face 5.4
Just right of an arete climb the easy face.

16. Beginners Lament 5.8
Climb the obvious arete at the left end of the boulder.

Ross Boulder
Many boulder problems can be done on the boulder behind *Rappel Rock*. The boulder is named after Nick Ross who pioneered problems on the boulder.

17. Ross Boulder Problem V0+
Climb past pockets at the left side of the arete. A V4 variation incorporates a sit start.

18. Ross Boulder Traverse V1
Traverse the *Ross Boulder* from either side.

19. Ross Center V0
Climb the center of the boulder.

For more climbing and bouldering areas that we couldn't fit into this guide-book.   Visit:

www.paclimbing.com

Notes

Notes

About the author

The author was born in Northeast Pennsylvania and has climbed in nearly all U.S. states and eight countries but has spent a great deal of time developing over 3,000 routes and boulder problems in Pennsylvania. He worked as an Access Fund coordinator for Pennsylvania for 5 years and is responsible for many areas in the state being open to climbing. He has also had dozens of photos and articles on rock climbing published and has been a consultant for FOX television and other networks for climbing programming. Besides freelance writing Holzman works as a practitioner in the field of orthotics and prosthetics. His web site is www.paclimbing.com. He, his wife, and dog Mia still enjoy Pennsylvania's best climbing.